Newspaper	Circulation*	
	Daily	Sunday
Daily Star, Oneonta, N.Y.	18,815 (AM)	—
Pocono Record, Stroudsburg, Pa.	18,920 (AM)	20,034
Press-Republican, Plattsburgh, N.Y.	22,610 (AM)	—
News-Times, Danbury, Conn.	40,483 (AM)	45,355
Times Herald-Record, Middletown, N.Y.	75,118 (AM)	85,754
Tri-State Gazette, Port Jervis, N.Y.	4,648 (PM)	—
Standard-Times, New Bedford, Mass.	**48,338 (PM)	52,154
Cape Cod Times, Hyannis, Mass.	39,569 (AM)	45,694
Daily Item, Sunbury, Pa.	26,945 (PM)	—
Herald, Sharon, Pa.	27,036 (PM)	—
Record-Eagle, Traverse City, Mich.	24,536 (PM)	—
Mail Tribune, Medford, Ore.	***29,832 (PM)	31,296
Globe, Joplin, Mo.	38,503 (AM)	43,423
Essex County Newspapers:	36,631 (PM)	—
Daily Times, Gloucester, Mass.		
Times, Beverly, Mass.		
Times, Peabody, Mass.		
Daily News, Newburyport, Mass.		
Free Press, Mankato, Minn.	26,976 (PM)	—
People's Press, Owatonna, Minn.	7,474 (AM)	7,637
Daily Independent, Ashland, Ky.	24,806 (PM)	27,137
Santa Cruz Sentinel, Santa Cruz, Cal.	27,735 (PM)	30,686
News-Sun, Sun City, Ariz.	15,846 (PM)	—
TOTAL	**554,821**	**389,170**

*ABC as of 12/31/84
**PM Monday-Friday; AM Saturday
***Does not publish Saturday

Medford

Santa Cruz

Sun City

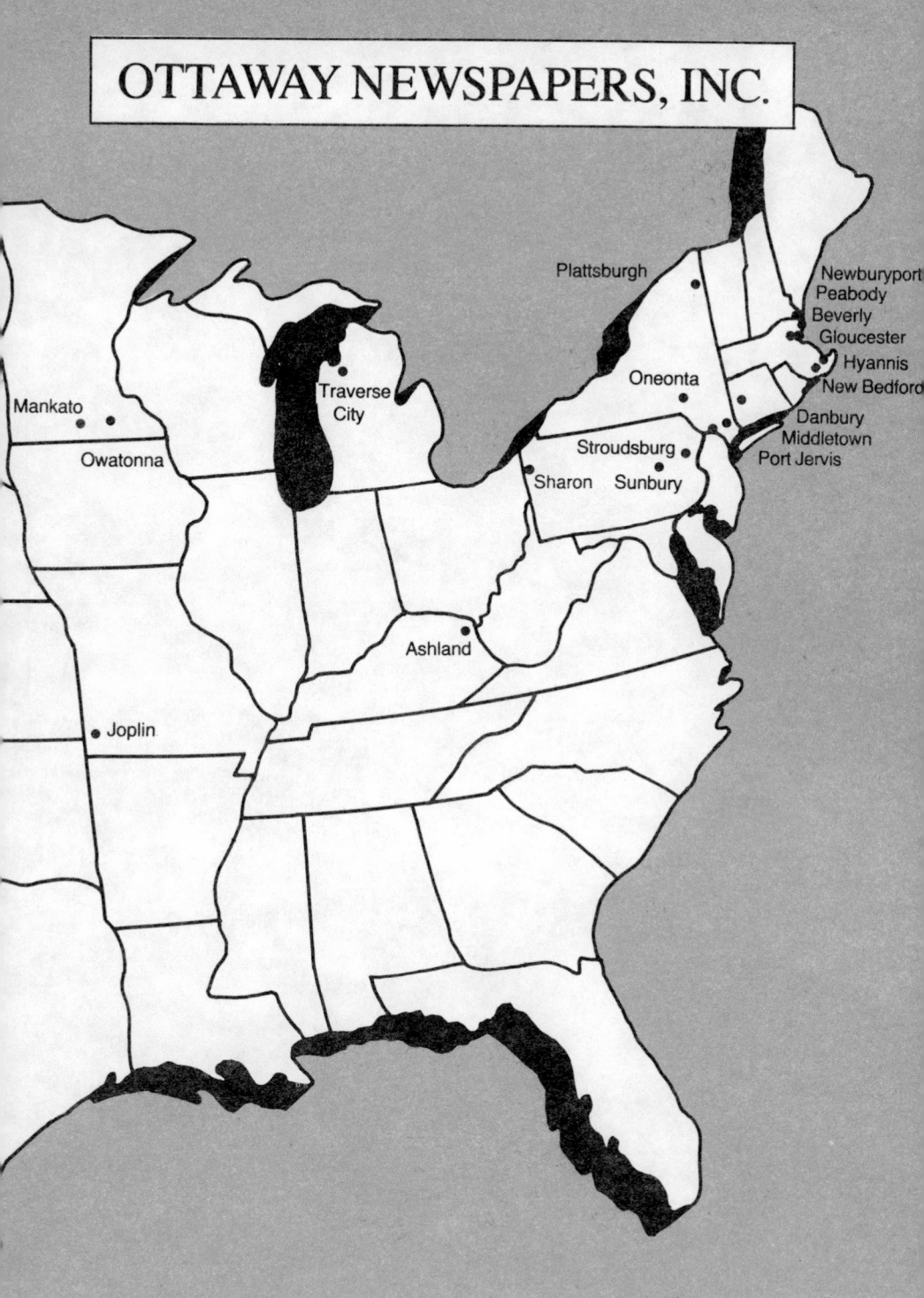

OTTAWAY NEWSPAPERS, INC.

Plattsburgh

Newburyport
Peabody
Beverly
Gloucester
Hyannis
New Bedford

Oneonta

Mankato

Traverse
City

Owatonna

Danbury
Middletown
Port Jervis

Stroudsburg

Sharon   Sunbury

Ashland

Joplin

Ottaway Newspapers
the first 50 years

by Charles A. King

Ottaway Newspapers, Inc.
Campbell Hall, New York

Since mid-1970 the community newspapers subsidiary
of Dow Jones & Company, Inc.

ISBN: 0-87094-781-8

L.C.: 85-63450

Printed in the United States of America

Cover design and map by James Detlef

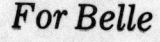
For Belle

Contents

Introduction

As a family and as a company, we wanted to mark November 1986 with a fitting tribute to the 50th anniversary of the founding of what has become Ottaway Newspapers, Inc.

So in 1981, we turned to Charles King, retired vice president for news quality. Earlier in his career he had been general manager of our first daily newspaper in Endicott, New York. Later he had served as publisher of our largest newspaper, in Middletown, New York. In partial retirement, Charles was still producing Ottaway News Extra, a six-times-a-year in-house publication of editorial praise and criticism that may be the best-of-show in the newspaper industry. At least our friends in the profession and in journalism schools often tell us so.

Would he undertake to write a history that not only would celebrate our 50th anniversary, but also would serve to remind our past, present and future staff members who we are, where we came from, why we are different from other newspaper groups and why we find constant challenge in this exciting and important profession?

He would. He did. He accomplished more than we and perhaps he expected. Charles King's remarkable book captures an era in a way that may interest, even captivate, many readers outside as well as inside the journalistic profession. Time will tell. What we know for certain is that he brought to the assignment the investigative zeal of a young reporter and the art, integrity and judgment of a peak-of-career newspaperman.

We imposed no rules, identified no sacred cows, demanded no frills, withheld no records. A handshake launched the project.

Charles King dug deep into our historical files and gave life to that data by talking to scores of present and past officers, publishers and staff members to capture the facts and feelings, the fun and the frustrations, the fundamentals, and the froth of our search for editorial excellence, our dedication to public service and our quest for financial stability during our first half-century.

He sought the truth when stories conflicted, memories faded, pride forgot or embellished the facts.

In terms of the assignment, Charles did uncommonly well.

His book reminds us who we are by relating stories about the people who built each newspaper in our group, with droll, illuminating and sometimes exciting anecdotes about their behavior at turning points in our history.

His book reminds us of where we came from — our roots — through stories about each newspaper in order of acquisition. The format makes it easy for readers to travel at their own pace and follow their own route down memory lane or the acquisition trail.

His book suggests why we are different from other newspaper groups. It chronicles our unique combination of public ownership by Dow Jones & Company, the most respected newspaper publisher in America, and private family management leadership over 50 years; our special commitment to editorial quality; our Washington and statehouse news service, unusual for a newspaper group of our size; our seminars, management development strategies and training programs, which go far beyond the efforts of many newspaper groups; our personal and corporate concern for our employees and their families' health and welfare.

Since the merger with Dow Jones in 1970, the people of Dow Jones have given us unwavering encouragement and support in our efforts to expand and improve this newspaper group, always challenging us to match or exceed their high standards of integrity and editorial quality.

Much is written these days about "corporate culture." This anniversary history tries to capture our corporate culture by telling the story of our half-century adventure in journalism.

This history is dedicated to all our employees — past, present and future — because without their spirit, talent and commitment there would be no Ottaway Newspapers.

Finally, this history was inspired by the creative energy, journalistic ideals and humanity of my father, James H. Ottaway Sr., our retired chairman and founder, who is 75 years old in this 50th anniversary year, and by my mother, Ruth B. Ottaway, who has contributed her common sense, warmth, energy and talent to our company spirit.

Constantly helped by this remarkable woman, my father built this newspaper group by attracting a lot of very good people to work with him, not for him. He is universally respected in the newspaper profession for the quality of his newspapers and his contributions to the industry, not the least of which is his 25 years of service to the American Press Institute.

I hope this book will inspire all of us charged with carrying on his journalistic work to follow his example in the pursuit of excellence, attention to detail, genuine concern for fellow workers and, above all, service to our readers and our communities.

Jim Ottaway Jr.
Chairman
Ottaway Newspapers, Inc.
January 1, 1986

1 A test of courage

Those were the days, my friend,
We thought they'd never end.
We'd sing and dance forever and a day;
We'd live the life we chose;
We'd fight and never lose,
For we were young and sure to have our way.

(Copyright 1962, by Gene Raskin)

The Ford V-8 sedan left Port Huron, Michigan, crossed the St. Clair River into Canada and headed eastward, carrying its passengers to a date with the proprietor of the *Endicott* (N.Y.) *Bulletin*. The 4,000-circulation semi-weekly, published Tuesdays and Fridays, was on the market.

The half-century publishing odyssey of Jim and Ruth Ottaway had begun. It was early fall, 1936.

The Ottaways would have preferred to acquire a small daily. But the *Bulletin* would do. If their plans clicked it soon would become one.

Conceivably their thoughts were dominated by money matters during the long drive from Sarnia, Ontario, to a Niagara Falls stopover and during the southeast tangent from the Falls to New York's Southern Tier. Could they swing a deal? Their own financial resources were limited. In terms of determination and resourcefulness, they were wealthy. Had not Ottaway already been dreaming of a multi-newspaper ownership?

It was a Saturday morning when the Ottaways appeared at the offices of the moribund *Bulletin* at 113 Washington Street

1

and introduced themselves to Harry J. Freeland, proprietor of the Bulletin Publishing Company, who was ready to sell on his terms — cash on the line.

The crusty Freeland — right out of central casting — had advertised his paper in *Editor & Publisher* through a phone broker of obscure destinies with the improbable name of J.B. Shale. Shale worked out of a tiny office in the Times Building in New York City.

It wasn't long before the pipe-puffing Freeland, feet on desk, said he wanted $50,000 for the *Bulletin,* cash or certified check. Or so the legend goes.

Ottaway didn't have $50,000. Would Mr. Freeland talk terms? A down payment, say around $20,000, with notes over a reasonable period?

Fencing for an opening that might weaken Freeland's stolid resistance, Ottaway asked to see some record of the paper's earnings. Freeland opened an enormous ancient safe and extracted a bank book.

"Well," he said, consulting the dog-eared passbook, "I had this much a year ago and I have this much now."

So much for Freeland's legendary financial disclosure technique, possibly a spur-of-the-moment elfin gesture. So much for folklore. So much for dimming memories.

Corporate files have yielded Bulletin Publishing Company audits for 1934 and 1935, pegging Freeland's net profit at $4,547 and $2,848 for those years, respectively. Freeland, certainly, wasn't getting rich.

It must be assumed that Ottaway later had access to the Freeland audits. In any case he commissioned Greene & Wolcott, a Binghamton accounting firm, to run an audit of the Bulletin for the period January 1 to October 31, 1936, which showed a 10-month operating profit of $4,481 and a net of $1,629.

Legend tells us further that Ottaway finally convinced Freeland to accept a $20,000 down payment and notes at the then unremarkable rate of four percent.

But brittle, yellowing documents show that Ottaway signed an option to buy the *Bulletin* on October 31, 1936. Freeland's price was $125 per share for the 450 shares of capital stock, or $56,250. The down payment was $22,500.

Ottaway exercised the option November 18. Terms called for the unpaid balance to be reduced by $2,250 every six months, with interest pegged at six percent.

That same day Freeland called a meeting of shareholders and directors, and, with his slate, stepped down.

Jim and Ruth Ottaway were elected president-treasurer and secretary, respectively, and directors.

The minutes were signed by Ruth Ottaway. Her signature was the first of hundreds that would appear over the years in a myriad of minute books.

The sale did not include the *Bulletin* building. Ottaway signed a four-year lease at $175 per month with an option to buy. Freeland valued the structure at $30,000. Terms of the lease enjoined the new publisher from subletting the building for use as a restaurant, beer garden, shooting gallery or bowling alley.

James Haller Ottaway, born July 8, 1911, had become a newspaper owner-publisher at 25.

Freeland's lawyer during negotiations was Jacob Yale Becker, attorney for the Endicott National Bank. As soon as the deal had been cut, Ottaway engaged Becker, who would remain a corporate counsel until his death in 1973. Jake Becker practiced law with verve and an imagination that matched Ottaway's spirited approach to journalism. He would be a major figure in the expansion that lay ahead.

Becker was born Yael Becher in Russia March 18, 1900 and came to the United States at six. His Hebrew given name was changed to the anglicized Yale. Yael, or Yale, is the Hebrew equivalent of Joel.

One of his grammar school teachers in Springfield, Massachusetts, told the lad that Yale simply wouldn't do for a first name and announced that henceforth it would be Jacob.

Jacob Yale Becker (or JYB, which would appear on hundreds of memos over the years) attended Northeastern University Law School, graduating magna cum laude in 1922.

The purchase was exhilarating for Ruth Blackburne Ottaway. She would be back east. She had become homesick in Michigan for her beloved Brooklyn Heights, where she and a sister had been reared by a grandmother and an aunt, her mother having died when she was five.

3

For Ottaway it was a welcome sense of freedom from family newspaper ties.

Elmer James Ottaway, Jim's father, who died in 1934, co-founded the *Port Huron* (Mich.) *Times-Herald* in 1900. (Today it is part of the Gannett Newspaper group.) His partner was Louis Weil Sr. The *Times-Herald* was, in part, to nurture and sharpen Ottaway's newspaper skills. He graduated from paper carrier to press fly-boy, and was classified and national advertising manager.

A far more sophisticated training ground, he said, was his 18-month experience (1934-36) as vice president and assistant general manager of the *St. Petersburg* (Fla.) *Times*. The Ottaway family owned 20 percent of the *Times,* which father Elmer had acquired in 1930 by paying off an overdue $100,000 newsprint bill owed to International Paper Company. The Ottaways also had acquired the rights to buy 50 percent of the *Times* stock at a fixed price.

"I was only 23 years old," Jim said. "It was a great experience. That's where I really cut my newspaper teeth."

Jim's half brother, William O., was running the *Times* with not much help from Paul Poynter, father of Nelson. Nelson would help bring the newspaper to the pre-eminence it enjoys today.

The Ottaway family sold its St. Petersburg interests in 1936. With options to buy all or sell all, it chose the latter course.

There was one more way station for Ottaway on the road toward personal independence. For six months in 1936 he was classified manager of the *Grand Rapids* (Mich.) *Herald,* owned by U.S. Senator Arthur Vanderburg, since deceased. During this period the first of three children was born to the Ottaways: Ruth Woodward, in Ann Arbor.

Jim Ottaway and Ruth Blackburne Hart met as students at Rollins College, Winter Park, Florida. Ottaway had transferred from the University of Michigan to a warm climate after suffering a severe bout with nephritis. He was a journalism major and editor of the weekly *Sandspur,* the Rollins campus newspaper.

Ruth had attended Packer Collegiate Institute in Brooklyn and had studied in Switzerland for a year before entering

4

Rollins, which she chose because of its Oxford tutorial system and because her father lived in nearby Leesburg. Ruth was a member of the *Sandspur* staff. She hadn't thought about newspapering before Rollins, but found herself indoctrinated by a sorority sister whose parents owned the *Tampa* (Fla.) *Times*.

Elfishly the two coeds had written a story for the *Sandspur* which was made up of whole cloth. Becoming nervous about the caper, they sought out Ottaway at a Winter Park boarding house, where he took meals.

"It (the story) never happened," Ruth told the editor.

"Are you prepared to pay the printer?" Ottaway asked.

They were.

If it wasn't exactly love at first sight, a romance developed.

As their senior year at Rollins wound down, Jim and Ruth decided to marry.

The wedding took place June 2, 1934, in Brooklyn Heights, just across the river from Lower Manhattan. The honeymoon was in New England. "They were made for each other," an intimate Ottaway associate said 50 years later.

Contrary to a report in *"Inside the Wall Street Journal,"* by Jerry M. Rosenberg, which contained a chapter on the Ottaway group, the new proprietor had not made any strategic errors in choosing Endicott. The village was a self-sustaining enclave in what was called the Triple Cities, the others being Johnson City and Binghamton. The three were linked by a narrow two-lane road. There was no head-to-head competition either from Frank Gannett's wealthy (and smug) afternoon *Press* or William (Billy) Hill's comparatively pallid morning *Sun*, both based in Binghamton. The *Press* did offer an Endicott edition, but it could not come close to matching the *Bulletin*'s local-area report.

The Rosenberg account also incorrectly charged Ottaway with a major judgmental error for investing in a location "tied to a single industry." The reference was to Endicott Johnson, a long-time giant in the manufacture of footwear. EJ was Endicott's largest employer. But there also was International Business Machines. In 1936 IBM's only plant, and therefore, its headquarters, was in Endicott. It also ranked as a dominant

5

force in the area economy and although its work force then was about half of EJ's, it was constantly expanding. IBM evolved from the Bundy Time Recorder Company, which was founded in Oneonta, 60 miles to the northeast where the *Star* would become Ottaway's second acquisition. The Oneonta area is heavily infused with ex-Bundy shareholders who became wealthy through IBM dividends and stock splits. There were other substantial industries in Endicott, albeit less important.

"One of the reasons we chose Endicott," Ottaway said, "was because of IBM."

But the Great Depression was in full flower. In 1936 EJ was a torpid giant.

Its work force was on a four-day week. Foreign competition in the shoe industry was tough.

There was little room for the *Bulletin* to expand its circulation reach. Binghamton effectively blocked any thrust eastward. A few miles to the south lay the Pennsylvania border. Ottaway had to court potential readers in the thinly populated western sector along the Broome County-Tioga County border. To the north, livestock outnumbered people.

Harry Freeland, in a burst of chauvinistic devotion to the cause of his little paper, had been guilty of a bit of outrageous plagiarism: His Page 1 flag bore the slogan, "Nearly everybody reads the *Bulletin,*" copied, of course, from the Philadelphia daily of the same name.

Ottaway's first objective (after dropping the hyperbolic catch phrase) was to increase circulation as quickly as possible from the 4,000 base he inherited. The planned expansion into a daily operation, he estimated, would required at least a 7,000 net paid floor, which, in turn, would justify an advertising rate card commensurate with a six-day operation.

The hard sell in home delivery soon began to pay off. More and more Endicotters and fringe dwellers took to the *Bulletin.* They found they liked the new editorial product.

Commercial radio had barely been born. Television was the stuff of science fiction. In the 1930s afternoon papers were the main source of news and information. The nation's reading habits called for a newspaper at the end of the day, not at breakfast time. Times would come full circle in four decades.

"We harped on concise writing," Ottaway wrote in a look-back article in 1983. "We harped on thorough local news coverage, all the local art that we could get through our ancient engraving department, and an editorial page that spoke out on local, state, national and world issues."

Selling advertising in the woebegone Endicott market of the mid-30s required more than dogged persistence. (And even in 1939, when the gods began to smile on the *Bulletin*, the super-hard sell continued as a way of life.)

It is conceivable that the fight for survival would have been even tougher had it not been for Byron E. (Barney) French, a Freeland holdover. French was a rare combination of undeviating loyalty to the new owner, mastery of selling strategies, unlimited ideas and a diplomat's sense of public relations. He also could have qualified as Ottaway court jester had there been anything about which to jest.

"He kept Jim's spirits up when things were darkest," a close associate recalled.

In 1932 the Freeland corporate title was the Bulletin Publishing Company, but by January 1, 1933, it had been reorganized as the Endicott Bulletin, Inc.

It was capitalized at $60,000. Harry and Harriet Freeland held 450 of the 600 outstanding shares. Par was $100.

(Becker's fee for organizing the corporation was $100, quite fair by Great Depression standards.)

At the same time Freeland granted French, the advertising manager, the right to purchase out of unissued stock 100 or fewer shares by cash or on the instalment plan. French had a five-year contract with Freeland, calling for a weekly salary of $65.

The stock agreement with French was dissolved four days before Ottaway took over. Whatever stock French had accumulated eventually would be purchased by Ottaway under a buy-back agreement between the two. No one can recall the extent of French's original holdings.

Any of smiling, cherubic, florid-faced Barney's intangible assets, as well as his revenue-producing talents, were more than welcome as the buildup toward daily publication continued.

7

The *Bulletin* went daily on October 4, 1937. Almost a year had elapsed since the acquisition. The premiere issue was doormat thick — 72 pages.

So much for the conversion. Most succeeding issues ranged between 12 and 16 pages.

Stories have circulated about broken merchant promises to support the new daily. "There was an Endicott-Binghamton rivalry," Ottaway said. "Endicott merchants did want their own daily. But the Endicott Johnson four-day work week and the shock when they received their bills meant that pride ran second to increased outlays for advertising."

Daily publication meant four additional work shifts. More newsprint and ink. Heat, power, light. The revenue wasn't there, yet somehow the bills got paid.

Ottaway took no salary while the *Daily Bulletin* was running deficit figures. (On paper it was $115 a week.) Ruth, Ruthie and Jim lived on savings, *Port Huron Times-Herald* dividends, Ruth's personal funds and loans from Jim's mother. "Mother acted like a banker," he says. She did. Literally.

Ottaway's mother had remarried in 1936 to Nikolai Sokoloff, the conductor of the Cleveland Symphony Orchestra when it was founded in 1918. After retiring in 1933, he established the La Jolla, California, symphony. Sokoloff had come to the United States from Russia as a boy. Mrs. Sokoloff's interests in music spanned the continent. As president of the National Federation of Music Clubs she met Sokoloff when he was working as a volunteer to find work for unemployed musicians.

And there was the Endicott Trust Company.

ETC held an Ottaway note for $50,000 and out of the blue decided, on the basis of the stagnant Endicott economy and Ottaway's palpably precarious position, to call it, even though payments were being made on schedule.

"It looks as though we're going to be in the newspaper business," one ETC executive was reported to have announced on Washington Street.

Ruth Sokoloff advanced the balance of the note to her son, insisting on full collateral, in this case part of Ottaway's life insurance.

Then, in an abrupt reversal, ETC decided it didn't want a

payoff. But Ottaway retired the note.

"In 1937," Ottaway recalled, "we were losing our shirts." But the *Bulletin* never missed a payroll. More often than not the proprietor and French could be seen trudging Washington Street collecting advertising bills. They couldn't always wait until the first of the month. But the publisher saw fit to give French a $5 raise to $70 a week.

Circulation continued to rise, proof that the burghers of Western Broome and a slice of neighboring Tioga knew a good daily when they saw one.

It proved an Ottaway adage then, as it would many times again:

"I've always figured that if we put out a good editorial product, the business end will take care of itself."

In 1938, the year James H. Ottaway Jr., their second child, was born, a war preparedness economy was taking form. It would not affect the Endicott area directly until the following year, but the shoe industry was stirring and IBM soon would be manufacturing Norden bomb sights.

On January 9, 1938, at the *Daily Bulletin*'s annual directors meeting, minutes show that "the directors reviewed business prospects for the coming year and authorized officers to place in effect all possible savings to offset the present recession in business."

Less than a month later Ottaway was authorized by the board to apply for a $15,000 line of credit at Endicott Trust and "temporary" loan of $3,000 at six percent.

Borrowing had become a way of life.

The *Bulletin* struggled through under Ottaway's relentless drive and in 1939 its books showed black ink for the first time. The breakthrough came concurrently with the birth of Ottaway's third child, David Blackburne Ottaway.

Triple Cities factories were beginning to hum with war orders from the government and some allies-to-be. The battle for sheer survival was over. There would be almost two decades of profitable publishing in Endicott before the *Daily Bulletin* perished in 1960.

There was more to the *Bulletin* than getting the story first or doing an even better job if it was scooped by the *Press* (which

9

was seldom). The paper was built on civic pride, as Ottaway put it, with Jim and Ruth indefatigable participants in activities ranging from Chamber of Commerce to the Community Chest to hospital and PTA. The collateral goodwill was priceless.

Older Ottaway watchers often have marveled at Ruth's tireless contributions (even shopping for employees when they were working long hours) in a setting that hardly rivaled the old school ambience of Brooklyn Heights. Were one to ask how she managed (also holding the office of corporate vice president and secretary) with three children, there's a quick answer: Their dwelling at 407 Shady Drive, Endwell, contained a live-in cook-housekeeper and a nursemaid who came daily but did not live in.

Live-in domestic help was easy to find and not at all expensive in the 1930s. Shall we say between $8 and $10 a week?

One reason Ruth sat on the Ottaway board from the start was Jim's mother's fate on the death of her husband. "Father never told mother anything about business. When he died, she was almost helpless."

In late winter of 1939 Ottaway borrowed $17,500 from his mother and $8,500 from his step-father, putting up *Bulletin* stock and, once again, life insurance as collateral. Interest was pegged at five percent. With the funds in hand, Ottaway offered to pay Freeland what was left on the 1936 notes — but at a discount.

"Send the money," Freeland wired from Florida.

A contract dated August 28, 1939, points to an effort by Ottaway to beef up his Monday edition, the one with the least advertising in most newspapers. He hired William M. Kerr of Binghamton as "solicitor" to provide a weekly business page, which was to consist of 75 percent advertising and news stories "of and for the benefit" of the advertisers. Kerr also would provide the "news." Whether the venture enjoyed a long run is lost in time. But it was a harbinger of things to come for a community newspaper group. Special pages and sections would proliferate. Perhaps the "tin cup" soubriquet applied at first, but, under Ottaway's constant prodding, recalcitrant editors eventually learned to match revenue linage with reader service

10

material several cuts above canned syndicate filler.

When the *Bulletin* emerged as a daily, its wire news was supplied by a rather obscure agency, Trans Radio Press Service. The *Binghamton Press* held territorial rights to Associated Press, United Press and International News Service. Ottaway presented himself before the AP board in New York City and asked for a membership, which was not forthcoming. But the board ordered the *Press* to divest itself of INS, which Ottaway used in Endicott starting in 1942. It cost him $1,600 to escape the 1938 contract with Trans Radio: $1,000 down and six notes for $100 each. After the UP-INS merger in the 1950s, the *Bulletin* used the United Press International wire report.

Endicott in 1940 continued to support a weekly, the *Endicott Times*. There is no known record of whether the *Times* advertising linage or circulation was a burr under Ottaway's saddle. But financially robust or not, its owners, Orlo Brees and Elwa Lloyd, struck a deal with the *Daily Bulletin*.

They would dissolve the *Times* and retain and hopefully enhance their job printing enterprise. Ottaway would dissolve his job printing operation and sell his equipment to the Brees-Lloyd company. Ottaway paid $1,000 for the *Times* name. His equipment went for $500, or pro rata advertising credit if its market value proved to be less.

A week later Ottaway hired Brees as a reporter for one year for a $325 retainer. He wanted access to Brees's news sources.

The year 1939 had seen the arrival of William C. (Bill) Lundquest at the *Daily Bulletin*.

Lundquest, who would become a key member of the Ottaway team, had worked on William Randolph Hearst's *Syracuse (N.Y.) Journal*. The *Journal* was acquired in June 1939 by Samuel I. Newhouse, who soon afterwards bought the *Syracuse Herald*, also an afternoon paper. Newhouse promptly merged the two. Hundreds of employees were dismissed. It is not clear whether Lundquest approached Ottaway before or after the merger. His first job on the *Journal* was part-time, selling classified advertising door-to-door at the rather uninflated "salary" of $5 a week, plus commissions. Evidently his drumming technique impressed the front office. He left

11

Syracuse University for a full-time sales job.

And, according to his widow, Margaret Kelly (Peg) Lundquest, Bill "concentrated his time and efforts learning all about newspapers, and as he would say 'the money end of the paper.'"

Lundquest heard that Ottaway was looking for an advertising hotshot and drove the 90 miles to Endicott to look things over. "He was so thrilled with this small paper that had just gone daily," Peg said, "that he offered to invest a two-week vacation in Endicott at no pay to prove his ability and sincerity."

"Well, we ended up in Endicott with two small children," Peg continued. Two more would be born to the Lundquests. One of them, Bill Jr., would become advertising director of the *Plattsburg* (N.Y.) *Press-Republican,* decades after his father presided over the newspaper as general manager eight years.

"I compare these newspaper ventures to having a child," Peg told the author. "You negotiate with God and nature...the often distressing situations, the proud times, the never, never quite finished product."

Lundquest's natural newspaper habitats were in the areas of advertising and production. He relied on others for editorial guidance. Ottaway himself was figuratively at the newsroom's helm while Endicott remained his only newspaper.

Lundquest was in part an irreverent soul, who found satirical release (but never sarcasm) in telling Ottaway (for example) that he ought to wear underwear patterned to match his trousers. It seems that the publisher, engrossed in his work, was coming to the office with holes in his pants. (This anecdote surfaced in Lundquest's 1970 memoirs and again in 1983 via his widow.)

Lundquest also poked fun at Ottaway's 1936 Ford, the front seat of which was "so worn that a driver needed three pillows to achieve road vision."

A generation of Ottaway executives will bear witness to Ottaway's behaviorial quirks or aberrations, one of which was to extend a dinner invitation and invariably turn up with empty pockets when the time came to pay the piper. Perhaps this particular trait hews to the saying, as Peg Lundquest said, that "newspapermen never carry enough money."

The Lundquests had been invited to a dinner and concert in Binghamton. First a drink at the Ottaways. Then to the Ottaway car. But the car keys were missing. They were found two days later in a fish bowl, where David had thrown them. Jim's wallet was empty. So was Lundquest's. Peg bailed them out. Let it be on the record that Ottaway always reimbursed his colleagues, usually without any reminder.

Lundquest's memoirs also suggested that lighting in the *Bulletin* building fell somewhat short of minimal requirements. "I used to lay out advertising at night by the light of a street lamp," he wrote.

"And there was Oscar the cockroach, who was my constant companion. Peg used to shake out my clothes every night because a roach or two would be in a coat pocket or trouser cuff."

Lundquest couldn't forget the story of Marty Mangan, a *Bulletin* compositor. Mangan, like hundreds of typesetters before and since, occasionally had an unconquerable urge to create an embarrassing misspelling. One this occasion the man of matrices substituted an "i" for an "o" in a business page story about a new "snapshot center." The headline, picture caption and story all carried the offending vowel. Much amused by Mangan's mischief, Lundquest found Ottaway in an uncharacteristic rage.

"He gave me hell and ordered me to go out and buy every *Bulletin* I could find. What I did find was that they were going to collectors for two dollars apiece." The episode was a staple of Washington Street conversational currency for days.

Barney French trained Lundquest in the mechanics of community newspaper publishing, radically different from the metropolitan way of life Bill had tasted. And when Jim Ottaway joined the Navy in 1944, Bill took over much of the community service role of the paper. He was chairman of War Bond drives and even staged mock enemy invasions on Washington Avenue with tanks and trucks borrowed from Army Ordnance in Rochester — plus free airplane rides if someone bought a bond.

French thought Lundquest was overdoing things and bade him slow down.

Several years earlier Lundquest had mischievously

13

complained to Ottaway that he was overworked. "I think I'll tie a broom to my tail and sweep the office while I'm rushing around," he told his prodding publisher.

Early associates of Ottaway recalled that Jim Jr. often accompanied his father to the office on Saturdays and was fascinated with the red ink Ottaway used to single out no-pay or late-pay advertisers on the early aging schedules. And David, they recall, once filled the family Ford's gasoline tank with water. Two reasons for this well-meant juvenile act of charity have been offered: He was moved by the continuing financial plight of the *Bulletin* or by the shortage of fuel under wartime restrictions.

When it came time to settle for the drained tank refill, Lundquest's memoirs related, "I had to pay the bill. Jim had no money."

The time had come to abandon the former Freeland rabbit warren at 113 Washington Street. The *Daily Bulletin* was profitable — marginally so, but profitable. Among other immediate requirements for continued growth was a modern press. Circulation still was rising.

The paper had become a pioneer in modern typographical design. Column rules were dropped. Headlines went lower case and flush left. Unheard of devices, such as bullets, were employed to tick off developments in a packaged story. Readers loved it.

And Barney French's Page 1 column, "Mainstreams," was a daily hit.

Early in 1941 Ottaway commissioned Truman A. Lacey, a Binghamton architect, to design a modest plant. Land had been acquired from the New York State Electric & Gas Company at East Main Street and Lincoln Avenue. An application for state review of the plans, dated May 7, indicated an estimated cost of $18,000. Cost of equipment at the time was estimated at $45,000, including press, typesetting equipment, furniture and fixtures.

Construction didn't move as speedily as Ottaway thought it should have. (Other builders of Ottaway projects over the years would hear the same lament.) But it was sufficiently closed in by the time of the Pearl Harbor onslaught to receive furniture. Ottaway's Binghamton jobber advised him to take the

14

merchandise then and there. The government war effort was closing in on supply houses.

Radio station WENE, which would start operations in 1947, would be housed in a second building, to be connected to the Bulletin structure by a sort of breezeway.

The 1942 annual meeting of directors was held in the new plant on January 10. Board minutes show that title was held jointly by the Ottaways "as builders." The *Bulletin* rented the building for $375 a month. Final cost was pegged at "about $35,000."

First recorded allusion to dividends appears on the same page. Ottaway was quoted as saying that a dividend "was not advisable," even though the company had returned a "small profit" in 1941. At any rate, the directors (Jim, Ruth, and Barney French) raised the salary Ottaway did not take from 1937 through 1940 ($115 weekly) to a more exalted $135. French's salary went from $70 to $100.

Two ancient documents show how Ottaway financed part of the plant and equipment.

One is an agreement dated December 3, 1941, between Ottaway and the trustees of his father's estate, in which the trustees loaned the publisher $12,000. As collateral Ottaway put up 400 shares of *Port Huron Times Herald* stock. The terms were five percent over five years with an option to extend payments over an additional five.

Once again Jim's mother emerged as her son's in-house banker. Her name appears on the document as co-trustee with William W. Ottaway, one of Jim's brothers.

The debt was discharged in 1947.

The other document bears the legend "Duplex Printing Press Company, Battle Creek, Michigan." It shows that sometime before October 1941, Ottaway had ordered a rebuilt 16-page, 20,000-per-hour tubular press with a half-page folder. The price for the press, folder and related foundry equipment was an unbelievable $12,546 net.

Ottaway traded in the old Duplex Model B (a flatbed) as part payment and Duplex took his notes for $10,546. In that era some manufacturers would finance purchases. Ottaway recalled that "we would take that route if the interest rate was favorable."

The press drive mechanism came from Shamokin, Pennsylvania, southeast of Sunbury, home of the *Daily Item,* which Ottaway would acquire in 1970. And Duplex erectors commanded $18 a day. That figure wouldn't cover an hour's work in the 1980s.

The Duplex contract data sheet does not indicate terms of the financing agreement. But *Bulletin* records suggest that Ottaway found a more favorable interest rate at Endicott Trust. On September 26, 1942, ETC loaned him $9,243 with the press as collateral. The mortgage was renewed in 1943 and 1944. On December 26, 1944, he reborrowed $5,146, renewed the note in 1945 and finally retired the obligation on November 30, 1946.

Add to the 1941 *Bulletin* financing picture a $12,000 Endicott Trust mortgage on the newspaper plant signed by Ruth and Jim Ottaway on August 11, with interest at six percent. The mortgage was extended on December 31 and assigned to the Endicott National Bank.

The year 1943 was marked by several firsts:

At the January 9 stockholders meeting, Ottaway discussed the possibility of establishing a pension fund for employees.

On June 29, the *Bulletin* bought the building at 911 East Main Street from the Ottaways for $24,000 and assumed a $10,500 mortgage held by Endicott National. The Endicott Bulletin Employes Retirement Fund was established. The corporation would contribute $6.25 per month per full-time employee. Marine Midland Trust Company of Binghamton was the depository.

The first (and only) pensioner in early Ottaway history was Bert MacKnight, head pressman on the old semi-weekly Bulletin. Perhaps the only employee known to have addressed the publisher as "Jimmy," MacKnight considered himself a grandfather figure to the Ottaway family. His loyalty and devotion to his job were legendary.

One day Ottaway found a strange and uninvited face in the backshop. It belonged to an investigator for the Wage and Price Administration. The publisher, one hand on the intruder's collar, the other on the seat of his pants, not so gently ushered him out the front door.

Weeks later another inspector turned up, politely identified himself and informed the publisher that MacKnight had approximately $1,000 coming to him for hours worked but not reported by the pressman. Ottaway cheerfully agreed to square the account. But MacKnight, in his fashion, refused the money.

At the time of MacKnight's retirement he was given a lifetime pension of $100 a month, with an extra $50 every July and December. MacKnight died in 1970. His widow continued to receive the same pension until her death in 1981 at 95.

On July 9, the *Bulletin* increased its par $100 capital stock from 600 to 1,500 shares.

On July 30, a $5 dividend was declared.

The board meeting of November 1, 1943, was significant. Jim Ottaway was preparing to enter service.

On his recommendation, directors fixed dividends for 1944 at $2 per share per quarter. Ottaway submitted his resignation and French was named manager of the corporation at Ottaway's salary of $135 per week.

Ottaway also suggested that since Ruth Ottaway "would represent his stock interest and him personally for the duration and because she would assume an active role in management," she be voted a salary of $250 monthly. Ottaway was voted a $335 monthly salary as long as he remained in service.

Ottaway entered service with the Navy on January 4, 1944. He had been sworn in the previous fall.

On August 1 of that year he dissolved the *Endicott Bulletin* corporation and set up a partnership with French. Division of profits (or losses) was Ottaway, 83 percent; French, 17. Title to the building and equipment passed to Ruth Ottaway for $1.

A new corporation, Empire Newspapers-Radio, Inc., would be formed January 21, 1946, less than two months before Ottaway was mustered out. The new corporate name was, in part, a harbinger of what was to come: radio.

As Ottaway left for service, the newspaper's long-term debt stood at $13,696, a rather remarkable figure considering the heavy 1941-42 capital investments in property, plant and equipment.

Even then there were inviolable rules of finance:

No short-term borrowing.

Annual payments would not exceed depreciation charges in a

given year.

And there was an ancillary rule (or maxim):

Always borrow money when you don't need it.

Jim and Ruth Ottaway were long-term idealists, but short-term realists.

Twenty years later long-term debt would reach $12 million!

And in 1941, as the *Bulletin*'s new building was going up, work had started on a project then totally unrelated to the newspaper's fortunes: a four-lane divided highway between Binghamton and Endicott. Because of the war, construction was halted until 1948. The highway was completed in 1951.

The George F. Johnson Highway (named for an EJ founder) in effect created a single community out of the Triple Cities. Year by year through the mid and late 1950s the Ottaways and French saw their newspaper market disappear. The *Binghamton Press* became the dominant force. The *Sun* would survive, but in a reincarnation that would include the *Bulletin*'s nameplate.

The final issue of the *Daily Bulletin* (now a five-day paper) appeared August 31, 1960. That story will be chronicled in the chapter devoted to the Middletown, New York, acquisitions.

2 Oneonta/Gene Brown

In mid-1944 word reached Lieutenant Ottaway at his Navy post in Philadelphia that the *Oneonta* (N.Y.) *Star* was for sale. He was interested. As it turned out, the war would not end for another year and he would not be mustered out until March 1946.

Herald of these tidings was Allen Kander, a veteran Hearst newspaper executive and now a newspaper and radio broker. Why Kander approached Ottaway, whose only track record was based on the Endicott struggle, is lost to memory. Perhaps, Ottaway said, he had chatted with Kander at a now-forgotten publishers meeting.

Kander, who would be point man for several Ottaway acquisitions through the late 1960s interchanged the trappings of a nabob with those of a churchmouse over the years. His mercurial financial status on one occasion found him chauffered from Washington, D.C., for a date with Ottaway. Next time he might appear in a suit rumpled from a less exalted mode of transportation. When Kander was living high, the odds were good that he had just completed a major transaction for Samuel I. Newhouse, who amassed a vast fortune in newspapers, broadcast and magazines. Kander, the record shows, more than once borrowed money from Ottaway.

Francis A. Lee was proprietor of the *Star,* whose physical plant and fixtures, not to mention the product itself, was a melancholy model of benign neglect.

But the newspaper held a commanding position in Otsego and Delaware counties both in circulation and advertising appeal.

Acquisition of the *Star* again would underscore the Ottaway

19

philosophy of choosing a market with growth potential and a relative minimum of competition.

Lee's father, Harry W., had founded the Otsego Publishing Company in 1890. Along the way he added a job shop and a weekly limited edition, made up of stories and art already used in the daily. The operation had been conducted since 1901 from a ramshackle structure on downtown Broad Street that in itself set the tone for the paper.

The *Star* had just over 9,000 audited paid circulation, providing, in effect, saturation in the city and neighboring towns. Oneonta was in an isolated section on the northwest edge of the Catskill Mountains.

At that time the Delaware & Hudson Railway had major car repair shops in Oneonta. There were two colleges and diversified small industries. The city lay on Route 7, the major highway between Binghamton and Albany. Oneonta also had dependable rail passenger service to those cities and back. In 1941 you could buy a sirloin steak in a D & H dining car for a buck and a half. Martinis were two bits. On some visits to Oneonta during the war, Ottaway rode the train.

Asked to compare his own market research of the 1940s and 1950s with today's involved techniques, Ottaway ventured that what he did in Oneonta was "adequate but not as sophisticated. Let's just say it was thorough enough."

When it appeared that Ottaway and Lee would agree on price and terms, it occured to Kander to ask if Ottaway had someone in mind to run the *Star*.

"I don't know," Ottaway replied. "Do you know anyone who might be available?" (French was busy minding the store in Endicott.)

Yes, Kander had a candidate. His name was Eugene Joseph Brown, advertising manager of S.I. Newhouse's *Long Island Star*. Brown also aspired to newspaper ownership, but would accept a general manager's post if the long-term future seemed bright.

Ottaway hired Brown after a meeting in Endicott at which "I was grilled thoroughly," Brown recalled. Presumably unsure of Ottaway's political shading, Brown volunteered that he was a Democrat.

"We are hiring a newspaperman, not a politician," Ottaway responded.

Besides Ottaway at the meeting were Ruth Ottaway, French and Stewart Newing, owner of the Ford franchise in Endicott. Newing was an Ottaway family confidant.

After Ottaway, French and Jake Becker were convinced that the *Star*'s receivables were valid at $34,000, Ottaway bought the properties for $260,000. Lee accepted a $50,000 down payment and notes payable over 20 years at four percent.

The weekly soon was discontinued, but the *Star* continued the job printing operation for several years.

Most of the negotiations for the *Star* had been conducted in New York City, where Lee had an apartment penthouse. Ottaway often rode the Pennsylvania Railroad from Philadelphia to New York to join French in the discussions. Occasionally Ottaway ran across a former *Endicott Bulletin* ad salesman in the Pennsy's Philadelphia 30th Street station. He was Elton P. Hall, who had been working for the railroad since the war began. In time, Hall would return to the Ottaway fold and would succeed Gene Brown at the helm of the *Star*.

In buying the *Star*, Ottaway acquired his first Associated Press membership. But in what might be regarded as an act of loyalty to Newing's Ford franchise, he stipulated in the contract that he wanted no part of Lee's corporately-owned Packard sedan. The document was signed by French, vice president of the new company, Oneonta Star, Inc.

The ancient building not only had acquired a pronounced slant, but sat atop a fast-moving stream. The publisher's office on the second floor (among other areas) was six inches higher at one end than at the other. The Lee rolltop desk soon would be leveled by the strategic placement of bricks and wood blocks.

And the new owner discovered another long-standing aberration, this one of the human variety. A good number of the *Star*'s production force were fond of hunting. When the season arrived, they refused to work overtime, just as though time for hunting was a right bestowed by contract.

Gene Brown did not get off to an auspicious start as GM. Most citizens of Oneonta were aware of Francis Lee's affinity for whiskey, which had manifested itself all through the

21

negotiations. (French and Lundquest had cheerfully done whatever drinking was deemed necessary to gentle Lee through the give and take.)

At the end of Brown's first day on the job — Ottaway and French having left the city — he received a call from the police after midnight.

"Will you come down to the hotel (Hotel Oneonta) and take Mr. Lee home?"

Brown found Lee in a serious state of disrepair and, in helping the weaving ex-publisher across the almost deserted but brightly lit Main Street, found himself stumbling to retain footing.

The word spread quickly downtown: "The new guy (Brown) is just as bad as Francis Lee."

Whether the street gossip ever reached Endicott or Philadelphia remains unanswered. Brown told the story on himself to the author.

In the next few years, Brown recalled, Lee helped him out of many tight situations that a new general manager was likely to encounter in a very conservative community that for years had been quite happy with Lee's product and that consequently was chary about journalistic innovations.

Perhaps the lassitude that seemed to pervade the *Star*'s newsroom was at least partially attributable to the editorial salary structure. Not very long after he became owner, Ottaway happened upon a bookkeeper drawing a non-salary voucher for the wire editor. "Why?" he asked the man of ledgers.

"This fellow washes the windows every month for extra money," was the reply.

R. John Van Kleeck, one of only two presently active newspapermen in the Ottaway group who served in Oneonta in the 1940s, recalled that he started as a reporter in 1947 for $25 a week. After three months his pay was advanced to $27.50. After a year of service it was raised to a lofty $30.

"Oranges and coffee were for Christmas," Van Kleeck said.

A few knew Van Kleeck as the "Trapper." The sobriquet derives from his Portlandville area avocational quest for pelts to augment his income.

22

The last Lee payroll before the Ottaway takeover showed that the publisher was paying himself a weekly salary of $163.46 after taxes.

Gene Brown's starting salary as the new GM was $125 a week and Gerald Gunthrup, editor, was at $42.50. Harold Rockwell, city editor, drew $40.

At the end of 1944 Ottaway and French each drew $48 a week as corporate officers.

An interesting sidebar to the Oneonta acquisition was an offer tendered some years earlier by Frank Gannett, founder of the then Rochester-based group. Lee spurned Gannett's advances because the teetotaling tycoon declined to make a personal appearance. One or more of his satraps would do the negotiating, Gannett reasoned erroneously, underestimating Lee's sense of pride.

It is not clear whether Jim Ottaway's mother appeared in Oneonta at the time of the closing or shortly afterward. Still one of her son's bankers, she had advanced most of the down payment.

In a burst of candor she volunteered to Brown that "Jim is awfully reckless with money. I don't think he'll ever be a financial success."

Ottaway has little doubt that his mother's colloquy with Brown took place. "She always thought I was too rash with money," he said.

Early in their association Ottaway suggested that Brown might do well to buy stock in the fledgling corporation, and arranged for his mother to lend Brown $7,000 after the general manager reported his pockets were bare. Brown was off and running, financially.

Ottaway's acquisition of the *Star,* without a solid financial background and with only the Endicott struggle to show for credentials, began a theme, or personality pattern that enabled the Ottaways to acquire newspapers from long-time owners who primarily wished their papers to be developed by people they could respect.

"Ottaway's mission was clear," Brown said. It was to give readers the finest newspaper he could produce. He was a journalist first, a publisher second.

"I participated in numerous negotiations with the Ottaways and their associates. Publishers in many cases could have demanded and received higher prices for their papers. Almost without exception the key to an eventual Ottaway purchase was their faith in Ottaway's publishing standards."

But Brown didn't always agree fully with Ottaway's traditional approach to potential acquisitions.

"I sometimes thought that in our negotiations Jim talked too much about ourselves and our publishing standards and neglected to address himself to the seller's tax and estate problems and any other troubling situations that might have arisen."

"However," he added, "in the light of Jim's success, my comment perhaps sounds like not fully ripened grapes."

Besides building an executive team, which at this point consisted of Jim and Ruth Ottaway, French and Brown, the Ottaways were developing close ties with key personalities in satellite publishing industries and trade associations.

In the war year of 1942 newsprint was in short supply. Shortly after the Oneonta purchase the Finch-Pruyn Company, the *Star*'s supplier, canceled Ottaway's contract. (Newsprint then, by the way, was $40 per ton. Today it costs about $570.)

The *Rome* (N.Y.) *Daily Sentinel*, in effect, bailed out the *Star* and the *Bulletin* for the duration. Wartime newsprint allocations were based on a given newspaper's usage over preceding years. That meant Endicott had no viable usage factor because it had gone semi-weekly to daily in 1937.

The *Sentinel*, like all newspapers, tightened its newshole during the war and was able to get by with plenty of newsprint to spare. Whether its proximity to the then-building Rome Air Base (known today as Griffiss Air Force Base) had anything to do with the surplus is open to conjecture. But Bradley Barnard, *Sentinel* proprietor, saw to it that extra tonnage was reconsigned to Endicott or Oneonta.

Charles C. Carpenter of International Paper Company helped originate and exercise the arrangement. Years before, as Ottaway was about to start the *Daily Bulletin*, he met Carpenter for the first time in IP's New York City headquarters. He sought a newsprint contract, his first.

24

(Ottaway had been buying paper from a Binghamton jobber at premium prices.)

"I'll need a contract for 50 tons," Ottaway told Carpenter.

"A week? A month?" Carpenter asked.

"No. A year," Ottaway replied.

Carpenter didn't bat an eye. Ottaway got his contract.

"He treated me as though I were ordering 5,000 tons," Ottaway said. They would remain lifelong friends.

At the board meeting January 2, 1945, directors improved Brown's salary status. His base remained at $125 a week, but he was allotted another $20 for "traveling, entertainment and other expenses." In addition, the new arrangement called for Brown to receive two percent of net profits up to $20,000 and three percent above $20,000. Ottaway and French were pegged at $5,000 each for the year. Pretty heady stuff for a venture that still was richer in romance than revenue!

On July 27 of that year, board minutes show, Ottaway was authorized to apply for a broadcasting license for Oneonta.

By 1946, Brown said, company indebtedness began to be "more comfortable."

"This made it imperative," he observed (tongue in cheek) "that we go into more loans. The imperative can always find a reason to be imperative."

Minutes of board meetings during 1946 leave little doubt that the operation was picking up steam under Brown's guidance. On November 1 directors voted Jim Ottaway a 1947 salary of $175 per week. Brown's base jumped to $155. And Ottaway and Brown each were voted princely $3,500 year-end bonuses. This time Ruth Ottaway was not forgotten. The hard-working corporate secretary was given a $25 weekly salary.

On December 7 Ottaway signed a contract with the Duplex Division of the Goss Printing Press Company, Battle Creek, Michigan, for a new 20-page standard tubular press and folder. Estimated price at the time was $46,000, according to the minute book, but by the time it was delivered the following April 9, it carried a price tag of $53,360.

Gene Brown stored the press at Strenger's Body Shop on River Street against the time a new *Star*-WDOS building would be built.

A laconic minute book entry late in 1947 reported that the Ottaways and Brown had been looking for a building site. In December the following year the company took an option for $1,000 on a parcel of land at Chestnut and West Streets. The site would cost $25,000.

The cornerstone of a new building was laid in 1949. That structure would house the *Star*. Its broadcast division, WDOS, would occupy an abutting frame structure. Building cost was estimated at $155,000.

Just a year later, construction started.

So into more loans went the Ottaways, French and Brown.

The *Star* borrowed $10,000 at four percent from Citizens National Bank, using a new Linotype as collateral. The Wilber National Bank advanced $40,000, accepting a chattel mortgage on the press at four percent. And another loan agreement was fashioned with the Oneonta Building and Loan Association, which would advance up to $100,000 as work progressed on the building. Advances were to be applied to construction "and no other purpose."

At the end of 1949 total long-term debt of the *Star* stood at $154,349. Total Ottaway long-term debt had risen to $366,000. His borrowings, obviously, were not confined to Oneonta, as we shall see.

Disaster struck March 14, 1950. The stored press and folder were severely damaged by fire at the River Street shop. Insurance covered the loss, and the machinery was returned to Duplex for complete rebuilding, which included a new press guarantee. The tab was $35,000.

Collecting the insurance proved to be a protracted task.

Why? "Probably because of the shabby place in which I stored it," Brown told the author.

The *Star* moved into its new quarters July 22, 1950. The move began after the Saturday edition had rolled off the old press. By Sunday afternoon all machines were in working order, including the rebuilt Duplex. First issue from the new plant went to press Monday morning, July 24, right on schedule. Station WDOS had moved a few months before.

Oneonta would not pay a dividend until 1955.

Directors were as one: "Let's pay off debts!"

Brown followed the traditional Ottaway pattern of becoming a community activist. He served as president of the Chamber of Commerce and for four years as president of Fox Hospital.

As was the case in Endicott, profits generated by the *Star* were plowed back into the operation. Better pay. Better equipment. A bureau in Cooperstown, the Otsego County seat.

That would be the key to continued expansion: "Borrowing and generating cash, putting it back into a better product," Ottaway said.

Gene Brown at times regarded Ottaway's penchant for local autonomy as a license to operate the *Star* — and later the *Danbury* (Conn.) *News-Times* — somewhat outside the philosophical and commercial parameters favored by the chief. The protracted early struggle for bedrock solvency had drawn Margo and Gene Brown into an intimate relationship with the Ottaway family. But the mutual affection did not preclude periodic arguments, which, according to Brown, became violent at times. "We always said what we thought, " Brown wrote in 1970.

(That year Brown was gathering material for a company history, but the project was dropped. His fragmentary notes form the basis for portions of this book. "I was thrown by contradictory information I received on incidents to which I was participant or a witness. I gave up with a sense of inferiority.")

If Ottaway ever had a general manager-publisher who functioned as a Cyclops of the cash register, it was Brown, especially in the area of payroll accounts. But his penurious bent did not dilute the esteem in which he was held by employees.

"You knew he was picking your pockets," one self-termed former "union radical" said. "He'd lend you a car. He installed an automatic shoeshine machine in the Danbury building. He'd make small, interest-free loans. And he'd bring in his son's old shirts for us. All in lieu of money."

"It was Gene's show all the way," another ex-employee said. "He wore the white hat. He was a master."

"You'd bust your butts for him," still another volunteered. "He endeared himself to everyone. Everyone trusted him. He

27

was like a benevolent father, always there when you needed him."

More than one of Brown's charitable acts drew Ottaway's ire. In Danbury he hired a former Oneonta editor who had been fired for incompetence. "I felt sorry for the fellow," Brown said, recalling the "monumental" chewing out he received from the not-so-compassionate chief. But Brown had learned to roll with the punches, knowing that Ottaway would be "smiling the next day." Brown never told Ottaway that the suggestion to hire the editor had come from Jim Ottaway Jr.

Throughout his Ottaway career Brown found time to write a daily column, "The Light Side." Started in 1944, it began with what he called an "acerbic" or "satirical edge." In the late 1950s Ottaway induced the author to "go all out for the humorous." Brown wrote in 1974 that "that's where it stands . . . on a shaky pinnacle." In later years he averaged $1,000 a year each from *Reader's Digest* and the *National Inquirer* for bon mots they picked up from the column.

Brown handled his own labor negotiations, which predictably resulted in minimal settlements and which were marked by breaks during which he lay on the floor of his office to doze or to meditate.

One former associate recalled Brown as a "health nut," who was partial to copper bracelets, tennis and golf. On the links Brown carried only three clubs, a five iron, seven iron and putter. And he excelled at tennis.

On company festive occasions Brown always was ready with just what his employees expected: a sort of shock treatment. After one dinner at the Yankee Drover Inn in Newtown, Connecticut, he announced from the head table "My God, you people ate a lot!" They loved it.

3 Stroudsburg

"Jim Ottaway," Gene Brown told the author, "never worried about all the loans floating around. His mother told him he would die owing money."

Ottaway confirmed Brown's observation: "I never worried because I knew we were going in the right direction toward a worthwhile end."

Total long-term debt of Endicott and Oneonta had jumped from $13,696 at the end of 1944 to $193,000 a year later. And considerably more borrowing lay directly ahead.

Distribution of *Bulletin* profits at the end of 1945 under the Ottaway-French partnership at the 83-17 percent ratio was $24,568 for Ottaway, $5,032 for his manager, for a total of $29,600. As *Bulletin* profits went, it was a good year. Oneonta recorded a net of $16,519 in its first full year of Ottaway operation.

As 1946 began, the Ottaway-French partnership (formed early in 1944) was dissolved. A new corporation, Empire Newspapers-Radio, Inc., took its place. At its first meeting in Endicott, January 23, Ottaway was authorized to apply to the Federal Communications Commission for a 250-watt Endicott radio station, which eventually would carry the call letters WENE. The Bulletin building was returned to Empire by Ruth Ottaway for 325 shares of Empire ($32,500). Ottaway held the titles of president and publisher, French vice president and GM. Ruth was named corporate secretary.

At the inception of Empire, Ottaway owned 599 of the 1,050 outstanding shares (57.05 percent); Ruth controlled 336 (32 percent) and French 115 (10.95 percent.)

29

But 1946 is remembered principally for the Stroudsburg, Pennsylvania, acquisition.

One of the folktales that has surfaced off and on since Ottaway acquired the *Daily Record* is that it was a birthday present for Ruth. Sort of a surprise gift on that July 29, as though the protracted negotiations had been carried out clandestinely. It was a "gift" in the sense that July 29 is her birthday and the closing just happened to have taken place that day. It is true that Ottaway had not chosen a gift. His thoughts, understandably, were focused on the acquisition and what Jake Becker had in mind with that certified check for $100,000 in his pocket.

Once again Allen Kander had approached Ottaway, who had just been mustered out of Navy service. Somewhat curiously, Ottaway was not aware the paper was for sale, even though he and Ruth owned an all-weather cottage at nearby Buck Hill Falls.

Not much is on record about the owner of Monroe Publishing Company. Edward J. Breece is described only as a "newspaperman from Phoenixville, Pennsylvania," in a 1976 newspaper article tracing the history of the Record. Breece bought the paper from Nelson Frantz, a former school principal, who became business manager of the then-weekly *Record* early in the century. It went daily in 1909, pledging allegiance to the Democratic Party. Frantz acquired control midway through his 35-year stewardship, besides buying out the pestiferous *Morning Sun* in 1938, at which time the *Daily Record* switched to morning publication.

Frantz obviously knew a hot item when he saw one. The *Sun* had been cutting into *Record* circulation, and it didn't take much research to determine that Stroudsburg area readers wanted a morning product.

Frantz sold the *Daily Record* to Breece in 1944, as one article put it, having "won respect as newsman and publisher."

Breece's mistake was acquiring the newspaper without federal tax consequences in mind. He bought the newspaper personally, without incorporating. As a result, whatever profits shaken off were taxed as part of Breece's individual returns. He was forced to sell.

As July 29 approached, Ottaway and Breece had about agreed on a price: $256,680. That included a $55,000 payoff over 10 years to Breece in exchange for an agreement not to compete. Sweetening the deal for Ottaway was $35,000 in cash and U.S. government bonds in the till.

Before leaving Endicott for what they hoped would be the final negotiation, Becker instructed Ottaway to give him $100,000 in the form of a certified check.

"I don't have $100,000," Ottaway protested.

"Get it," Becker shot back.

Ottaway got it in the form of a demand note from his old friends at Endicott Trust. The transaction was unique for Ottaway. It violated his Rule No. 1: No short-term borrowing.

Breece's lawyer was Arlington Williams, who, three decades later would become president judge of the 43rd Judicial District, encompassing Monroe and Pike counties in Pennsylvania.

Breece and Williams, Ottaway remembered, were holding out for four and a quarter percent on the notes Ottaway would sign. Ottaway and Becker stood fast at four. Negotiations began to deteriorate.

Finally Becker arose and with a theatrical flourish waved the check at his adversaries.

"This is too bad," he intoned mournfully, "seeing that Jim and I came down here with $100,000 ready to close the deal."

Breece and Williams caucused. Becker flashed a thousand-watt smile at Ottaway.

The interest rate was pegged at four percent. Becker's gambit had carried the day.

"Really and truly a banner deal," Kander would write in retrospect. His subjectivity may be excused. For the second time he had acted as Ottaway's broker. He would return to the publisher's side on more exalted occasions.

First meeting of the new ownership, Pocono Record, Inc., was held September 3 at the old *Record* offices on Seventh Street, from which the company would operate for the next 11 years.

Capital stock of Pocono was authorized at $30,000, consisting of 3,000 shares with a stated value of $10 per share. Pocono, in effect, merged with Monroe Publishing Company and became

31

the surviving entity.

The Ottaways, Barney French and Gene Brown comprised the board.

There is an allusion to broadcasting in Section 3, Article of Merger, which says one purpose of the corporation is "the ownership and operation of radio broadcasting stations in or near the Borough of Stroudsburg." Station WVPO was around the corner.

Merle Ostrom, then national advertising manager of the *Binghamton Press,* an old friend (and friendly competitor) of Barney French in the Triple Cities advertising wars, was hired to run the *Record.* He was given the title of vice president and business manager. As far as can be determined, Ostrom had no editorial experience.

But unlike the situation Ottaway inherited in Oneonta, the 7,000-circulation *Record* had a cadre of executive talent. John S. (Jack) Remaly was brought in from Endicott as editor. Bill Deering, the incumbent, had reached 80. Horace Heller, city editor, in a rather strange move, was given the co-title of business manager, even though Ostrom was running the show. Why? "To assuage Horace's feelings when we bought in Remaly," Ottaway recalled.

Lowell H. (Red) Cross was a very successful advertising director and would become a legend over the remainder of his long life span, partly because of his affinity for, and heroic skirmishes with, ardent spirits.

Cross, according to Brown, had a sort of airy sense of humor, so that working with him "was an adventure in light comedy. He fit the mold of the old-time drinking newsman, but in his (Cross's) opinion, he carried liquor well enough so that it did not impair his competence."

Red Cross wasn't the only Stroudsburg staffer so inclined.

It was an effective staff, however rambunctious.

The first Ottaway payroll is in the newspaper's vault. Starting on September 1, 1946, it had Ostrom pegged at $100 per week, Remaly at $75 and Cross at $55. Listed at $50 weekly was an ad salesman named Elton Hall, back in Ottaway harness after his wartime stint with the Pennsylvania Railroad.

Hardly munificent compensation. But that's the way it was in

1946, and not only in small-town publishing.

Edward J. (Ed) Somers, today publisher of the *Sun City* (Ariz.) *Daily News-Sun,* who joined Ottaway in Stroudsburg as a radio time salesman in 1952, found that his first experience with newspapers hardly was calculated to invest him with abiding faith that it was financially rewarding.

In pre-Ottaway days, Somers was a no-pay *Record* sports stringer, lured into virtual bondage by Heller.

"For two years in high school, " Somers recalled, "I covered local football, basketball and baseball. My prose was torn to shreds by Heller, Bill Deering and Art Everitt. After Navy service I continued my career as a stringer covering East Stroudsburg State College. During my high school days in lieu of pay I received a letter from Heller, which identified me as an accredited reporter. This was intended to get me into games without charge. My total pay consisted of 50 cents when I begged for supper money for an out-of-town contest."

Hepatitis struck Ottaway in the fall of 1946. He was hospitalized in Stroudsburg for two weeks, and returned to the Buck Hill Falls cottage to convalesce. The Ottaway children attended school in Barrett Township for the 1946-47 academic year. French supervised Endicott, Oneonta and Stroudsburg operations from the Endicott command post.

The *Daily Record* returned an operating profit of $12,620 between August 13 and December 31, 1946, the first segment of Ottaway ownership. Ruth and Jim Ottaway controlled 86.66 percent of outstanding stock. French and Brown each held 6.67 percent.

Minute books of Pocono Record, Inc., contain little other than borrowing resolutions and normal takeover problems between 1946 and 1952, when the board decided it was time to seek new quarters. The Seventh Street plant was aging and lack of space was becoming a more acute problem each year.

But entries reveal that you could get home delivery of the *Daily Record* for 15 cents a week in 1946. Ottaway, historically never bashful about raising the price of anything, jumped the price to 20 cents early in 1947 and at the same time set up Pocono's first advertising rate card that included display and classified contracts. And he renegotiated the $100,000 demand

33

note with Endicott Trust, coming up with a four percent term loan. Concurrently, Empire found it necessary to advance $10,000 to Pocono to cover a debt installment.

Ostrom was promoted to general manager early in 1948. The move suggests only that he had earned the board's full confidence, and that his on-line leadership was beginning to pay off financially. The paper recorded a net profit of $23,280 that year.

Ostrom in 1948 also acquired 100 shares of Pocono Broadcasting, the same number held by French and Brown. He was the only executive outside the original Big Four ever to own stock in an Ottaway venture.

Meantime, Ruth Ottaway was urging the board to speed debt reduction on $11,000 worth of mortgage bonds on the Seventh Street property, and Ottaway was voted a salary increase from $75 to $200 a week "as business was improving."

First mechanical improvement came that year with the arrival of a $13,169 Intertype linecasting unit, which was promptly chatteled for $10,000.

Other needed capital investments in Stroudsburg would be held back several years. Profits elsewhere were being funneled into three radio start-ups and the new plant in Oneonta.

The flamboyant Heller became editor in 1950, and after Ostrom's retirement was named assistant general manager. In mid-1950 he became general manager.

By December 31, 1950, total Pocono long-term debt had been shaved to $113,500. The newspaper was paying its way handily. Circulation had inched to 8,000. During the year, Pocono minutes tell us, Marshall Brooks retired as circulation manager of the *Endicott Bulletin* and was named promotion manager for all three papers in the expanding group. Ottaway was thinking bigger.

Back at Endicott headquarters, meantime, the Empire board abandoned the 1943 retirement trust fund program because of "employee lack of interest." A hospitalization-surgical plan was substituted. It would be almost 30 years before the Ottaways set up the present pension fund.

Three financial maneuvers marked the end of the 1940s for Empire. The *Endicott Bulletin* building was mortgaged to

Security Mutual Life Insurance Company of Binghamton for $60,000 (to help finance the WENE studios) and, because the board decided that "there was a need for additional financing," Ruth Ottaway bought 185 Empire shares, her husband 115 and French 45 at $100 per share, enriching the parent treasury by $34,500. In retrospect it was big money. At about the same time, Ottaway returned to Endicott Trust and negotiated a $45,000 term loan at five percent.

Empire board minutes of January 3, 1949, relating to the Endicott editorial product and burgeoning circulation give insight to the careful attention French was giving to the Bulletin. They are worth reprinting:

"Mr. French discussed at some length the news coverage of the *Endicott Daily Bulletin*, with special emphasis devoted to extended coverage of the communities adjoining Endicott. He said that additional correspondents had been hired in Endwell, Vestal, Maine and similar outlying villages, and that he felt that this had resulted in far superior news coverage. He also said that the Endicott news coverage was being stepped up considerably. At the end of 1948 he said that the *Bulletin* circulation had passed 7,800 net paid for the first time and that this represented a net gain of about 600 to 700 subscribers compared with the same period in 1947.

"Mrs. Ottaway said that she had noted considerably improved news coverage in Endwell, and that in her discussions with women about the area she had found that the improved news coverage was winning more readers. Mr. French also pointed out that Donald Munro, formerly city editor, was assigned to cover Binghamton and the county news in December 1948, and that William Rising had been hired as city editor to serve under Editor Harvey Travis. He said that this had further strengthened the *Bulletin* news coverage.

"Mr. Ottaway said that because Endicott, Vestal, Endwell, Maine, Owego and other communities of the so-called Greater Endicott Area were all separate politically, he felt that the name of the newspaper should be changed to the *Daily Bulletin*, which would more adequately represent the area the newspaper serves. Mr. French said that he felt this should be seriously considered, and Mrs. Ottaway added that she felt it

35

was a sensible idea, too."

By the end of 1951 the Ottaways had acquired three newspapers, had built two newspaper plants and had started three radio stations. Two replacement presses had been installed, together with a wide range of improved hot metal typesetting equipment.

Despite the labyrinthine financial maneuvers these exploits required, Ottaway found time to ensure that his general managers and editors produced not merely good newspapers, but what he called great ones. Ascending circulation and profits were solid evidence that his primary credo was viable: Publish a great newspaper, plow back profits to make it even greater and success would be assured.

4 Enter Lyn Boyd

November 1949 saw the arrival of a personality who would complete the Ottaway summit management structure, which remained intact virtually up to the mid-1970 merger with Dow Jones.

At the time, Gene Brown was searching for a human catalyst to increase the *Oneonta Star*'s advertising volume. The new plant was under construction; a new replacement press had been ordered.

It would have been perfectly understandable for Brown to have mentioned his quest to one or more of the ad service drummers who called at the *Star* periodically.

The traveling salesmen historically not only carried presentation kits, they knew (or thought they knew) what publishers were in the market for advertising talent. Most of the time they were right. The dropped word was just as effective as a six-line help wanted ad in *Editor & Publisher*. And it was free.

Not only publishers confided in (or hinted to) the men of mats. Advertising directors, managers and even salesmen let it be known that they were ready to move to bigger and better opportunities.

In such a way did a future president of Ottaway Newspapers-Radio, Inc., find his way to Brown.

Lyndon Ray Boyd, a graduate of Union College, at 36 was retail advertising manager of the *Union-Star* in Schenectady, 75 miles east of Oneonta. Boyd was doing well; retail display linage in the *Union-Star* was running substantially ahead of that in the *Gazette* (which would survive as the city's only daily).

But Boyd was unhappy. Or shall we say stymied? His superior, also a comparatively young man, was performing creditably. Boyd wanted out.

Boyd's ambitions were known to at least one member of the advertising services fraternity, who confided via a long distance call that there was "an opening" in Oneonta. "Perhaps," Boyd's informant suggested temptingly, "you could become ad director for the whole (Ottaway) group."

No harm in looking, Boyd decided, and drove westward on Route 7 for a date with Brown.

After meetings with Brown and Ottaway, a deal was struck. Boyd was hired as ad director. He would supervise retail, classified and national linage.

Brown's and Boyd's memories jibe on the new director's starting salary: $10,000. But the yellowing payroll journals of the *Star* peg Boyd at $100 for his first week's work. No matter.

"Brownie had a habit of giving people titles instead of money," Boyd said. "I had to eliminate the titles before I could get anything done." This was not accomplished by giving more money in lieu of titles. People knew their place when Boyd was in charge and as a generation of staffers who worked under Brown will tell you, Brown would give you just about anything except money. He was frugality incarnate.

Lyn Boyd had served throughout the war and had emerged as a major of infantry. Picture him as a somewhat diminitive martinet line officer with swagger stick, reviewing evening parade. He could be tough.

Those who managed, through various types of nonfeasance, to incur his displeasure would agree in spades. Some union negotiators included.

And there are those who cringed before Boyd's fusillades of profane memory. Some recovered as the taskmaster applied salve to the wounds. Salve was for salvageable penitents.

Boyd volunteered that he had to conquer an industrial-strength temper during his early career.

"Boyd's 'tough' demeanor," Brown surmised, "was a calculated ploy to get things done his way. Immediately. Lyn did have a soft side, but he used it sparingly, primarily with general managers and publishers. He was committed to them wholeheartedly. They, in turn, gave Lyn their loyalty."

"Brownie," Boyd said, with tongue in cheek, "is wrong. I was a sonofabitch. I'm still a monarchist at heart."

His associates remembered Boyd as quite disposed to listen to all sides of an argument. But they all came to know that there was a flash point where he invoked cloture, announcing, "This is the way it's going to be." Boyd always had his facts marshaled. Seldom did he have to yield.

Secretaries recalled he did most of his work on the telephone.

They also remembered spasmodic outbursts when the person on the other end of the line began to overstate a case: "God damn it, let me get a word in!"

One secretary, transcribing a Boyd dictation belt about skunks in his back yard, came up with a sentence that included the phrase "pathetic skunks." Boyd's adjective was "peripatetic." The embarrassed typist could relax on this occasion. Boyd thought it was funny.

Brown recalled that Boyd believed "implicitly" that the success of day-to-day newspaper operations was entirely dependent on the managers and didn't hesitate to press on Ottaway his belief that they deserved all the recognition (including certain perquisites) that reasonably could be given.

"He fought for them without ever retreating," Brown said, "even when in my opinion they didn't deserve such extraordinary treatment."

So it was only natural that Boyd would find himself officiating whenever matters headed toward "a final solution," i.e. discharge at the executive level.

From the start Boyd was a resounding success in Oneonta. Advertising graphs showed constantly ascending curves.

When misfortune in the form of hepatitis struck Brown, Boyd ran the *Star* for the better part of two months. Ottaway had sent the general manager to Florida to recuperate. Gene, Margo, and son Jonathan stayed at Captiva on Sanibel Island on the west coast. Boyd's leadership talents did not go unrecognized. He felt he was ready for another move — upward.

Boyd remembered a melancholy incident that occurred during Brown's absence. An advertiser complained that there was an $800 discrepency between his records and what the *Star* said he owed. The business office employee who might be able to unravel the apparent snarl had left for the day, but it was his wont to stop off at a neighborhood deadfall en route home. Boyd sent for the man of ledgers.

One quick question. One quick answer.

"I took the money," he told Boyd. "Mr. Brown wouldn't lend me any. I had no choice. I was desperate."

He opened his wallet and extracted a paper listing the defalcations, which came exactly to the sum in dispute.

A call to Jim Ottaway in Endicott brought the publisher to Oneonta the next day.

The embezzler was transferred to a non-sensitive post on the *Star*. He died four months later.

"That," Boyd said, "tells you a lot about Jim Ottaway. As Barney French used to say, 'I never knew Jim to do a mean thing'."

Brown's version of the incident differed from Boyd's.

"I had loaned him money from time to time without knowing what he needed it for. He was a close friend and I admired him. In my opinion, he embezzled to pay off horse betting losses."

In the early 1950s Ottaway concluded he needed an executive assistant. His first choice was Brown, who declined gracefully.

"Our publishing philosophies are so different I don't think I could work that closely with you," he told the proprietor.

Apparently the matter was tabled during the soon-to-be-started negotiations for the *Plattsburgh* (N.Y.) *Press-Republican*. Concurrently, Boyd had received an attractive offer from Howard Parrish Associates, a Miami-based classified advertising service. Boyd said he was tempted.

Brown eventually told Boyd about his decision to turn down the post as Ottaway's assistant. "Too much traveling, among other things," Brown confided.

Boyd's response was to the point.

"I want the Plattsburgh job," he told Brown, making it clear he wanted a general manager's slot.

"We're sending Bill Lundquest to Plattsburgh," Brown said. "We have other things in mind for you."

"I was frank with Brownie," Boyd said, "I told him I was

looking, told him about the Parrish offer and assured him this was no holdup."

Brown, Boyd said, even urged him to visit Parrish, which he and Eda did. "It's worth a look," Boyd quoted Brown.

Indecision followed. Boyd said he was "hesitant."

Then, according to Brown, he assured Boyd that his (Boyd's) future lay with Ottaway.

"You'll become president in time. There's no limit to what you can achieve."

Brown's remark was prophetic.

Boyd must have sensed that Brown knew what he was talking about. He declined the Miami offer.

Shortly after the Plattsburgh acquisition, Ottaway, French and Brown marshaled their advertising executives in Cooperstown for a sales clinic. Boyd was summoned to Ottaway's room in the Cooper Inn and was offered the job as administrative assistant to the president. He accepted on the spot.

"I had no authority," Boyd recalled. "I was a sort of caddy for Jim."

"Caddying," as Boyd put it, "was a sort of guessing game as to just how far I could go" without the titular trappings of power.

During one visit to Stroudsburg, he found a new air conditioner on the floor of Merle Ostrom's office. The *Daily Record* boss said he had been urged to buy it and one other for the darkroom. The urging, Boyd discovered, had come from Ruth Ottaway. Ruth had followed up a suggestion from daughter Ruthie, who had been an intern that summer. Ruthie had been approached by the staff photographer.

Back in Endicott, Boyd reported Ruth's role as intervenor and told Jim Ottaway he thought it was "dead wrong."

"You're right," Ottaway said. Nothing further was heard of the matter. But Boyd felt Ottaway had backed him.

"If I hadn't moved on this, everybody in the plant would have demanded air conditioners," Boyd said. In the early days ACs were not part of the Ottaway standard complement of office fixtures.

Ruth Ottaway remembered giving Ostrom the green light.

She said she was motivated by Stroudsburg's geographic susceptibility to heat and humidity which at times assumed Saharan proportions.

As the group expanded, its exposure to labor problems widened. At best, negotiations could be handled locally. Some were simple. Some were beyond the bargaining talents of Ottaway's general managers. And some GMs had no stomach for the give-and-take, which, at times reached the strike-threat stage. These early battles involved only the printers' and pressmen's unions. Years later there would be confrontations with the Teamsters and unions bent on organizing newsrooms.

Boyd emerged as the one who answered an SOS from the bargaining table. He reveled in combat, winning most but losing a few skirmishes as he developed negotiating skills via the trial-and-error route.

"He was a great labor point man for Jim Ottaway," Brown said. "He had a knack of knowing just how far he could go."

Boyd underscored his thirst for battle with what he considered the unreasonable and power-mad type of labor spokesman.

"Jim Ottaway was not a good negotiator," he said. "He had no patience and quickly tired of the nonsense that you have to put up with. Jim would say 'Give 'em $2 a week more. The hell with it'."

Brown offered another side of Jim Ottaway on the labor front:

"Once Jim gave me hell because I had gone 25 cents an hour over the previously-agreed offer to get a settlement. Lyn insisted to Jim that I had full authority to make the best possible deal. In fairness to Jim, I think he resented the settlement because he wrongly insisted I had not conferred with Lyn. Lyn couldn't convince Jim that I had consulted with him and that my authority indeed was implied.

"It was one of my many heated discussions with Jim. They never bothered me because in 24 hours Jim would be praising me to the skies."

Ottaway always introduced Brown and Boyd as "my associates," in Brown's view an extremely courteous and welcome gesture.

42

Boyd was a conservative who carried well the classic description, "well to the right of a John Bircher."

Candor would compel a biographer to write that Boyd was at least conversationally guilty of some caustic putdowns when his dander rose.

"Lyn's positive traits so far outshone the negative we all overlooked that," Brown said. "It was just his way, just talk."

☆ ☆ ☆ ☆ ☆ ☆

Another figure of legend, especially to those whose responsibilities encompassed accounting matters, arrived on the Ottaway scene in 1950 via Riga, Latvia, and a Mobil filling station in Oneonta.

Arthur and Austra Beiniks fled the post-war Soviet-controlled country, and, sponsored by the First Baptist Church of Oneonta, went to work as filling station attendants. Their living quarters abutted the garage.

Beiniks, proficient in four languages, held a bachelor of commerce degree. He was determined to return to the world of credits and debits as soon as his displaced person work contract with the church was fulfilled. Together the Beinikses speedily established a reputation for super service at the pumps. No windshield left the station untouched. Nor did head lamps. Boyd went out of his way to patronize the station during his tenure as the *Star's* ad director.

To keep his accountant's eagle eye in trim, Beiniks moonlighted, keeping books for a dry cleaner at $35 a week. In 1952 he spotted a help wanted ad in the *Star*. Gene Brown needed a bookkeeper. Beiniks was turned down. "Overqualified," he was told.

The following year the *Star's* chief accountant died. Once again Beiniks approached Brown.

"I know more about you than you do about me," Brown told Beiniks. "The job is yours." Perhaps Boyd had spoken to Brown about the hard-working political refugees. Perhaps Brown had read the newspaper stories about Beiniks's talks before area service clubs. Beiniks wasn't sure.

Beiniks remained at the *Star* until 1956 (the Danbury acquisition year) when he was transferred to Endicott headquarters. He would move to Middletown after the 1960 merger there as comptroller of the *Times Herald-Record*.

☆ ☆ ☆ ☆ ☆ ☆

Details of the birth of Ottaway's national advertising sales department apparently have not been preserved. Corporate minute books of the late 1940s and early 1950s contain no mention of the individual or agency first retained, but assembled fragments of fading memories indicate it came into being about 1950.

It is known that Walton Deming of Oneonta was the second representative. Deming said in a telephone conversation in April 1984, "I didn't replace a person. I replaced a small upstate company."

Long, lonesome hours on the road and Mrs. Deming's death from cancer took their toll, and in 1955 Deming stepped down.

His successor at Endicott headquarters was Philip Gage (Phil) Daniels, who had been Upstate New York representative of the Julius Matthews advertising agency until what he called his totally unexpected discharge "for no apparent reason."

Daniels had turned to selling linage for radio pages (program listings in tabloid format) and tie-in ads for church pages.

"I was completely crushed. It was a terrible blow to my pride," he recalled.

Daniel's travels for the Matthews agency had brought him into frequent contact with Deming and Boyd. Indeed, Daniels says, he signed all the then-four Ottaway papers as Matthews clients. (Ottaway's national sales department did not represent radio. Peggy Stone handled broadcasting time spots from a New York City office.)

With Deming departing, Daniels said he pleaded with Boyd for the job and was hired in 1955 in Cooperstown during a general managers' meeting. Daniels said he was "rocked" by his starting salary of $5,000. "I was making $15,000 with Matthews." But he was beginning a solid second career that would end in 1970 when he became 65.

Apalachin, N.Y., is a hamlet a few miles from Endicott and the home of Joseph Barbero. Barbero was host to the notorious November 14, 1957, convocation of Mafia chieftains which was rudely interrupted by state police, who wanted to ask lots and lots of questions. The story rated Page 1 treatment across the country.

The raid, according to the attorney general's staff, led directly to the creation of New York's organized crime task force.

Phil Daniels knew Barbero in a different role, that of beer distributor. Through the Mafia grandee, Daniels wrote barrels of linage for the *Endicott Bulletin*. The connection fazed neither Daniels nor Jim Ottaway. Business was business.

When the salesman in Daniels failed to sway a prospect, his unmatched persistence paid off. Boyd would tell you that more than one space buyer caved in just to get Daniels out of town.

The Boyd deal with Daniels included hiring an assistant as the newspaper group expanded. After the Danbury acquisition in 1956, Daniels was joined by Homer Somers, then advertising manager of the *Ansonia* (Conn.) *Daily Sentinel*.

When Daniels stepped down in 1970, Somers was named head of the sales unit, remaining until Ottaway dissolved its own agency and appointed Branham/Newspaper Sales as it representative in 1976.

Merchandising inserts in the 1970s and 1980s became staggering revenue producers for most newspapers across the land. But some Ottaway publishers and general managers in earlier years recalled that at the outset of the phenomenon there was somewhat less than a positive attitude on the part of the headquarters oligarchy.

Boyd was perceived by many of his old colleagues as having

taken an anti-circular position. But he insisted that he was not opposed to circulars per se.

"I was against running inserts at give-away prices, at prices lower than the Postal Service charged. Run at reasonable rates, many inserts could be attractive additions to newspapers. Most printed in color were superior to anything we could produce. A favorable price per thousand should be computed without the cost of composition, presswork and newsprint."

Brown's recollections differed. He said Boyd was "sharply opposed" to carrying circulars and that Ottaway tended to agree. "Jim took a neutral position and let me give them a try. Lyn never resented it if I had my way."

"Gene was way ahead of all of us," Ottaway said decades later.

In mid-1961 Brown drafted a lengthy memo exploring the possible effects of shopping centers and preprints on retail linage over the ensuring five years. He worried about dying downtowns in Danbury, Plattsburgh and Middletown. "Downtowns," Brown wrote, "need all our circulation. Will shopping centers need it all? Will they demand fringe (expensive) circulation?"

"It is possible," he continued, "that use of circulars will grow with the influx of chains and new shopping centers. Thus we should consider the possibility that we may have to set up a system whereby we take the customer's own circular pre-printed with our dateline and distributed by our carriers."

Ottaway's reaction: Let's sit down and discuss it with Boyd before we commission a research project.

On the last point raised by Brown, Ottaway expressed his distaste for preprints:

"My own reaction, Gene, is that it would be very difficult to handle preprinted circulars, either within our newspaper or delivered separately by carrier. I have a feeling that we would be destroying our own medium, and if we did this for one customer, we would be in a position where we would have to do it for all."

Times and outlooks would change.

In a little more than a decade, Ottaway newspapers would

bulge with inserts.

It was a rare instance of the chief having been upstaged.

5 Plattsburgh

The 1950s would see four more newspapers added to the Ottaway group, three in New York and one in Connecticut. A new building would house the *Daily Record* in Stroudsburg. Long-term debt would soar from $399,669 to $1,384,812.

And, significantly, the decade marked the end of the era when an Ottaway could acquire a medium-size property for $250,000 - $500,000. Publishers eager to sell were pricing their papers nearer $1 million.

On January 20, 1953, Dwight Eisenhower was sworn in as the 34th president. Eisenhower's "free market system," promulgated over two terms, with an absolute minimum of government economic interference, was cut to order for entrepreneurs such as Ottaway. "Those were great years," the publisher sighed, wistfully.

As 1952 opened, the Oneonta debt reduction program was proceeding smoothly. Almost $100,000 had been pared from the borrowings for the new plant, machinery and the notes held by Francis Lee, Mrs. Sokoloff and local lending institutions.

Down in Stroudsburg the story was different. The *Daily Record* was financially sound, but its annual debt amortization of $23,800 so hobbled cash flow that Merle Ostrom told the board that it was "difficult to pay bills." And to add to Ostrom's worries, he had to shoehorn an additional $4,000 from the treasury to repair the aging building on Seventh Street.

A rather tart observation by Ruth Ottaway appeared in the Pocono Record, Inc., board minutes on February 4: "In the future the building should be kept in better condition." The search for a new building site and a larger-capacity used press would not start for another year.

The *Endicott Bulletin* had returned a net of $12,000 in 1951 after a rather marginal $4,200 the previous year. As yet there existed no symptoms of the economic squeeze that soon would take place with the completion of the divided highway through the Triple Cities.

Early in 1952, Allen Kander again approached Ottaway. His attache case contained a copy of the *Plattsburgh* (N.Y.) *Press-Republican.*

"It was," Ottaway said, "the worst-looking newspaper I'd ever seen."

A glance at Page 1 of the August 15, 1952, issue announcing the Ottaway purchase would confirm his dour appraisal. The headdress was a potpourri of serif-laden condensed cheltenham and light tempo with words spaced full-line flush right and left. Everything under 24-point was in capitals, an aberration that in itself would chill the publisher's blood.

But, Ottaway figured, "if a paper's bad enough, you can be a hero."

Gene Brown was assigned to conduct a survey of the area and its potential and to determine if it fitted into the realm of Ottaway management philosophy. There was much to consider.

"My survey was conducted on a street corner," Brown reminisced. "The first person I approached asked if I had a light. We struck up a conversation and during it he said he worked for a 'fine newspaper, the *Press-Republican.*' That was about enough of a survey. My report went out in a single sentence: 'Let's buy it.' "

The next and most compelling question was: With what?

"We still were strapped financially, installing new equipment in our three newspapers and outfitting three AM radio stations. And to make matters worse, a much larger newspaper group was trying to buy the property, and presumably would (and could) offer more," Brown said.

Ottaway thought Hearst Newspapers must have been the other potential buyer. The morning *Times-Union,* published in Albany, was the *Press-Republican*'s chief circulation rival in the North Country.

The *Press-Republican* was owned by Mrs. Mary Mannix

Dunphy and a niece, Miss Mary C. Oliver. Mrs. Dunphy, in her 70s, knew she had to improve the property or dispose of it. One albatross was a antediluvian flatbed press, which Ottaway knew he would have to replace — immediately.

Mrs. Dunphy wanted $400,000 for the run-down 7,500 circulation *P-R*.

But among the corporate assets was $100,000 in government bonds.

Mrs. Dunphy's attorney, Charles M. Harrington, turned out to be a schoolmaster type, whose North Country practice seldom, if ever, had pitted him against a voluble and imaginative Jake Becker.

During negotiations in his office, he decreed when and when not Becker could fire up his corona and stiffly informed Ottaway counsel that every agreement had to have an index.

"Fine," Becker told the stuffy man of torts, "you write the index and I'll write the agreement."

Which is what happened.

In effect Ottaway proposed to use Mrs. Dunphy's $100,000 as the down payment.

An outraged and out-maneuvered Harrington turned to his client (after doing "a double flip-flop" according to Brown) and, pointing to Ottaway, inveighed that "this man is buying your newspaper with your money!"

"Tax lawyers," Brown reflected wryly, "will understand the reason."

Balance of the purchase price was in two sets of installment notes bearing four percent interest, one for $176,307, the other $123,693.

Mrs. Dunphy's 325 shares of Plattsburg Publishing Company, Inc., went to Ottaway, then to Mrs. Dunphy's bank to be held under terms of an escrow agreement.

Brown didn't think Harrington "ever quite forgave us" for taking Mrs. Dunphy's cash and paying it back to her, but he described the septuagenarian as "a shrewd lady who knew what she was doing."

Why did Mrs. Dunphy sell to Ottaway?

Ottaway and Brown felt deeply that she believed they would carry on the traditions of what she felt was a good newspaper.

Brown doubted if any other prospective purchaser had a chance to acquire the *Press-Republican.*

"She was thoroughly sold on Ruth and Jim," he recalled. "They showed a genuine interest in all she stood for in the community and, after the purchase, continued the close friendship."

Mrs. Dunphy's old press, as Ottaway had feared, eventually managed to get out a morning run, but often just in time for late brunch reading. A new press was ordered, an auxiliary building was constructed to house it, together with a "floating" concrete press pad. The new owner had built on quicksand.

The "new" press was a 48-page Hoe, purchased from the Gillespie Brothers of Stamford, Connecticut, owners of the *Stamford Advocate*. It was reconditioned in Poughkeepsie, New York, by the John Griffiths Company.

The old Dunphy 12-page flatbed was sold to the Kennedy family, owners of the *Hudson* (N.Y.) *Register-Star,* for $8,500, less 10 percent to Griffiths.

Ottaway remembered warning the Kennedys that it was a dog. Finally, Eddie Webber, *P-R* press foreman, was sent to Hudson to show the new owners how it was supposed to operate. Ottaway feared he would lose the friendship of a fellow publisher despite the red flag he had raised.

The Hoe press went into operation in December 1952, five months after Ottaway control began. The start-up was hardly trouble-free. The Hoe Company had to assign one of its erector-mechanics to bail out Griffiths. A year later the Griffiths bill still was in dispute. It was resolved when Boyd and Lundquest managed to get $2,000 chopped off.

The Dunphy newspaper offices were not included in the transaction. Ottaway rented the inelegant rabbit warren until 1955.

It would be more than two decades before Ottaway would build a modern plant in Plattsburgh.

Endicott's ebullient Bill Lundquest was tapped to run the *P-R.* Almost overnight he transformed the newspaper into one of editorial integrity and a lucrative bottom line.

In 1959, on the occasion of Stephen W. Ryder's succession to the general managership, Ottaway characteristically wrote to his appointee:

"Management of a newspaper — whether it be the *Press-Republican* or another newspaper — is no picnic. It requires almost the same attention a mother gives a baby. Bill Lundquest has built the *Press-Republican*. . .to a very high position in Clinton and Essex counties. He has also made it an outstandingly successful newspaper financially. . ."

Lundquest discovered immediately that the *Press-Republican* literally had been shunning its advertising potential. Coming off the *Bulletin* hard sell, he took in so much local linage the first week that he ran out of newsprint.

The frowsy typographical look, it turned out, was not a facade. Things had been somnambulant in sales and service, too.

Before Ottaway, Brown and Becker left Plattsburgh, Jake had urged the new owner to set up a transition fund for Lundquest, whose name now appeared on the bank signature cards. But Ottaway left without attending to this detail. His general manager was out shaking hands with community leaders.

When Ottaway returned a couple of weeks later, he looked at the bank statement and shot a question at his lieutenant: "What the hell are you paying bills with?" There was less than $1,000 in the checking account. "I was keeping accounts current via financial chicanery I learned in Endicott," Lundquest wrote.

The *P-R* advertising department, Lundquest recalled, "consisted of a Frenchman. He was the sole salesman. He built a home, did upholstering and fished — all on company time." (The Frenchman was not identified further.)

Typical of the newspaper's utter indifference to revenue was the serio-comic case of the J.C. Penney Company, which had just built a store on Margaret Street. The manager called the *P-R*'s sleepy ad department to set up a schedule for the grand opening (Why are all openings grand?) but no one responded. Thoroughly perplexed at the *P-R*'s icy attitude toward the windfall of linage, he went to New York City and had the layouts prepared.

The opening schedule amounted to seven and a half pages over four days. The *P-R,* in its inexplicable philosophy of abstinence, agreed to accept two and a half pages, no more.

Lundquest's brother-in-law, eastern manager for Chesterfield cigarettes, encountered the same attitude when he fought unsuccessfully to place the equivalent of eight and a half pages of advertising in the *P-R.* (Liggett & Myers had chosen the isolated Plattsburgh market to test a new brand.) One and a half pages were all the paper would accept.

But that was all pre-Lundquest, one of whose first moves was to hire John Fournier, a combination radio time salesman and sports announcer. The linage began to roll in.

During the second week of Lundquest's stewardship, Mrs. Dunphy, in passing by, became engaged in conversation with William M. (Bill) Lynch, who had been retained by Ottaway as business manager. Lundquest and others overheard Lynch's melancholy tongue-in-cheek pronouncement:

"Mrs. Dunphy, they're going to run this newspaper into the ground. They're getting so much advertising and news that this Ottaway group will fail within the next month or so."

Jim Ottaway also would write to Ryder in 1959 that the *Press-Republican* "has a special place in the heart of Gene Brown because Bill Lundquest and his gang have given the *Danbury News-Times* 'the best run for its money advertising-wise of any of our newspapers'."

One of Lundquest's most fortuitous moves was the hiring of Donald J. Clifford as classified manager in October 1952. Clifford's career began on the *Rutland* (Vt.) *Herald,* and, like other Plattsburgh alumni, he was destined to become an Ottaway publisher.

The acquisition year ended with a company dinner at the Cumberland Hotel. All the top Ottaway brass attended with wives. *P-R* employees sat through appropriate speeches by Ottaway, Barney French, Gene Brown, Bill Lundquest and Merle Ostrom. As if that wasn't enough Eddie Webber entertained with his repertoire of magician's sleight-of-hand.

At Christmas each department head received a $25 bonus. Everyone else was given a turkey. Small potatoes by today's standards, but the gifts marked the beginning of Ottaway's human relations campaign in the North Country.

Albert D. (Al) DeLuca was another Lundquest find, joining

the *P-R* in 1955 as an advertising salesman. In six years DeLuca rose to advertising director and in 1964 was named general manager, replacing Steve Ryder, now a corporate vice president. DeLuca eventually would succeed Lundquest as publisher of the *Cape Cod Standard Times*.

DeLuca had had both radio and print experience. He worked in radio in Olean and Elmira, New York, and held sales positions on both the *Olean News* and *Olean Times Herald* and the *Watertown* (N.Y.) *Daily Times*.

Contemporaries of both Fournier and DeLuca agree that, because they were such extraordinary linage producers, there wasn't room for both in the old building on Clinton Street. When DeLuca was named ad manager in 1960, Fournier joined the Clinton Press, a top-flight job printing firm in Plattsburgh. He rejoined the Ottaways in the early 1960s in Middletown — as a printer.

In 1954, the *P-R* became a member of the Audit Bureau of Circulations. Just in time, too. Advertisers could be excused for wondering if Lundquest's claim of just under 10,000 net paid was realistic. It was.

William K. (Bill) Babel moved up from Endicott as editor. Lundquest raised the home-delivery rate to 30 cents a week and slipped into his first five-figure annual salary, $10,800.

Ottaway bought the Dunphy properties on Clinton Street in May 1956 for $30,000. The terms dovetailed nicely with the publisher's fondness for protracted payouts: No principal payments for eight years, with interest at 10 percent. In 1964, the principal was to be reduced $500 a month, with interest pegged at five percent on the unpaid balance. Ottaway — as usual — had more pressing obligations to meet.

Board minutes reflected Lundquest's warning in mid-year that space problems were becoming intolerable. For one thing substantial linage increases and steady circulation gains required commensurately more newsprint and the Post Office added to the storage problem when it ruled the *P-R* had to sack its own mail on premises. So Lundquest was authorized to buy the abutting Judge building, also on Clinton Street, for $13,750 in cash.

The Judge property purchase obviously was a stop-gap

remedy. Lundquest at year-end was authorized to erect a one-story building behind the former Dunphy property to house the mechanical departments. This $37,000 venture was financed principally by a $30,000 loan from the National Commercial Bank & Trust Company at five and one half percent over three years.

With few exceptions, newspaper acquisitions by Ottaway prior to the 1970 wedding with Dow Jones provided the publisher with economic bonanzas completely unforeseen at the time of purchase.

So it was in Plattsburgh.

In December 1953 the U.S. Air Force announced it would establish a base in Plattsburgh on the shore of Lake Champlain. Ground was broken Janury 19, 1954. Eighteen months later the base was designated as home for the 380th Bombardment Wing. By the mid-1980s the 380th had become the largest tactical wing in the Strategic Air Command.

The overall annual dollar impact of the base on the North Country exceeded $164.5 million in 1984.

For almost three decades, 50 weeks a year, the *Press-Republican* has published the *"Champlaner,"* an air base newspaper. The *P-R* sells the ads, sets the type and prints the tabloid. The base prepares the copy and pictures.

It has been a profitable sideline.

6 Training: an Ottaway lodestar

In 1944 the Ottaways had acquired a second home at Buck Hill Falls, Pennsylvania, in what is known to the Falls community as a "cottage settlement." Ruth Ottaway's family, of Unitarian persuasion, for years had been summering there, in the heart of the Pocono Mountains.

The settlement was founded in 1901 by a group of Philadelphia Quakers. In the mid-1980s it consisted of more than 200 dwellings, ranging from modest, summer-only cottages to what one promotional brochure described as "palatial year-round homes." The 1944 cottage cost $5,500, Ottaway recalled. Two years later he bought a larger unit, which he would call neither modest nor palatial.

Buck Hill Falls lies 17 miles due north of Stroudsburg, Pennsylvania, Monroe County seat, and the home of the *Pocono Record*, then known as the *Daily Record*, which Ottaway acquired in 1946.

The Falls home over the years would be not only an all-weather family retreat, but an important Ottaway command post. During the 1950s and 1960s its ample living room and veranda overlooking the Delaware Water Gap was the sylvan setting for pre-dinner attitude adjustment by Ottaway executives registered at the nearby Inn for seminars unending. Not until the late 1960s did the Inn shuck its Society of Friends heritage of abstinence from strong drink.

During the first Eisenhower term the Ottaway cottage somehow acquired the irreverent sobriquet "Camp David," an obvious allusion to both David Ottaway and the president's Catoctin Mountain retreat in Maryland.

Innumerable (and improbable) stories spring from the verdant hills.

Ed Somers, whom we met as a sports stringer for the *Daily Record*, first met the Ottaways while working the front desk at the Inn.

"I was aware of a place called the Ottaway cottage," Somers recalled. "And I knew that there were three Ottaway kids who ran wild over the Buck Hill property."

In 1952, after service in the Navy, Somers went to work for Ottaway's Stroudsburg radio station (WVPO), which had been acquired in 1948. At the time he lived in Mountainhome, a hamlet a few picas east of Buck Hill.

One of Somers's extracurricular duties during the summer was to pick up whichever one of the Ottaway children was currently interning at the *Daily Record*.

Jim Jr. was my first rider, followed by Ruthie and then David," he recalled. It was from David, Somers said, that he learned Ottaway newspapers "never fire anyone...they just promote them."

And, if Somers wasn't available, the interns might make the trip to the depot in East Stroudsburg via the Delaware, Lackawanna & Western. The DL&W had a convenient early morning run between Scranton, Pennsylvania, and Hoboken, New Jersey, which took on eastbound passengers at Cresco, a couple of miles from the cottage.

Jim Ottaway Jr.'s newspaper career, however, predated summer stints at the *Record*. It started in 1949 with an *Endicott Daily Bulletin* carrier route, which he was forced to give up two years later when he entered Phillips Exeter Academy, Exeter, New Hampshire at age 13. His parents were not admirers of the educational format at Endicott High School. One of the family friends who recommended Exeter was Chuck Carpenter of International Paper Company, himself an alumnus.

The paper route interfered with my sports program," Jimmy said, "but it gave me my first experience with money."

"Yes, I am sure father suggested I deliver the *Bulletin*."

Jim Jr.'s informal introduction to newspapering began even earlier, perhaps at age eight. He spent Saturday mornings pitching pennies with the Endicott press crew and wrapping coins from carrier collections. And there was an entrepreneurial sideline: shining employees' shoes in the *Bulletin* offices. He charged 10 cents a pair.

"Father didn't push me into the profession," Jim reflected. "He introduced me to the wonders -- and the fun -- of the business in a very subtle way. So I had a feeling early on for the excitement that captivated him."

It is hardly pure coincidence that Jim Jr. stressed "the fun" of newspapering. No doubt he, like two generations of Ottaway executives, was reminded occasionally that if one can't find fun in the same package with the headaches, one has no business in journalism.

Ruth and Jim, we are told, made a point of keeping the children busy. And starting at age 10, Jim Jr. caddied at Buck Hill summers. The charge was $2 per bag for 18 holes, he recalled. Either a one-bag or two-bag job was good for a $1 tip, so it was possible to clear $10 a day if the right combination came up morning and afternoon.

One of Jim's golfing clients off and on was William F. (Bill) Kerby, who would become chairman of Dow Jones & Company, Inc. which was destined to acquire the Ottaway group in 1970. Kerby, too, was a Buck Hill cottager.

The caddying experience whetted Jim Jr.'s enthusiasm for golf, and he took up the game at 14. Like his father he became a star performer.

Colleagues rated Jim Jr. as a 12-14 handicap player. "If he played regularly he'd be under 10," one said.

David Ottaway also caddied, but did not pursue golf as an avocation. In later years he preferred tennis and fishing.

Another Buck Hill cottager was John R. Tappan, vice president of the American Reinsurance Company, who became trustee of the Ottaway children's trusts. Tappan was an investment advisor to the family and would help guide the Ottaways in the merger discussions with Dow Jones.

"John Tappan," Jim Jr. said, "came up with the formula that led to the marriage."

In 1955 the youngster spent the summer as a reporter on the *Daily Record*. He was apprenticed to City Editor Jim Riley. On one occasion he was assigned to do a feature on a long-neglected monument, covered by growth. Picking through the innocuous-appearing vines in an effort to read the inscription, the legman contracted a world-class case of poison ivy. He was on his back two weeks.

Jim Jr. credits Reporter Leonard Randolph and Chief Photographer Roderick MacLeod with catalyzing his interest in good writing and pictures. Stroudsburg contained a plentiful supply of talented staffers who helped the future Ottaway chief executive step off on the right foot. And he wasn't pampered financially. He received the minimum wage.

One of Jim Ottaway Sr.'s greatest strengths was his early commitment to damn-the-expense coverage of big stories. The annals of many newspapers in the group reflect hundreds of thousands of dollars in overtime worked, newsprint and ink consumed, travel and even the rental of helicopters and conventional aircraft.

The Ottaway children's first experience with their father's insistence on the best, whatever the cost, came in August 1955. The family had just returned from Michigan, where they had attended the funeral of Jim Ottaway's mother. Mrs. Ruth Ottaway Sokoloff, who had gently chided her son in 1944 for his "recklessness" in spending, had lived to see him attain financial stability.

Jim Sr. was in Endicott when Hurricane Diane struck the northeast and turned normally placid Brodhead Creek into a raging wall of water a mile wide in some places. The creek separates the twin boroughs of Stroudsburg and East Stroudsburg. More than 50 drowned in the floods. Ruth and the children were at the Buck Hill cottage.

Newsprint deliveries were disrupted, Lackawanna trackage and trestles having been ripped apart. Lyn Boyd's bite became just as severe as his bark as he chewed up a recalcitrant newsprint sub-executive who didn't seem to grasp the urgency that gripped the newsroom and WVPO radio staffs. People were missing. Only the *Record* and WVPO could provide answers.

Boyd got his newsprint via long-haul trucks. And for more than two weeks the *Daily Record* did whatever it had to do — and more.

Bypassing washed-out roads and bridges Ruthie, Jim Jr. and David made their way to Stroudsburg and helped the beleagured newspaper and radio staffs for the duration of the crisis. Among other assignments Ruthie worked the switchboard. Jim Jr. recalled he handled survivor lists, mainly for WVPO. David filled in wherever help was needed.

It was community service at its noblest.

The year 1955 also saw Ottaway named president of the New York State Publishers Association.

Proprietors of newspapers Ottaway acquired in the 1940s and early 1950s rarely, if ever, sent executives to national conventions. If anyone went, it was the owners, who presumably filled in staffers on what they had learned that might redound to the paper's overall benefit.

Nor is there any evidence that staffers in Oneonta, Stroudsburg and Plattsburgh even had attended regional convocations. Ruth and Jim Ottaway had ranged widely in behalf of the *Daily Bulletin,* but back then he was a publisher with an intimate, hands-on approach to every department.

So it came to pass that intra-company seminars started at Buck Hill Falls.

And it was to be expected that some of the Ottaway management flock, out on their own for the first time, would kick over the traces after school had closed for the day. The newly-discovered camaraderie was exhilarating.

During the dry era at Buck Hill Inn some participants would arrive burdened by suitcases that gave off gurgling sounds as they were borne from lobby to rooms. And on more than one occasion the Buck Hill Inn chief of police was summoned by aggrieved guests of the Inn, who did not appreciate the sounds of midnight revelry from a handful of Ottaway's tippling employees.

The chief happened to be Thomas Somers, father of Ed, and a close friend of the Ottaway family. On a few occasions, the chief simply quit trying to restore order. Things had gotten too far out of hand. The hellions knew the boss was in his cottage, a quarter mile distant. The chief's sense of diplomacy, it must be clear, was superb.

Another incident has a permanent place in Pocono lore:

One day, during an Ottaway board meeting in the cottage, there came a knock on the door. On the stoop stood the wife of one of Ottaway's executives, obviously sorely agitated.

"Mr. Ottaway," she blurted, "my husband is seeing another woman. I know it was he in her bedroom. I followed him to her house."

"How do you know? Are you sure?" the publisher asked.

"I know his cough. I was right by the window. I heard him coughing."

"Well," replied Ottaway, "I'll talk to my associates and see what we can do. I'll get back to you."

Having relayed this intelligence to Ruth, Barney French, Gene Brown, Lyn Boyd and Jake Becker, Ottaway posed the question: "What do you think we should do?"

Brown, with an elfin sense of humor second only to French's, gave a straight-faced answer: "I think, first, we should cure his cough."

Seminars in the early days also were held in Cooperstown, New York, the Otsego County seat 20 miles north of Oneonta. The setting was the Cooper Inn, built in 1936 and opened in June of that year with plenty of civic fanfare — but without liquor. A taproom would not come until the mid-1950s but by that time the Ottaway management forces had almost outgrown the Cooperstown hostelry.

Whether Ottaway and his lieutenants chose Coooperstown because the Inn was dry is a matter of conflicting memories. Survivors of the seminars said he wanted to minimize after-hours gaiety. He said he thought he chose Cooperstown because of its central location.

At any rate the same handful of Buck Hill revelers found postprandial happiness just one block south on Main Street in the subterranean grotto of the very wet Tunnicliff Inn. "The next morning," a present Ottaway publisher recalled, "they showed up looking like nothing so much as the remnants of a defeated army."

Part of the Ottaway legend has Lyn Boyd conducting room searches of one or two participants for contraband bottled goods. Boyd denied ever having been assigned this detail. It doesn't, however, defy imagination. But it was no legend that

Ottaway had his share of drinkers.

Starting in 1964 the Inn at Buck Hill Falls each June was the scene of an Ottaway social get-together. Top executives and their wives were invited, along with a few corporate friends from the fields of law and banking. Guests arrived Thursday afternoon and departed after breakfast Sunday. The outings were Lucullan examples of wining and dining, interspersed with golf, tennis, lawn bowling and at night, dancing and various games of chance. And with just enough business scheduled to make the happening a legitimate business expense.

As the newspaper group expanded and seminars became a way of life, erudition and sophistication triumphed. Training programs were stepped up after the Plattsburgh acquisition in 1952. But it would not be until the mid-1960s that the seminar system embracing every major newspaper department would come to full flower.

Its development was a cornerstone of Ottaway management philosophy.

Training programs were designed primarily to improve the quality of newspapers already in the group. A secondary reason derived from the fact that acquisition possibilities were constantly springing up. Should deals be struck, trained leaders might be needed to manage the new properties.

Among community newspapers Ottaway looked at seriously in the early days were in Hanover, Easton and Bradford, Pennsylvania; Monterey, California; and Auburn, Cortland and Lockport, New York.

Correspondence files show that feelers, at least, were received from or directed to properties in Ansonia and Norwalk, Connecticut, and Glens Falls and Corning, New York. (The *Hanover Evening Sun* was the last two-cent paper in the U.S.)

Lyn Boyd believed the Ottaway management training

movement had its deepest roots in the American Press Institute, which first operated at the Columbia School of Journalism in New York City and later moved to Reston, Virginia.

Boyd recalled going to the very first API seminar for advertising executives. Until the early 1950s seminars were only for editorial personnel.

"Publishers were cool to the idea," Boyd said. "API was struggling to attract participants. Ottaway helped bail them out by sending me, Bill Lundquest and Red Cross." (Oneonta, Plattsburgh and Stroudsburg).

Walter Everett supervised the seminar and, as might be expected, had to depend on the participants to carry the first program.

"If ever I have had any success in newspapering, it began right there," Boyd said.

Post-API came planning sessions with Ottaway and Brown. "We must have had 25 to 30 meetings," Boyd said. "Eventually we started to hold meetings for ad salesmen. Then circulation people, then business office employees." Editorial meetings widened as well. Outside experts in all fields were called in.

"One of the best ways to keep subscribers is to see that our people are well trained," Ottaway insisted. "We need training not only in the art of writing and reporting, selling, advertising and subscriptions and providing a top-flight newspaper typographically, but also in that difficult art of human relations - inside and outside the plant."

Ottaway's first official association with API was as one of 27 members of a Management and Cost seminar at Columbia University in 1951. He was identified as "president and publisher, the *Daily Bulletin*, Endicott."

As "president and publisher of Ottaway Newspapers-Radio, Inc.," he attended a second seminar for Publishers, Editors and Chief News Executives in early 1957. Also participating was Ruth Ottaway. It was one of the rare occasions when husband and wife attended an API seminar together.

"Why did we go? Because we felt we might be getting so immersed in the bottom line that we would forget the ever-present necessity for editorial quality. We didn't want our concern for the P&L to obscure our editorial vision. Two weeks later we returned from the refresher course more determined than ever to make our newspapers as outstanding as humanly and financially possible," Ottaway said.

Ottaway attended a third API seminar, its first for publishers alone, in 1975. He long had urged API to offer a seminar for publishers, but according to Malcolm F. (Mal) Mallette, API director of development, the staff demurred, believing "such distinguished persons" should not be housed in the ramshackle King's Crown Hotel at Columbia. By 1975 API had moved to Reston. Participants were housed in the Sheraton Reston Inn.

Ottaway served three times as an API discussion leader. Two of his sessions were for newspaper persons from abroad. For a domestic seminar on Management and Costs, he presided over the segment on general management.

In 1959, he was appointed to the API Advisory Board by the then president of Columbia University, Grayson Kirk. He became Advisory Board chairman in 1968, succeeding Barry Bingham Sr., of the Louisville newspapers. At the time it was apparent that API must seek larger quarters than the makeshift and cramped facilities on the ground floor of the Columbia Journalism Building. The Advisory Board continued until API left Columbia in June 1974 and overlapped the present board of directors established when API incorporated in 1972 as a non-profit educational organization in Virginia.

Thus Ottaway was at the helm during most of the planning for the move from Columbia to Reston. He continued as chairman until June 30, 1978, when he voluntarily stepped down after also providing leadership for the settling-in years at Reston. He was' a central figure in raising $2.6 million for the building fund for the original building in 1973-74 and was chairman of the 1979-80 campaign that raised $1.9 million to enlarge the building.

He continued on the board of directors until June 30, 1984. He could have continued indefinitely, as a former board chairman. At the API annual meeting April 4, 1984, in Atlanta, his fellow board members adopted this resolution:

"Resolved, that the Board of Directors expresses its

appreciation to James H. Ottaway, who is resigning from the Board effective June 30, 1984, when he will have completed twenty-five total years of service on the fore running Advisory Board of the Institute of Columbia University and the present Board of Directors. Mr. Ottaway was three times a Seminar member and three times a Discussion Leader. He was Chairman of the Board of Directors from 1968 to 1978 and guided the relocation of the Institute to its own building in Reston, Virginia. He was also a key figure in raising funds for the 1974 relocation and chaired the committee that raised funds for an addition to the building in 1979-80. He currently serves as chairman of the Bequest Committee. The Board congratulates Mr. Ottaway on his unparalled record of leadership and devotion to the Institute and extends to him its best wishes."

Ottaway still is chairman of the Bequest Committee, which over time should play an important role in building financial strength for API.

Fellow board members and the API staff appreciated the energy and leadership he gave API during the crucial decade in which he was chairman. Thus they arranged for a bronze plaque, mounted in the building lobby. It reads:

In Appreciation
To James H. Ottaway, Chairman of the Board of Directors, 1968-78: His foresight, leadership and dedicated effort contributed immeasurably to the construction of this building and to the American Press Institute.
April 1978

Starting about 1950, Ruth and Jim Ottaway began sojourning in the West Indies each February and March. At various times they vacationed on Barbados, Jamaica and St. Croix. Communications from the sun and sand arrived at executive desks in the states in the form of Ottaway longhand, hieroglyphics that would baffle a military cipher expert.

When they returned from their 1967 trip, they found that the

65

unused second floor of the latest Campbell Hall addition had been converted to a conference center. Furniture, fixtures, carpeting. First class. Boyd, weary of travel, motels and hotels and occasional attendant dyspepsia, had ordered a citadel of training into being. Approximate cost: $5,000.

Ottaway was delighted even though "I never intended to finish the room." The entry soon bore a bronze plaque with the legend "Lyndon R. Boyd Conference Center."

"Eventually," Boyd said, "we worked out rules calculated to bring about frank discussions. No brass was ever at a seminar except as discussion leaders. If their bosses were present, participants would say only those things they thought the bosses would want to hear."

Ottaway recalled that in the early days "we found out we really didn't know our people, so we had to shape a training philosophy that would bring out their personalities."

Boyd, as did a score of other Ottaway executives, lectured many times at API seminars.

At one of the first of those API sessions with classified advertising managers, he recalled, he set the stage for a no-nonsense exchange of views with this exhortation:

"You've already lied to each other about your salaries. And you've lied to each other about how much you pay your people. You've gotten it out of your system. So let's have a frank and honest discussion!"

Boyd not only got away with such sallies, his audience savored them.

Publishers across the U.S. looked with unalloyed admiration at the continuing intensive quest for excellence, knowing that Ottaway training had created a fertile source of talent for any department of a newspaper. If one wanted to leave Ottaway, one could find plenty of opportunities elsewhere. Few defected.

"There was a feeling of family within the organization," Mary Ryder (Mrs. Stephen W.) said. "When I suffered a ruptured appendix in Endicott, Jim Ottaway and Barney French came often to Ideal Hospital. I was assured that 'whatever the cost' I was not to worry; if a specialist was needed one would be called."

"You don't forget things like that," she said. "You stay. You simply don't go to a 'better job'."

Associates eventually mastered the hieroglyphics Ottaway fashioned with his felt-point pen, but memos he fired off to new acquaintances during and after acquisition negotiations left some in utter confusion.

Robert A. (Bob) McCullough, one of the principals in the 1979 sale of the *Ashland* (Ky.) *Daily Independent* to Ottaway, recalled that he received rune-like memos which he was never able to decode.

Ken Berg, then editor of the *Mankato* (Minn.) *Free Press,* also acquired in 1979, wrote to Jim Jr. that year: "I see I have a new challenge — learning to interpret Jim Ottaway's handwriting. I'll get better with experience. Jared says 'he, too'." Jared How was owner of the Free Press Company.

Lyn Boyd once suggested that Allied forces in World War II could have shortened the conflict simply by dropping reprints of Ottaway memos behind enemy lines and confusing them into surrender.

The author of this volume submitted samples of the chief's baffling messages to a graphoanalyst, who concluded "he has a very forceful personality and will usually get what he wants — one way or another." The graphological description included these other character traits: "Plans far ahead, strong and enduring will power and vision, extraordinary persistence, acquisitiveness and aggressiveness."

"I have rarely seen so many forceful traits in one specimen," the analyst reported.

7 Radio

Broadcasting spanned 23 of the first 50 years of the Ottaway saga.

It was born in Endicott in 1947. It ended in mid-1970, a few weeks before the merger with Dow Jones, when the Ottaway family sold its three radio properties to a group of long-time executives at a virtual fire sale price.

The radio venture was financially rewarding in the long run, but minuscule in relation to the newspaper investment. Two of the original three stations were only marginally successful for the first decade of their existence.

But broadcasting produced a completely unforeseen windfall. Never thought of as a source of newspaper executive talent, it spawned four successful publishers, two of whom rose to further prominence at the corporate level.

Even though Ottaway radio, comparatively speaking, was a small fragment of the whole, it undeniably helped Ottaway achieve a national presence. We have met some of the broadcast personalities in earlier chapters. Others presently will appear on the scene. Most will reappear later.

Radio did not wear the ermine of noble purpose.

The establishment in 1947 and 1948 of stations in Endicott, Oneonta and Stroudsburg, in that order, simply created in effect what Gene Brown called "small town monopolies," designed to protect the newspapers from advertising and news incursions.

Station WENE in Endicott went on the air September 17, 1947. But the radio story actually started in Oneonta on September 30 the previous year.

Stephen W. (Steve) Ryder had graduated from Syracuse University the preceding June with a bachelor of arts degree, which framed majors in the liberal arts and journalism. About the same time Barney French was seeking an individual to lay a foundation for Ottaway radio. French called Dr. Kenneth G. Bartlett, director of the university's radio/speech department. Bartlett told French he had a strong candidate — Ryder.

Coincidentally, French knew Ryder, who had come down to Endicott from Syracuse months before to investigate a report that Ottaway interests were thinking about establishing a station there. Ryder's source was his wife-to-be, who had heard rumblings about local broadcasting during a visit to the Southern Tier.

As Ryder put it, "My subsequent wife discovered my subsequent job."

French and Ryder talked. Barney must have liked what he saw. Ryder was directed to Oneonta, where he was hired by Gene Brown.

"I signed on with the understanding I would move on to Endicott," Ryder recalled. "My job was to soften up the Oneonta area for radio. Among other things, I wrote a column for the *Oneonta Star* two or three times a week. It was called 'Dial Tones'."

In reality, the Oneonta slot was a stopgap, designed to keep Ryder from straying before Endicott was ready to begin the preliminaries leading to actual broadcasting.

WENE's conception took place January 23, 1946, when the newly-formed Empire Newspapers-Radio, Inc., authorized Ottaway "to make application to the Federal Communications Commission for licenses, permits and/or franchises for the construction, maintenance and operation of a 1450-kilocycle, 250-watt radio station" in Endicott.

The call letters WENE have no specific meaning. Ottaway had applied for WEND, for Endicott, but the FCC could come no closer.

(The way had been cleared for an Ottaway application by an old friend, Thomas J. Watson, president of IBM. Watson called Lieutenant Ottaway, based in Philadelphia, and the two met at Buck Hill Falls. Watson told the publisher he no longer was interested in a radio venture and volunteered to surrender his construction permit.)

Ryder's stay in Oneonta was brief. On December 7 he married Mary Knappenberger, a Syracuse classmate, and took a week's leave for a wedding trip. On January 2, 1947, the Ryders moved to Endicott. He had been named program director of the hoped-for-but-not-realized radio station. Gene Brown, Ryder said, loaned him a *Star* circulation truck to move the household gear.

For the next six months Ryder was occupied with the permit and license work requisite to setting up shop. Getting a permit, in effect, means putting all the facts together including detailed programming plans for the Federal Communications Commission. Getting a license puts you on the air.

WENE also required construction of a studio, which went up next to the *Daily Bulletin* building and which, according to Ryder, was on the extravagant side. It lacked nothing. Gene Brown called it "a palace." There is no available breakdown of costs, but Brown told the author that Empire couldn't get a fixed-price building contract immediately after the war, suggesting the tab was well above expectations. Corporate records indicate that it cost $121,000 in building and equipment to put WENE on the air. "We didn't know any better," Ottaway said. The station incurred an operational loss of $6,008 during the four months following start-up.

Ottaway was thinking frequency modulation, too. Minutes of an April 1, 1947, board meeting show that he was authorized to apply for an FM license for Endicott, five months before WENE was operational.

Meantime, preparation for an AM-FM operation continued in Oneonta.

Ottaway had been authorized to apply for a license as far back as July 27, 1945.

WDOS-AM started operations December 1, 1947. FM broadcasting started the following February. Radio was set up as a division of the *Star*.

"When a radio station was losing money," Ottaway said, "we operated it as a division of the newspaper to offset the losses. When a station became profitable, we'd have to file all financial data if it was lumped with a newspaper. We didn't want that."

Walton F. Deming came over from the *Oneonta Star* advertising department to run the operation.

The AM operation showed a red figure of $17,637 for the single month in 1947, obviously reflecting heavy initial expense.

Board minutes of April 1948 contain an "expectation" by Gene Brown that "the station" would be in the black by year's end. Whether Brown alluded to AM, FM or the combination is not clear.

But his hopes for profit in 1948 were smashed. The FM project was a loser from the start and was abandoned November 12, 1949, after less than two years. "It was at my insistence that we promptly went into FM," Brown recalled, "and just as promptly we lost $50,000. It was an impossible project. Unfortunately, we were about 15 years ahead of our time. Losing $50,000 that we didn't have was a searing experience."

The $50,000 figure represents Brown's estimate of his own responsibility in terms of money. Actual losses were higher.

"Jim Ottaway never said a word, then or later."

Consolidated financial report for 1948 shows a loss of $7,215 for the *Oneonta Star*'s radio division. The AM operation, apparently, could't quite cover FM losses.

The land, property and equipment accounts of Oneonta's radio division on December 31, 1949, included $20,774 of the FM station's assets, which were acquired by the New York State Electric & Gas Company. Hours after the purchase, a storm wrecked the mountain tower, which the utility planned to use for communication with its truck fleet. (Loss on the sale of FM assets are on the books at $11,544.)

The WDOS call letters stand for Delaware, Otsego and Schoharie counties, into which the station piped its programs.

Ottaway faced far fewer problems in Stroudsburg. Harold B. Newman's Station WHAB (For HArold B) was a 250-watt daytime operation, as Brown put it, a "ready-to-wear-business." There was no need for heavy up-front outlays.

Through Pocono Broadcasting, Inc., incorporated January 27, 1948, Ottaway acquired the Newman station for $75,000, one of his most fortuitous deals. The call letters under the new ownership became WVPO (Voice of the Poconos) which went on the air October 1. Even in the face of the impending Oneonta FM disaster, Ottaway received authorization from the Pocono board to apply for an FM license.

Pocono's start-up, unlike Oneonta's and Endicott's, was not inundated with red ink. It showed a marginal three-month loss of $1,543 in 1948 and the next year posted a solid operating profit of $12,626, and a net of $8,352.

Just who ran WVPO for the first three months is not clear. More than likely it was Elton Hall, of the *Stroudsburg Daily Record*'s advertising staff. At any rate, Hall's name first appeared as station manager in board minutes of February 1949.

Hall did not make the switch from newspaper to radio unprepared. He had taken a cram course in broadcasting from Ryder in Endicott.

March 1, 1949, saw the arrival of a broadcasting personality who would ascend to a high position in the overall Ottaway management structure.

Francis H. Brinkley was destined to become a corporate vice president and treasurer by 1960.

Ottaway, with a few years of radio experience under his belt, had come to realize that his newspaper and radio advertising arms were not operating on a competitive basis. Bill Lundquest, for example, was selling space for the *Daily Bulletin* and time for WENE in Endicott. It wasn't working.

Ottaway reached out to the Delaware Broadcasting Company, based in Wilmington (WILM) and hired the 36-year-old Brinkley, a courtly southerner, to be managing director of his three stations.

Ottaway's financial arrangements with Brinkley might be considered on the short side today, but a guaranteed salary of $10,400 with a base of $7,800 bought a lot of groceries back in 1949. The modest wage would be adjusted upward "if the profits of the three stations so justify," the contract read. Brinkley's moving allowance from Wilmington to Endicott, for a then family of four, was a less-than-breathtaking $200.

Brinkley was a native of Portsmouth, Virginia. He attended Duke University, graduating in 1931. A concert pianist at 11, he was active in the Duke Glee Club and was an accomplished organist.

His first job was with Vick Chemical Company in Greensboro, North Carolina. When Vick moved its headquarters to New York City in 1934 he became assistant advertising director. Vick used a lot of radio time to push its Vaporub, cough drops and other products, and Brinkley's responsibilities put him in touch with many in the broadcast field.

In 1947 Brinkley entered radio management at WILM and as part owner of the property. When the majority stockholders decided to get out of radio, they turned to the Washington law firm of Morris Jansky, which just happened to be handling Ottaway's broadcasting affairs. Brinkley needed a job; Ottaway needed a radio manager.

Brinkley's arrival cast an immediate shadow of rank over the fortunes of Ryder, Deming and Hall. No longer would the station managers report directly to Barney French, Gene Brown and Merle Ostrom. Now there was a middleman stranger. Some rough edges developed.

Ryder told the author that "despite some initial resentment due to the circumstances," Brinkley subsequently became a close friend of his and the other radio managers.

Deming also felt some resentment. In 1984, when he was a retired Congregational minister living in Santa Rosa, California, Deming said he did like Brinkley. But when an opening popped up in Ottaway's national advertising sales department (based at Endicott headquarters), Deming asked for and received the job. Deming left ON-R in 1956 "because I needed a change of life-style" and joined the *Grand Junction* (Colo.) *Daily Sentinel*.

There remains not a wisp of memory as to how Hall fared at the outset with the new radio boss.

"Brink did a reasonably good job in setting up the radio division," Ottaway said. "It wasn't easy to create that separate piece of pie. Don't forget that the news-side general managers were the big toads in the puddle before 1949 and it could have been that they resented the new alignment."

When WENE began operations, station manager was Keith Field, a Massachusetts import. Little is known of Field except

73

that he was not well regarded by French. Ryder supplanted him as station manager in 1948.

In 1948 WENE's operating profit was a respectable $14,201. Whatever optimism this may have generated was dampened in 1949 when the comparable figure came in at $5,303.

Ryder remained boss of WENE until April 15, 1958, when he was transferred to the *Danbury News-Times* for newspaper training under Gene Brown. The switch didn't come any too soon for Ryder, who said he told Ottaway as far back as 1949, the year of Brinkley's arrival, that his radio job seemed not to have an attractive future.

In 1950 WDOS moved its studios from the Hotel Oneonta to new quarters in the dwelling that today is contiguous to the *Daily Star*'s plant.

At the 1950 year-end meeting of the Oneonta board, Brown announced that the radio division "apparently" would show an operating profit of "about $7,000" — the first time in the black. But he reminded the board that capital losses on the sale of the FM tower and transmitter facility would reduce the net.

The Ottaways, French and Brinkley all agreed that WDOS should become a separate company, a subsidiary of the *Star*, a proposal that had surfaced before. "Better morale" was the rationale. But they were advised against any change until Congress had acted on the then-pending excess profits tax.

French waxed enthusiastic about WENE's performance as 1950 drew to a close. "It enjoyed the best year since it went on the air in 1947," he told the board. The "best year" could have meant many things for WENE profitability was elusive. Board minutes did not clarify French's remarks.

Construction of a new 5,000-watt facility was progressing slowly, French reported, due to inclement weather. But he believed it would be operational by March 1951.

A glimpse at the Empire debt structure was provided in the December 11 board minutes: "Mrs. Ottaway said that due to the necessity for the company to borrow additional funds to finance construction of the 5,000-watt station, she felt no action should be taken in regard to declaring a dividend. Mr. French and Mr. Ottaway agreed. She pointed out that all available cash would be needed to repay company loans.

74

"Mr. French said that the building mortgage would be reduced to $46,500 by December 31; and that $15,000 was owed the Endicott Trust Company as first part of a $45,000 term loan negotiated to finance radio station construction; and that balance on chattel mortgages on the *Daily Bulletin* press and for a new linotype machine would be approximately $21,825. He said that the balance of $30,000 available to the company on the Endicott Trust radio loan would not be needed until 1951.

"He said that the chattel mortgages were being reduced at the rate of $5,700 annually; the building mortgage at the rate of $6,000 annually, and that, beginning in July 1949, the company would start repaying the radio loan at the rate of $6,000 or $500 monthly for the first 12 months thereafter, increasing after 12 months to $750 monthly for a year, and then to $1,000 per month until paid in full.

"Mr. Ottaway said that with completion of the 5,000-watt station, there were no plans for any major capital investments and that it appeared that the company should be able to make major reduction in its debt during 1951."

On March 12, 1952, Ottaway Stations, Inc. (OSI) came into being, with the corporate purpose of acquiring the assets of the radio division of Empire Newspapers-Radio, Inc. (WENE) and the WDOS division of Oneonta Star, Inc. The transaction was completed the following June 1. (Pocono Broadcasting remained a separate corporation, but in 1953 control of the company passed from the Ottaways to Ottaway Newspapers-Radio, Inc., in an exchange of stock.)

Whether OSI was designed as a vehicle to propel Ottaway into television was not specifically spelled out in its minute books, but developments in 1953 indicate it was. By now all three stations were profitable, one marginally so, with WVPO leading the way with a gross of more then $100,000 in 1952.

TV first entered the discussion stage in August 1953. At a WVPO board meeting Ottaway told the directors that "there was an opportunity" for Pocono Broadcasting to loan money to Ottaway Stations "if that company receives a TV grant."

Since no channels were available in Stroudsburg, Ottaway said, "it would be to the advantage of Pocono to assist Ottaway Stations in erecting a UHF station in Endicott."

The directors voted to have Pocono lend OSI $75,000, with no repayment for two years, then $2,500 a year over 30 years.

Exactly one month later, Brinkley presented the OSI board with a draft of a proposed TV program policy "for WENE-TV," which medium he loftily described as "the new dynamic of mass communication."

The TV application had to have been filed with the Federal Communications Commission in the fall of 1953, because on January 4, 1954, Ottaway reported to the OSI annual meeting on the "heavy cost" involved. Almost a year later OSI had invested in excess of $10,000 in its quest for a channel, which would turn an anticipated 1954 WENE profit of $5,000 into a $5,000 book loss.

The end was not long in coming. On January 3, 1955, WENE was denied a channel, which was awarded by the FCC to Southern Tier Broadcasters of Binghamton (WINR). The FCC award noted that WINR did not have newspaper affiliations.

On February 28, 1955, OSI minutes show, the corporation had decided not to continue its TV venture and the $75,000 WVPO commitment was canceled.

Gene Brown called it a "very successful" failure for Ottaway. The UHF channel eventually was sold to the *Binghamton Press,* "which ran it well, only losing $200,000 to $300,000 a year."

During the TV experiment radio managerial shifts had been taking place.

In May 1952 Chester Miller became sales manager of WVPO under Elton Hall. And Ed Somers joined the staff as a "radio want ad" salesman. Somers also worked the news broadcast side and did play-by-plays of major sports. No longer was the term "station manager" applied to the radio bosses. They had become general managers, in terminology, at any rate, the equal of their newspaper counterparts.

An interesting bit of Empire stock byplay was recorded in the minutes of the board meeting October 27, 1952:

"Mr. Ottaway said that on December 31, 1947, he purchased an additional 115 shares of stock in the company at $100 (par) per share, or $11,500.

"He said that at a directors' meeting held December 20, 1947, the matter of sale of the stock to himself was discussed and the following terms approved:

"The company owed Mr. Ottaway $3,500 for funds he had advanced during the year. This left a balance of $8,000 due on the 115 shares of stock, on which he paid $2,025 on December 31, 1947, the day the stock was issued, leaving a balance of $5,975.

"Later Mr. Ottaway paid $1,000 on the balance due, leaving a $4,975 balance due to the company, which still exists.

"Mr. Ottaway said that at the time he purchased this stock, it was done so that he would maintain a 51 percent control of the company, which he had previously enjoyed. However, in December 1947, Mrs. Ottaway bought 185 shares and Mr. French 45 shares to help finance radio station WENE. This made it necessary for Mr. Ottaway to buy additional stock to maintain his control, or the company would have had to apply to the Federal Communications Commission for change in control, which the company could not do at the time conveniently as it had just gone on the air September 17, 1947, and had not received its regular license from the FCC.

"Mr. Ottaway asked if the board of directors would like to buy the stock into the company's treasury at par, $100 per share. This would reduce outstanding stock issued to 1,345 shares, giving Mr. Ottaway a 49.37 percent interest versus 51.18 percent he now has; increase Mrs. Ottaway from 37.35 to 38.74 percent and increase Mr. French from 11.47 to 11.89 percent.

"Mr. French moved that the company buy from Mr. Ottaway 100 shares of the common stock of the company at par, $100 per share, or $5,000. Seconded by Mrs. Ottaway. Unanimously adopted."

In 1953 more personnel shuffles occurred. Harold E. (Hal) Graves, program director of WENE under Ryder, became general manager of WDOS in September. Graves found himself short of sales help and tapped a veteran salesman-announcer he had met earlier that year in Endicott.

Benjamin M. Turnbull had come to WENE to audition for a sportscaster job while Graves was still program director. He didn't get the job because no job materialized. WENE had lost the rights to broadcast games of the Binghamton Triplets of the Eastern League.

77

Turnbull returned to his radio job in Ogdensburg, in upstate New York. Previously he had worked in upstate radio in Massena, Plattsburgh and Syracuse.

Graves kept in touch with Turnbull, even passing on a report that had come his way that Ottaway was going to buy a Plattsburgh station.

Indeed Ottaway was interested in acquiring Plattsburgh's WEAV. He offered George Bissell $100,000 plus the equivalent of the station's net quick assets, which totaled approximately $13,000 as of October 31, 1952. (Net quick assets represent the difference between current assets and current liabilities.) He also offered Bissell a five-year consulting role at $3,000 a year.

The proposed deal never came to fruition.

Turnbull reported for work in Oneonta as a time salesman late in 1953. He was the first at WDOS to broadcast ad-sponsored schoolboy football. The following year Turnbull became sales manager.

Also in 1953 Elton Hall left WVPO and returned to the *Daily Record* as assistant general manager. Chet Miller advanced to general manager of the station. Concurrently, Somers was promoted to sales manager. He had come a long way, he said, from what could have been a "lifetime of selling shirts, socks and ties at a Stroudsburg haberdashery."

Ruth Ottaway appears to have been the principal corporate monitor of programming at WENE and WVPO. She listened to WENE in Endicott and WVPO while at Buck Hill. Programmers in Oneonta, on the other hand, had comparatively few worries about the opinions of the secretary.

There are frequent RBO allusions in the minute books to the "excellent" music on WVPO and it's "good news coverage and public service programs."

She was not as pleased with the musical offerings provided by WENE. On several occasions she recommended that the musical "standards" of WENE be raised, suggesting that announcers enjoyed too much latitude of selection. At one directors' meeting in the 1940s she conceded that "all tastes must be served," but she registered strong disapproval of "so much boogie-woogie."

Barney French said he agreed and would pursue the matter

"more" with Steve Ryder. It may be assumed some foot-dragging had occurred.

But she extolled WENE's broadcasts by church choirs during the Christmas season. Also on the positive side was a minute book reference to her having set up a Girl Scout radio training course that "was proving popular" at the station.

Eventually WENE brass got the message. In July 1957 the station adopted officially what it called a "middle-of-the-road" music policy. It was not defined.

Former station programmers will confirm that RBO was a relentless critic.

She did not confine her criticism to radio. At the annual meeting of the Oneonta board at Buck Hill Falls in 1952 she chided the *Star*.

"More care should be exercised in editing crime and sex stories," she declared, "with an eye toward maintaining the *Star* policy of publishing a paper for all ages and all homes."

"Some Associated Press stories do slip through," replied Gene Brown, laconically.

Ruth Ottaway, like her husband, was a shrewd judge of people. More than one member of the Ottaway board told the author that this innate characteristic was at its best when staff promotions were being discussed.

"She has always had a lot to say," Jim Jr. said, "and her opinions were deeply respected."

Brown left the *Oneonta Star* in 1956 and moved to Danbury, Connecticut, to run the *News-Times*, which Ottaway had acquired that year after an arduous struggle. At the same time Elton Hall was named general manager of the *Star*, the first of four radio executives who achieved No. 1 ranking on a newspaper.

Ryder was the next to leave radio. He joined Brown in Danbury April 15, 1958, to enter a newspaper executive training program. Howard Johanson, sales manager of WENE, took the helm. Ryder would become general manager of the *Plattsburgh Press-Republican* the following year.

Fire destroyed the WVPO studios on Main Street in the summer of 1958. The station offices were on the second floor of the Rea & Derick drug store. The third floor contained priceless bound volumes of the *Daily Record* and its predecessors, all of which went up in flames.

Ed Somers recalled the August blaze, which started in the drug store basement: "I was a volunteer fireman back then, and I managed to rescue the station log and commercials. But we lost our receivables schedule. We didn't lose any broadcast time. We operated from the tiny transmitter building on Godfrey's Ridge until a rented house trailer could be moved in. Our sales office was shifted to the *Daily Record*."

Before the end of the year WVPO studios had been relocated on South Sixth Street. Land and building were bought for $23,500. Modernization of the building and replacement equipment cost $33,500, all of which was covered by insurance.

WVPO was easily the most profitable Ottaway station. It paid its first dividend, $1.50 per share in 1955. (Ottaway Newspapers-Radio, Inc., held all 3,000 shares.) In 1957 the dividend rate rose to $3. By 1965 it was $6 and in 1969, $7.50 per share. Truly a money-maker!

The radio table of organization remained constant until 1962.

On January 1 Brinkley separated Johanson, whose leadership had been ineffective. Hal Graves moved back to Endicott as boss of WENE. At the same time Turnbull moved up to general manager of WDOS.

Station WENE — not surprisingly — was sold the following September to C. Alan Bengston of Binghamton, former general manager of WINR and a veteran executive of the National Broadcasting Company. The price: $170,000. The sale included the radio tower and transmitter site, but not the studios, which Bengston leased.

In a letter to WENE employees dated September 24, Ottaway reminded them that he had been asked many times since the sale of the *Daily Bulletin* (in 1960) whether WENE would be sold. "We always replied in the negative, which was true," he wrote. "It was only when Mr. Bengston approached us and said that he was interested in purchasing our station that we actively entered in negotiations with anyone."

In announcing the sale, Ottaway also alluded to the 1961 move of corporate headquarters from Endicott to Campbell Hall: "Since moving from the Endicott area we believe it is in the best interests of Endicott and the Triple Cities to have local ownership. Mr. Bengston's previous local radio management experience eminently qualified him to own and operate the station."

The WENE staff, with the exception of Hal Graves, remained intact. Graves moved to Danbury as retail advertising manager of the *News-Times*.

Another round of executive shuffles took place in 1964, two involving Station WDOS.

Ben Turnbull became advertising manager of the *Plattsburgh Press-Republican*. Ed Somers succeeded Turnbull as WDOS boss.

The Turnbull move was a checker player's dream. He was summoned to Ottaway headquarters by Lyn Boyd, not knowing what was about to unfold. Francis Brinkley, Turnbull's boss, was not at the meeting. "You are going to Plattsburgh," Boyd told the rather shocked Turnbull, "and you are not to discuss it with anyone until I say so." Turnbull cajoled Boyd into giving him permission to talk to Elton Hall at the *Star*. He simply had to confide in a newspaperman who once had been in radio.

Turnbull reported to Ryder the next Monday morning. Next day the full scenario unfolded along with the reason for Brinkley's absence and Boyd's directive for silence. The following afternoon Ryder announced he was leaving Plattsburgh for a corporate vice presidency. Albert D. DeLuca, *P-R* advertising chief of staff, was introduced as the new general manager.

"I felt very insecure when Ryder left," Turnbull said. "Al DeLuca was supposed to train me, but how could he when he had a newspaper to run?"

But DeLuca and Ray Slater (another Ottaway advertising hotshot) did train Turnbull. So well, in fact, that he succeeded DeLuca as publisher in 1970, when DeLuca was transferred to the *Cape Cod Standard-Times* (now the *Cape Cod Times*).

"I believe I am where I am because of Francis Brinkley," Turnbull told the author. "Brink must have told Lyn I deserved a shot in Plattsburgh."

The full story of the Ottaway acquisition of the *New Bedford Standard-Times* and the *Cape Cod Standard-Times* will be chronicled in Chapter 13. But there was an important radio-related development in the negotiations with E. Anthony & Sons.

On December 7, 1965, Ottaway signed an agreement (with Ottaway Stations, Inc., as the vehicle) to buy WNBH, AM-FM, New Bedford and WOCB AM-FM, West Yarmouth, Massachusetts, from Anthony, subject to FCC approval. OSI, in effect, sought to acquire the broadcast assets of Anthony, while Ottaway Newspapers-Radio acquired the non-radio assets (newspapers).

The FCC approved only the WOCB purchase, which was consummated on May 5, 1966. The price was $600,000. OSI borrowed the down payment from ON-R. (WOCB was sold in late 1983 for in excess of $3 million.)

Jim and Ruth Ottaway were the sole shareholders in Ottaway Stations, Inc. Ten shares were outstanding at $100 par value. In mid-1966, they exchanged their shares (JHO seven, RBO three) for 130 shares of Ottaway-Newspaper- Radio, Inc., voting stock. Thus OSI became a wholly-owned subsidiary of ON-R.

On May 8, 1967, Chet Miller was appointed vice president of all radio stations, retaining his post as general manager of WVPO. A newcomer from Washington, Pennsylvania, Ronald Drescher, became assistant manager.

And the fourth radio GM departed for newspaper work. Ed Somers reported to the *Middletown Times Herald-Record* to start on a training program. In less than a year Somers would become general manager of the *Union-Gazette* (now *Tri- States Gazette*) in Port Jervis. By 1969 Somers had become No. 2 executive of the *Times Herald-Record,* and in 1974 became publisher in Oneonta. Al Sayers replaced Somers at WDOS.

In 1984 Somers was named publisher of the *Sun City* (Ariz.) *Daily News-Sun,* acquired by Ottaway in June of that year.

Paul Stiles was general manager of WOCB at the time of the Ottaway acquisition. He elected early retirement in 1969. Miller took over on the Cape, resigning as radio vice president. Drescher was promoted to GM at WVPO.

The end of Ottaway radio came on May 27, 1970.

The Ottaway merger with Dow Jones was only a few weeks away. Dow Jones wanted no part of broadcasting. "Too much governmental regulation" was the reason.

"That was Bill Kerby's attitude," Jim Ottaway Jr. said. "It was purely an editorial decision on his part." (At the time Kerby was president of Dow Jones.)

The answer was clear: Ottaway had to sell. Fast.

He had had the stations appraised early in the year. Their combined value was pegged in excess of $1.5 million. But he realized that the appraisal figure was contingent on finding the right buyer over a time span no one could estimate, plus a possible protracted wait for FCC approval.

The solution: Sell the stations to a group of his top corporate and line executives.

Thus, the board of directors of Ottaway Stations, Inc., (WDOS and WOCB), in solemn session May 27, passed a resolution "in conjunction with Pocono Broadcasting, Inc., (WVPO) to sell all three stations to Seamount Radio Corporation of New York and its subsidiaries, Seamount Radio Corporation of Massachusetts and Seamount Radio Corporation of Pennsylvania, for $765,000."

Present were Ottaway, chairman; Ruth Ottaway, vice president and secretary; Gene Brown, vice chairman; Lyn Boyd, president; and Jim Ottaway Jr., vice president. In effect the decision was made by Ottaway Newspapers-Radio, Inc., which had acquired the 10 outstanding OSI shares from the Ottaways in 1966.

It was an extremely generous act by the Ottaway family, a high point in its long personal and corporate tradition of excellence in human relations.

The price to executives was half the estimated market value of the stations.

Seamount was formed to embrace those who would be invited to participate in the can't-miss investment. There were two classes of stock: voting and non- voting. Boyd, Brown and the three station managers would own voting stock. Sixteen others, all but two either newspaper publishers or general managers, each would acquire 26 non-voting shares.

The Ottaway family assumed the full debt.

FCC approval of the sale came comparatively swiftly. The agency historically looks benignly on takeovers by employees.

Bruce O. Becker (Cornell Law School 1958), Jake's son, handled the sales agreement and applied the pressure to FCC counsel for quick approval. Bruce eventually became an Ottaway general counsel, "a long way from carrying Dad's briefcase," as he put it.

From the outset, criticism arose over the division of spoils by a few non-voting shareholders.

Boyd was outspoken on the subject:

"The arrangement was made primarily to reward Gene Brown and me. And I set it up as chairman of the board so that Gene and I could control the vote. And Gene was an active managing director. He did the traveling. He supervised the stations. And he found the broker who negotiated the eventual sale."

The gross profit on 26 shares of non-voting stock was approximately 29 times investment. Voting shares returned much more.

One shareholder built a lakeshore retreat with part of the proceeds.

He named it Camp Seamount.

8 'the years of risk have passed'

Jim and Ruth Ottaway never worried what the future held, even in the hand-to-mouth days in Endicott. Jim played to win; Ruth confidently backed his hand.

Jim's exceptionally shrewd business sense, his ability to calibrate financial risk with actuarial acumen, his publishing philosophy and dedication to superior human relations carried the organization across the last threshold of doubt in 1953.

"Jim," Gene Brown told the author, "had a vision. He wanted people to help him make it come true."

The realignment of Empire Newspapers-Radio that year was an important development.

It was ratified by the board in special session November 27 in Endicott and resulted in the formation of Ottaway Newspapers-Radio, Inc.

The move, Ottaway wrote, meant that "the burden of debt amortization on the part of all but one company (Plattsburgh) had eased and the early years of development and risk have passed."

Earlier in the year, Ottaway had obtained a favorable ruling from the Internal Revenue Service in a bid for tax-free reorganization involving exchange of capital shares of five separate corporations "for the purpose of establishing one operating-holding company with the four operating companies as wholly-owned subsidiaries."

Empire was to be the parent of the other companies: Oneonta Star, Inc., Pocono Record, Inc., Plattsburgh Publishing Company and Pocono Broadcasting, Inc.

Ottaway's petition to the IRS said in part:

"After several years of experience publishing the *Endicott Bulletin,* the other four companies were organized from time to time as independent corporations to acquire newspaper and radio businesses with the Ottaways as principal stockholders. That form of organization was deemed most desirable at the time because of problems of financing new companies upon their incorporation, the relatively weak financial status of Empire, the desire to keep each company entirely independent because of substantial long-term debt to outsiders and liens which existed against assets of the respective companies and for other similar reasons."

The letter to the IRS mentioned that "Empire" might be changed to "Ottaway" when and if the charter was amended. It was. The change was made, Ottaway said, "partly because of ego and because there were a number of other enterprises in New York bearing the 'Empire' label."

Not only had the early years of "development and risk" passed, Ottaway wrote (with Jake Becker's coaching), "management and personnel have become experienced in carrying out the ideas and ideals of the Ottaways, and the chief executives of the companies have gained, over the years, experience and knowledge of the problems of the respective companies and the manner in which they can best serve the local communities.

"The period is at hand when the greatest benefits can be derived from the formation of a closely-knit organization with one common corporate parent, instead of the existent five separate, independently-owned corporations. After the proposed reorganization, executives now holding minority shares of the capital stocks of the separate companies will become stockholders of one parent company with a consequent incentive to plan and work for the organization as a whole. The personnel of the five companies will be encouraged to perform to the best of their ability with the knowledge that they are members of a large and successful organization and that there may be more opportunity for reward and advancement than heretofore. Futhermore, shares in the new operating-holding company will be available for sale to other key operating executives to permit them to become stockholders and to share in the future earnings of the organization."

The stock-sharing program never materialized. It was abandoned, Ottaway recalled, at the urging of Ernst & Ernst, long-time Ottaway auditors, who pointed to the perils of stock eventually reaching unfriendly hands through non-family bequests.

Only Barney French, Gene Brown and Merle Ostrom held stock at the time. Ottaway had buy-back rights to their shares.

Ottaway listed these other benefits that would result from the reorganization:

Savings in interest expense in financing subsidiaries.

Better control of short and long-term borrowing.

Centralized purchasing.

Enhancement of prestige.

Greater power for expansion through acquisitions.

The letter to the IRS then alluded to the possibility that Ruth and Jim Ottaway might have to relinquish control:

"The proposed reorganization will also permit the establishment of a capable management team to assume responsibility for management and operation of all the companies in the event of the death or disability of Mr. and Mrs. Ottaway. It is only natural that at the present time the managers of the several companies should regard themselves as responsible only to Mr. and Mrs. Ottaway; and in the event the latter should become unable to participate actively in running the business, there would undoubtedly be some dissension among key employes. By developing a strong management group in the parent company, which would naturally control the operations of the subsidiary companies through voting power, it is hoped to create a permanent and coordinated management policy for the entire group."

As of December 31, 1952, total long-term debt of the five separate companies stood at $593,000, an increase of $208,500 over the previous year. The Plattsburgh acquisition, of course, accounted for the difference.

The following is a summary of net profit for the years 1948 through 1952 as furnished to the IRS in the reorganization petition:

	Empire Bulletin WENE	Oneonta Star WDOS	Stroudsburg Daily Record	Plattsburgh P-R	Pocono Broadcasting WVPO
1948	$26,857	$28,712	$23,280	—	—
1949	19,886	20,396	23,328	—	$ 8,352
1950	18,820	11,819	12,559	—	7,465
1951	7,916	15,562	16,758	—	7,666
1952	9,362	19,826	17,377	$2,908*	10,753

*Incorporated August 8, 1952

The Empire figures reflect dramatically an extension of Ottaway's earlier comment that the *Daily Bulletin* and Station WENE comprised a "relatively weak" property.

The next seven years would see the Ottaway children (then in their teens) recipients of substantial stock gifts from their parents.

The 1952 net recorded by Empire was more than disappointing because retail display linage for the year was the second highest in the *Bulletin*'s history. Classified sales had set an all-time high. Paul Morrissey had succeeded Lundquest as retail ad manager. A whirlwind named Beverly Moyle had become classified manager. Morrissey soon would succumb to cancer. Ms. Moyle would remain with the *Bulletin* until the end. But offsetting the good news from the *Bulletin* side were severe losses sustained by WENE, which Empire sold to Ottaway Stations, Inc., on May 31.

Donald Munro was editor of the *Bulletin;* William K. (Bill) Babel, managing editor. When Babel was promoted to the editor's job in Plattsburgh, he was succeeded by John Van Kleeck, who, like Babel, had joined the group in Oneonta.

Also in the early 1950s ON-R minutes recorded the promotion of Jean Reilly to the position of chief auditor. Now Mrs. John Gunn of LaGrangeville, New York, and mother of a son, Jean Reilly joined the organization in December 1941, when it consisted of the pioneer *Daily Bulletin*. She was hired as a bookkeeper's assistant and, like many on the payroll in those primeval days, found herself with more than one assignment.

"I worked in display and classified for Bill Lundquest and for the circulation department, trying to collect from deadbeats," she recalled. "Jim Ottaway's idea was to give me broad experience and eventually to make me bookkeeper. About 1946 I was made an internal auditor (Oneonta and Stroudsburg were in the fold by then) and I did an awful lot of traveling — mostly via public transportation. I didn't learn to drive until 1951 and that came about because Ottaway heckled me into it."

Jean Gunn would appear in Ottaway business offices just ahead of Ernst & Ernst audit teams, confirming ad balances, depreciation and fixed asset schedules. With Ottaway, she said, "everything — everything — had to balance."

As chronicled, Ottaway was traditionally eager to play the host and did so charmingly, but often he was oblivious to the fact that he was not carrying the wherewithal to pay the piper.

One day in 1956, Jean Gunn recalled, she had boarded the Delaware, Lackawanna & Western's westbound Phoebe Snow in East Stroudsburg, bound for Vestal (hard by Endicott) when she was greeted by Ottaway and his long-time confidant, John Tappan, who were on their way to the dining car. Ottaway also had been visiting the *Daily Record*.

She accepted the publisher's invitation to share his luncheon table. All went delightfully until the steward placed the tab in front of Ottaway, who once again found his pockets empty. Tappan came to the rescue.

Mrs. Gunn was named assistant treasurer of ON-R in 1956.

When the Endicott base of operations was abandoned in 1960, she joined the corporate move to Campbell Hall, New York, (which will be described in detail in Chapter 11.) She retired in 1965 to become a homemaker-parent.

While still active she set up the Blackburne Farm books and in retirement kept the Seamount and Ottaway Investment Company ledgers. OIC was a post-merger operation involving the family, completely divorced from publishing operations.

Blackburne Farm was a horse-breeding partnership venture of Jim and Ruth Ottaway, that was founded in 1966 on farmland adjacent to Campbell Hall headquarters. The Ottaways dealt solely in Arabians, a swift, graceful breed. The venture ended after 12 years.

One of the very few commonalities of the Ottaway properties is what each business office knows as the uniform system of accounts.

The basic idea was developed by Ottaway, who rejected a suggestion that it was unique. He spent the academic year 1931-32 at the School of Business of the University of Michigan, studying accounting. "I simply wanted to be able to understand figures," he said.

It is a matter of record that, unique or not, the Ottaway system figuratively stunned more than a few publishers, general managers and comptrollers at American Press Institute Management and Costs seminars. They had been content with a bottom line figure, not overly concerned with isolating factors that created a profit or loss situation.

Jean Gunn said there was a "primitive sort of chart of accounts" when she joined the organization. "After Francis Brinkley arrived in 1949 it began to develop into a more cohesive document," she recalled.

At the end of 1953, long-term debt stood at $554,531, down $38,296 from the preceding year. All properties were paying their way. The debt would shrink to $528,490 a year later, the last drop that would be recorded under Ottaway ownership.

Jim Ottaway's play-to-win inner drive embraced more than acquisitions and excellence in publishing. It extended to leisure-time pursuits, such as golf and gin rummy.

Two generations of executives will attest that he did not always accept defeat with grace.

One day in the clubhouse at Buck Hill Falls after a golf trouncing at the hands of one of his publishers, Ottaway was moved to suggest that perhaps his opponent was spending too much time on the links and not enough in the office.

The piques were short-lived.

9 Danbury

Jim and Ruth Ottaway had a profound grasp of the role an attractive newspaper plant could play in a community. Their innate artistic talents, combined with a sharp perception of cost awareness, were demonstrated amply in the new construction in Endicott and Oneonta.

It was part of the internal and external good neighbor policy they demanded their local managers pursue. As quickly as prudence allowed, every work place was upgraded or eventually replaced.

So it was in Stroudsburg.

During 1953 land was acquired south of the commercial center of the city in a prime residential area at Broad and Lenox streets. Ottaway hadn't given another downtown location a second thought.

Ottaway and Merle Ostrom personally sold the idea to adjacent home owners, displaying architect's renderings and touting the elegant landscaping that would be installed. Counterpart to their paeans of civic betterment was Ottaway's salesmanship. Obviously it worked. "It'll be a lot better than what we have now," property owners chorused.

Also in 1953 the *Daily Record* bought from Ottaway "all his rights" to a proposed corporation to be called Record-Sun Printers, Inc. Ottaway had struck a deal with George B. Forster, owner of the East Stroudsburg job printing enterprise, known as the Sun Printing Company. Purchase of Sun was not consummated until January 1960. The price was $100,000 with $20,000 down and $6,666 yearly until paid. The new company eventually was named Sun-Litho Print, Inc., and was a marginal money-maker until its sale in the early 1980s.

Meantime, Elton Hall left WVPO to become assistant general manager of the *Daily Record*. Hall was placed in charge of commercial printing and "several departments" of the newspaper.

To round out the year on another positive note, Ottaway acquired a 20-page Duplex press from the *Attleboro* (Mass.) *Sun* for $20,000, paying $9,000 down with the balance due on arrival. Board minutes contain no reference to borrowing for this third press replacement within the organization, so it must be assumed that the *Record* had sufficient cash reserves to cover the tab. Not quite unalloyed prosperity, but things were looking up!

The Teletypesetter Age came to Ottaway in the early 1950s. The major wire services and some syndicates now delivered news and features in the form of perforated oiled tape, which was fed into Linotype or Intertype line-casting machines via an apparatus that activated the letter keys. TTS offered the cost advantages of steady 11- or 12-lines-per-minute production of type with the further blessing that the machines didn't take coffee breaks or insist on vacations. But editors were at the mercy of whoever filed the wire reports. Resetting type defeated the TTS concept of economies.

Oneonta received its first TTS unit in 1952. Endicott followed two years later. The latter was promptly chatteled to Endicott Trust for $9,000.

Even as the ink was drying on the Plattsburgh acquisition documents in August 1952, fate was beckoning to Ottaway from rich Fairfield County, Connecticut.

Severe friction had developed among stockholders and directors of the *Danbury News-Times*. Some wanted to sell. Others did not. Some were on the fence.

Once again Ottaway was approached by the ubiquitous Allen Kander, who correctly appraised the Danbury area as a lucrative market, largely untapped by a leadership composed of well-meaning men with little knowledge or understanding of a newspaper operation.

Exactly how Kander discovered that some *News-Times* shareholders and directors were eager to sell is lost to memory.

Ottaway suggested the broker might have struck it rich with one of his "feeler" letters to publishers, which simply probed for possibilities.

Whatever the process, there were others who eagerly sought the combination for control of the 6,000 outstanding shares of *N-T* stock. They included the Miller family of Pittsfield, Massachusetts, owners of *The Berkshire Eagle;* Kingsley Gillespie, publisher of the *Stamford* (Conn.) *Advocate;* and Robert M. Feemster, at the time chairman of the Executive Committee of Dow Jones. Feemster also was owner of the now defunct *Alexandria* (Ind.) *Daily Times-Tribune.* There also was a local bid. It, too, was doomed.

Negotiations for the *Danbury News-Times* (Danbury would be dropped from the nameplate in 1962) extended over more than five years, requiring an atypical approach as the saga of the financial give and take will underscore.

"No conventional approach would have worked," Ottaway said. "We had to do things we ordinarily would not do."

Gene Brown, who would move from Oneonta to manage the *News-Times,* called the Danbury acquisition the most difficult ever undertaken by Ottaway and his associates.

Who was the principal architect?

"I am best prepared to answer that," Brown told the author. "I am best because Jim and I have differed in many areas, therefore I can be completely dispassionate. Jim was the principal architect and in my opinion there wasn't another man who could have put that deal together."

Ottaway, in turn, credited Kander and Jake Becker with major roles in the protracted struggle.

"Kander twisted arms, cajoled and finagled," Brown recalled.

"He was an ingenious bulldog," Ottaway added.

Ottaway described Becker as less a lawyer of theory and more an unwavering advocate of teamwork, which made the difference in this particular quest.

"There wasn't much in the way of humor to lighten the acquisition period," Brown recalled. "Highways between Endicott-Oneonta and Danbury hadn't been improved then and it was a tortuous trip, which gave Jim plenty of time to tell me how to run the world. We would meet in a motel near Ridgefield so no one would know what was going on. We all felt like conspirators.''

Which, in a sense, they were.

To understand the complications faced by Ottaway it is necessary to identify the major shareholders and their relationship to the founding fathers of the *Danbury Evening News* and the *Danbury Times*.

The *Evening News* became a daily September 8, 1883, under the aegis of James Montgomery Bailey, known as the "Danbury News Man." Bailey died in 1894.

George W. Flint, Bailey's brother-in-law, who had served as general manager, and William L. Smith, a half-brother, were Bailey's principal heirs. They formed a partnership, Flint & Smith, to continue the *News* operation. Flint was the guiding force over the next 20 years.

During that period another *Evening News* managerial force emerged — Frederick B. Dalton, a nephew of Flint. When Flint died in 1919, his ownership and responsibilities passed to Dalton. Smith died in 1918.

In 1927 the *Danbury Times* was established, financed by Frank H. Lee Sr., a Danbury industrialist, who was president of the flourishing Frank H. Lee Hat Company.

Economic circumstances of the 1930s precluded the operation of two competing dailies. The *Evening News* and the *Times* merged January 31, 1933. But there was another reason for the merger. The *Evening News* was weakened by the embezzlement of substantial sums by its advertising manager, who was considered to be a special protege of the childless Dalton.

Dalton continued as publisher of the merged operation — The *News-Times*. The first Mrs. Dalton had died and Dalton married Mrs. Elizabeth Hull, widow of T. Clark Hull Sr. of Danbury. Dalton thus became step-father to three children. One was T. Clark Hull Jr., future lieutenant governor and Superior Court judge, and then a member of the Connecticut Appellate Court, founded in 1983.

Dalton died October 3, 1935. Mrs. Dalton inherited her husband's holdings.

Frank H. Lee Sr. died in 1937.

By 1955, a year before the Ottaway takeover, records show that three major shareholding factions had emerged: Elizabeth Dalton, the Frank H. Lee Company, owned by his four children and Ralph A. and Florence Griffing.

The provenance of the Dalton and Lee holdings is clear.

Florence Griffing was the daughter of Ella L. Smith, widow of William Smith of the old *Evening News* partnership. Ella Smith had inherited her husband's holdings. Over the years Ella Smith's stock passed to the Griffings. Ralph Griffing had interests in real estate and among other things was the builder and landlord of the Palace Theatre in Danbury.

One veteran Danbury newsman remembers that on Dalton's death Griffing was a frequent presence at the *News-Times* until 1938 when the Lee and Dalton interests set up a voting trust and took control.

Charles F. Stevens, one of four brothers who had come from Bridgeport to help start the *Times* in 1927, had taken over as general manager and continued during the trust until his death in 1941.

The Lee family stock, 1,612 shares, and 1,399 Dalton shares were in the voting trust. The trustees in 1955 were T. Clark Hull Jr., representing his mother (Dalton); Leonard McMahon, counsel to the Lee Hat Company, representing the Lees and Kenneth M. Hooper, president of the old City National Bank and Trust Company as the neutral trustee.

The voting trust was formed in January 1938 and renewed in 1948 for 10 years — or less if the Lees and Mrs. Dalton decided to dissolve it.

Neither the Lees nor Mrs. Dalton, especially the latter, were admirers of the Griffings. Contemporaries surmise that she had litle faith in Ralph Griffing's ability to help guide the *News-Times* as the now senior board member.

There was another, more solid, reason. Just before the merger, the *Evening News* partnership between Dalton and the Griffings had become strained to the breaking point. The Griffings went to Superior Court and obtained an order placing the operation in the hands of a receiver. Auditors for the receiver uncovered the defalcations of the advertising manager.

William A. White, Mrs. Dalton's brother-in-law, with minor Danbury business interests, set up the voting trust with McMahon.

The relationship between Mrs. Dalton and the Lees, a competent source said, was "not close" but "devoid of animosity." The Lees apparently had no adverse personal feelings toward Ralph Griffing, but like Mrs. Dalton, felt he was not competent in newspaper matters. Another contemporary however, insisted that the Griffings "detested" the Lees.

Some minor holdings were as follows:

William A. White, 201 shares; William J. Stevens, composing room foreman, 40 shares; Frank S. Stevens, general manager as of 1950 and former circulation manager, 125 shares.

(William J. Stevens was succeeded as composing room foreman by Thomas E. Purcell, who eventually became an Ottaway corporate vice president in charge of production.)

Frank P. Rollins, from 1941 to 1950 publisher and general manager, held 133 shares. Rollins was lured from the *Evening News* in 1931 and became the *Times*'s editor. The stock, it must be assumed, was a reward for risking the jump to an untested newspaper.

The remaining unidentified shares of non-voting trust stock were in the hands of employees or their heirs.

Recapitulation shows that the voting trust shares totaled 3,011, or 50½ percent. Free stock totaled 2,989 or 49½ percent.

Frank Lee Jr., then James, had succeeded their father as president of the hat company. The other Lee children were Thomas and Josephine Lee Robinson. Frank and James, contemporaries said, were eager to sell the *News-Times*. Mrs. Robinson staunchly opposed any sale. She felt she had an obligation to carry out her father's belief that the paper should always be locally owned and operated. For a while, at least, Thomas sided with his sister.

There had been more than just a division of thought on selling the paper. Frank Lee Sr. had left the extensive family farm to Josephine, plus any shares of *News-Times* stock registered in his name. A intra-family battle erupted over the issue of whether the shares had been in Lee's name or were company owned.

Thomas eventually joined his brothers in favoring the sale of the paper, but, with Josephine, opposed selling the hat company. The family friction resulted in at least one lawsuit. The courts stepped in and appointed trustees to manage what Lee assets were left and to keep the factory operating.

Lee Hat Company eventually was sold to Stetson, which then owed the Mallory Hat Company, also of Danbury.

The Lee brothers were critically short of cash. Mrs. Dalton, a contemporary suggested, depended on *News-Times* dividends to a great extent, but had other income. None of the principals had the means to buy out the others.

Even in the face of cash flow problems. Mrs. Dalton turned down an offer of $500,000 for her shares. It came from Lazarus Heyman, described as a lawyer, real estate operator and would-be politican. Heyman aspired to an influentual role in Danbury affairs.

Mrs. Robinson had no comparable money problems. Her husband, Frederick F. Robinson, owned an accounting firm in Danbury. But one close observer offered another reason: "She was not a spendthrift like some others" in the cast.

The acquisition battle plan, as recounted in a seven-page step-by-step "primer" for Jim Ottaway Jr. by his father, was simple in concept but devilishly difficult to bring to fruition. At the time Jim Jr. was a freshman at Yale University, but remained close to the operations of his father's growing organization.

The Ottaway-Becker strategy called for formation of a new Connecticut corporation (Danbury Publishing Company, Inc.) with 6,000 shares of common stock, same as the News-Times Company.

Ottaway Newspapers-Radio, the parent corporation, had authorized Ottaway to act as its agent to sign contracts for buying stock. ON-R also advanced cash to Ottaway. Cash would be a key element in two of the three major transactions. Ottaway also was empowered to lend money to acquire options as necessary. Any options would expire in January 1958 when the voting trust ended, or sooner if the Lees and Mrs. Dalton agreed to dissolve it.

First breakthrough came on June 24, 1955. Ottaway acquired an option on the 2,000 shares owned by the Griffings. The $40,000 option price would be applied to a down payment of $75,000 with the balance payable over six years at 7¾ percent. Total cost would be $300,000 or $150 per share.

Ralph Griffing had been booted off the *N-T* board and when the voting trust was organized found himself exiled. Patently he and Mrs. Griffing were the logical targets for Kander's first thrusts. They were, to put it mildly, ready for retaliation.

The 1,612 Lee-Robinson shares actually were in the name of Leonard McMahon, who had acquired them as trustee from the Lee Hat Company for $100,000. The Lees and Mrs. Robinson had an option to repurchase from McMahon the stock that would expire July 1, 1955. Price was the same: $100,000.

It must be assumed that Kander cut the crucial deal with the Lees. With only three days remaining on the option with McMahon, they agreed to repurchase the stock by July 1 if Ottaway would lend them the $100,000.

It was an historic moment.

Kander called Jake Becker. Becker appeared at Ottaway's Endicott headquarters only to find that the publisher was fishing in Canada, a guest of Chuck Carpenter at International Paper's Oriskany camp.

As the Fates would have it, Gene Brown was in Endicott, possibly for a meeting with Barney French. Brown thought Lyn Boyd and Jim Ottaway Jr. were present, but wasn't sure. Jim Jr. said he could have been, but didn't remember. Where was Ruth Ottaway? Surely she would have been consulted at this critical stage if she had been in Endicott. No one could recall her whereabouts.

At any rate, Brown and Becker placed a call to Oriskany to get approval of a loan to the Lees. French opposed the idea.

"The connection was so poor," Brown said, "that Jake and I didn't know if Jim agreed or not. But we decided to take a chance, not in a spirit of bravado, but because if we didn't, all of Jim's work would have gone up in smoke. We didn't have any options."

"They may not have heard me, but I heard them," Ottaway recalled. "I said okay."

In consideration of the $100,000 loan, the Lees agreed to sell 1,612 shares to Ottaway at $150 per share or 1,209 shares (403 each) if Mrs. Robinson did not sign before January 1958, when the trust would be dissolved.

They also agreed to place the 1,612 voting trust certificate shares in escrow as collateral for the six percent loan and to start court action to divide the trust certificate into four parts if Mrs. Robinson did not sign.

The $100,000 loan was to apply to the purchase price, leaving a balance for the 1,612 shares of $141,800, which was to be retired over three years in equal installments.

Thus the Lees paid roughly $62 a share to McMahon and received $150 from Ottaway.

Jim Ottaway didn't get all 6,000 shares at a unit price of $150.

Mrs. Dalton had become concerned at the thought of being a minority stockholder, and was fearful that a rival newspaper might come into being. Her son (Trustee Hull) also had qualms about the *News-Times* directorate. Its directors meant well, he reasoned, but actually knew little about the newspaper business.

Mrs. Dalton, like the Lees, needed cash. Although she basically didn't want to sell, Ottaway and Kander arranged a deal that proved attractive enough to sway her.

Of the 1,799 Dalton shares, 1,399 were in the voting trust; 400 were "free."

Ottaway advanced $64,000 to Mrs. Dalton in terms of a loan and acquired two options: To purchase 400 shares at any time before the trust dissolved and to buy 1,399 shares in January 1958 or before, if the trust expired before deadline.

The loan, advanced at six percent interest, would pay for the 400-share block at $160 per share. Ottaway agreed to pay $238,840 for the remaining shares, again at a unit price of $160. The deal called for a five-year installment payout with interest pegged at 7¾ percent.

Ottaway then loaned William White $30,150 for an option to buy his 201 shares at $150 each. The loan would apply to the purchase price. One of the White shares was in the voting trust.

Leonard McMahon died in July 1955, shortly after the Lees repurchased their 1,612 shares. Kenneth Hooper, the neutral voting trustee, resigned the same month. That left Hull as the only voting trustee. The trust, in effect, was unable to operate.

Hull called a meeting of the Lee brothers and Mrs. Robinson in September to name a successor to McMahon. Mrs. Robinson was not present. Frank Lee represented her by proxy.

At that point Ottaway won an agreement from the Lees to name Lyn Boyd as their trustee.

On January 23, 1956, a week before the annual meeting of the News-Times Company, Hull and Boyd named Ottaway as the third trustee.

The day before the meeting, Oneonta Star, Inc., acquired 2,000 Griffing shares. It put up $35,000 cash in addition to the $40,000 option money already paid. Ottaway bought 400 shares from Mrs. Dalton and canceled the $64,000 loan. He also bought White's 200 shares for $30,000 and canceled that loan. (One White share still was in the voting trust.) There had been no action on the Lee-Robinson block.

Between January 22 and April 1, 1956, Ottaway had acquired for cash all the loose shares, 388 in all, for $150 a share.

On the day of the annual meeting, 5,999 shares were voted for an Ottaway board. Mrs. Robinson was present but abstained from voting.

At this point Ottaway owned 49½ percent of *N-T* shares outright; the voting trust, 50½ percent.

Winter and spring of 1956 saw the Lee-Robinson faction engaged in more intra-family squabbling. In short the Lees were hard up for cash. The solution to their fiscal dilemma came on June 22 when the Lees and Mrs. Robinson signed over the 1,612 shares to the Frank H. Lee Company. The company agreed to sell them to ON-R, Inc., according to the original agreement.

A concession was made to sweeten the deal: Ottaway agreed to pay the $141,800 purchase balance in cash instead of over three years.

At the same time Ottaway (as agent) bought Mrs. Dalton's remaining 1,399 voting trust shares with a down payment of $11,942, with the balance, $226,896, payable over five years. Add White's single voting trust share, bought for $150.

Ottaway had paid just short of $1 million ($932,990) for the

6,000 shares.

But he had physical possession of 5,999.

Mrs. Robinson, secretary of the old company, had needed at least one share of *N-T* stock to serve on the board, a requirement under Connecticut law. Frank Stevens had loaned her one of his shares, for which she sent him a check for $150. Stevens returned the draft, saying he didn't want to sell.

Mrs. Robinson refused to give up the share. Ottaway, understandably miffed, urged Jake Becker to bring suit. Jake calmed the publisher. "Let her keep it," he advised. "We've paid Stevens for it. Why waste your money on a lawsuit?"

Frederick Robinson brazenly suggested to Ottaway that his wife ought to be named secretary of the new company at a modest stipend, so as to carry on the Lee name in Danbury journalism. If Ottaway agreed, Mrs. Robinson would turn over the elusive share.

Josephine Robinson still has the share. Ottaway would have no truck with her husband's proposition.

Ralph Griffing did not go unrewarded for opening the way to Ottaway control. He received a 20-year consultant contract at $3,000 a year.

Gene Brown was tapped to run the *News-Times*, resigning as general manager and treasurer of the *Oneonta Star* March 31, 1956. His title in Danbury would be assistant publisher and executive vice president. Ottaway had always retained the title of publisher at each newspaper.

There were heavy borrowings from Endicott Trust Company in 1956 ($394,000) and again in 1958 ($226,600).

The reason for the first was clear: helping to finance the acquisition. But improved typesetting machinery was needed to handle burgeoning advertising volume. Tommy Purcell's name can be found in the minutes of a July 1959 board meeting as recommending an outlay of $43,000. The same year Brown rented sorely needed space in an adjoining building, and the board was considering buying the adjacent Capital Theatre building to relieve overcrowding.

A replacement press was bought right after the Ottaway takeover. It was a five-unit Goss letterpress, four plates wide, capable of 30,000 impressions per hour. It had been used to print comics in Montreal.

One of the Ottaway legends that is difficult to authenticate relates to the Goss. As the story goes, the Ottaway board, save for the chief, vehemently opposed the purchase. As usual, he prevailed. Memories of the incident have become blurred.

The *News-Times* soon eclipsed Plattsburgh in profitability and long would remain No. 1 on the earnings chart. Ottaway also had inherited a superb editorial staff, which was unabashedly exuberant over the acquisition by a man totally committed to the pursuit of journalistic perfection.

The *News-Times* celebrated its centennial in September 1983.

Writing about the Ottaway takeover in a commemorative edition, Stephen A. (Steve) Collins, editorial director, said: "It was a time for me to keep my eyes and ears open and mouth shut, but that did not stop me from hoping it would be the Ottaway firm that bought the paper, a name I had picked up rather early. I had attended an American Press Institute seminar for editors and publishers. . .early in 1953 with two Ottaway editors. I was impressed with the quality of their publications. I was even more impressed with the information I picked up during informal shop talk about how an Ottaway paper operated."

Robert (Bob) Lauf, now editor of Ottaway's *Daily Item* in Sunbury, Pennsylvania, was on the *News-Times* copy desk when ownership changed. Here's how he recalled the first day:

"It was an event that remains vivid — the moment Jim Ottaway came into the third-floor newsroom and was introduced as the new owner!

"I remember vaguely his speech about who the Ottaways were and what they stood for in journalism. I remember vaguely his assurance that we would not be losing our jobs, but would be sought after to make the *News-Times* a better paper than it was.

"I remember much more vividly Jim Ottaway's admonition about 'no sacred cows.' I remember something to the effect that 'If Jim Ottaway gets arrested, make damn sure his name appears in the paper like anyone else's.'

"I came to realize, over the next 25 years, that he meant every word he said, and that any attempt by anyone 'in the know' to keep his or her name in or out of the paper failed — especially if they tried to get through to headquarters.

"I came to realize, over the years, that the same credibility and adherence to high journalistic ethics were passed on to Jim Jr., whose first on-the-job assignment was as a reporter in our newsroom.

"How did people in the newsroom feel that day when they learned the Ottaways had purchased the *News-Times* and a man by the name of Eugene J. Brown would be our publisher?

"Somewhat afraid — but it was strictly fear of the unknown. Most of us had been around long enough to know that when a company changed hands, changes are sure to follow.

"In subsequent years there were some bad changes. Some people were pushed out the door to make way for someone else's choice when they didn't deserve it. But there were 10 good changes for every bad one, and it didn't take long to realize we were becoming a truly independent newspaper, free of local hamstrings.

"A significant number of us were concerned about some tight monetary policies in these early days, even though there were indications the overall treatment of employees would be better than that of the previous ownership. I remember being irate at finding out our new owners would not pay my expenses (beyond dues) as president of the Danbury Lions Club after the former owners had encouraged me to accept the nomination and agreed to pay. At the time, I was disheartened, but later realized that most other situations were treated more openly and honestly than in the past, including a much fairer system of salaries."

During the period immediately preceding the actual closing in Danbury, Lyn Boyd was promoted to vice president of the newspaper division of ON-R from executive assistant to Ottaway. Concurrently, Francis Brinkley was advanced to vice president of the radio division and was given the additional title of controller.

The Oneonta board, in a heady gesture reflecting still greater prosperity, declared a $6 dividend for 1955. This would rise to $12 in 1958, to $18 in 1961, to $24 in 1963 and to $30 per share in 1964.

In Stroudsburg, meantime, Merle Ostrom had become assistant publisher. Elton Hall had been named general manager and Horace Heller assistant GM.

On April 1, 1956, Hall was picked to succeed Gene Brown as GM in Oneonta. And when Ostrom retired at the end of that year, Heller became boss of Stroudsburg operations.

And James A. (Big Jim) Somers, a cousin of WVPO's Ed Somers, was named chief of the job printing department.

Ottaway well might have been excused had he deferred action on the new *Daily Record* building, what with the hefty Danbury outlay on the books, which would reflect a long-term debt of $1.3 million at the end of 1956.

But the project moved ahead. The first construction estimate came in at $150,000 on April 8, 1956, at a board meeting in Cooperstown. But the bids, opened November 30, all were in excess of $200,000. Wayne Edwards of Endicott got the job. Edwards had been general contractor for the *Daily Bulletin* building and later the WENE studios in Endicott.

Financing was achieved through borrowings of $125,000 from Security Mutual Life Insurance Company of Binghamton and $100,000 from First Stroudsburg National Bank. The Security loan waived payments during the first year, but carried a term-end balloon of $45,000.

There is a further reference to the borrowing in the minutes of July 25, 1957, which describes one of the lenders as the Fidelity Philadelphia Trust Company of Philadelphia "participating with the Stroudsburg National Bank" to the tune of $125,000 at six percent over 11 years. The exact purpose was not explained. It is mentioned here because Fidelity Philadelphia was destined to play a further role in Ottaway financing in the decade ahead.

The new Stroudsburg building opened for business in June 1957, and on November 9-10 Ottaway held open house for the community. The event was commemorated with an ad-heavy 16-page supplement. Every contractor and supplier with the remotest connection to the structure bought congratulatory space. It was what might be called a tin cup bonanza.

During 1958, a relaxed year by Ottaway standards, Ruthie was married to Dunham Baldwin Sherer II, of Brooklyn Heights. The ceremony took place June 28 at the Canadensis Methodist Church, with the Reverend Samuel Little officiating. Like the Ottaways, the Sherers were Buck Hill Falls cottagers. Mr. Little, pastor of the Endwell Methodist Church to which the Ottaways belonged, was an old family friend. (The hamlet of

104

Canadensis is next to Buck Hill Falls. Endwell is an Endicott suburb.)

The file shows that Ottaway personally handled his daughter's announcements, which went to the *New York Times* and the now defunct *Herald-Tribune* and *World Telegram & Sun*. The *Times* responded, explaining that there would be no charge for news items on the "society page," but that publication could not be guaranteed.

The chief had no misgivings about the play his own *Endicott Bulletin* and *Stroudsburg Record* would give to the nuptials.

And just a few months before the Ottaway Middletown adventure began, Jim Jr. married Mary Wells Hyde on June 16, 1959, at the Brick Presbyterian Church in New York City. Jim, who had risen to board chairman and editor of the *Yale Daily News*, would graduate in 1960 with a bachelor's degree, and shortly start his family newspaper career with Gene Brown in Danbury.

Two stories suggest that Jim Jr. wasn't sure he wanted to join the family business immediately. Jim Sr. said that his son visited Louisville right after graduation at the behest of John Macauley Smith, his roommate at Yale. Smith's father, a judge, was close to the Binghams, owners of the Louisville newspapers. Whatever discussions might have taken place in Kentucky have faded from memory. "I can't remember my thought processes at that time," Jim Jr. said. (Mac Smith worked for Ottaway for a while in the Goshen bureau of the Middletown *Times Herald-Record*.)

Jim Jr. and his bride went on a belated wedding trip in 1960, spending five months in Greece. The honeymoon was financed with $1,500 he earned on the *Yale Daily News*, which sum was matched by his father. "We spent $1,500 for transportation and lived on $10 a day," he recalled.

In Athens, Jim Jr. interviewed for a job on the *News*, an English language daily. The salary was to be $60 a week, or so he thought. When he discovered the $60 was a monthly stipend, he backed off.

"That was the only serious job interview I can remember," he said.

Jim and Ruth Ottaway visited the newlyweds in October,

their last month in Greece.

One day father and son took a boat ride to the island of Aegina to view a temple. They discussed Jim Jr.'s future. Just this once.

"Father never pressured me. He stayed very cool."

Jim Jr.'s next stop was the *Danbury News-Times*.

"Considering what was at stake for him I was amazed. I admired him."

10 Middletown

It was a serendipitous meeting.

One day in February 1959 Ruth and Jim Ottaway were at Broome County Airport, which serves the Binghamton-Johnson City-Endicott area. They were about to fly to New York, then change planes for their annual vacation in St. Thomas.

Jacob Merrill Kaplan, who sat on the Endicott Johnson Shoe Company board, also was at the airport. Kaplan, then 66, was, in effect, proprietor of the *Daily Record* in Middletown, New York. The *Record*, founded in 1956, was the first daily paper in the United States to be assembled by photo-composition (cold type) and printed by the offset process. It was an upstart tabloid, tightly edited, and had achieved a respectable circulation of 19,000 in less than three years.

But it was losing money. Lots and lots of money.

A Goldman Sachs executive, a friend of John Tappan, the Ottaway financial advisor, introduced Ottaway to Kaplan.

Quite predictably, Kaplan opened the conversation by asking Ottaway what he did for a livelihood.

"I'm in the newspaper business," the publisher replied.

"Oh? I have a morning paper in Middletown. We have problems," Kaplan volunteered. "I want to talk to you when you get back from vacation."

Jack Kaplan, born in January 23, 1893, was a man of immense wealth. He organized a molasses firm in 1921, merged it with another in 1925, and sold the company for what "Who's Who" describes as a "large sum" in 1928. In 1929-30 he held a seat on the New York Stock Exchange, became president of the National Grape Corporation in 1934, and between 1945 and 1960

107

was president of the Welch Grape Juice Company. He also established and presided over the J.M. Kaplan Fund, Inc. The trust was widely believed to have financed the fledgling *Record* but the report was firmly denied by Kaplan and his associates.

At that point Jim Ottaway couldn't talk further to his new friend. Unknown to Kaplan, he had opened serious negotiations for the other Middletown property, the afternoon *Times Herald*.

Ottaway would meet Kaplan again before long.

Even on that February day, Ottaway's long-range strategy included buying out Kaplan's Middletown interests.

"We figured the *Record* was losing a hell of a lot of money," Ottaway said, "and we concluded that a successful businessman like Kaplan wouldn't put up with it for long."

Call it a hunch. Call it inspiration.

The Fates would deal Ottaway a royal flush.

Another broker, Vincent J. Manno, had been watching the expanding Ottaway group, and, as the publisher said, "kept in touch with us." Manno's principal client was Gannett. Manno had called Ottaway in late 1958 in Endicott to announce that he had "something to talk about."

The "something" was Ralph McA. Ingersoll's *Times Herald* and Port Jervis *Union-Gazette*. First discussions were in the living room of Ottaway's Pheasant Lane home.

"We went down to Middletown and took a look at the market. We made as thorough a study as we could," Ottaway recalled. "Then we took a look at the linage figures and checked the P&L. The *TH* was making a few dollars — without much management. We figured we could at least tread water."

Ingersoll carried a unique pedigree as a metropolitan and national journalist: He was managing editor of the *New Yorker* magazine in its infancy; manager of *Time, Life* and *Fortune* of the Henry Luce group (he was a founder of *Life*); and creator of the *March of Time* and of *PM*, the pre-war New York evening newspaper that carried no advertising and soon perished.

Ingersoll returned from the war with seven battle stars and the Legion of Merit and set about creating a chain of community newspapers in the northeast. The *TH* was one of them. The *TH* had been acquired from the Harriman family by Charles E. Marsh, who, until 1950, was in partnership with

108

Ingersoll. Ingersoll's R.J. Company incorporated in 1950, and bought Marsh's Middletown interests for $500,000. Marsh, a publisher whose principal interests lay in the southeast, had retired by 1958.

Marsh and Kaplan had come to Middletown for the same and yet different reasons.

Middletown originally was an important railroad hub. In the 1950s it was an area of rapidly growing farming and livestock operations and boasted a diversity of manufacturing enterprises.

It is located in mid-Orange County, 60 miles from New York City. The county still remains the last undeveloped area within 75 miles of New York.

In a 1959 memo to Lyn Boyd, Ingersoll wrote: "Orange County. . .must inevitably become industrialized within the next 10 years. The fact is that to date this expansion has not begun. On the other hand the stability of this area's income is extraordinary, based on diversification of small industries and backed up by the fantastically productive black dirt farming country and the rich dairy farming area serving New York. I don't want to try to sum up this situation in a paragraph, but the prospects for industrial development of Orange County were what induced Charles Marsh to buy the *Times Herald* from the Harrimans, and is a prime reason why Mr. Kaplan thought he could start a competitive paper here."

Perhaps not the prime reason. Kaplan, one knowledgeable source said, had become concerned with the trend toward decreased newspaper competition and had commissioned a survey of upstate New York and Connecticut communities for a growth site for a new newspaper to compete with an established one. Any new publication, Kaplan reasoned, should be printed by the offset process to whet competition.

Others have suggested that Kaplan's survey also sought to identify the most vulnerable properties — financially, editorially, or both.

Kaplan selected Middletown "because of the growth potential and because the paper there wasn't doing a good job," according to an article on the Middletown newspaper "war" in the May 11, 1959, issue of *Newsweek*. The article also quoted

Kaplan as "hoping to see black ink at the *Record* in a year's time."

Seven months later Kaplan told *Editor & Publisher* that "it would be dishonest to say that the *Record* is making a profit . . . but that will come in a short time. One reason we are not showing a profit is that we are using the *Record* as a training ground for people we will put in charge of other newspaper properties as we start or acquire them."

The *Times Herald,* by any publishing yardstick, hardly could have been considered a weak target when Kaplan established the *Daily Record* in 1956. Perhaps not a diadem in the Ingersoll crown, it nonetheless was returning a comfortable profit to its mostly absentee owner, who preferred life in Culpeper, Virginia.

Ingersoll visited Middletown five or six times a year and "seldom meddled" in company affairs, one staffer recalled.

There may be a third reason.

A competent source said that Kaplan tried to buy the *Times Herald* from Marsh in 1949, but was "cruelly rebuffed" in a chilling meeting.

Kaplan, the source said, left the Marsh apartment seething with "frustrated rage." Was Kaplan's Middletown plunge motivated by a desire to get back at Marsh through Ingersoll, who in 1956 still owed Marsh more than $200,000 for the property?

If Kaplan indeed sought revenge via Ingersoll's pocketbook, he achieved it in no small measure. Seventeen months after the *Daily Record* start-up, Marsh agreed to waive the $25,000 annual principal payment "pending determination of the competition" with Kaplan. A year later Marsh waived both principal and interest and in December 1958 loaned Ingersoll an additional $20,000 on a no-interest demand note to help defray costs of the *TH's* new $250,000 building at West Main and Mill streets.

At the end of 1959 it was clear something had to give. Kaplan's losses were mounting. Ingersoll's now marginal profit was shrinking. He had given thought to discontinuing the unprofitable Saturday edition to pare costs. But his editors persuaded him not to make the move.

Early in January 1960 one of Kaplan's confidants asked, "How is Middletown going?" Kaplan is quoted as replying "Oh, you've always been right. There is room for only one paper there."

On November 5, 1959, Jim Ottaway added the *Times Herald* and the *Union-Gazette* to his string of five dailies.

Purchase price for Ingersoll's stock in the R.J. Company, Inc., was $8,500, plus $91,500 to repay Ingersoll for funds he had advanced to R.J. for working capital. To consummate the deal, Ottaway formed Middletown Publishing Company, Inc., which in effect became the purchaser.

Ingersoll had given the staff no advance notice. On the day of the sale someone affixed a bare-bones announcement to the bulletin board.

Ingersoll had acquired the afternoon *Union-Gazette* (Tri-States Publishing Company, Inc.) in 1958, relying on the Fred D. Salmon family's representation that it was "doing $190,000 a year of business of which the Salmons were retaining in excess of $35,000."

Audited annual statements never had been prepared for the *U-G* prior to 1959.

Minutes of Tri-States's annual meeting June 4, 1958, show Fred Salmon Sr.'s salary as president-treasurer was $9,880; Mrs. Helen Salmon, vice president, $4,420 and Fred Salmon Jr., secretary-publisher, $8,840.

The $100,000 was advanced to Middletown Publishing Company by Stroudsburg ($25,000); Oneonta ($30,000) and Plattsburgh ($45,000).

The Middletown-Port Jervis acquisition left Ottaway with not a few long-term obligations.

Ingersoll, who also operated a newspaper management service company (General Publications, Inc.) was given a four-year consulting contract at $13,750 a year, 1959-63. Middletown Publishing also assumed the Marsh $220,000 debt to be repaid over 10 years and mortgage and chattel loans of $150,000.

Then there was the Salmon-DeWoody contract, also inherited from the R.J. Company. The Salmon family for decades had been proprietors of the Port Jervis property and at the time of purchase by Ingersoll, Fred D. and Helen Salmon entered into a 20-year consulting agreement worth $400,000, assuming the Salmons did not die first. The agreement was set up in four five-year increments, the payments to be halved when one beneficiary died and canceled on the death of the other. Fred Salmon did not live into the second tier of the contract.

The Ingersoll management corporation was to receive the Salmon payments on the same terms between 1963-1978 if one or both of the Salmons died.

Fred Salmon Jr. had been elected to the R.J. board in 1958 and had been given a 10-year contract at $13,000 to run the *Union-Gazette*. The junior Salmon eventually turned up as an "Ottaway consultant" from the family's new base in Florida.

Finally, the Salmons held $40,000 worth of notes due in 1978 in connection with the sale of the *U-G* to Ingersoll.

So, at the end of 1959, total Ottaway long-term debt stood at $1.38 million, up about $260,000 over 1958.

And he had signed a $45,000 contract with Manno for "financial and consulting services," payable over five years.

Bill Lundquest was brought down from Plattsburgh to run the *Times Herald* and Steve Ryder went north from his Danbury executive training slot to operate the *Press-Republican*.

Keeping the *TH* afloat in the face of the nagging competition from the *Record* was for Lundquest nothing short of a reenactment of the fight for survival in the old pre-war Endicott days. Plattsburgh had been profitable from the very start of Ottaway ownership. If Lundquest missed the halcyon days of solid gold P&Ls and an occasional sail on Lake Champlain, he didn't complain.

As the group expanded, Lyn Boyd found himself forced to draw up a transfer policy for general managers.

"If I had a choice, they had a choice," Boyd said. "If I didn't, they didn't."

Peg Lundquest said that her husband looked on the new assignent as a challenge he couldn't bear to duck.

Curiously, Gene Brown said he advised Lundquest not to move. "He was doing a great job in Plattsburgh. I thought he'd be crazy to take on the Middletown headache."

"Peg and I were told to come to Middletown," Lundquest

wrote years later. "We met Ottaway and Boyd for dinner and we thought this was going to be a trial run. But Jim asked if I had brought my picture. That was that."

Under Ingersoll ownership, both the *TH* and *Union-Gazette* were composed and printed in the Middletown plant. The press was a Scott 64-page octuple with twin folders, which were used simultaneously. By the time the pressmen got the ink set for the *Times Herald*'s 13,000 run, most of the *U-G*'s 4,000 copies had been printed — in the loosest sense of the word.

A mellowing Jack Kaplan must have watched the Ottaway takeover of the *Times Herald* with mixed emotions. A close Kaplan associate wrote early in 1960 that for the first time in three years the financier wasn't "visibly disturbed" when Middletown came up in conversation.

His choice was simple: Buy out Ottaway or sell Ottaway his *Daily Record.*

Kaplan began pursuing Jim Ottaway right after the *TH* purchase. With Lyn Boyd at his side, Ottaway met several times with Kaplan in New York.

"He was a brilliant man," Ottaway said. "A skilled negotiator. Very creative. Once he set a price, he never changed."

And Kaplan thought well of Ottaway. Asked by a confidant in mid-January 1960 about the possibility of an Ottaway takeover, Kaplan volunteered that Ottaway "is a first-class fellow and I like everything I've heard about him, and I understand now why Jim couldn't talk to me: he was negotiating for the afternoon property."

Kaplan's first effort involved getting Ottaway out of Middletown.

"Because of his connection with Endicott Johnson, he tried to get us to buy Billy Hill's *Binghamton Sun,*"Ottaway recalled. "We'd looked at the *Sun.* We knew all about it. We weren't interested."

Kaplan, of course, wanted the *Times Herald.*

ON-R board minutes dated April 7, 1960, quoted Ottaway as saying "that after some discussion, Kaplan had now decided he was willing to sell us the *Record* instead."

On a fateful spring day in New York City, Ottaway said, Kaplan announced jovially "I have great news for you, Jim. I will sell you the *Daily Record* for what I have in it — $1.5 million."

With Kaplan was David Bernstein, his editor and publisher. Bernstein, by all accounts, went into virtual shock. He had had no advance warning.

Ottaway and Kaplan agreed on a $300,000 down payment, with the balance to be paid over 20 years at an incredibly favorable interest rate of 2½ percent.

"While the price is high," board minutes quote Ottaway, "I do not feel it is an unreasonable price to pay in order to consolidate the newspaper field in the prosperous Middletown market."

Note the word "consolidate."

The sale was heralded in banner headlines by both Middletown papers on April 19. Ottaway was quoted in the fourth paragraph of the announcement as saying that all three papers — the *Record, Times Herald* and *Union Gazette* "would continue to publish separately."

Ottaway watchers must have been stunned by his proclamation, which contained no visible escape clause. As one former *Record* executive observed: "He did continue publishing two newspapers in Middletown — until he didn't."

There was no way the competitors could survive. The *Record* alone had been losing $30,000 a month, which Kaplan had underwritten since July 1956. And the *TH* was borderline — if that.

Orange County Publications, Inc., was formed to absorb Community Newspaper Publishers, Inc., owner of the *Record*. And Ottaway returned to his old friends at Endicott Trust Company for another loan, this time for $200,000.

In December 1959 capital stock of Ottaway Newspaper-Radio was increased by providing for an issue of 5,000 shares of second preferred at $100 par. The 1,500 shares of preferred were reclassified to first preferred at $100 par.

That fall came the first known mention in writing of Jim Ottaway "shifting control of ON-R to his sons, who will be active in the business." "Purely theoretical," he explained. Blocks of stock had been transferred piecemeal to the children's trust by Ruth and Jim since 1955.

Bernstein's journalistic credentials were not particularly imposing. Born in 1915, he worked as a reporter in Ithaca, New York, and New York City prior to World War II. Before entering service and afterward, he held public relations posts in and out of government and served as an advisor to two Philippine presidents.

Bernstein's partner and general manager, Harry Milligan, was born in 1929, reported for papers in Ohio and North Carolina and also worked in public relations.

Exactly how their paths crossed and how they were drawn to Jack Kaplan cannot be determined.

Lundquest was tapped to run the *Record*.

His memoirs suggest that in 1959 he expected the Kaplan sale to Ottaway.

"My pipeline to the *Record* told me that the attitude over there was 'What the hell do we do now?' after Ottaway acquired the *Times Herald*," he wrote.

Lundquest's No. 1 aide at the *Record* was Frederick Philip (Phil) Blake, a taciturn native of Maine, who joined the *Record* three months before it started publication. Blake's background was principally in advertising. His two previous posts were the *Lewiston* (Me.) *Sun and Journal* and *Keene* (N.H.) *Sentinel* as an ad representative.

Reports of the pending *Record* start-up had reached Keene. Blake called Harry Milligan. He was given the post of advertising director.

Was Blake fearful then that the Kaplan-Bernstein dream might explode?

"When you're making only $49 a week in New Hampshire, you don't think about things like that."

On May 1, 1958, Blake was promoted to business manager, with supervision over the advertising and circulation departments.

Phil Blake was destined to spend the rest of his long career with Ottaway, becoming publisher of first one, then another, Pennsylvania newspaper and achieving further recognition as a corporate senior vice president and board member.

Blake, who lived in a Middletown suburb, indulged in an improbable avocation — 10 Siberian huskies, some of which he

115

occasionally entered in weekend races far to the north. To gain access to the Blake dwelling, visitors first would have to mince their way through a sort of canine minefield. The Blakes were assiduous with their pooper-scoopers, but couldn't keep up with the dogs, each of which had a world-class appetite.

If Blake occasionally was missing from his post at the newspaper, the odds were favorable that he was back at the corral, chasing down huskies that had torn loose from their moorings.

The task of running the *Times Herald* was assigned to Howard Jordan Brown, hired by Ingersoll in April 1959 as his personal assistant "with the hope I could make a publisher of him."

Brown's one-year contract for $13,000, which was to expire June 1, 1960, contained an option to buy 20 percent of the common stock of R.J. Company. "Ralph," Brown told the author, "thought I was wealthy."

Brown, a Princeton graduate, had been associated the previous five years with Forest City Publishing Company, owner of the *Cleveland Plain Dealer,* as assistant promotion manager. Realizing that the future was bleak on the shore of Lake Erie, he started looking. Exactly how his path first crossed Ingersoll's, Brown did not remember, but eventually they talked at the exclusive Brook Club in New York City. Brown was dispatched to Middletown as the absentee owner's general manager. "I was not received warmly," he said.

Uppermost in Brown's mind during his hitch with Ingersoll and Ottaway was owning his own paper, or acquiring a significant equity position in one.

In December 1961 an opportunity to acquire the *Kenosha* (Wis.) *News* arose, and, with his lawyer father's help, Brown became a publisher.

"The first person I told was Jim Ottaway, " Brown said. He was delighted, assuring Brown that he remembered the thrill of acquiring his first property.

"Jim Ottaway always has been a sort of guiding spirit for me. I still feel as though I'm a member of the Ottaway family."

Merger of the two Middletown properties was high on Ottaway's priority list at least as early as July 1960, three

116

months after the *Record* purchase.

On the 27th he wrote to Boyd, "When the time comes that for (tax) carryback loss reasons we desire to merge Middletown Publishing and Orange County Publications, it seems to me that this should be done without any thought in regard to the Marsh agreement and any agreements we have with Ingersoll . . . It is my feeling that Brink and Ernst & Ernst should go ahead with their explorations of merger on the basis of what will be most advantageous to us tax-wise."

On September 26 a combined meeting of shareholders and directors of Orange County Publications and Middletown Publishing Company was held at group headquarters in Endicott. Listed as present besides the Ottaways were Francis Brinkley, representing Ottaway Newspapers-Radio, Inc., holder of all issued and outstanding shares of the two corporations, Bruce Becker, Lyn Boyd and Gene Brown. The session was called, according to the minutes, "to consider the consolidation of OCP and MPC."

A Becker statement, the minutes show, said "that surveys of the Orange County area. . .indicate that the area will not adequately support two local daily newspapers. A single strong newspaper would have a decided advantage in meeting the competition of other newspapers distributed in Orange County."

Now to the heart of the meeting:

"Past division of the market," the statement continued, "had resulted in drastic financial losses for both parties" and "the two corporations had competed needlessly for editorial, advertising and printing personnel."

The vote to consolidate was unanimous. But no merger date was set.

The summer of 1960, as related in Chapter 1, also saw the melancholy demise of Ottaway's pilot newspaper in Endicott — the *Daily Bulletin*. As the Triple Cities fused via a modern highway, the doormat-thick *Binghamton Press* came to dominate the *Bulletin*'s old market and at least half its subscribers had defected. Fowler's, the largest Binghamton department store, decided that the remaining *Bulletin* circulation wasn't worth the candle. The *Bulletin* toward the end had dropped its Saturday edition in a goal-line effort to cut costs, publishing a "Weekender" on Fridays. There was no money for raises. Union printers and pressmen backed off when they were shown the books.

"Gene Brown had been urging me to sell the *Bulletin* for some time," Ottaway recalled. "But sentiment was too strong."

Back to Jack Kaplan.

On July 1, 1960, he bought Hill's morning *Binghamton Sun* for Bernstein and Milligan. The *Sun* was the very property Kaplan tried to thrust on Ottaway early that year.

Obviously Jack Kaplan felt an obligation to his old Middletown associates after the abrupt sale of the *Record*. Shall we call it corporate salve? Price for the 34,000-circulation Morning Sun., Inc., has never been revealed. But Dun & Bradstreet records through 1960 offer two hints — an equipment chattel mortgage of $200,000 and a real estate mortgage, also for $200,000.

The Ottaway-Kaplan-Bernstein saga came full circle on August 31 when the *Sun* bought the ailing *Daily Bulletin's* name, subscription lists and good will for $75,000 without interest. Circulation had dropped to 6,500. Price per *Bulletin* subscriber was an unbelievable $11.54.

Next day the paper appeared as the *Sun-Bulletin*.

Terms called for five percent of ad billings for 1961 and 10 percent annually thereafter. Ottaway retained the plant, equipment and receivables.

Certainly one of the principal reasons Kaplan invested in the *Sun* was the $100,000-a-year advertising contract it held with Endicott Johnson. The linage was of the "in-house" variety, pertaining to the benevolent employee relations concept that was a hallmark of EJ. But shortly after Bernstein and Milligan took over, the EJ ad budget was cut in half.

By March 1965 the Bernstein-Milligan debt to Ottaway had been reduced to $42,000, but the partners again were mired in long- and short-term debt. In August Bernstein asked Ottaway to forgive $17,000 in return for "guaranteed" monthly installments of $1,000 until the remaining $25,000 was retired. Very reluctantly, Ottaway agreed. On September 15, 1967, the books were cleared. Gannett acquired the *Sun Bulletin* after

118

Bernstein's death at 59 in 1974.

The slow demise of the *Bulletin* fortunes began during the Roger Hildenbrand regime. Hildenbrand, a former executive with the New York State Publishers Association, had replaced Barney French as general manager. French, as could be expected, was slowing down.

Hildenbrand departed in April 1958. Donald W. Diehl replaced him the following August. Diehl was a business administrator with little newspaper background.

In March 1959 the author of this book came to Endicott from St. Louis as editor of the *Bulletin*. King had worked 16 years on Gannett's morning *Utica Daily Press* and evening and Sunday *Observer-Dispatch*. Late in 1958 he joined an old friend from Syracuse, now publisher of S.I. Newhouse's recently-acquired St. Louis *Globe-Democrat*. Newhouse had sent Richard H. (Dick) Amberg west from the Syracuse *Post-Standard*.

King's stay in St. Louis was brief. The *Globe-Democrat* was struck by the American Newspaper Guild in a long, bitter struggle over a pension plan.

Mutual friends in the industry knew Ottaway needed an editor. They knew also that Lois King was homesick and that money would be running out.

After an interview in Endicott with Ottaway and Diehl, King was hired. But not before Ottaway checked with an old friend, Fritz Updike, editor of the *Daily Sentinel* in Rome, New York, just west of Utica.

In retrospect King felt he knew that all wasn't well economically with the *Bulletin*. But he didn't know how near the brink it was until Diehl was transferred to Danbury for advanced training under Gene Brown.

On Diehl's departure King was named general manager. One look at the P&L indicated the situation was terminal. The rear-guard action to hold retail display linage and circulation was heroic but futile. Only classified held its own. National linage was virtually non-existent.

When the *Daily Bulletin* succumbed, much of the staff was retained by Bernstein for his Binghamton *Sun-Bulletin*. Some printers and pressmen found work in job shops. Others simply retired.

119

Characteristically, Ottaway broke the sad news to his employees in person, implying that it was as much his fault as anyone's. And after the goodbyes he stood at the doorway of King's office and quietly offered the GM an as yet undefined post with the headquarters group "if you choose to remain with us." One other staffer was retained, Arthur Beiniks, whom we met earlier in this history.

King, like Howard Brown, was named assistant to Lyn Boyd, and was assigned to help improve news-gathering techniques of the Stroudsburg, Oneonta, Plattsburgh and Danbury operations, and, if there was time left, to help sell off the Endicott typesetting and pressroom machinery.

A 1960 file has yielded a November 25 memo from Lyn Boyd to the then six Ottaway general managers, explaining in detail King's first intra-group assignment. Part of it is reproduced here to underscore the first-of-its- kind Ottaway commitment to improving newsroom techniques:

> "First of several special project assignments for Charles King in his new job is to satisfy what has been a long-standing desire on the part of general managers and editors.
>
> "That is, a detailed analysis of each of our newspapers' editorial departments and the several details listed below and many others not on the list.
>
> "Following his individual analysis of the departments and the end products themselves, the whole project will be culminated in an editorial session wherein all the many facts can be summarized and discussed at length in assisting managers and editors in formulating future plans, etc.
>
> "Some, but not by any means all of the factors on which Charles will touch in his visits to the newspapers will be:
>
> "A. Personnel — to include number, deployment, wage scales, etc.
>
> "B. Organizaton — desks, wire editing, departments, correspondents, coordination.
>
> "C. Procedures and techniques — coordination with other departments, control of news flow, setting editorial policy, training methods, hiring procedures, physical lay-out department, phone hook-ups, public relations, promotion and many other items much too numerous to mention.
>
> "D. As a matter of fact, it's a little difficult at this time to know precisely the path that will be followed, and it will probably be determined largely in conference with general managers and editors as we go along."

11 Laying the keel of the flagship

It was a foregone conclusion that the *Daily Record* would be the surviving Middletown paper. In just four years it had attracted 20,000 subscribers in Orange and Sullivan counties. It was printed by the then-new offset process in a handy tabloid configuration. And, apart from its acceptance by an ever-increasing number of readers, it literally was receiving worldwide attention as an upstart pioneer in a more sophisticated type of community journalism.

Circulation of the *Times Herald,* born of a merger in 1927, was static at 13,000.

The *TH* practiced its own brand of community journalism, as did Ottaway's five other dailies. But unlike the *Record,* they were to varying degrees victims of outmoded traditions and questionable habits acquired over generations. The *Record* set its own state-of-the-art policies at the very start, policies that would occasionally aggrieve both reader and advertiser, but would eventually set loftier editorial standards for the other papers in the group.

What was the *Record*'s idea of community journalism?

One of its early editors put it this way:

"Coverage of mainstream issues at the hometown level. It is semi-metropolitan journalism, which is to say metro standards with a smalltown sense of proportion. It is depth reporting, which is to say rocking the boat, breaking through the establishment web. It means not aspiring to becoming or being a mirror image of the community. It means a courageous publisher telling special interests to go to hell and telling advertisers (if necessary) that the advertising dollar buys only

121

advertising space."

The *Record* also unlimbered another big gun when it felt the need: a strident editorial voice, often of liberal persuasion.

Long used to the conservative *Times Herald* and quite comfortable with its complement of home-grown editors and reporters, not a few old-line Middletowners snubbed the *Record* prior to merger. They asked each other in the Middletown Club (no Jews admitted) about Kaplan and Bernstein and conjectured on why the carpetbaggers had come to Orange County and what they intended to do to it.

The *Times Herald* was a good newspaper by most standards of journalism. Editor was Edward P. (Eddie) Dougherty. E. Bradley (Brad) Boyle was his ME. Both were taskmasters: Dougherty by gentle persuasion, Boyle by gruff approach. They had assembled a competent staff, whose intimate knowledge of the county easily gave it a leg up on news background. In retrospect, it seems clear that, because so many *TH* staffers had worked the area vineyards for so long, some had become too close to friends in news-sensitive areas. At any rate, the *TH* seldom rocked the boat. And it must be remembered that its publisher was largely absent.

Observers of the 1956-60 Middletown newspaper war — even those on the *Record* — agreed that the *TH* rose to the challenge in its final years but could never have repulsed the invader, assuming continued financial support for both properties.

"The *Times Herald* is a better paper than when we started," *Editor & Publisher* quoted Kaplan on December 19, 1959. "Shortly after we started the *Record* Mr. Ingersoll called us up to say: 'It will either be you or me who will go out of business within five years'."

At the time of merger, editor of the *Record* was Avrom N. (Al) Romm, from 1949 to 1957 city hall reporter for the *Springfield* (Mass.) *Union*. Romm had been reading in trade journals about the *Record*'s auspicious start and because a glut of newsroom talent appeared to have blocked his chances for advancement in Springfield, he applied for a post in Middletown. He joined the Bernstein-Milligan team in June 1957 as city editor. He soom became managing editor. Ottaway named him editor in the spring of 1960.

Romm later became an Ottaway corporate officer, serving as director of news quality and training for the entire group.

Romm's managing editor was Robert S. (Bob) Van Fleet, who started his career as a reporter for the *Times Herald* in 1946. After a five-year hitch he turned temporarily to Middletown politics. His next newspaper stop was Newburgh, New York, at Gannett's *Evening News*, the *TH*'s arch-rival in Orange County. Van Fleet returned to Middletown in the fall of 1957 as county editor of the *Daily Record,* rising to city editor and then to ME.

As No. 2 on the *Record's* editorial team, Van Fleet brought to the challenger something it needed badly — a bedrock knowledge of the area's mores, traditions and who was who. Van Fleet also gave the *Record* its first home-grown editorial executive.

Besides being a top-flight reporter-turned-editor, Van Fleet offered newsroom administrative expertise, desperately needed during the *Record*'s period of rapid growth.

The reporter in Van Fleet prevailed in the end. In 1963 he approached Jim Ottaway and proposed that the group set up its own news service. The answer was an enthusiastic "Yes!" The story of Ottaway News Service, today a four-bureau network with headquarters in Washington, will be told in later chapters.

Romm said his memories of the immediate pre-merger period are "mercifully blurred. It was not a pleasant chapter (in my career)."

"When Jim Ottaway acquired the *Record* in April 1960, I assumed but wasn't told that merger with the *TH* would certainly come to pass. I assumed also that the *Record* would be the survivor, representing the wave of the future.

"It was to be the *Record,* but Bill Lundquest confided that that decision was a lot closer than I would have suspected. Only a handful of newspapers had joined the cold-type, offset ranks since the *Record* started. The *Times Herald* had just invested in a new building and a better press. Offset was a completely new ballgame.

"In either late August or early September Bill Lundquest asked me and Bob Van Fleet to draw up a newsroom plan for a merged operation. There were two ground rules: We could hire no more than five *TH* staffers and we were forbidden to discuss it with them or anyone else until the *TH* closed shop. The rule made matters ticklish. If any of our selections were to say no, for instance, the replacement would almost certainly know he or she was a second choice.

"Bob and I argued unsuccessfully for a larger complement from the *TH* newsroom on the theory that rapid turnover would solve over-staff problems within a short time.

"Further, we were told that Dick Milburn, who wrote the popular *TH* column Bittersweet, had to be on the list and that we could invite Eddie Dougherty or Brad Boyle, but not both. It was like a wartime triage or, using contemporary imagery, a Sophie's choice.

"We had settled on Dougherty after much soul-searching when we were called to a top-secret meeting in Lundquest's home. Howard Brown, general manager of the *TH*, was present to mount a spirited campaign in Boyle's behalf. But we stuck to our guns.

"The anguish, in retrospect, could have been prevented by a more lenient merger policy. Events rather quickly conspired to create vacancies at the merged paper. Boyle was called back within a year. So were many of the other editors and reporters. Thank God they still were available. All of them speedily and nobly subdued any residual ill feelings."

(Immediately after the *Record* purchase Ottaway, Boyd and Lundquest had terminated several of its employees, including a personnel director, with severance negotiated as part of the purchase contract with Kaplan.)

That Ottaway had agreed to add even five editorial staffers to the merged paper was in itself remarkable, considering the financial pressures. It more than underscored his philosophy of enhancing staff, rather than diluting it in order to achieve a faster return on investment.

TH staffers from other departments were also brought over, including hot-type linecasting operators, production and advertising personnel.

The *Record* and *Times Herald* combined October 3, 1960. First issue of the merged properties that Monday morning bore a new flag: The *Times Herald-Record*. It was priced at seven cents and announced that Middletowners would henceforth have a Saturday morning paper. (The *Record* did not publish Saturdays.)

After the first week of merged operation, circulation shook out at 23,000. It is significant that the *TH*'s circulation was 10,000 in pre-*Record* days. In less than four years, because of spirited competition and despite negligible population growth, more than three times as many newspapers were being sold in roughly the same circulation area.

Merging the two properties, Gene Brown said, "was a horrible experience for Bill Lundquest." Operating the *Times Herald-Record* after the consolidation was equally painful.

Basically the strategy involved selling at least the same number of lines of advertising that both papers had run before merger, and slashing expenses. The latter meant that holdover *Record* department heads had to be reminded even more strongly of Ottaway's operational philosophy: The paper must pay its own way. It may be assumed that some of Bernstein's executives had to be taught the difference between Jack Kaplan's "bottomless" money well and Ottaway's relative frugality.

For one thing, few at the *Record* had ever heard of a budget, which shortly would become a way of life.

As he did at the times of the Oneonta, Stroudsburg and Plattsburgh acquisitions, Ottaway found himself situated in a dilapidated rabbit warren. The North Street, Middletown, building was next door to the about-to-be completed and truly magnificent County National Bank building. Even so, the run-down pile was in some ways superior to the vacated *Times Herald* building on West Main Street. Ralph Ingersoll had contrived to erect that structure abutting a siding along the eastbound right-of-way of the Erie Railroad's main line between Chicago and Jersey City. Ingersoll's plan called for rail delivery of newsprint right to the front door, so to speak. But no one ever figured out how to get the rolls to the loading dock, 25 feet below the siding. Ingersoll also apparently had ignored parking requirements. Six spaces lined the east side of the building, all metered. When the time came to sell the *TH* building, lawyers discovered a minute encroachment on railroad (now Erie-Lackawanna) property, which became a serio-comic chapter in Ottaway's corporate history. It will be recounted later, along with the story of the Charles Botti circulation contract, which had not appeared on Ingersoll's disclosure schedule and which made a temporary process server of Lyn Boyd.

Newsprint delivery was also difficult at North Street. Trucks could back into the *TH-R* loading dock, but only if a detachment of pressman raced out to halt traffic on North Street. And there was parking in the loading dock area — if newsprint wasn't being delivered.

Directly across the street was one of Middletown's sleaziest deadfalls — Jules' bar. Its late night patrons provided another lingering headache, using the *TH-R*'s parking lot, and often blocking circulation trucks. Getting half-gassed revelers to move their cars required the diplomacy of a Metternich, but on one melancholy occasion an affronted guest of Jules loosened several of Phil Blake's teeth.

Prior to merger, type for the *Record*'s classified advertising was set off premises in a job shop. Three of the former *TH* hot metal linecasting machines and related equipment were brought up to North Street and reactivated in a rented building next door to the paper, to compose classified and legals. The "hot shop," as it became known, stayed with the *TH-R* until the computer age.

The plant of the *Union-Gazette* in Port Jervis occupied the basement and first floor of 112-114 Pike Street, a 19th Century edifice with creaking floors and mismatched paneling covering the most unsightly of the walls. Pressed tin adorned the high ceilings. "It was the only building where you wiped your feet when you came out," one Ottaway home office executive remarked.

When Ottaway took over the Ingersoll properties Ralph Frederick became general manager of the *U-G*. Frederick in every sense was "Mr. Port Jervis." During the last years of the Salmon proprietorship, he had been editor. Now he found himself in a strange world of Ottaway budgets, weekly reports and strict cost controls. The new stringencies never daunted Frederick, who wore a perpetual smile and who was worshipped by the small staff.

The author helped Frederick prepare his first budget at the GM's hideaway camp in an improbably-named backwoods clearing called Cahoonzie, west of Port Jervis. The first trial balance came up red. "You can't budget a loss, can you?" he remarked, still smiling.

Frederick got the hang of things in short order.

During his brief remaining life he operated the *U-G* at a profit, albeit a narrow one. He died in August 1964. Most of Port Jervis attended the funeral.

Three days later Daniel Dwyer was named editor and general manager.

Curiously, the tabloid *Record* that Ottaway acquired in April 1960 wasn't a tabloid at all.

On April 6 it had adopted the broadsheet format. In a lengthy Page 1 editorial that day, Bernstein proclaimed the reason to be that the growing paper had to be printed in two to four tabloid sections and then collated for distribution.

Inserting, his announcement said, had become a bottleneck. Bernstein blamed the manufacturer of the *Record*'s $45,000 stuffing machine, who was quoted as saying his equipment could not collate tab-size signatures.

But competent observers branded the Bernstein apologia as only part truth.

"The Sheridan stuffer actually was working, but admittedly with lots of grief," one said.

"There was another reason Bernstein went broadsheet. It was to get the 'A' food chain advertising schedules."

It was clear to Ottaway, Lundquest and Blake that the tabloid format had been a prime reason for the paper's public acceptance. If any proof was needed it came in the form of an opinion survey by Ruth Ottaway and Peg Lundquest: "Give us back the book!" respondents chorused. The *Record* returned to tabloid size June 27.

The *Record*'s first press was a Waldron Trail Blazer, capable of printing four tab pages at a time. Thus a 24-page issue would require six press runs and some frantic stuffing. Bernstein and Milligan put up with the Waldron for only six months.

The beleaguered *Record* brass then turned to the George M.

Hantscho Company of Mount Vernon, New York, manufacturer of highly-regarded offset presses for the commercial printing industry. Bernstein bought three two-plate-wide units, capable of turning out 24 tab pages.

If quality printing was all the *Record* sought, the Hantscho equipment turned out a product of unsurpassed excellence. Not long after merger, Ottaway bought two additional units, increasing capacity to 40 pages. But the *TH-R* was averaging more than 50 pages per day, so the stuffing headaches continued.

Another segment of the Hantscho story would begin in 1963, when Ottaway placed an order for a four-plate-wide press, which would be mated with a Wood-Scott folder. Almost a decade of problems ensued, problems that would dwarf even those encountered by pressmen and stuffers on the infant *Record*. Call it a chapter of demonology in the folklore of the industry or call it the price of pioneering in cold-type composition and offset printing.

The *Times Herald-Record* continued the task of composing and printing the *Union-Gazette*. Syndicated material, such as columns, comic strips and features with little or no time element reached Middletown well in advance of publication. Current news and pictures were delivered by a *Gazette* staffer early in the morning and deadline news, if any, was phoned in.

A constant concern was misplaced *U-G* copy. On one occasion an entire envelope of news and features inexplicably found its way to apparent oblivion. Two eagle-eye, never-say-die composing room staffers found the packet in the Middletown dump. But that's the way operational spirit went at the *TH-R*. On a wall in the display advertising department was the legend "Today the Goldenarea, Tomorrow the World!" (The phrase "Goldenarea," meaning Middletown and suburbs, was then a fashionable sobriquet, perhaps more visionary than descriptive.)

Like others before him, including the author, Romm had difficulty in reading Ottaway. When was a suggestion a suggestion? When was it an order?

"Jim liked his associates to agree of their own free will," Boyd said, "But it didn't always work out that way."

The author remembers a typical case:

"When are you going to buy 'Tiger'?" Ottaway asked one day. ("Tiger" was a comic strip of no great pedigree.) King had no intention of adding "Tiger" to the stable of strips and dismissed the query as so much banter.

A week or so later the same question. And no action.

There followed periodic allusions to "Tiger" until The Message came through. The *TH-R* has carried the strip ever since.

During the dark red ink days, there were murmurings by a few of Ottaway's top aides that the entire Middletown venture might have been a mistake.

Stockholders had been divided on the *Times Herald* acquisition. When it came to the *Daily Record* purchase, only Ottaway voted in favor of the move. But he held the controls.

It was at this fateful meeting that David Ottaway voiced his now-famous one-liner: "Okay. But just keep those dividend checks coming!"

At one executive session, which can be described only as melancholy, Ottaway listened patiently as a few of his top lieutenants unburdened themselves of anxiety that the venture might be too perilous to continue.

The publisher had no thoughts of surrender. He said he was going to see it through by actually increasing investment, such as a bureau in Goshen (the county seat) and other betterments as soon as prudence permitted.

If the meeting accomplished nothing else immediately, the message was clear: There would be no turning back.

Interviews with all principals make it clear that few other than Jim Ottaway had the 20-20 vision of what lay in store for the *TH-R*. But even he probably never dreamed it would emerge as his flagship, both in editorial quality and substantial profitability.

The fallen flag in Endicott meant that corporate headquarters would be moved. Station WENE was still a part of the organization, but it, too, would be sold just two years after the *Daily Bulletin*'s demise.

With the departure from Endicott, title to the Ottaway Williamsburgh-style dwelling on Pheasant Lane generously passed to the Endwell Methodist Church, where the family worshipped. The Reverend Samuel Little, long-time family friend, was pastor.

Mr. Little's church lacked a steeple for years. Construction funds had run out. The spire finally went up in 1983. The Ottaways went back for the dedication ceremony. The steeple fund included gifts from the Ottaways, Gene Brown and Lyn Boyd.

Selecting a new location for HQ was simple: Put it in the center of Orange County, less than a day's drive to any of the newspaper or radio properties, much on newly-constructed superhighways. The comparatively narrow world of Ottaway moved a lot slower in the early 1960s. The first corporate aircraft was years in the future.

The choice of Orange County also underscored Ottaway's faith in the *TH-R*.

Early in 1961 Ottaway Newspapers-Radio, Inc., the parent company, began its move to Middletown-Goshen. Jim and Ruth Ottaway leased an apartment on Main Street in Goshen, the county seat. (It was the same apartment Ralph Ingersoll had used during his visits to the *Times Herald*, much more frequently during the competitive period). Jim also established an office at the vacant *TH* building in Middletown. For a while Ottaway, King and Carmen Kaczmar, a secretary, were the only ON-R presences there.

The chief wasn't happy in the *TH* building. For one thing, the Scott press had been sold to a publisher in South America and the Spanish-speaking mechanics who were dismantling it had literally contrived to choke Mills Street with Grace Line sea-going freight containers and were monopolizing Ottaway's telephone link to the world.

If Ottaway couldn't be found at West Main Street, he might be found back in Endicott or at his other command post in Buck Hill Falls. If he wasn't at any of those locations, odds are he was scouting the countryside for a home and acreage adaptable to eventual use as the new operational hub.

For two months the Kings lived in Middletown's famous Mitchell Inn while seeking a permanent Middletown residence. The author remembers the hotel room, located on the second

130

floor front. The hotel flag pole jutted over James Street from a window sill outside his quarters. Precisely at eight each morning an old retainer would let himself into the room with a pass key to set out the flag — regardless of what its occupants might be doing at the time. Appeals to management failed. Who was King to interrupt Old Glory's unfurling?

Lyn Boyd found property in Goshen in March of 1961 and built atop a mini-mountain. Francis Brinkley also joined his colleagues in Goshen. Brinkley, his closest associates recall, was not a bit enthusiastic about leaving Endicott and actually considered resigning.

In early June 1961, the Ottaways found just the property they had been looking for. For $50,000 they acquired the Strasser estate in Campbell Hall, five miles east of Goshen. The original dwelling, on five and one-half acres, was constructed in 1916 of native stone and shingles. An addition, which eventually became Ottaway's spacious office, was built in the 1920s. No one remembers exactly when. The villa fronted on Route 416 behind a stand of magnificent ancient maples. It was built by William K. (Billy) Dickerson, who came to Goshen in 1903 to work as horse trainer for the Harriman family. Dickerson became general manager of Historic Track in Goshen, retiring in 1947. Embedded in a hearth off the entrance is a horseshoe that legend says was worn by Dan Patch, a trotter of redolent memory.

Jim and Ruth Ottaway had title to the property where they would live until they built a new home just west of the former Strasser dwelling.

Back in March Ottaway Newspapers-Radio had bought the former *TH* building from its subsidiary, Orange County Publications (owner of the *TH*) for $223,043. Of that sum, $74,435 was used to retire the mortgage held by County National Bank. The balance was applied to OCP's debt to its parent.

ON-R of course, promptly put the 80 West Main Street property on the market. It soon had a tenant — the Salvation Army — which leased the building in December 1961 for $500 per month, with an option to buy. Asking price was $97,000. The Army exercised the option in May 1962 only to discover that a tiny portion of the building (630 square feet out of 12,000) encroached on Erie-Lackawanna property. It took Jake Becker and lawyers for the Salvation Army and railroad more than nine years to settle the matter. The affair caused much grief to Brinkley and Jake and Bruce Becker, charged with disposing of the case. Ottaway didn't like corporate loose ends.

Ottaway formally notified the ON-R board that because of the scheduled sale of the *TH* building, office space would be needed at Campbell Hall for the management division of the company.

The strategy was simple: Ottaway would sell the (Strasser) home to ON-R which in turn would build an addition (it did so in 1962, the first of several) and the Ottaways would, meantime, make available sufficient room for the then small HQ staff when the *TH* building was sold.

Despite the conflicts inherent in combining work and play under the same roof, the resettling continued unabated. Jim and Ruth Ottaway had begun a getting-to-know-you campaign in Goshen and Middletown, and cocktail parties became frequent as community leaders at all levels came to meet the publisher, his wife and corporate associates.

The Ottaways commissioned a Middletown architect, Gunther Heinzel, to design their new home. Construction started late in 1961. The Ottaway-Heinzel relationship was established via the Middletown Rotary Club, whose meetings the publisher attended every week he was in the city. And if he was in Goshen on the appropriate day, he attended Goshen Rotary. The familiar "Hi! I'm Jim Ottaway!" began to be heard at almost every conceivable social and business function.

The Heinzel-designed frame-and-brick-veneer dwelling, which the architect described as "contemporary," contained an enclosed swimming pool, haven of relaxation for the harried publisher of the still profitless *Times Herald-Record.*

The former Strasser home and the easterly portion of the land were conveyed to ON-R on November 26, 1962. In 1964 Ottaway added 95 acres of farmland to his holdings, part of which abutted Orange County parkland, and in 1980, when the Ottaway conference center was built, ON-R acquired 27.8 acres of the farmland for sewage disposal.

With Ottaway in residence, so to speak, Lundquest's heroic struggle to turn the profit corner acquired a new dimension:

constant input from the top, vigilant follow-up from the top and often irritable complaints from the top that things weren't being done quickly enough. Lundquest's phone or the author's well might ring as late as 10 p.m. It would be Ottaway, checking whether action had been taken on some agreed strategy or offering a new idea. The workdays in 1961 (and for some time to come) ended only when Ottaway said goodnight.

And there were the hundreds of old *Times Herald* circulation tubes. The *Newburgh Evening News,* Lundquest discovered, was using *TH* tubes to sample its afternoon product. The general manager dispatched three trucks and crews to uproot every tube they could find. The result was a pile of tubes and stakes 50 feet in diameter and 30 feet high.

Proving again that nothing is impossible if you're working for Ottaway, Lundquest sold "the entire mess, *TH* logos and all," to an upstate publisher. Even at a fire sale price, it was a coup.

Jim and Ruth Ottway at the time were driving his (black)-and-hers (white) Thunderbirds, underscoring his continued preference for Stuart Newing's Ford products. The chief traveled several different routes between Campbell Hall and Middletown and kept a running log of the number of Newburgh tubes on each. He also tallied the hostile tubes on Route 6 out of Middletown, enroute to Buck Hill Falls. The count was inscribed on a series of Kleenex boxes which lay athwart the car's console, and relayed via King to the circulation department for action. Ottaway wanted only *Times Herald-Record* tubes in his territory. It wasn't long before they were.

There also were extra-curricular duties, such as the shoe detail.

During the publisher's temporary stay in Goshen and before his new Campbell Hall home was built, he would appear at the interim West Main Street HQ with grocery bags or small cartons filled with footwear to be shined. Both Lundquest and King shared the task of delivering the Ottaway wingtips to the Erie-Lackawanna station a block away. A venerable master of the bootblack's calling presided over an ornate two-seat walnut stand with solid brass foot rests. At day's end, one of the couriers would retrieve the shoes and enter the fee plus tip on his expense account. Even if Ottaway carried the cash, he didn't proffer any. And in those days you always had to have enough in your wallet for a few packages of Robert Burns panatelas, which the chief savored at the time.

The dogged pursuit of profitability and the search for a new HQ site didn't stop Ottaway from accepting an honorary degree from Hartwick College in June of 1961. And September 6 saw the first van load of office furniture and fixtures arrive in Middletown from Endicott.

On September 9 the indefatigable publisher established a $300,000 line of credit at the County National Bank in Middletown.

King's diary fixes the date as Sunday, September 17, 1961. He and Lundquest were summoned to Campbell Hall, where they found a not-so-cheerful Ottaway sitting on the front steps of the combination home and office.

The publisher wanted to hash things over — again.

"How can we make a go of it?" he asked rhetorically.

There was little new to offer. Advertising still was far short of the total run by both papers before merger. Even circulation appeared to be in the doldrums. The trio on the steps apparently had done everything it could to cut expense.

The rump session produced no fresh strategy.

Ten days later, September 27, Ottaway called another strategy review meeting, this time with Boyd and King. Another frustrating, inconclusive session. The next day Boyd met with Lundquest. On September 29 he called King to his office in the former *TH* building to announce that Lundquest had been promoted to a corporate vice presidency and that on October 1 King would become general manager of the *TH-R*.

Lundquest's basic assignment was in the realm of group-wide plant and production technology, which he proceeded to handle with inordinate skill.

Lundquest was bone-tired. For almost two years he had borne the crushing pressures endured by no GM other than a younger Jim Ottaway himself in the pre-war Endicott days. Now others had a chance to build atop the still shaky base he had helped fashion.

When the 1961 books were closed, the *TH-R* showed a

12-month operational loss of $10,155. Compared with the financial cataclysms of 1959 and 1960, one might even say things were looking up.

Total Middletown operational losses under Ottaway ownership from November 1959 to December 31, 1961, have been estimated at more than $200,000.

For several years the *TH-R* would remain the offset showcase of the industry. As a direct result Lundquest and Blake, then King and Blake, periodically found themselves without key mechanical employees who had been lured to distant climes by almost obscene wage offers from visiting publishers panting to go cold type.

Staff defections usually followed visits to Middletown by participants in the American Press Institute's New Processes seminars. They came by the busload in the evening, the better to watch paste-up and camera work for the early morning press run.

One by one, most of the best were picked off, starting with Ben Wiggins, a foreman, who resettled on the West Coast.

The personnel raids stopped only after API was urged strongly to take its field trips elsewhere.

If Jim Ottaway ever had an inseparable companion besides Ruth, it was a worn cowhide briefcase, basically an office within an office. Principal contents were profit-and-loss folders for his now six newspaper and three radio properties. The P&Ls were updated monthly, and showed not only current earnings, but income and expense compared to budgeted figures and the previous year's performance.

His associates marveled at the chief's penchant for mental retention of figures, no matter how insignificant some might seem in the light of overall performance.

Ottaway's managers knew they were expected to have the answers when he asked by phone or memo why the classified average rate was down (or up) or why the mechanical cost per page was fluttering. And why is your circulation cost 18 cents per dollar of income when last year it was 16½?

Strictly realistic budgets, prepared and painstakingly reviewed between September and December, gave managers the information they needed if all went according to plan, but that rarely happened. Ottaway wanted to know why matters weren't taking the charted path.

In 1957 Francis Brinkley came up with the idea of six-month budget reviews for the purpose of adjusting in mid-stream for unexpected major developments.

As further check and balance there were weekly reports, which pinpointed activity of key business elements, intended, as Lyn Boyd put it, "to put out brush fires before they became four-alarm blazes."

The system was no more than an extension of Ottaway self-discipline. His and Boyd's persistent attention to detail irritated a few of their field generals, who complained that the "nit-picking" was driving them crazy.

During the money-losing Middletown acquisition period and subsequent merger, the publisher's briefcase bulged with cheerful financial tidings from Oneonta, Stroudsburg, Plattsburgh and Danbury.

Broadcasting also was doing well.

The *Star* paid dividends of $12 per share in 1959 and 1960. In 1961 the payout was $18. Under Elton Hall's leadership the debt to Oneonta Building & Loan Association had been more than halved, so Ottaway instructed the GM to renew it to $100,000 at 4½ percent. Was this an example of Ottaway's maxim, borrow when you don't need the money? Board minutes are silent on the subject.

The *Daily Record* in its sparkling new building in Stroudsburg was thriving under Horace Heller, but it must be assumed that debt reduction had first call on profits. Not until the end of 1962 would the directors declare a dividend, $3 a share. But despite the enormous investment Ottaway knew he soon would have to make in Middletown, directors were even discussing a switch to cold type and offset printing in Stroudsburg. Bill Lundquest was assigned to investigate.

Up in the North Country the *Press-Republican* , with Steve

Ryder in command, had switched to a Bodoni head dress and was making ready for its first teletypesetter unit.

Reflecting bullish performance on the shore of Lake Champlain was a $30-per-share divided declared in 1958, but only after Ottaway had gotten a waiver of restriction from Mrs. Dunphy, to whom he still owed money. He was voted a $12,000 salary at the start of 1959. Another $30 dividend came in 1960, the year Plattsburgh Publishing Company merged with Ottaway Newspapers-Radio.

On January 1, 1962, Barney French retired after a 26-year association with the Ottaways. He was named honorary chairman of the board. Three years before he had sold back his stock to the company, leaving Gene Brown as the only shareholder outside the Ottaway family. Merle Ostrom's tiny holding had been bought back (at Ostrom's request) a year earlier.

☆ ☆ ☆ ☆ ☆ ☆

When the then *Daily Record* invaded Middletown in 1956, Ingersoll's *Times Herald* had no carrier organization (or even a circulation manager). Those copies that were home delivered were sold to Charles W. Botti, a newspaper and magazine distributor, who had developed an informal carrier system. Botti, in turn, sold the papers to the boys.

It didn't take the *Times Herald* brass long to conclude that competitively the system was impractical. It was decided to incorporate Botti's carriers into its own "little merchant" organization to enable the *TH* to vie more effectively for circulation. As compensation to Botti for his equity in his carrier group, Ingersoll set a rate of 90 cents per 100 on approximately 1,600 sales per day. Actually all Botti did was to deliver 45 bundles to carrier drop points in Middletown and suburbs.

Botti's 15-year contract with the *TH* took effect September 18, 1958. It also affirmed his control over delivery of the paper to newsstands in and adjacent to the city.

137

On October 3, two days after the Middletown merger, Botti came to pick up his papers at the North Street plant but was turned down on the grounds that the *Times Herald* "no longer existed" and that there was "nothing (for him) to perform" under the 1958 contract. Botti turned to his attorney for "rights and remedies."

Thus ensued a three-year skirmish — with some overtones of bitterness — between Ingersoll and Ottaway, over what Jake Becker called a valid contract that was not included in Ingersoll's disclosure schedule at the time of the sale.

Ingersoll insisted he went over the Botti-*TH* relationship with Lyn Boyd. Boyd said he did not remember the discussion.

At one point, after what he called a "bewildering visit from Becker," who evidently threatened legal action, Ingersoll formally offered to buy out all Ottaway's Middletown holdings "and with a reasonable profit to you (Ottaway) to boot."

"I do not know the details of your deal with Kaplan," Ingersoll wrote, "but I have confidence enough in you to be willing to buy it sight unseen."

In mid-1960 Ottaway and Ingersoll met over lunch in Mahwah, New Jersey. Ingersoll promised to try to convince Botti to cancel the contract and replace it with a more favorable one-year agreement subject to renewals. Ingersoll did talk with Botti, but without results. Another year passed. Botti sued the *TH-R*.

The struggle was exacerbated in July 1962. Boyd met with Ingersoll at the select Brook Club in New York City in another effort to advance Ottaway's case. The luncheon discussion led nowhere.

"It was clear Ralph wasn't going to do anything," Boyd said. "So after we finished, I served him with papers seeking $160,000 in damages."

A petulant Ingersoll immediately wrote Ottaway, saying he "could only conclude that this business of involving me is the brain child of an over-ambitious lawyer," a direct slap at Becker.

"You are not the kind of a man whose reputation is based on that way of doing business," the lettter continued. "You'd be a son of a bitch, businesswise, and you are not. Your very fine reputation testifies to that fact!"

Ottaway was not impressed. He had been miffed ever since Ingersoll first referred to the undisclosed contract as "breakage."

The matter was not resolved until November 1963 when Ingersoll agreed to concessions on his consulting contract. At that point Ottaway and Botti signed a new 10-year contract, which included a $9,000 payment that canceled the Ingersoll-Botti agreement.

Ingersoll had been told by counsel that his position was indefensible.

☆ ☆ ☆ ☆ ☆ ☆

Profitwise, the *Times Herald-Record* turned the corner in 1962, returning an operational net of $87,670 and setting the stage for a dramatic series of capital commitments that dwarfed any single betterment program Ottaway ever had undertaken.

In January 1963 King was dispatched to Cicero, Illinois, just south of Chicago, headquarters of the Goss Company, press manufacturers. A foresighted Ottaway wanted a four-plate-wide offset press to replace the two-plate-wide Hantscho units, and eliminate the costly and time-consuming stuffing nightmares.

Goss executives turned out not to be as prescient as Ottaway. They told King there was no market for a wider offset press and tactfully suggested that a Goss letterpress would fill the bill nicely. Less than a decade later, Ottaway's vision would become the norm as more and more newspapers, large and small, took the offset route.

Goss's position forced the publisher to turn once again to George Hantscho. It seemed logical that if Hantscho could manufacture a successful two-plate-wide press, he could design and build a four. The matter, board minutes say, "was at a point of urgency."

Circulation of the *TH-R* had passed 28,000. Each issue of more than 40 tab pages required multiple press runs and concurrent increased costs. But Ottaway was most distressed by his perceived quality of the paper, which he and others felt was being compromised by too-early deadlines forced by limited production capacity.

On April 9, 1963, the directors took the plunge. They voted unanimously to buy a three-unit Hantscho press, with provisions for a fourth. The price tag was $335,810.

Arrangements were completed at Hantscho's Mount Vernon plant. The chief was assured that he had contracted for the best money could buy. But as the Ottaway delegation was leaving, a churl in the accounting department not so subtly asked about Ottaway's credit.

Once in his car Ottaway could be heard mumbling something about the lineage of the indiscreet Hantscho aide. It was one of the very few times he was heard to indulge in disparaging epithets.

Hantscho's commercial printing design capabilites did not nclude a folder for his pioneer effort on a strictly newspaper ᵣress. The contract went to the Wood-Scott Company for the folder, substructure, balcony and reels, tensions and automatic pasters, with provision for a fourth installation. The price: $181,892.

Terms called for a typical Ottaway long-term repayment arrangement: 10 percent down, 30 percent during the 12 months after signing and the balance in 48 payments after completion of installation.

The same equipment, if bought from Goss in late 1984, would have cost more than $3.5 million — before installation.

Meantime, Bill Lundquest had been searching for a new home for the *TH-R*, which would have to be ready in time to receive the new press and folder. He found what would be the nucleus of a new plant on the fringe of Middletown's urban renewal area. It was the office complex of the Master Rule Company, whose executives had moved west. Ottaway bought the 7,000-square-foot brick and glass block building on Mulberry Street in March 1963 for $65,000 and the following July committed $200,000 to start the necessary addition, which would be erected on adjacent UR land, acquired from the city that same month for $9,500. The building program eventually cost $324,000.

In July 1964 four departments moved from North Street to the new building. The move was completed over the Labor Day weekend. Camera, platemaking and presswork, however, continued at the old location while erectors from Hantscho and Wood-Scott assembled the new press and folder.

The maiden press run took place December 3, with Ottaway filling the traditional role of jabbing the start button. The Hantscho managed to get through the run, but well off schedule. Reproduction was mediocre, the automatic pasters failed and the folder delivered a somewhat uneven product. With Ruth and the Boyds, the chief stayed on the deck for part of the run. He was not happy. He had provided the best equipment the industry then could produce.

As if the last tie to superb press work had been cut, the old two-plate-wide Hantscho was sold to Offset Multicolor, a Mexico City company, for $80,000, a fire sale price.

Orange County Publications board minutes a month after the press start-up reflected Ottaway's faith in the Hantscho. "Operating difficulties," he said, "were finally being straightened out, and it is expected that the quality of reproduction of the paper would soon be as good or better than it had been, and that operating economies and schedule improvements which were anticipated should soon be realized."

But they never would be realized. Countless dollars went down the drain in the form of newsprint waste, late papers, overtime and constant repairs, some of major dimensions.

During one Christmas shopping season when the Hantscho was at its infamous worst, Ruth Ottaway found herself in a Middletown haberdashery choosing gifts.

"May I help?" asked the proprietor.

"I'm looking for something for Jim."

The boor's retort bristled with sarcasm: "Why don't you buy him a new press?"

The remark touched off a contretemps over which this historian prefers to draw the veil.

The early 1960s also saw the arrival at the *TH-R* of three individuals who would have profound influence on the paper's future. Jim Ottaway Jr. came over from Danbury, where he had served as a reporter and associate editor; Stroudsburg's John S. (Jack) Haswell was named circulation manager and John Van Kleeck returned to the Ottaway fold after several years as a proprietor in the weekly field in upstate New York.

Jim Jr.'s two-year hitch included hands-on experience in every phase of the *TH-R* operation as a management trainee. He never eased off a self-imposed work week of 55-60 hours, which led him to King's office one evening after completing his usual outsize file of stories.

"Why is it," he asked the general manager, "that I'm turning in 10, 12 or more stories a day and the other reporters maybe come up with five, six or fewer?"

"The reason is simple," King explained. "You aren't on my payroll. I don't even know your salary or who pays you. But you're working twice as long as my staffers every day. They're on a 40-hour week. And your father doesn't happen to like overtime outside budgeted figures."

It was clear that Jimmy shared his father's passion for newsroom enterprise but as a major shareholder he understood what unbridled expense could do to the Ottaway balance sheet.

The subject was dropped.

Jim Jr. also had a principal role at the outset of the *TH-R* bureau expansion program, yet another example of Jim Ottaway's policy of plowing back profits into betterments. He opened offices in Goshen (the county seat) and Monroe, southeast of Middletown. Five others would follow, almost one each year. The former *Record* always had had an office in Monticello.

☆ ☆ ☆ ☆ ☆ ☆

The youngest of the Ottaway childen was married July 18, 1963 in Milan, Italy. After graduating magna cum laude from Harvard in 1962, David Blackburne Ottaway went to Europe to continue his studies. While at the Goethe Foreign Language Institute in Munich, Germany, he met his bride-to-be, Marina Seassaro. She had also studied at the University of London, he at the Sorbonne University in Paris. The entire Ottaway family attended the wedding. So did a United Press International photographer. A picture went to all Ottaway clients of the news service.

Tragedy struck David and Marina on October 12, 1967. Their first-born, Nicholas, 2½ was killed in a traffic accident northwest of Milan, Italy. The child was a passenger in a car driven by his grandfather, Giovanni Seassaro. David, Marina and the Seassaros escaped serious injury.

In a magnificent gesture to honor the infant's memory, David and Marina established on December 29 the ˜Nicholas B. Ottaway Foundation, described in its charter "for charitable, religious, scientific, literary or educational purposes."

The trustees were Jim, Ruth, Jim Jr., Ruthie, David and Marina.

The foundation's basic philosophy, Jim Sr. said, was to help those communities "that gave us what we have."

Over the years, the minute books show, members of the family have contributed tens of thousands of dollars to its charitable works, which at first embraced mostly scholarships for the disadvantaged. Eventually hospitals, civic betterment groups, United Way appeals, college building funds and even the American Press Institute received gifts. In recent years the focus had tended to narrow to student financial assistance.

The child's death hit Jim Ottaway particularly hard.

It was the only time his intimates saw him weep.

Unlike Jim Jr. David was disinclined to join his father in business. During David's brief period of reporting from the *Times Herald-Record*'s Monticello bureau, Ottaway (then living in the former Strasser home) attempted to sway his recalcitrant son.

"When I feel I need your advice, I'll ask for it," David replied, with no filial disrespect. It was simply David's way of underscoring his preference for foreign correspondence.

Most of David's career has been with the *Washington Post,* which he joined in 1971. In mid-1974 he was assigned to Addis Ababa, Ethiopia. Three years later he was stationed in Luska, Zambia. He returned to Washington in mid-1979.

In May 1981 David became the *Post's* bureau chief in Cairo, where he served through 1984. During 1985 he was assigned to the State Department in Washington.

David previously served as a *New York Times* stringer in Algeria and in 1968-1969 was a reporter for Ottaway News Service in the Federal City.

He has won two Overseas Press Club awards. One was shared with a fellow *Post* reporter for their 1973 forecast of the petroleum shortage. In 1981 his first-person account of the assassination of Presdient Sadat of Egypt earned him his second award. Ottaway was only 17 rows from Sadat in a reviewing stand.

David and Marina have co-authored three books: "Algeria: The Politics of a Socialist Revolution" (1970); "Ethiopia - Empire in Revolution" (1978); "Afrocommunism" (1981). Marina wrote "Soviet and American Influence in the Horn of Africa" (1982).

12 A $2.5 million refinancing

Jim Ottaway and Lyn Boyd were in Springfield, Massachusetts late in 1963, hats in hand, for an appointment with financial officers of Massachusetts Mutual Life Insurance Company. As they waited in the company's magnificent rotunda, Boyd remarked slyly: "I wonder if one of the side benefits to a policy holder is being laid out here on a catafalque?"

Boyd's allusion to mortality was not in the spirit of gallows humor. Massachusetts Mutual was quite willing to lend Ottaway $2 million for a refinancing program, which, concurrently, included $500,000 loan from Fidelity-Philadelphia Trust Company.

"Actually we didn't need the money," Ottaway recalled two decades later. "But we had been advised that such a move would stand us in good stead later on."

The notes were signed on March 25, 1964. Half of the proceeds went to Ottaway Newspapers-Radio, Inc., half to its subsidiary, Orange County Publications, Inc., owner of the *Times Herald-Record*. Both were at 5⅞ percent interest, the former over 10 years, the latter 15.

It was the largest single borrowing in Ottaway's then 28-year history. The loan agreement itself, 23 bound pages of 10-point type with cross indexing (plus six pages of exhibits) cost $5,000. Lawyers' fees came to $7,500. "The fees were breaking us," Gene Brown lamented.

(Two years later Ottaway would borrow $12 million. That loan agreement consisted of a couple of typewritten pages.)

Part of the proceeds, board minutes of the previous February 4 indicate, hopefully would be used to pay off the debt to Jack

145

Kaplan, which stood at $990,000 — in exchange for a discount of $137,500. Another Ottaway hunch proved to be correct. Over luncheon in New York, Kaplan accepted the offer. The chief, understandably, was in a jubilant mood as he and Ruth left for their winter vacation in Barbados.

The Charles Marsh notes also were retired.

Jim Ottaway Jr., having completed training in Middletown, was reassigned by his father to Stroudsburg in 1963 as editor of the *Daily Record*. (During his stay at the *Times Herald-Record*, Jim Jr. had even managed a stint as statehouse correspondent in Albany, helping Bob Van Fleet cover the legislature one or two days a week during the winter-spring session.)

The publisher had asked King and Blake: "Is he ready?" The answer was easy: "More than ready."

Jimmy's boss in Stroudsburg was Horace Heller, flamboyant as an editor and as much so as general manager. Heller could be found in his office as early as 4 o'clock in the morning, but his wherabouts eight or nine hours later was open to some conjecture. A reasonably safe bet was the men's bar of the Penn Stroud Hotel (now Pocono Best Western.)

One of Jimmy's first moves was to recommend that the nine-column *Record* be changed to eight because "it would be easier to read." But there was another reason offered, reflecting the shareholder side of the new editor: an opportunity to trim newsprint costs.

As 1963 drew to a close, the *Pocono* board agreed to purchase a four-unit, 32-page Goss Urbanite press. Bill Lundquest and Heller had been assigned to investigate the feasibility of going offset. Consideration had been given to bringing in Middletown's old two-plate-wide Hantscho, but that idea was rejected. On July 28, 1964, the Goss was ordered. Net cost was $148,000. Trade-in on the letterpress was just what Ottaway had paid for it.

The offset research and preparation under Lundquest's leadership, with nights on end spent in motels, took its toll on the vice president. He suffered a heart attack in mid-summer and was taken to Pocono General Hospital. Within a week he demanded to be released, and returned to Middletown in the Lundquest Oldsmobile to recuperate. But Peg drove. The move was typical for Bill. Bedpans were not his style.

The new press made its debut Februry 3, 1965. The press and related offset equipment were chatteled to the First Stroudsburg National Bank to offset a loan of $135,000 at 5½ percent over five years.

At the same time the name plate was changed to *Pocono Record,* reflecting a more vigorous circulation expansion policy.

Jim Jr. wasn't around to celebrate the advent of offset. In January he was transferred to Danbury as second in command to Gene Brown, at a salary of $15,000.

He also was sitting on the Ottaway board, which in the previous month had voted a $6 dividend, the first for Danbury Publishing Company.

"I promised Mary it would be a permanent, last move," he said. The Fates were hiding smiles. They would decree otherwise.

At the end of the year Jim Jr. was voted a $10,000 bonus after Brown suggested "his contributions and accomplishments had not been adequately rewarded."

And in May 1965, Heller stepped down as general manager. Board minutes give the reason as "failing health."

Phil Blake, assistant general manager in Middletown, was tapped to replace Heller. But not before Ottaway and Boyd gently suggested that Blake divest himself of all but a couple of his huskies.

Blake found the former Ottaway editor's chair occupied by Robert L. (Bob) Clark — a sort of interim appointee. Clark had been sports editor of the *Record.* He ran the news operation until the arrival in October 1966 of Alan Gould Jr.

Gould, who also was destined to become an Ottaway publisher, joined the group in Oneonta in 1960 as editor of the *Star*. The second refugee from Gannett to achieve executive rank, he was the son of Alan J. Gould, then executive editor of the Associated Press.

The junior Gould, whose chief responsibility in 1960 had been the *Elmira* (N.Y.) *Sunday Telegram,* wanted an editor's post on a paper he could think of "as his own," unencumbered by unending directives from on high. But he soon discovered that although life with Ottaway was generally pleasant, the chief's philosophy of local autonomy did not preclude periodic comments from Campbell Hall, both congratulatory and critical.

Blake needed a solid editorial presence. He asked Campbell Hall for help. Gould was tapped.

Gould arrived in Stroudsburg with the impressive title of assistant general manager and executive editor. In 1967 he regained the services of James J. Riley. Jim Riley, a 13-year veteran, had gone to Lancaster, Pennsylvania, after having been denied the editor's job by Heller. Now it was his.

In Oneonta, meantime, Elton Hall (now with the title of publisher) was racking up ever-increasing profits. The *Star* paid a $30 dividend in 1965 and in a further heady move directors voted Ruth and Jim Ottaway their first salary increases in six years, she to $3,100, the chief to $17,200. Hall was the second field marshal to become publisher. Gene Brown had been the first.

Don Clifford, who had come to Oneonta from Plattsburgh in 1956, had become assistant general manager. Another future publisher was appointed advertising manager. He was Milton D. McLean, who joined the *Star* as classified manager in 1959. McLean had come to Oneonta from the *Burlington* (Vt.) *Free Press*, where he was an ad salesman.

McLean would move to Campbell Hall as executive assistant to Ottaway in 1966. McLean was the first of several talented middle-management types who eagerly accepted transitory assignments at headquarters, which hopefully would help prepare them for executive roles in the field. The demand for executive replacements would grow in direct proportion to the number of newspapers in the group.

With Gould's departure from Oneonta, Francis A. (Frank) Perretta took over the newsroom. Perretta, too, was destined to become an Ottaway publisher.

In the wake of Lundquest's heart attack Ottaway proposed in August 1964 a "strengthening of the management division staff" at Campbell Hall, recommending that Steve Ryder move down from Plattsburgh as a vice president. Al DeLuca was chosen to replace Ryder. Ben Turnbull of Oneonta's WDOS replaced DeLuca as advertising manager.

In 1962 Ryder had hired an ad salesman who also was destined for high-level Ottaway posts. He was Richard A. (Dick) Barker, whose newspaper career started with the now defunct *Burlington* (Vt.) *Daily News* circulation department. Barker soon became circulation director of the *Press-Republican.*

Barker would spend a brief period as an administrative assistant at Campbell Hall before moving to New Bedford, Massachusetts, and then to Joplin, Missouri, where he attained publisher rank.

In spite of the continuing crisis with the Hantscho, the *Times Herald-Record*'s circulation continued its rather astonishing climb. During the 1960s growth was catalyzed by three strikes that shut down all New York City newspapers. One lasted from December to April. TH-R competition, it became clear, was mainly in the form of the tabloid *Daily News*. Readers by the thousands turned to the *TH-R* and discovered its four-hour news deadline advantage meant a daily blue plate serving of late news (especially sports) that the metropolitan paper could not offer in Ottaway territory. Jack Haswell, who normally operated on an eight percent returns policy, banned dealer returns during the strikes. It was the most profitable sampling campaign in Ottaway history. At least 8,000 newcomers liked the *Record* enough to stay aboard.

Haswell became a legendary figure, not just because of his triumphs as a circulator, but also for his malapropisms. Invariably he referred to the Barbizon Plaza as the "Barbasol Plaza." He exhorted his carriers to achieve their "gools." "Instinct burners" replaced incense burners in the Haswell lexicography, and Barca-Loungers became Barcelona lounges.

When Phil Blake was tapped to run the *Pocono Record* King found himself in a sticky predicament, having lost the one executive who was most knowledgeable about the unpredictable Hantscho, not to mention the waves of other more sophisticated offset equipment that were appearing on the market. There was no time for King to try to capture Blake's expertise, even if, in fact, he could have.

King knew whom he wanted as Blake's successor: John Van Kleeck, who had returned to the group in 1963 after leaving Endicott to buy weekly newspapers in Oxford and Greene, New York. Van Kleeck, who joined Ottaway in 1947 in Oneonta as reporter, had risen to managing editor in Endicott. He had even aspired to Barney French's job, and, in fact, asked Ottaway if there was a chance of getting it. He quoted the publisher as saying "there's not much I can do about Barney."

Van Kleeck also shared an interest in another nearby weekly, the *Whitney Point* (N.Y.) *Reporter*.

Van Kleeck's experience with the weeklies was more rewarding in terms of entreprenurial experience than bottom-line dollars. Facing an uncompromising balance sheet, meeting payrolls, selling advertising and circulation and keeping some antediluvean machinery operational brought him face to face with the verities of publishing life. Shall we say the rewards were not commensurate with the time and energy invested?

At the time of Blake's departure neither Ottaway nor Boyd spoke up immediately about a replacement, leaving King free to propose Van Kleeck. Early in June 1965 J.V.K. was installed as business manager, a favorite Ottaway catch-all title that seldom fitted the job description.

Ottaway asked one favor: "Tell Van Kleeck to stop wearing those clip-on bow ties."

King carried the message. He also asked Van Kleeck to oversee the obstreperous Hantscho.

The same month brought sad tidings to Campbell Hall. Barney French, the first of Ottway's executive aides, died in Endicott. His association with the Ottaway family had spanned 29 years.

Up in the North Country Al DeLuca recommended purchase of the Spencer property in downtown Plattsburgh, consisting of five dwellings on four parcels. DeLuca, backed by Lyn Boyd, was thinking of the new *Press-Republican* plant that Ottaway would have to build sooner or later. The board approved the $80,000 asking price, authorizing a $20,000 down payment, with the National Commercial Bank & Trust Company taking a mortgage on the balance at 5¼ percent.

Knowing the burgeoning Middletown operation would have to expand, King and Van Kleeck began acquiring properties contiguous to the *TH-R* as they came on the market. Eventually the newspaper would own an entire city block. In 1966 the birthplace of the former *Daily Record* was sold to an electrical supply wholesaler. The rabbit warren where newspaper history was made went for $36,750. There were no tears.

J. Allan Meath, a mercurial advertising hotshot, appeared on the Ottaway scene in 1965 as assistant general manager of the *Danbury News-Times,* reporting to Gene Brown. Meath's career, coincidentally, began on the *Schenectady Union-Star* in 1951. Lyn Boyd also was a *Union-Star* alumnus.

Meath went to Florida in 1953 and served in various executive capacities in St. Petersburg, Tallahassee and Miami. In 1961 he became ad director of the *Augusta* (Ga.) *Chronicle and Herald* newspapers and three years later joined Ralph Ingersoll's *Trenton* (N.J.) *Trentonian* as business manager.

Over the years Meath lectured often at American Press Institute advertising seminars and on occasion found himself sharing the program with Boyd. During his Augusta tour Meath talked at length with Boyd about joining Ottaway but decided not to accept Boyd's offer. Brown sat in on the discussions.

At Trenton, Meath said, he was affronted by a management policy of not printing anything unfavorable about a prime source of advertising revenue. He resigned. Jobless, he turned to Boyd and Brown.

Gene Brown, now almost 60, needed help at the top. Don Diehl had departed in 1964 for the top job at the *Easton* (Pa.) *Express.* Almost a decade after acquisition, the affluent *News-Times* was bursting at the seams. Directors were talking about a new building, and a switch to cold type and offset printing. To tide things over, Brown purchased additonal property adjoining the *News-Times,* but at best it was a patchwork situation.

One stop-gap measure was strengthening the composing

room floor, which was vibrating in an alarming way under the four high-speed, tape-fed linecasting machines ordered by foreman Tommy Purcell in the late 1950s. Bill Lundquest was assigned to help Brown, Purcell and a Danbury engineer to cure the problem. It was decided to replace the entire floor. Lundquest proposed that the old floor be removed from the top. The engineer wanted to take it down from the ceiling below.

"This he did," Lundquest's memoirs said, "only to be greeted in the advertising department by about five tons of metal shavings that had settled in over 50 years."

The replacement floor, wiring and plumbing was done over a weekend. Lundquest wrote a complimentary note to the construction company, only to receive what he called a "sharp rebuke" from the parsimonious Brown.

"I don't care how good a job they did," Brown snapped. "I wanted to chisel them some more."

Presumably the old Ludlow (used to set headlines of 24 point and larger) had been fully depreciated. At any rate Brown approached Purcell and bade him sell it. The proceeds, Brown said, would be used by Purcell to set up an "employee fund." Purcell found a buyer for $500.

At the time Brown had befriended an inmate of Danbury's Federal Correctional Institution, who was incarcerated as a result of some stock maneuverings that had drawn the displeasure of the Securities and Exchange Commission. Herbert (Johannes) Steel was in a work-release program. Brown was his sponsor. Besides writing a column on stocks for the *News-Times* Steel tipped Purcell on penny stocks. It wasn't long before the $500 had burgeoned to more than $3,000. Brown and Purcell made several employee loans but had a difficult time getting back some of the advances.

After the Ottaway merger with Dow Jones in 1970, Steel predictably was dropped as a Danbury columnist.

Whether the Brown-Purcell fund or the Steel column ever were run past the headquarters staff is lost to memory. Probably not. Gene Brown liked to do things on his own.

☆ ☆ ☆ ☆ ☆ ☆

Dominick Sportelli's barbershop occupied a site at 42 West Main Street in Middletown, a short block from Ottaway's temporary offices at No. 80, from which he operated until the Campbell Hall complex opened.

The Sportelli menage included his wife, Mollie, and an ageless parrot, Polly, who, under the tutelage of the tonsor, had mastered a substantial repertoire of earthy remarks. Polly's cage, of course, was lined with old pages of the *Times Herald-Record*. Mollie's conversational gambits could be as salty as the parrot's.

So it came to pass that Jim Ottaway joined Sportelli's somewhat elite clientele. Mostly old Middletown money came to Sportelli. New money patronized salons where hair was styled and where no parrots confused the customers.

Snip by snip Sportelli learned of Ottaway's station in life and concluded that he was trimming the locks of a veritable Croesus.

The friendship mellowed over the years. The tips were generous, especially at Christmastide.

One winter Ruth and Jim departed for their annual winter vacation in Barbados without telling the man of cologne and talcum powder. They would be gone two months, a span over which Ottaway surely would have had at least three haircuts.

When Ottaway's normal time for a trim came and went, Sportelli asked another long-time client if he knew the whereabouts of the publisher. He solemnly advised Sportelli that Ottaway from then on would be getting his haircuts elsewhere.

"Jim Ottaway bought a second-hand barber's chair and had it installed at Campbell Hall," the wag said. "He hired a retired Goshen barber to cut his hair. His assistants are getting haircuts there, too. He doesn't want them wasting time driving to barber shops."

Sportelli, by all accounts, was crushed. Not only was a munificent meal ticket gone, but an uncommonly valued friend as well.

Ottaway showed up in March. Never was Sportelli happier to go to work on the publisher's West Indies overgrowth.

In the 1970s Sportelli spent a morning as the chief's awestruck guest at Campbell Hall, among other things inspecting Ruth's stable of Arabian horses, but from a respectable distance. He thought they might bite.

The prankster had had his laughs.

If Ottaway was amused he didn't show it. Friends like Sportelli were not to be hoodwinked.

It was a singular example of Jim and Ruth Ottaway's empathy for everyone with whom they came in contact. They made it a special point to know lower level employees and their wives and husbands. They listened carefully to expressions of hope and fears — and remembered. They wrote personal letters in an unending stream. And they answered every letter no matter how trifling.

As the group expanded countrywide after the merger with Dow Jones, Ruth and Jim understandably found themselves unable to continue the long tradition of attending every annual company party. Jim Jr. took up the slack, making certain that at least one Ottaway would be on hand.

The Ottaways reveled in the company get-togethers, which ranged from clambakes to punk rock dance-a-thons. And when the band — whatever its instrumental make up — started they were among the first on the floor. They danced the night together and with employees of high and low station. Often they were the last to leave. After one Middletown party the author received a thank you note from Jim Jr., which read in part: "As for my poor father and mother, they enjoyed your party too much. I dragged them away at 2 a.m. and drove them home safely."

Most employees invited to dance by Jim Ottaway tactfully described his floor style as "very enthusiastic."

The dancing highlight of some parties in earlier years was a snappy Charleston, starring Ruth and Jim Jr. The troops loved it.

Jim Ottaway was the owner of three newspapers when this picture was taken in Endicott in the late 1940s.

His first building was completed just before U.S. entry into World War II and right after his pioneer *Daily Bulletin* began to turn a profit. If the structure looks spartan, cash was on the scarce side.

William C. (Bill) Lundquest, left, joined Ottaway in Endicott in 1939. Barney French was advertising manager of the semi-weekly Endicott Bulletin at the time of its purchase by the Ottaways.

In 1952 all the Ottaway brass attended an end-of-year dinner for employees of the *Plattsburgh Press-Republican,* acquired the preceding August. Ottaway, then 41, was principal speaker. Gene Brown, left, ponders the chief's remarks.

$17,500

Endicott, New York
March 20, 1939

In accordance with terms of this agreement, I promise to pay to
the order of Ruth Ottaway Sokoloff $17,500 with interest at the
rate 5 per cent per annum, payable semi-annually, and I hereby
pledge and assign to Ruth Ottaway Sokoloff as collateral
security for this indebtedness the following securities:

                Certificate #34, Times Herald Co., Port Huron,
                        Michigan---------150 shares

                Certificate #5, 40 shares, Endicott Bulletin, Inc.
                Certificate #6, 40 shares, Endicott Bulletin, Inc.
                Certificate #7, 40 shares, Endicott Bulletin, Inc.
                        Endicott, New York

I hereby agree that said Ruth Ottaway Sokoloff may demand
repayment of 20 per cent of said indebtedness, upon 30 days
notice, at any time within the period between March 20, 1939
and March 20, 1941, or a total not to exceed $3,500, and I
agree that if said 20 per cent payment is not made within 30
days, that the entire indebtedness may be declared due and
payable;

I hereby agree to repay said $17,500 on the following terms and
at the following dates:

        March 20, 1941----$1,500   March 20, 1943---$2,500
        Sept. 20, 1941---- 1,500   Sept. 20, 1943--- 2,500
        March 20, 1942---- 2,000   March 20, 1944--entire
        Sept. 20, 1942---- 2,000   balance to be paid.

I hereby agree to assign to said Ruth Ottaway Sokoloff life
insurance in the sum of $17,500, as additional collateral;

And, I hereby agree to all the conditions of said note, with
the understanding that a grace period of 60 days will be
allowed by said Ruth Ottaway Sokoloff on the payment of any
principal or interest payments as they become due, and I agree
that after said 60 day period expires and said payments have
not been made in accordance with this agreement, the entire
balance may be declared due and payable.

In 1939 Jim Ottaway's mother was literally his principal banker. Blood
ties notwithstanding, she always insisted on full collateral. The *Bulletin,*
now a daily, moved into the black that year. It had been a protracted
struggle.

DUPLEX PRINTING PRESS COMPANY
BATTLE CREEK, MICHIGAN

DATA RELATIVE TO CONTRACT FOR ROTARY EQUIPMENT AND DETAILS
REGARDING SHIPMENT AND INSTALLATION

Date_____

Publisher **Endicott Bulletin, Inc.**_____ City and State **Endicott, New York.**___

Style of Press **Rebuilt 16-page Standard Tubular** Folder **Half Page**_____

Stereo or Other Equipment **1 rebuilt regular mat roller, 1 new speed scorcher, 1**___ **3,000-lb. metal pot and furnace, 1 new metal pump, 1 new full automatic Burdett** **Burner, 1 rebuilt casting box, 1 rebuilt finishing machine with motor, 1 new elevating**

Sheet Cut___ **22-3/4"**_____ Kind of Mats **Dry** **table, 16 new chases.**___

Center Margin **7/8"**_____ age Size_____ **8**_____ **12**_____ **6**___

Web Widths **34" and 17"**____   Cols.   Ems   Pt. Rules

Contract Shipping Date **Octobe.** __41 Insurance **$10,546.00**_____

Cash with Order	$ **2,000.00**
Cash Before Shipment	$ **none**
Cash on Erection	$ **none**
Notes	$ **10,546.00**
Allowance for Old Machinery	$ **included**
Total	$ **12,546.00**

Drive Equipment Furnished by _ **Duplex**_____ Arranged for Speed of **~~30,000~~ 20,000 per hour**

Drive to Be Placed on *plating side of press*

Current **220**_____ Volts___ **3**_____ Phase_____ **60**_____ Cycle

Blankets Furnished by_ **Duplex**_____

Composition Furnished by_____ **Duplex**

Erector's Transportation Paid by_	**Customer**
Erector's Living Expenses Paid by_	"
Erector's Services Paid by_	"
Erector's Services Rate per Day $ **18.00**	
Freight Paid by_	**Customer**
Cartage Paid by_	"
Common Labor Paid by_	"
Electric Wiring Paid by_	"

Machinery Taken in Part Payment_ **Duplex Model B Press**___

Cost Dismantling Old Press Paid by **Common labor only to be paid by customer**___

Cartage on Old Press Paid by_ **Duplex**_____

Chases and Extras Property of_ "___

Motor for Old Press Property of_ "___

PLEASE ANSWER FOLLOWING QUESTIONS

Will paper be wound on sulphite cores? *Yes*___ Do cores have metal ends? *Yes*___

Will 36¾" height of form tables be O. K.? _____

To whom shall we ship roller stocks? **No answer needed**_____

Route desired_____

Do you desire to inspect press during testing at factory? **No answer needed**_____

Signed_____

The year is 1941. Jim Ottaway has contracted to buy his first replacement press. At the time some equipment manufacturers would accept notes. Rates for erectors were an unbelievable $18 per day.

Lyndon R. (Lyn) Boyd, left, was a no-nonsense taskmaster, but one who fought for his field generals all the way. The foliage and their attire suggest the early 1950s picture of Jim and Ruth Ottaway was taken at a now-forgotten newspaper convention in sunny climes.

At the Ottaway cottage in Buck Hill Falls in 1967, from the left: David, Jim Sr., Ruth, Ruthie and Jim Jr.

There were seminars unending at Buck Hill Falls. Above, center, Ottaway and Phil Blake engage in some pre-dinner badinage in the Ottaway cottage. Ruth Ottaway and Francis Brinkley are in the foreground. Dinner is over in the picture below, which portrays, clockwise from the left, Gene Brown and Leroy Paltrowitz (Danbury); Bob Whittemore (Oneonta); the late E. Bradley Boyle, the author, Al Romm, Phil Blake and Bob Van Fleet (Middletown). The pictured dates to the early 1960s.

The year is 1960. The Ottaways, having just acquired the *Middletown Daily Record,* posed for a court portrait by Manny Fuchs, then its chief photographer. Merger with the *Middletown Times Herald* was just around the corner.

THE MIDDLETOWN DAILY
RECORD

VOL. 4 NO. 185 . LATE FINAL EDITION • • TUESDAY, APRIL 19, 1960 3 SECTIONS 22 PAGES 5 CENTS

AROUND THE WORLD

Daily Record sold to Ottaway; Lundquest is named manager

S. African police jail 400 natives

Police yesterday raided a shantytown to arrest 400 African natives and fanned out in a show of force to other Negro areas to try to head off a threatened stay-home strike by Negro workers. Two police officers, both Negroes, were beaten by fellow natives, but this was the only violence in the racially tense country. Police said their arrests were carried out peacefully. There was danger that blood would flow today, however, should Negro nationalist leaders succeed in staging a large-scale stay-home strike against white supremacy laws.

Police said they seized about 400 "troublemakers" and "gangsters" in the East London Negro area, 500 miles south of Johannesburg. But they denied that they had arrested 40 Negroes in the Johannesburg area. Police insisted that those arrested were mostly "antiindustees" who might try to force African natives who might otherwise go to work to stay home. Bootleggers were among those arrested on the theory that alcohol might inflame the Africans, who are forbidden such beverages by law.

* * *

Cuba

New reports of internal disorders and threats of an all-out anti-government military campaign plagued Cuban Premier Castro. Castro appeared tired and worn on his return to Havana from Manzanillo in Oriente Province by airliner. He apparently left behind the 5,000 troops in the Sierra Maestra Mountains which he had been personally leading against roving bands of guerrilla fighters. Castro's return to Havana coincided with threats of open war against his regime voiced by the so-called Cuban anti-Communist rebel army, an organization of exiles abroad which claims 5,000 members.

* * *

Taxes

As thousands of New York State taxpayers struggled against a deadline for filing their federal and state income tax returns, Gov. Rockefeller signed a measure to make the job easier next year. The governor approved legislation to simplify the tax return form by having state standards of income conform to those set down by the federal government.

* * *

Segregation

A Negro sitdown demonstrator and a white man engaged in a fist-swinging incident at a Savannah, Ga., dime store, and were arrested. Anti-segregation demonstrations occurred again in Chattanooga, Tenn. A Mississippi Negro physician reported that he was arrested for swimming at an "all white" public beach at Biloxi.

National pastime

President Eisenhower, acclaimed in recent years for his own interest and prowess in another popular sport, rears back to throw out the first ball to officially open the American League baseball season yesterday at Washington's Griffith Stadium. The President was a baseball and football star at West Point some years back. Mr. Eisenhower, along with numerous other dignitaries, then sat back and watched the Washington Senators overpower the Boston Red Sox, 10-1. (See story on Page 8A.)-- UPI Telephoto.

Times Herald, Union-Gazette to continue

(See related stories on Page 2A.)

The Middletown Daily Record has been purchased by Ottaway Newspapers–Radio, Inc., of Endicott, N.Y.

Announcement of the sale was made yesterday by James H. Ottaway, president of the company; J.M. Kaplan, president of Community Newspaper Publishers, Inc., which owned The Record since its founding in 1956; and David Bernstein, editor and publisher of The Record.

The Ottaway organization, which acquired The Middletown Times Herald and The Port Jervis Union-Gazette last November, now operates eight newspapers and three radio stations.

Mr. Ottaway said that all three Orange County newspapers will continue to publish separately and that -- with the exception of several management positions -- no changes in personnel are contemplated.

The Record will be operated by Orange County Publications, Inc., a wholly owned subsidiary of the parent Ottaway organization at Endicott. Mr. Ottaway is president of the new company. His wife, Ruth D. Ottaway, is secretary.

* * *

William C. Lundquest, executive vice president, treasurer, and general manager of The Times Herald since November, will take over today with the same titles at The Record. A new manager of The Times Herald will be named today.

Harry S. Milligan, general manager of The Record since its beginning, will continue in Middletown during a transitional period before he and Mr. Bernstein move on to another as yet unannounced newspaper enterprise.

Mr. Ottaway spoke yesterday of The Record as "the leading offset, cold-type daily in the country," and said he pledged "to carry forward the original principles established by the previous management ...including editorial assistance and leadership in the development of Middletown and the Goldenarea."

He paid tribute to Mr. Bernstein and Mr. Milligan for bringing to reality "the dream of a new kind of daily newspaper."

Mr. Kaplan praised Mr. Ottaway as a newspaper publisher "with the highest ideals" who would "continue to build upon the standards of quality and service that have been the hallmark of The Record."

Mr. Bernstein, who said his future plans for "a newspaper enterprise in another city" could not yet be announced, thanked the members of The Record staff for their dedication. He said the newspaper under Mr. Ottaway could "move forward toward even greater accomplishment."

* * *

The purchase, completed last Thursday in New York City, brings to eight the number of papers operated by Ottaway Newspapers.

They include the Stroudsburg, Pa., Daily Record; the Danbury, Conn., News–Times; The Endicott Daily Bulletin; The Oneonta, N.Y., Star, and the Plattsburgh, N.Y., Press-Republican. The Ottaway radio stations are WENE in Endicott, WVPO in Stroudsburg, and WDOS in Oneonta.

Third death in three days:

Long Island youth is killed; Woodbourne crash

a Sullivan County as many days earlier. Four others were injured in the automobile crash, one critically, Ferndale state police reported.

The deceased was identified as Arnold Weiner of Seaford, L.I. He died at Monticello Hospital at 3:30 a.m., less than three hours after the accident. A coroner's verdict by Dr. Ralph S. Breakey of Monticello has been withheld pending further investigation.

In critical condition in a Kingston hospital is Michael Joseph Thomas, 19, also of Seaford. State police said he suffered a brain concussion.

Reported in satisfactory condition at Monticello Hospital last night were Henry Robbins of Queens, 15; Phyllis M. Gold, 14, of Brooklyn and Laury Jay Gaynes, 17, of Seaford, the driver. They suffered minor cuts and bruises.

Gaynes, police said, lost control of his auto at 12:35 a.m. on the Hasbrouck Rd., a mile north of Woodbourne. The vehicle, a station wagon, swerved off the right side of the highway, struck three small trees, and then cracked head-on into a larger one.

jured. The accident took place on the Hasbrouck Rd. near Woodbourne early yesterday.

-- Photo by Paul Gerry

Red-hot baseb dent Eisenhow munch away as League baseba on Page 8A.)--

Plane c

of nine crashed Air Force Base from Dover, D Azores. The Service.

Rocket

of its Scout, nearly gone i "live" engines ule, but that the

Execution

scheduled execu fense lawyer triple execution four years, is se

Election

Police, makes today for the nominee Jimmi Party color-bea whelming Davis

Antony Arms of the royal fan becoming an ins the idea. They photography with the decora

"He takes same old Elvis sleeps all day," describing Elvis 'emy.

* * *

"A friend of rock 'n' roll singer Elvis Presley, describing Elvis's adjustment to civilian life after a hitch in the

New owners

David Bernstein, former editor and publisher of The Daily Record, discusses the paper with the new owners, Mr. and Mrs. James H. Ottaway. The Ottaway organization now includes eight daily newspapers in New York, Pennsylvania, and Connecticut, and three radio stations. -- Record Photo by Larry Mulvehill.

WEATHER

Local forecast

Generally fair with temperatures reaching the 50s and near 60. West to northwesterly winds, under 15 miles an hour, Increasing cloudiness and warmer tomorrow with a chance of showers in the late afternoon or early evening.

Yesterday's facts

	High	Low
Middletown	68	39
Boston	69	48
Chicago	45	33
Miami	80	74
New York	65	51
San Diego	77	56

State forecast

Generally fair with moderate temperatures reaching into the mid 50s. West to northwesterly winds, under 15 miles an hour.

Based this railing prognosis authorized at Middletown, N.Y., under the act of March 3, 1897.

The *Middletown Daily Record* came into the Ottaway fold April 18, 1960. The drop head (top right) pledged continuation of the *Times Herald*. But it was not to be. The following October 1 the inevitable merger was announced. Bill Lundquest (inset) was tapped to run the *Times Herald-Record*.

VOL. LIX.   No. 6.   Plattsburgh, N. Y., Friday, August 15, 1952

Costello Starts Jail Term Today, First in Years

Kingpin of New York-Miami Underworld Convicted of Contempt of Senate

NEW YORK, (P)—Frank Costello, one of the rulers of gamblers, is slated to switch his residence today from a swank Manhattan apartment to a prison cell.

His attorney said no more legal maneuvers were contemplated to further delay the start of his 18 months sentence for contempt of the United States Senate. He will be eligible for parole in six months.

Court sources said the term probably would be served in the Federal Correctional Institution at Danbury, Conn., although there was no official word in advance.

A jury found the 61-year-old Costello guilty of contempt for walkouts and refusal to answer questions concerning his finances at a Senate Crime Committee hearing witnessed by millions of televiewers in March, 1951.

The stocky fashion-plate protested at being televised and for the most part the tv audience seeing a view of an underworld figure saw only his clasped hands or his single.

Law enforcement officials regard Costello as the kingpin of New York-Miami gambling and his prison term starting today will be his first in 37 years.

Served a short stretch behind bars for illegally carrying a gun long before he rose to the underworld ladder and retired with politicians on an estate on Rhode Island, in addition to and told the Crime kept as much as in a cafe at his...

SYSTEM FOR COLLECTING DIESEL FUEL TAX CHANGED

ALBANY, (P)—The State Tax Commission announced yesterday it had adopted a new system of collecting the state's 6-cent-a-gallon tax on diesel fuel, effective Oct. 1.

The new law, enacted earlier this year, makes retail dealers and bulk users responsible for payment of the tax. The former system gave this responsibility directly to individual operators of diesel trucks.

The tax yields the state about $2,000,000 a year.

Among those affected by the new law are about 500 retail dealers in diesel fuel. These dealers will be required to register as "diesel motor fuel district distributors" and file monthly reports on the tax before Nov. 30, to cover sales in October.

AUTO INDUSTRY SEEKING STEEL ALLOTMENTS BOOST

WASHINGTON, (P)—Auto industry, contending that the government has exaggerated the prospective steel shortage, asked yesterday for sharply increased steel allotments after Oct. 1.

Auto makers told the National Production Authority in their appeal that unless allotments are increased, auto production in the last quarter of the year will fall to 72 per cent of the present rate.

This would indicate a loss in auto output of more than 700,000 cars for the year—about 400,000 resulting directly from the steel strike during the present quarter—July through September—and more than 300,000 because of curtailed allotments in the last three months of the year.

Rapid improvement in the steel supply is indicated, the auto men said, asserting that the military will be unable to use all the metal now earmarked for its use.

Therefore, it was argued, the industry should be allowed material to make 1,100,000 cars in the coming quarter and 1 1/2 million cars a quarter after Jan. 1.

ANOTHER RUSSIAN 'FIRST' CLAIMED—BATTLE ROCKET

MOSCOW, (P)—The Russians added rocket artillery yesterday to their list of claims for Russian inventions.

By account of the Soviet Navy newspaper Red Fleet, the War of 1812 rocket to which Francis Scott Key referred in writing "The Star Spangled Banner" was only an inferior British copy of Russian rocket models.

The real creator of battle rockets, Red Fleet said, citing a new book on the weapon by a Russian author, was not the British but a Russian general, Alexander I. Kartmazov during the Napoleonic war hero, A. D. Zasyadko.

The Encyclopaedia Britannica says Congreve is chiefly remembered for his battle rockets, first fired in 1806, but notes: "The origin of the rocket is lost in time and the invention of the rocket is as yet unknown. Only this much is certain—it has been lived long before the beginning of the Christian era."

Asks Indictment For Perjury be Killed by Court

Justice Best to Rule on Motion by James A. Leary on September 3

GLOVERSVILLE, (P)—Republican boss James A. Leary asked yesterday that the State Supreme Court dismiss the perjury indictment brought against him by the extraordinary grand jury probing gambling in Saratoga County.

Justice Willard L. Best indicated he would rule on the motion Sept. 3.

The 71-year-old Saratoga Springs lawyer was given until Aug. 30 to reply to an affidavit filed Monday by Special Prosecutor Paul W. Williams. The prosecution must answer by Aug. 27 any briefs Leary might file next week.

Williams' affidavit was in support of the grand jury's charges of first and second-degree perjury against Leary.

The jury accused Leary of lying when he told them he did not own stock in the Saratoga National Bank.

The prosecution contends that Leary owned 668.5 shares through a "dummy," Herbert L. Stone, a Gloversville television repairman.

Leary asked for dismissal of the indictment on the ground that: 1. Gov. Dewey's order to convene the jury pertained to gambling and crime and not to stock ownership. 2. Williams' "tirade" against him in court April 3 violated Leary's constitution rights. 3. He was not permitted to answer more than yes or no about stock ownership when he appeared before the jury. 4. The grand jury was impaneled illegally.

Leary asserted secret data drawn on prospective jurors were prepared by the prosecutor and consulted by Justice Leo J. Hagerty. He contended that the alleged data sheets were withheld from the Court of Appeals when it recently upheld the legality of the grand jury.

EXECUTION IS DELAYED BY ORDER OF GOVERNOR

ALBANY, (P)—Gov. Dewey yesterday delayed the scheduled execution of a Kingston man from Aug. 25 until the week of Oct. 27 to permit the man's appeal to be reargued in the Court of Appeals.

The state's highest court upheld the first-degree murder conviction of Edward H. Kelly on July 14.

The 33-year-old man was found guilty of shooting Elnoise McHugh, the mother of four children, on a Kingston street on May 27, 1950.

Kelly actually was found guilty twice by Ulster County Court juries. However, the Court of Appeals reversed the first conviction and ordered a new trial.

Dewey said the delay of execution was requested by Louis B. Brahn, Ulster County district attorney.

At his trials, the prosecution contended that Kelly killed Mrs. McHugh because she had refused to marry him and because he objected to her going with another man. Kelly contended that he was temporarily insane at the time of the shooting.

Sale of Press-Republican by Mrs. M. M. Dunphy Announced

Sale of the Plattsburgh Press-Republican to a company headed by James H. Ottaway, newspaper publisher from Endicott, N. Y. is announced today by Mrs. Mary M. Dunphy, president of the company.

Associated in the sale of the newspaper, which has been in the Mannix family for 60 years, are Mrs. Mary M. Dunphy's niece, Miss Maria C. Oliver, part owner of the company with Mrs. Dunphy.

The new owners include: Mr. Ottaway, president and publisher; Byron E. French, Endicott, vice-president; Eugene J. Brown, Oneonta, treasurer; and Mrs. Ruth B. Ottaway secretary.

William C. Lundquest, formerly business manager of The Daily Bulletin, Endicott, has been named general manager representing the new ownership. Mr. Lundquest is married, father of four children, and with Mrs. Lundquest will move to Plattsburgh as soon as they locate a home.

William M. Lynch, associated with the company as business manager, and T. Harold Weldon remains as editor.

"The present personnel of the newspaper will be continued without any changes planned," Mr. Ottaway said.

"We are proud to have become owners of the Press-Republican and we are also proud to become a part of Plattsburgh, Clinton and Essex counties.

"We pledge the full support of the Press-Republican in the development and growth of this area."

The Press-Republican began publication on October 6, 1942, as the result of the consolidation of the Plattsburgh Daily Press and the Plattsburgh Daily Republican.

The Press was founded in 1894 and the Republican in 1811. Prior to the consolidation the Press was politically Republican and the Republican was identified with the Democratic party. The consolidation resulted in the Press-Republican becoming an independent newspaper.

If a history of the newspaper publishing business in Plattsburgh were to be written, it is probable that three names would be outstanding—Thomas F. Mannix, Mrs. B. Theresa Mannix and Thomas H. Weldon. Mr. Mannix took over publication of the Plattsburgh Daily Press in the early 1900's and, following his death in 1909, Mrs. Mannix for the next 18 years was the publisher. Mr. Weldon, by virtue of his keen editorial mind, plus his brilliant writing served to establish over a period of 30 years until his death in 1942, the groundwork whereby the consolidation of the Press and the Republican was accomplished.

ANOTHER CHINESE ATTACK REPULSED BY MARINES

SEOUL, (Friday), (P)—Fighting U. S. Marines today turned back a fifth Chinese Red attempt to recapture strategic Bunker Hill on the Western Korean Front.

The attack was a stone punch launched without the usual artillery warning.

Two Chinese companies—about 500 men—struck in the dark before dawn.

One company was moving up the valley between Siberia Hill and Bunker Hill when Marine lookouts spotted the Reds. Allied guns opened fire.

"We clobbered them," at 1st Marine Division spokesman said.

The other Red company launched a direct frontal assault and a raging fight developed.

The Communists poured in artillery shells at the rate of 100 a minute. Their fire pulverized the shell-pocked slope.

The leathernecks blazed away from their pre-fabricated bunkers. Allied artillery joined in the roaring engagement.

In two hours the Chinese were beaten off.

The assault climax was the worst in 24 hours. Early Thursday morning the Reds launched a half-hearted assault that sputtered out in four minutes.

Wire Briefs

LICK-ATHENY, France, (P)—Deaf leaves last night to underground explorer Marcel Loubens, 34, thousand feet down in the Pyrenees, just before the midnight hour when rescuers hoped to bring him out. His back was broken yesterday in a fall down a fissure, one of the world's deepest.

WASHINGTON, (P)—President Truman refused yesterday to increase the duty on imported Swiss watches, declaring he could not find that the $6-million-dollar-a-year traffic was injuring American manufacturers.

If special measures should be needed to preserve the domestic watch industry for defense purposes, the President said, "it is by no means certain that an increase in import duties constitutes an effective approach to that objective." This was Truman's answer to a recommendation of the Tariff Commission that cheaper imported Swiss watches be priced significantly higher.

CAMP DRUM, (P)—The 6,200 men of the 43rd Division, New York National Guard, spent a busy day in the field yesterday as their annual two-week training period neared the half-way mark.

Every outfit moved out early and many didn't return to camp until well after sundown.

MARK SULLIVAN, NOTED COLUMNIST, DEAD AT 78

WEST CHESTER, Pa., (P)—Mark Sullivan, dean of America's newspaper columnists, died of a heart attack Wednesday night in Chester County Hospital. He would have been 78 on Sept. 10.

A working newspaperman, author and political analyst for 44 years, Sullivan was stricken at his farm home in nearby Avondale. This farm, built by his Irish immigrant parents, was his birthplace.

He returned there several years ago and continued to write his twice-a-week column for the New York Herald Tribune and other newspapers almost to the moment of his death.

Sullivan was the author of several books, including his own autobiography, and once wrote for the Ladies Home Journal. He also served several years as editor of Collier's magazine.

One of 10 children, all of whom made a mark for themselves in life, Sullivan is survived by a son and two daughters. Tentative plans for the funeral have been set for Saturday at nearby West Grove.

ROSCOE TURNER, VETERAN PILOT, IS AWARDED DFC

WASHINGTON, (P)—The Air Force yesterday awarded the Distinguished Flying Cross to Roscoe Turner, veteran speed pilot, for his contributions to the advancement of aerial flight.

Turner, president of an Indianapolis Aeronautical Company, is the first civilian in 20 years to receive the decoration.

The medal was presented in a Pentagon ceremony by Gen. Nathan F. Twining, acting chief of staff of the Air Force.

Turner was cited for his accomplishments in winning the Thompson trophy race three times, breaking the transcontinental air speed record seven time, and for World War II training of more than 3,500 cadets and instructors.

New Officers of Press-Republican

JAMES H. OTTAWAY, President

WILLIAM C. LUNDQUEST, General Manager

WILLIAM M. LYNCH, Business Manager

Eisenhower Turns Down Invitation to Take Part In White House 'Briefing'

Reminds President Truman That He Has Lived With World Danger Spots and Problems For Many Years—GOP Applauds Rejection

(By The Associated Press)
Gen. Dwight D. Eisenhower gave a firm no-thank-you reply yesterday to President Truman's invitation for a White House "briefing" on world danger spots—and a tart rejoinder that he has lived with such problems for many years.

Eisenhower told the President he wants to steer clear of any direct contact with the White House as he can remain free to criticize the administration's policies in his role as the Republican presidential standard bearer.

Moreover, the general said: "I believe our communications should be only those which are known to all the American people."

A few hours after Eisenhower's reply was announced, Truman told his news conference that if Eisenhower planned to make public anything he had said to him, the general was at liberty to do so.

Truman went on to say Eisenhower has spent a great many things the President has told him—and some of them have been kind of garbled, Truman said. He didn't say what he thought Eisenhower had garbled.

The President said he decided long before Gen. Adlai Stevenson visited the White House on Tuesday that Eisenhower should also be invited to a briefing on the international situation.

Republican critics have contended that Truman invited Eisenhower only as an afterthought after the GOP blasts at Stevenson's briefing.

CARBORUNDUM CORP. TO BUILT PLANT AT AKRON

NIAGARA FALLS, (P)—The Carborundum Corp. yesterday announced it would build a $3,442,000 plant in Akron, N.Y. for production of rare metals used by the Atomic Energy Commission.

A subsidiary company, the Carborundum Metals Company, Inc., has been formed to build and operate the new plant, which will provide more strontium and hafnium metal.

Carborundum said it had arranged with the AEC to supply 500,000 pounds of the metals a year over a period of five years. It said the plant will double the construction of nuclear reactors.

The announcement did not say when construction would begin, or how long it would take. The plant will occupy an 18 1/2 acre tract just outside the village limits of Akron, which is 30 miles southeast of here.

HANDYMAN, 43, HELD IN SLAYING OF POLICEMAN

WEST CHESTER, Pa.—A routine ballistics test caused a 43-year-old Negro to be held on a homicide charge yesterday as the slayer of Patrolman James McMillan, 32-year-old father of three children.

Police said Henry Jefferson, a handyman, of St. Albans, had admitted shooting the policeman in an argument on a Harlem street.

The police found Jefferson in Jamaica early this week, brought him here for questioning in connection with another shooting affray Tuesday, the same day Mr. Gillion was slain.

Authorities told this story—Jefferson bought a Spanish revolver with the intention of shooting a girl friend, Sarah Goodman, 20, and himself if she refused a reconciliation. She refused and he fired at her, inflicting a superficial wound.

She ran screaming into a store and Jefferson was arrested on a felonious assault charge.

The gun was subjected to a ballistics test, and laboratory experts declared it was the same weapon that had killed McMillan about 12 hours before the girl was wounded.

WARREN, O., (P)—Ousting robbers ran a bank manager's car a residential street yesterday and fled with $71,000 in a daring daylight holdup.

It was the second multi-thousand dollar daylight robbery here in just over a year, and Paul J. Pilipe, agent—in charge of the Cleveland FBI office, declared, "We need all the help we can get."

NEW YORK, (P)—Spokesmen for three railroad brotherhoods squadrons of pennmen yesterday on the progress of mediation to avert a strike against the New York Central Railroad's lines east of Buffalo.

Saratoga Hotel to be Razed

SARATOGA SPRINGS, (P)—The famed old Grand Union Hotel, fashionable 19th century rendezvous of rich and famous horse-race followers, will close forever at the end of this month and is scheduled to be torn down, Mayor Addison Mallery said yesterday.

Mallery said an officer of the Tithe Guaranty and Trust Company in New York City had informed him that sale of the 680-room hotel was being negotiated and that the hotel would be razed.

The mayor said he was told the bank was acting for a client, whose identity was not disclosed.

George and Ryman Siegel, proprietors in Albany, reported they had bought the furnishings of the big landmark and would sell them at auction in October.

The auction involved in the sale was not disclosed. However, real estate sources put the purchase price of the hotel at about $300,000 and the Albany Times-Union said the auctioneers were reported to have paid $190,000 for the furnishings.

The Times-Union said a New York City syndicate was buying the Broadway Saratoga Corporation, headed by Louis Ginsberg and his son, Martin, both of Glens Falls.

Martin Ginsberg confirmed that negotiations for sale of the property were under way.

The Grand Union is the last of the two sprawling hotels that once dominated the main street of this Spa. The United States was torn down several years ago.

The Grand Union was built in 1864, the same year the Saratoga Racetrack opened. Its appointments were the ultimate in luxury in their day.

The hotel grounds cover seven acres and the front porch is billed as the longest single porch in the world—one-quarter mile.

Many of the Grand Union's rooms lack private baths, however, and the original steam elevators still are in place.

In recent years, it has been open only for conventions and from mid-July until the end of August, for the same.

Mayor Mallery reported there was one possibility of saving the historic structure. He said he had been informed that the purchasers might consider selling the property to the State as a Site for Champlain College, now located in Plattsburgh.

The Air Force is taking over the Plattsburgh property, formerly a military barracks for a bomber base.

Eden, Niece of Churchill Wed

LONDON, (P)—Deborah Foreign Secretary Anthony Eden married blue-eyed Clarissa Churchill, planned niece of Britain's Prime Minister, in a brief civil ceremony yesterday at a London registry office.

The bride's uncle, Winston Churchill, beamed irresistibly in signing the registry as a chief witness, bringing into his family the man who some day may become his successor as leader of the Conservative party.

Thousands of cheering well-wishers milled around in the bright noon sun outside Caxton Hall, where civil marriages are performed daily in solemnity this fashion, as the bridal party entered and as it departed few minutes later for a private wedding breakfast at Churchill's official London residence, 10 Downing Street.

Some spectators fainted in the heat and excitement. Housewives hurried out of line at ration shops as women managed to squeeze through the police cordon to slip a horseshoe to Eden's private car.

Anxious to leave, the foreign secretary was married by a registrar, not a clergyman. The church of England refuses to marry divorced persons. The new marriage of identification and signing the register. The Church of England refuses to marry divorced persons. Eden's first wife, Beatrice, divorced him in 1950, and he has since then scarcely played away from their mutual marriages.

After the wedding formalities Eden proudly kissed the radiant bride.

The whole side of the bride, too, is uneven in temperament that I walk?" he asked.

"I fear, sir, that I am not an expert in rush matters," grunted Mr. Registrar Holiday Jones and told Eden in reply to it the right.

The Plattsburgh Press-Republican, was, Ottaway said, "the worst-looking newspaper I'd ever seen." This is Page 1 of the August 15, 1952, edition, announcing the sale. Note the incompatible headline type faces.

SERVING THE GREAT E-V-E AREA
WESTERN BROOME COUNTY,
EASTERN TIOGA COUNTY

The Daily Bulletin

THE WEATHER

E-V-E and vicinity: Partly cloudy and not so cool followed by scattered thundershowers late tonight or Thursday. Low 60-65. Thursday warmer and more humid with scattered thundershowers. High 83-88.

Vol. 109, No. 23 — Endicott, N. Y., Wednesday, August 31, 1960 — Telephone STillwell 5-3355 or for Owego MUtual 7-1939 — 5 Cents

Daily Bulletin Sold to Binghamton Sun; 1st Combined Issue Tomorrow Morning

New International Uproar

Castro Charges U. S. Helped Plot Ambush of Plane

HAVANA (UPI)—Premier Fidel Castro whipped up a new international uproar today with charges of a U.S.-supported plot to shoot down an airliner carrying Cuban Foreign Minister Raul Roa home from San Jose, Costa Rica.

The charge — sprung by the bearded revolutionary leader in a speech from his palace balcony Tuesday night — was spread throughout the island by the government controlled press and radio to give impetus to a mass rally set for this Friday in Havana.

Castro called the demonstration to show Cuba's contempt for the anti-Communist declaration issued last Monday by 19 hemisphere foreign ministers in San Jose and its determination to stick by its new Soviet and Red Chinese "friends."

Called "War" Airplanes

The premier claimed that "two airplanes of war based in Guatemala" had been alerted to attack Roa's Cubana airliner over the Carribean on its return from San Jose.

He said the aerial ambush was to have been carried out "by international gangsters who are supported by the United States" but that the lot was foiled when Roa left five hours earlier than scheduled on a secret flight arranged by the Costa Rican government.

"You all know how many bandits there are, how many killers, gangsters and mercenaries who find work assured in the intelligence service of the U.S. State Department," Castro told a hushed street assembly of an estimated 5,000 persons. Roa stood by his side.

Arrest American Newsman

The premier said Costa Rican authorities were notified of the alleged plot by the Cuban delegation and cooperated fully in arranging the special flight, while keeping Roa's regular airliner on the ground as a decoy.

(Informed sources in San Jose stressed that steps taken to protect Roa were perfunctory and did not imply Costa Rica's belief that the plot charges had foundation. They said local authorities first heard of the alleged danger in a handwritten note from the Cuba foreign minister).

Cuban officials also arrested without explanation U.S. newsman Harvey Rosenhouse, Mexico bureau chief of Time Magazine who was on a brief stopover on his way to Puerto Rico.

Whites Quizzed On Firing Shots At Death Car

JACKSONVILLE, Fla. (UPI)—Three white men who fired pistol bullets at Negroes in a speeding car were questiond today by police investigating the first death in four days of racial violence here.

The car slammed into a utility pole, killing the driver and injuring a Negro passenger. An autopsy Tuesday disclosed that the victim, ex-convict Charlie Edward Davis, 27, had been shot in the head.

But police declined to say whether Davis died from the bullet wound or from injuries in the crash.

"He could certainly have been killed in the car accident," said homicide Sgt. W. C. Barber. "He was torn up bad—real bad."

Experience Calm Night

Questioning of the white men, attendants at a service station about one block from the scene of the accident, began as Jacksonville experienced its calmest night in a half-week of racial tempests which have left some 70 persons injured and more than 150 arrested.

The three men, whose identities were withheld, told police earlier they had fired a barrag of bullets at Davis' car as it sped by in a police chase. Their service station had been shot up in an earlier incident Tuesday morning.

Barber said a coroner's inquest probably would be called into the incident which left Davis' companion, 47-year-old Willie Green, severely injured.

Question Police Officers

There were no immediate plans to place charges, pending further questioning, authorities said. Statements also were taken from police officers who took part in the chase of the stolen car Davis was driving, or were at the service station.

The chase began when police officers, patrolling an area which had been hit by vandalism and violence, asked Davis to stop. Instead, he sped away. A fusillade of bullets erupted from the service station as the cars whipped past, and the Negroes' vehicle served out of control and wrecked seconds later.

No gun was found in the car and officers found no bullet holes in the vehicle.

Lawlessness Tuesday night appeared confined to vandalism in some Negro areas despite attempts by the NAACP to break up Negro gangs which have roamed the streets at night.

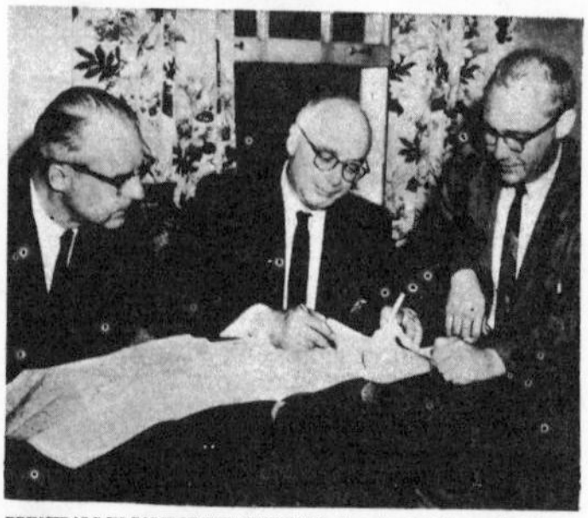

PRINCIPALS IN SALE OF THE BULLETIN—From the left: James H. Ottaway, president, Ottaway Newspapers-Radio, Inc., former publisher of The Daily Bulletin; David Bernstein, president and editor of The Binghamton Sun and Harry S. Milligan, vice-president and general manager, The Sun.

Minimum Wage Fails

Congress Ends Tonight?

WASHINGTON (UPI) — Congress, having spurned the legislative program of Democratic presidential nominee John F. Kennedy, moved today to wind up the rest of its business quickly and go home.

The most optimistic members hoped for adjournment late tonight. The more realistic ones talked about quitting Thursday night.

The drive for speedy adjournment began after a collapse in the efforts to work out a compromise bill to increase the minimum wage from $1 an hour to $1.15 and expand its coverage.

The failure of Congress to produce any minimum wage legislation plunged the issue into the presidential election campaign.

Kennedy, leader of the Senate negotiators, said he would rather measure which conservative conhave no bill than accept the trolled House conferees were willing to give him. So would leaders of organized labor.

The Democratic candidate promptly announced he would "take this fight to the American people." He already had stated he would make campaign issues of other items in his legislative program.

Kennedy also failed to get what he wanted on medical care for the aged, school construction and housing. Congress passed a medical care bill sharply scaled-down from his proposal, while the school and housing measures were bottled up in the House Rules Committee.

The two big issues still to be resolved by Congress were:

—What should be done about President Eisenhower's urgent plea for additional foreign aid funds? This issue probably will be settled on the House floor today. There was a chance that the President would get a part—probably a small part—of the $190 million in extra funds which the Senate voted in response to his appeal.

—Will the lawmakers give Eisenhower the power he wants to stop the Dominican Republic from getting a "windfall" quota to market sugar in the United States? The House approved compromise legislation Tuesday to grant this authority, but the measure ran into trouble in the Senate.

Nixon Banks on Lodge To Pick Up the Slack

WASHCNGTON (UPI) — Vice President Richard M. Nixon counted today on his running mate, Henry Cabot Lodge, to help take up the slack in the Republican campaign while Nixon recovers from a knee infection.

Lodge will not replace Nixon in any of the three out-of-town campaign appearances the GOP presidential nominee had planned for the next week in Jackson, Miss., Charleston, W.Va., and New York City.

But Lodge, who will quit Saturday as United Nations ambassador, will hit the road Tuesday for four consecutive days of campaigning. Lodge's bookings for Tuesday and Wednesday may be announced today. He will appear in Worcester and Lowell, Mass. on Thursday and in Boston on Friday.

Nixon was reported progressing satisfactorily" from the knee infection which will keep him in Walter Reed Army Hospital for about two weeks.

Doctors said the vice president had no fever, a good appetite, and was in good general physical condition, except for "some pain in his left knee."

With Lodge ready for the campaign circuit, Nixon was making the best of his hospitalization by dictating drafts of future speeches and having long telephone consultations with his staff members.

President Eisenhower visited Nixon for 45 minutes late Tuesday and discussed politics, legislation and foreign affairs. Eisenhower also compared his old "football knee" injury of West Point days with Nixon's ailment.

Nixon's infection, medically diagnosed as hemolytic staphylococcus aureus, was being treated with combinations of five antibiotics, primarily erythomycin.

May Ask U.N. Aid

AMMAN, Jordan (UPI)—King Hussein may seek United Nations aid in obtaining the return from the United Arab Republic of two Jordanians suspected of planting the time bombs that killed Premier Hazza Majali and 10 other persons, informed sources said today.

The assassinations Monday of the pro-Western premier and Hussein's accusations of UAR complicity in the plot touched off rumors of troop movements throughout the tense Middle East.

Main Stems

Congratulations to **Barbara (Endicott) Hoagland** who graduated from her teens yesterday with a 20th birthday celebration.

Miss Beth Andrea Paynter, daughter of Mr. and Mrs. William E. Paynter, 205 Hooper Road, Endwell, getting ready to start her college career at Cedar Crest Cottage, Allentown, Pa. She will begin on Sept. 18 a one-week orientation period before classes open.

Ellis (Al) Williams, Endicott, noting that he will have another birthday tomorrow. Insists that he is still 29.

Renamed Sun-Bulletin; WENE Not in the Sale

The Daily Bulletin has been sold to The Binghamton Sun and will be combined with The Sun to be published as a morning newspaper, effective tomorrow.

This announcement was made today by James H. Ottaway, president of Ottaway Newspapers - Radio, Inc., publishers of The Bulletin, and David Bernstein, president of Bernstein & Milligan, Inc., Sun owners.

The combined newspaper will be called The Sun-Bulletin. It will carry full coverage of Endicott area news every day, Monday through Saturday.

Endicott offices of The Sun-Bulletin will continue in the Daily Bulletin building, 911 East Main St., and the editorial, advertising and circulation staffs of The Bulletin will become part of the Sun-Bulletin staff. C. Bernard (Bun) Kuhl, managing editor of The Bulletin, will be in charge of Endicott news coverage for the Sun-Bulletin. John D. DeBiase, Bulletin advertising manager, will head The Sun-Bulletin advertising staff in Endicott. Charles W. Brunner, Bulletin circulation manager, will be the Sun-Bulletin circulation manager in Endicott. Beverly Moyle will be in charge of classified advertising for the Sun in the Endicott office.

Mr. Ottaway said that Radio Station WENE, owned by Ottaway Stations, Inc., will continue to operate at 909 East Main St.

He added:

"Our station is not included in the sale of The Bulletin, nor is the radio station for sale."

Building Not Included

Sale of The Bulletin did not include The Bulletin building at 911 East Main St., nor did it include any of the machinery or other assets of the Bulletin division of Ottaway Newspapers-Radio, Inc.

Charles A. King, editor and general manager of The Daily Bulletin, will remain with the Ottaway organization, which publishes newspapers in Oneonta, Plattsburgh, Middletown, Port Jervis, Stroudsburg, Pa., and Danbury, Conn.

The company also operates radio stations in Oneonta and Stroudsberg in addition to Station WENE in Endicott.

The acquisition of The Bulletin by The Binghamton Sun marks a new chapter in the 138-year history of the oldest newspaper in the Triple Cities, and one of the oldest in New York State.

The Sun, which has a circulation of 31,000, was purchased by Mr. Bernstein and Harry S. Milligan on July 1. Long an organ of the Republican party in Broome County, it was transformed into an independent newspaper. In the two months during which it has been operated the new ownership, many improvements in appearance and content have been made in the newspaper.

The End of an Era

The sale of The Bulletin also marks the end of a newspaper era in Endicott, which began in 1914 when Harry J. Freeland and his wife, Harriet, started publication of The Bulletin as a weekly newspaper.

Five years later it became a semi-weekly, and in November, 1936, it was sold to Mr. and Mrs. James H. Ottaway, with Byron E. French, general manager for many years, retaining an interest in the company.

On Oct. 4, 1937 The Bulletin was changed to a daily newspaper and continued to be published at 113 Washington Ave.

Four years later on Oct. 4, 1941, just before Pearl Harbor, The Bulletin occupied its new newspaper plant at the corner of Lincoln Ave. and Main St.

Radio Center, built in 1947, is

(Continued on Page 2.)

Statement by Ottaway

Sale of The Daily Bulletin and its absorption by The Binghamton Sun naturally brings a tinge of sadness to those of us who gave birth to The Bulletin as a daily in 1937 and who have helped it grow over the years.

But this is tempered by the fact that the best features of The Bulletin will become part of a Sun-Bulletin that will serve Bulletin customers in Western Broome and Eastern Tioga counties exceptionally well.

An equally important and over-riding consideration has been that many employes will continue with The Sun-Bulletin and serve our same customers.

We have great confidence in David Bernstein and Harry Milligan, owners of The Sun, and we are sure that they will serve our local area with a deep interest in its future growth.

This is an interest that has been basic in Bulletin policy the past 24 years. This included support of such civic projects as the original Community Chest (now the United Fund), the local Chamber of Commerce, new schools, expanded hospital facilities and other civic projects essential to our growing communities.

Bulletin employes; Byron E. French, formerly general manager; Charles A. King, editor and general manager; Mrs. Ottaway and our associates would like to thank our many friends for their wonderful friendship and loyalty over the past 24 years.

We still will be in the radio business with Station WENE, but the daily newspaper side of our operation has been acquired by Mr. Bernstein and Mr. Milligan.

We believe you will find yourselves in very good hands, and that The Sun-Bulletin will serve you with distinction and complete satisfaction.

Our thanks again to our many local friends, and especially to The Daily Bulletin staff for its loyalty and good work over the past 24 years.

—James H. Ottaway, Publisher.

Statement by Bernstein

In absorbing The Endicott Daily Bulletin into The Binghamton Sun, we pledge to the people of Endicott, Vestal and Endwell, and to all our readers everywhere, a bigger . . . better . . . stronger . . . more valuable newspaper.

We shall enlarge our coverage of local news of the E-V-E area, as well as of Binghamton, Johnson City and the surrounding countryside.

We shall maintain within this enlarged newspaper the features which have given The Bulletin its personality in the past, adding columns and comic strips to make this newspaper one of the most complete in the country.

We shall absorb into our own organization many of the employes of The Bulletin, who will be needed to produce the larger newspaper.

We shall offer to merchants in Endicott and throughout the Triple Cities an advertising medium geared to their special needs and requirements.

★ ★ ★

To working newspapermen like ourselves, there is no joy when a fine newspaper ends its existence. But the changing scene in the E-V-E area—and its relationship to the Triple Cities, has made continuation of The Bulletin impractical. As part of The Sun, its tradition of service and enterprise will be maintained.

We renew our pledge, made when we purchased The Sun two months ago, to provide the Triple Cities with a first-rate, independent, alert, readable, and intelligent newspaper, that will deserve the respect of its readers. Such a newspaper should properly seek to be the home town paper of all the people in the area it serves, and that is our earnest ambition. This new chapter in the life of The Binghamton Sun, with which The Daily Bulletin is now inextricably interwined, is another step toward the fulfillment of that ambition.

—David Bernstein, President,
Bernstein & Milligan, Inc.

2 Policemen Injured, One Seriously

Gunman Killed in Rockefeller Center Battle

NEW YORK (UPI)—Four young hoodlums fought a running gunbattle with police in tourist-packed Rockefeller Center after a spectacular $10,000 stickup in the RCA building Tuesday.

One gunman was shot dead. Two policemen were injured and in serious condition today. Another gunman was captured and police sought two more, whose identities were known.

No bystanders were hurt.

The gunbattle was witnessed by thousands of shoppers and tourists.

It began after the robbers fled with $10,000 from the currency exchange firm of Lionel, Perera, Manfsa and Brookes, just across from Radio City Music Hall.

The men, their pockets and two paper bags stuffed with U.S. and foreign bills, ran outside and separated, mingling with the crowds.

Thomas Byrnes, 19, a West Side hoodlum believed to be the leader of the holdup team, and a companion hailed a cab driven by Al Greenbaum, 60, and ordered him to "keep on going."

One of the gunmen shot at police through the cab's rear window. The frightened driver slowed down and dashed from the cab to hide in a doorway. All around, pedestrians fled for cover.

One of the gunmen's shots felled Patrolman Donald Baeszler, one of two policemen in Radio City who fired at the fleeing cab. A bullet ripped through his shoulder, chest and back.

The other policeman, Peter Gallagher, 30, a patrolman near retirement age who hadn't used his pistol in 31 years, was grazed on the forehead by a gunman's bullet. He later suffered a heart attack.

Byrnes and a confederate, who eluded police, jumped from Greenbaum's cab and Byrnes commandeered another driven by Patrick Baggio, 23. Baggio drove only a couple of blocks before he was halted in traffic. Byrnes, who had been firing at police from the cab, leaped out and ran.

Byrnes was at the top of a six-foot fence he had scaled when Patrolman George Maine brought him crashing down with four shots. Byrnes staggered to the kitchen entrance of a restaurant, stumbled in and fell dead in front of several horrified employees.

Elsewhere, Dick Jennings, an NBC employee, had seen the gunmen leave the currency exchange firm office and decided to follow one.

Jennings followed the man down the Avenue of The Americas and saw him fling a jacket and a revolver into a trash receptacle. The gunman got in a taxi and told driver William Silverman, 34, to take him to Hoboken "to see my aunt."

Jennings got in a cab and followed, and at the entrance of the Holland Tunnel, while the gunman's cab was stalled in traffic, a patrolman Jennings picked up along the way arrested the suspect at gunpoint. The fleeing man was identified as Charles Tritschler, 25.

The arresting officer was Joseph Vacchiano, 37.

Katange Warns 'Might Destroy Belgium Base'

ELISABETHVILLE, The Congo (UPI)—The Katanga government today threatened to destroy the base of Kamina if the United Nations does not guarantee that Congolese troops will be barred from landing there.

The threat was made in a communique issued by Katanga President Moise Tshombe. The Katanga leader feared the base, which is only lightly held by the U.N.'s 33rd Irish Battalion, could be captured by troops of Congolese Premier Patrice Lumumba and used to subdue the secessionist province.

Following the threat, the U.N. of 100 Swedish troops into Kamina to strengthen the garrison.

The U.N. spokesman in Elisabethville, New Zeland's Jan Berendsen, announced the Swedish movement and also confirmed that the United Nations has "neutralized" the base.

King Appointed To New Post With Ottaway

ENDICOTT — Charles A. King, editor and general manager of The Daily Bulletin, will remain with Ottaway Newspapers-Radio, Inc., it was announced today.

Lyndon R. Boyd, executive vice-president of the Ottaway organization, announced the appointment of Mr King as his assistant.

The appointment is effective tomorrow.

Mr. King came to The Bulletin in 1959 from newspaper posts in Utica and St. Louis, Mo.

Route 17 Crash Is Fatal to 3

MIDDLETOWN (UPI) — Three persons were injured fatally late Tuesday in a two-car head-on collision on the Route 17 Quickway here.

State police said Drew Bickerstaff, about 25, of Miami, Florida, driver of one of the cars, was pronounced dead at the scene.

Mrs. George Stanley, 45, Brooklyn, a passenger in a car driven by her husband, also was killed instantly.

Sarah Williams, about 45, another passenger in the Stanley car, died several hours later in a Middletown hospital of a skull fracture. Police said she also was from Brooklyn.

Troopers said the accident occurred at the intersection of Rts. 17 and 87 when Bickerstaff's car was heading north in the southbound lane of the Quickway.

Bickerstaff, a summer worker in the Catskill resort area, was alone in the car at the time of the accident, police said.

Mrs. Stanley's husband was in critical condition at a hospital.

The end came for the pioneer *Daily Bulletin* August 31, 1960. Next morning it appeared with a temporary joint nameplate.

Jim Ottaway's not-so-cursive handwriting baffled many in the organization. This is a letter to the author dated March 5, 1966, written while vacationing at Water Isle in Barbados. It is decoded at the end of the history.

PROMISSORY NOTE

$12,000,000

New York, New York

January 31, 1966

The undersigned, OTTAWAY NEWSPAPERS-RADIO, INC., a New York corporation (the "Company"), FOR VALUE RECEIVED, hereby promises to pay to BANKERS TRUST COMPANY ("Bankers"), or order, on or before December 15, 1975, at the office of Bankers at 16 Wall Street, New York, New York 10015, the principal sum of Twelve-Million Dollars ($12,000,000) in lawful money of the United States.

The Company promises also to make instalment payments on account of this Note at said office as follows: $400,000 on January 31, 1967; $450,000 on the 31st day of July and on the 15th day of December in the year 1967; $500,000 on the 15th day of each June and December in the years 1968 and 1969; $600,000 on the 15th day of June and on the 15th day of December in the year 1970; $650,000 on the 15th day of June and on the 15th day of December in the year 1971; $700,000 on the 15th day of each June and December in the years 1972 and 1973; and $850,000 on the 15th day of each June and December in the years 1974 and 1975.

The Company promises also to pay interest upon the unpaid principal amount hereof in like money at said office from the date hereof until maturity at the rate per annum of 5-3/4%, and after maturity at the rate per annum of 6%; such interest to be payable quarterly on the fifteenth day of March, June, September and December of each year, commencing March 15, 1966, at maturity (whether by acceleration or otherwise), and upon any prepayment hereon (to the extent thereof).

This Note is referred to in the Loan Agreement dated as of January 31st, 1966 between the Company and Bankers (the "Agreement") and is subject to prepayment, in whole or in part, in certain cases with and in other cases without premium.

In case an Event of Default, as defined in the Agreement, shall occur and be continuing, the principal of and accrued interest on this Note may be declared to be due and payable in the manner and with the effect provided in the Agreement.

OTTAWAY NEWSPAPERS-RADIO, INC.

By _____

This is the note that financed the *New Bedford Standard-Times* and *Cape Cod Standard-Times* acquisition. It marked the largest borrowing in Ottaway history as of 1966, $12 million.

In January 1970, the Ottaways gathered at the *Danbury News-Times* as it entered the world of offset with a brand new press in a brand new building. Jim Sr. pushed the start button as Ruth, Jim Jr., Ruthie and David watched with varied expressions of emotion.

In late 1982 Jim Sr. and Jim Jr. posed for a picture that would appear in *The Bulletin,* a magazine published by the American Society of Newspaper Editors. It illustrated an article on publishing philosophy, written by Jim Sr.

It is September 1967. Lyn Boyd is president of Ottaway Newspapers-Radio, Inc., and Jim Jr. is publisher of the *New Bedford Standard-Times.* The picture was taken at Whiteface Inn near Lake Placid, N.Y., at a meeting of the New York State Publishers Association of which Boyd also was president.

Ottaway headquarters lie in Campbell Hall, N.Y., 60 miles north of New York City. Sometimes elfishly referred to as Camelot, the complex expanded four times over 20 years as the organization grew. The latest addition, the James H. Ottaway Conference Center, appears in the photo below.

William F. (Bill) Kerby, above, president of Dow Jones at the time of merger with Ottaway, became chairman in 1972. He retired in 1977.

Warren Phillips, upper right, succeeded Kerby as president. He was named chairman when Kerby stepped down.

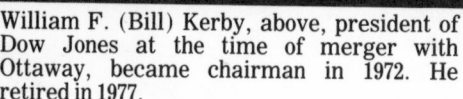

Gene Brown reached age 79 in 1985 and sat for this portrait in the newsroom of the *Danbury News-Times*. He had joined forces with Jim Ottaway back in 1944 in Oneonta.

13 New Bedford/Cape Cod

The precise date has vanished with yesterday's snows. Either late in 1964 or early in 1965, Allen Kander approached Ottaway for the fifth time. The newspaper, radio and television properties of E. Anthony & Sons, Inc., of New Bedford, Massachusetts, were for sale.

Ottaway Newspapers-Radio board minutes of June 23, 1965, indicate that preliminary negotiations had started early that spring, and acknowledge receipt of "necessary financial information" from Charles J. Lewin, president of Anthony, who invited Ottaway, among others, to make a cash offer by July 1 for all the Anthony holdings.

The properties included the daily and Sunday *New Bedford Standard-Times,* the daily and Sunday *Cape Cod Standard-Times,* WNBH, AM/FM, New Bedford; WOCB, AM/FM, West Yarmouth; and a 55 percent interest in WTEV, Inc., a television station serving southeastern Massachusetts, Rhode Island and much of Connecticut. Still another Anthony property was Massachusetts Air Industries, an air taxi service. And there was real estate.

Board minutes quote Ottaway as "summarizing the feeling of all board members . . . that the financial information received from Anthony, backed by our research . . . has created great enthusiasm for this large potential acquisition."

"The question at hand," he said, "was what kind of offer should be made for this long-established, profitable company whose volume (without television) is as great as the volume of ON-R and its subsidiaries combined, and whose position in its area is one of dominance."

Research was handled by Gene Brown, Lyn Boyd and Jim Jr. Observations by all three were positive, but one of Jim Jr.'s comments was ecstatic: "We should do everything we can to get this paper (sic). It will not require a special genius to make it pay for itself many times over."

All agreed that retail display and classified linage "had nowhere to go but up."

"I know," Brown wrote, "that we shall be backing up our observations with a wealth of statistics and other impressions, but on the whole my impression is that if the purchase can be handled financially, it can be operated successfully. Which is sort of redundant, as that is exactly what they (Anthony) have been doing."

Only Jim Jr. alluded to the radio stations: "They look like moderate though healthy businesses. They can't hurt us and would probably allow us to improve all our stations with better management and more attention by a radio specialist at the top."

The board was less than enthusiastic about the TV operation, which had lost money since it opened in early 1962. Lewin's figures, however, suggested the operation could be in the black in fiscal 1965-66.

The first Ottaway offer to Lewin on June 30 for all properties was $10.3 million, with $3 million down and the balance payable over five and one half years at five percent. Lewin declined the installment offer. He wanted cash.

Ottaway returned to his friends at Massachusetts Mutual and Fidelity- Philadelphia for another loan. Not surprisingly, he was turned down.

Newspaper balance sheets do not show material assets, such as inventories, that usually induce bankers to lend. And lending institutions have loan limits. A newspaper's greatest asset is an intangible — the market it serves.

On a Saturday in early July, Ruth and Jim Ottaway were lazing by the indoor pool at Campbell Hall when the phone rang. They had to have been wondering where to turn in the quest for the Massachusetts prize.

The caller was Harold (Specs) Kinsey, a New Jersey resident and Dupont executive. Like the Ottaways, Kinsey was a winter visitor to Water Isle, St. Thomas. He was a member of the self-termed "Gang of Five," who vacationed together, and which included John W. Hannon Jr., first vice president of Bankers Trust Company. All were friends of Ruth and Jim. The Kinsey and Hannon homes were back to back in Upper Montclair, New Jersey.

Kinsey told the Ottaways he had occasion to visit the Hudson Valley and asked for directions. Soon he found himself at Campbell Hall, listening to the chief's financial problems. Kinsey said he might be able to help.

Less than 48 hours later Ottaway received a call from Hannon, who opened the conversation on an airy note: "Hi, Jimbo! I hear you're wheeling and dealing!"

"It requires a very imaginative banking officer" to sponsor a loan of the magnitude Ottaway was seeking, Gene Brown wrote in 1970. The description fit Hannon perfectly. He invited Ottaway to make a presentation.

The Ottaways, Brown, Boyd and Brinkley went to work, "starting from zero," as Brown put it. The company's publishing philosophy, which accounted for its eminent reputation in the Northeast, was restated. Then came group newspaper exhibits, detailed reports on each community Ottaway served, and a five-year cash projection for ON-R and each subsidiary.

The projection of course included anticipated earnings of Anthony, which dwarfed the best of the Ottaway figures. The simple fact was that ON-R earnings were not sufficient to support a loan of the size Ottaway needed.

"In effect we literally pledged our entire assets. Few banks lend on that basis," Jim Jr. observed.

Bankers Trust also studied the Ottaway executive lineup and asked if younger men were being trained for the years ahead. And Hannon asked if continuing Ottaway expansion might dilute the brand of leadership that would insure continuing profitability.

A sidebar stroke of luck found Walter B. Thayer sitting on the Bankers Trust board of directors. Thayer, president of Whitney Communications, believed that newspapers were sound investments. Thayer, Ottaway said, was "very helpful."

The evolution of the loan that sealed the New Bedford deal came in two steps. First, Bankers agreed to lend Ottaway $10.3 million at 5¾ percent to back a cash offer to Lewin. On August 31 Ottaway senior and junior met with Lewin in Boston. Lewin was willing to accept the bid, but excluded the TV station from the package. At the meeting, Ottaway told the board, he was "led to believe" that there was a "substantial number of other prospective buyers "whose offers were substantially higher than ours."

The following day the Ottaway board convened in New York City to "consider the crisis." The chief felt that a "substantially revised offer" should be forwarded immediately to Lewin. He had just returned from another meeting with Bankers, which was willing to back ON-R with a 10-year term loan of up to $12 million, again at 5¾.

The board then voted unanimously to offer Lewin $12.5 million cash for the Anthony properties, excluding the TV station.

Board minutes show Ottaway senior and junior and Lyn Boyd had a "very successful meeting" with Lewin in Boston on September 10. A decision from Lewin "was expected shortly."

Win or lose, Ottaway didn't forget Bankers Trust. Typically he suggested the bank become one of ON-R's corporate depositories. It did, to the tune of $100,000.

It was the least Ottaway could do. Intimates of John Hannon later told the Ottaways that he had put his job on the line. His imagination had not been shared by all his colleagues, including what he called the "beady-eyed" accountants in the loan department.

Hannon had one piece of unfinished business as negotiations came to a head. "Let's take a trip," he said to Ottaway, "to make sure all your properties are where you say they are." The chief shepherded the banking contingent through each location in rugged weather, winding up the arduous tour in Danbury. Hannon and associates also looked over the New Bedford and Cape Cod plants.

Just how many others were in the bidding cannot be determined. But Ottaway knew that the *Boston Globe*, Gannett and Hearst were among them. Jim Jr. recalled Lewin saying that Hearst had offered to top the highest bid by $1 million.

Sometime between September 13 and October 4 word came from Lewin that the Ottaway offer had been accepted. At the October 4 board meeting resolutions were approved ratifying the purchase and the borrowing, and empowering Lyn Boyd to consummate the transactions. Ruth and Jim Ottaway were going abroad. They wanted no delays in their absence.

At the end of the year Orange County Publications, Danbury Publishing Company and the *Oneonta Star* were merged into ON-R "to obtain the necessary financial strength" for better financing terms for the New Bedford purchase.

Kander, despite having given Ottaway entree, took no part in the negotiations. He was confined by illness. Jim, Ruth, Jim Jr. and Boyd carried the load.

Although Lewin, as president, was point man for Anthony, Mrs. Basil Brewer, conservator of the Brewer estate, was in charge. Brewer was a former Scripps- Howard executive from Missouri, who in 1930 took over the 80-year-old New Bedford *Evening Standard* and *Morning Mercury*. After a depression era economic war, he merged them with the *New Bedford Times* in 1932.

Brewer became a majority owner of E. Anthony & Sons and led the company in its development, starting the *Cape Cod Standard-Times*, acquiring radio stations, and founding WTEV-TV and the airline. Because of illness Brewer withdrew from active management in 1962. He died in 1975.

The Cape newspaper was born October 19, 1936, as a special news section of the New Bedford product. It had 22,000 circulation. Thus, of New Bedford's 70,000-plus circulation, nearly a third was sold on the Cape, stuffed into the Cape *Standard-Times*.

Mary Minot Brewer had been anxious to sell to someone who shared the feelings she had about publishing: a deep sense of community responsibility.

"The deal was made because we meshed ideologically," Ottaway said.

Much as they had charmed Mrs. Dunphy in Plattsburgh 14 years before, the Ottaways became close friends with Mrs. Brewer during the weeks preceding the Anthony decision in their favor. That there was an implicit continuity in operational philosophy in the person of Jim Jr. also impressed Mrs. Brewer.

Mary Brewer and Ruth Ottaway even found they shared a persuasion for Unitarianism. The discussion arose during one of their rides through Boston, which took Ruth, Jim and Mrs. Brewer past a Unitarian house of worship, which the women agreed was an architectural triumph.

In the car was a fourth passenger, William H. Carey, counsel to the Brewer estate. During the period leading up to the closing on the Anthony properties, Bill Carey's punctilious manner made a resounding impression on Ottaway and his principals.

Carey would become chief counsel to ON-R. "Integrity plus," Ottaway commented.

"Bill Carey was a tough adversary," Jim Jr. said. "We wanted him on our side."

For the first time Jake Becker did not represent the Ottaways. Bankers Trust insisted that ON-R have a New York lawyer.

Carey would share legal responsibilities with the Beckers for some years, but with what Jim Jr. called the then "Ottaway center of gravity" moving eastward, more and more assignments went to the Bay State attorney.

"There was no aspect of an auction in the sale," Ottaway said later. "The so-called bid deadlines were extended because Mrs. Brewer wanted to study us. I very much doubt she seriously considered anyone else."

On December 7, 1965, a contract was signed for sale of the newspapers, Massachusetts Air Industries and other land, buildings and equipment to Ottaway Newspapers-Radio, subject to approval by Anthony stockholders. At the same time an agreement was signed to sell the New Bedford and Cape radio stations to Ottaway Stations, Inc., subject to shareholder and FCC approval.

Charles Lewin's role under imminent Ottaway ownership was spelled out in a six-point employment contract, also dated December 7, which would take effect at the formal closing, scheduled for January 31, 1966. Lewin held the title of editor and general manager under Anthony ownership. His five-year

160

contract with Ottaway would make him editor and publisher of the *New Bedford Standard-Times* and general manager of what then was to be called the E. Anthony & Sons Division of ON-R. Lewin's salary under Ottaway was pegged at $42,000 for the first year and $50,000 per year for the next four.

Lewin, a native of Wisconsin, started as a police reporter in New Bedford in 1924 after service with the *Rockford* (Ill.) *Morning Star*. He later served as city editor, news editor and managing editor. He was named editor-in-chief in 1937. In 1943 he became editor and assistant publisher and in 1947 was appointed editor and general manager of Anthony.

In 1962 Lewin took over as executive manager of Anthony because of Basil Brewer's illness. Shortly after he was elected president.

Jim Jr. was to move from Danbury to New Bedford as associate publisher. "I was a hostage in the acquisition," he said. "It was $12 million plus me, a sort of guarantee of continuity of operation under Ottaway."

Being a "hostage" also was an oblique allusion to his promise to Mary that the 1965 move to Danbury would be their last. "Mary indeed was unhappy at first," he said. "Our home in Redding was near Newtown, where her parents lived."

Once again he promised Mary there would be no more moves.

"No one wants to move unless there's a challenge involved," his father said. The challenge, the biggest of all, would arise in less than four years.

Mrs. Brewer helped the couple get settled. She found the home they were to occupy, and in Jim Jr.'s words, "found us our friends."

At the time of Mrs. Brewer's death in August 1984, Jim Jr. wrote:

"Mary Brewer was a beautiful human being in every way. She loved and supported her family and friends with her special feminine warmth and spiritual strength. She was a very good friend in spite of our difference in years. When my father and I were negotiating with her . . . Mary Brewer was primarily interested in the welfare of her employees, her newspapers and her communities. She did not sell to the highest bidder."

Among the many documents that changed hands December

7, 1965 was a memorandum from Ottaway to Anthony "confirming our understanding that the death or incapacitating illness of Charles J. Lewin prior to the time of closing shall not be deemed to be a material adverse circumstance in the business or financial condition of Anthony . . ."

It was a legal formality that turned out to be tragically prescient. Charles Lewin, 63, died of a heart attack at his desk December 29. According to the *Standard-Times* story, the indefatigable Lewin had been unable to sleep and had arrived at his office at 7 a.m. G. Everett (Ed) Hill, a Lewin assistant, said both doors to Lewin's office were locked. It was assumed he didn't want to be disturbed.

A farewell editorial said, in part: "The Lewin newspaper day had 24 hours. It began before most employees had taken off their coats. It continued after they had left for the day. It carried into the nights and the weekends. His . . . neighbors knew those late nights meant that the editor was poring over that day's edition. The Sunday schedule meant a careful reading of the newspaper at home or at the office.

"The Lewin newspaper day was lifelong, to the ultimate minute at his desk."

Charles Lewin, in effect, had worked himself to death.

Purchase of the Anthony properties was completed January 31, 1966. The price, after adjustments, was $10,927,212. Ottaway announced creation of a new newspaper division, the Standard-Times Publishing Company, which would operate the New Bedford and Cape Cod papers and the airline.

Long-term debt of ON-R and affillitates had reached $12,392,000 as 1966 began. Bankers Trust was owed $12 million. The balance consisted of family, real estate and machinery loans that Ottaway chose not to retire as part of the BT arrangement.

The 1964 notes held by Massachusetts Mutual and Fidelity Philadelphia were retired.

As if John Hannon's role in the acquisition was not pivotal enough, he refused to raise the 5¾ interest rate set in mid-1965, even though the prime lending rate had advanced several points by the time of the closing.

Jim Jr., predictably was appointed publisher and general

manager at 27. Lewin's death had thrust him into the No. 1 post, for which he had been preparing since 1960.

He settled into a fifth-story office well before the closing, working with the management team. And at graveside services for Lewin he met most of the community leaders with whom he would be dealing.

"When I took over, it was a terrifying moment," he said. "I was nervous, having had no previous experience as the overall chief. But the department heads rallied around me and gave me the support I needed."

Jim Jr.'s responsibilities at the outset included running the *Cape Cod Standard-Times*. But it wasn't long before he told Lyn Boyd that he couldn't be the publisher of two papers and do the job properly. His decision flowed from an operational concept laid down in a memo dated January 8, 1966, which urged an immediate study of the feasibility of splitting the New Bedford and Cape papers.

Lewin had had three executive assistants, Dan Gaylord, Robert O'Neill and Ed Hill, the latter having been appointed in 1964 after years in Italy as editor of the *Rome Daily American.*

Gaylord, business manager in New Bedford, soon was dispatched to the Cape as general manager. Jim Jr. and O'Neill had a serious falling out and O'Neill was terminated. Hill became assistant to the publisher. "Ed thought he was going to be fired," Jim Jr. recalled, presumably on the last-in, first-out principle. Instead, Hill would shuttle between New Bedford and Campbell Hall over the next 12 years, serving as general manager of the *Standard-Times* and as an assistant vice president at corporate headquarters.

The Gaylord appointment didn't work. In 1967 he was replaced by Bill Lundquest, who was given the titles of publisher and general manager. Lundquest had served as a corporate vice president since 1961.

Rumors that the Anthony empire would be sold first had surfaced in 1965. Gerald T. (Gerry) Tache, then advertising director in New Bedford, said the Ottaway name never came up in the "apprehensive" water cooler discussions over who might acquire the properties.

Just days before his death Lewin broke the news of the sale to

Ottaway at a meeting of department heads. Jim, Jim Jr. and Lyn Boyd were introduced.

Tache said he was ecstatic. He had reason to be.

In 1964 Lewin, who was not considered an enthusiastic promoter of the American Press Institute, sent Tache to an advertising seminar. Rather he "allowed" me to go, Tache said. The first discussion leader was Boyd, whose principal subject was budgeting. "Boyd was outstanding," Tache recalled. "It was my first impression of what the Ottaway organization must be like. We hadn't done much budgeting in New Bedford."

"When I spotted Lyn at the introductory meeting I had the greatest feeling. I knew we were in good hands. And I told everyone just that."

Veterans of Cape publishing say that Basil Brewer never visited his Hyannis outpost. So it was with Lewin, whose only link to Hyannis was the telephone. (Lewin detested driving. If he had to travel, he was chauffeured.) Lewin's intra-plant visits were just as limited. "He visited the ad department once during my tenure," Tache said. "He never set foot in the composing room. But he did involve himself with the editorial department."

In contrast, Tache recalled, Jim Jr. "was everywhere."

If the new publisher was nervous, Tache said, it wasn't perceived by department heads. "I would say he had a quiet confidence, knowing of the great back-up talent he had at Campbell Hall and at New Bedford. He wasn't a tough publisher. He was even handed, fair."

Jim Jr. followed the same exhausting routine he had practiced in Danbury, Middletown and Stroudsburg. Sixty or seventy-hour weeks were common. Weekends were not for relaxation.

At one point a solicitous Francis Brinkley warned the publisher against burnout. "Many people are depending on you," the treasurer counseled.

Part of the time was invested in cultivating community leaders. "He met and cultivated every important person in our circulation area," Hill said.

When Hill was assigned to Campbell Hall in 1968, Tache

became assistant to the publisher and on Jim Jr.'s ascension to the presidency in 1970 was elevated to general manager, then publisher. Tache would go on to become a corporate vice president.

Orren B. Robbins, publisher of the *Traverse City* (Mich.) *Record-Eagle* since September 1979, was a classified ad salesman on the Cape when Ottaway ownership began. Shortly after he was promoted to classified manager.

"Once the Ottawazation process began," he recalled, "there was an obvious division of employees into two distinctly different camps: those of us who saw the change of ownership as positive — a real opportunity to learn something about the business and to have some kind of future — and those who resented the fact that the party was over and that things had to be done in a certain way at a certain time, and that there was an accounting for one's actions at last.

"I was amazed that anyone could possibly not think that we were much better off under the new ownership. But some people just couldn't stop grumbling about how bad things had gotten. Most of those who were unhappy dropped by the wayside in the first year or so."

So much for Brewer-Lewin absentee management style.

Robbins recalled that the first employee party ever held on the Cape was staged by the Ottaways. There was an open bar (another first for most of the guests) with the new owners very much available and eager to listen.

One of the obligations inherited with the Anthony acquisition was an employee retirement plan, which was directly responsible for the formation of an overall Ottaway pension program, started in June 1967. It carried the formidable title of "Retirement Plan for Employees of Participating Divisions and Subsidiaries of Ottaway Newspapers-Radio, Inc."

Before 1967 ON-R was handling pensions on what Ottaway called "a case-by-case basis" in the form of deferred compensation agreements. Application of that system was limited to corporate executives, publishers and general managers. The new program encompassed all employees.

The deferred compensation agreements for the most part were scrapped when the new pension plan took over, it, in effect, being more generous. The pension system, however, could not match retirement awards to Gene Brown and Lyn Boyd. Their agreements continued.

Retirement plans of newspapers joining the group from 1976 on eventually were absorbed into the Ottaway system. Today the program, administered by Bankers Trust, has assets in excess of $18 million.

Jim Jr.'s first appointment was that of J. Richard (Dick) Early as editor. Early had been executive editor since 1962.

"The *Standard-Times* had always been a very conservative, right-wing paper," he said. "My challenge was to attain a more moderate, midstream stance. Dick Early supported this concept with vigor."

John H. Rogers remained as editor on the Cape.

During his research tour in New Bedford and on the Cape in 1965, Jim Jr. must have realized that although the combination package had served a useful purpose when the Cape *Standard-Times* was founded, there now were compelling reasons to split the two dailies but retain the Sunday link.

The *Cape S-T* was created in 1936, just 10 days after the appearance of a new daily in Hyannis, the *Cape Cod Colonial*. The *Colonial* threatened the circulation which the *New Bedford S-T* had established on the Cape. The *Colonial* prided itself on being the first Cape daily and championed itself with the slogan "We Build the Cape, Not the Off-Cape City." After 13 months the *Colonial* folded. The *Cape S-T* had an enormous advantage over the *Colonial,* with a news-gathering and distribution staff already at work for the New Bedford paper. It started with a paid circulation of almost 8,000.

In 1966 the forced, home-delivered combination of the dailies on the Cape cost 42 cents a week. It meant that the *New Bedford S-T* was literally given away six days a week. With 22,000 Cape circulation the newsprint bill alone for that segment then was running about $200,000 a year. Circulation revenue split was

166

55-45 percent, with the smaller portion going to the Cape, which absorbed the full cost of distribution.

Jim Jr. also discovered that a "fierce spirit of independence" permeated the Cape staff, from publisher on down. The mood was for breaking away.

Cape advertisers resented the combination. They felt New Bedford advertising was hurting them. Some New Bedford advertisers also were displeased, feeling they were paying for circulation which was unproductive. Sears Roebuck, for example, considered that its ads were helping its own outlet on the Cape, which did not have to foot the bills.

Tache's department was selling New Bedford linage on the basis of 46,000- 50,000- off-Cape circulation and telling advertisers the Cape circulation was a bonus. The rate card, Jim Jr. concluded, was reasonably calibrated for 50,000 circulation, but not for 70,000.

Back in 1966 Tache called the shot on what would happen to the rate card if a split was sanctioned — nothing. "We'd simply take away their 'bonus,' " he told the publisher, "with a minimum of trouble." Which is exactly what happened when the break finally came January 1, 1971.

The "split project," as it was known, was literally studied to death over four years. Successive reports came to the same conclusion — let's do it!

The Sunday *Standard-Times* editions were divorced in September 1973. The final bridge was burned exactly two years later when the nameplate was changed to the *Cape Cod Times*. Nine years had elapsed since the Cape began its struggle to end what it believed was a damaging identity gap.

When Bill Lundquest retired in 1969, he was succeeded by Al DeLuca, publisher in Plattsburgh. When DeLuca retired in April 1972, he was replaced by Scott Himstead, the present publisher. Himstead joined Ottaway in Danbury in January 1967, working in the classified and editorial departments. Five months later he was assigned to Campbell Hall as an assistant to Jim Ottaway Sr. His career on the Cape began in 1968 as assistant to Lundquest. He was promoted to general manager under DeLuca.

Successively, Lundquest, DeLuca and Himstead on the Cape

side, and Jim Jr. and Tache on the New Bedford side, never were far apart in principle. A succession of operational vice presidents also smiled on the plans. It was best for both papers economically. And for the Cape there was a spiritual advantage. Call it manifest destiny.

Then why the filibuster after all intra-organization differences had been resolved, not to mention documented reader and advertiser preference for a true Cape Cod daily?

The thick "split file" is remarkable for what it does not contain —— explicit reaction from Jim Ottaway, now chairman of the board. A few memos carry the notation "Please see me on this," or "This is too vague, pin it down." There is not one clue that Ottaway either opposed the split or favored it.

Yet it is logical to assume he kept it on the back burner. With the acquisition of the *New Bedford Standard-Times* he had become the prideful owner of a 70,000 circulation newspaper. It was the flagship of the 1960s. Understandably he was reluctant to lop off the piggy-back Cape's 22,000 subscribers.

At the time of the split New Bedford ranked No. 1 in terms of total dollars of operating profit. It would remain in first place until the mid-1970s, when Middletown took the lead.

Jim Jr.'s publisher's chair was barely warm when the New Bedford paper was struck by a Teamster local, embracing district circulation managers and delivery truck drivers. The strike centered on Ottaway's refusal to grant the unit a closed shop.

"They thought they had a pigeon in me as the new publisher," he said. The strike lasted almost a year.

Lyn Boyd, still eager to do battle on the union front, took charge. He marshaled 15 circulation managers and district managers from other Ottaway locations, set up a war room with specific assignments for *Standard-Times* executives, hired off-duty police and had his troops drive and ride shotgun. The strike finally was settled by union members themselves.

Revulsed by Teamster harassment, beatings and threatening phone calls to wives, they decertified the union.

The *Standard-Times* was able to continue publication because the printers, led by Henry Tabet, president of the local, were instructed to honor their contract. The word came from Joe Bingel, an International Typographical Union officer. Joe Bingel had always been a good friend of the Ottaway organization.

Jim Jr. lost 10 pounds during the tumult. Soaking wet, he weighed in at 110.

Four years after the New Bedford acquisition Gene Brown asked Ed Hill to set down his impressions, before and after Ottaway ownership.

"I was impressed at once with what I might now call the triple-A qualities of the new owners — the autonomy entrusted to each newspaper, the availability of expert guidance from headquarters, and the top-level attitude toward people as human beings, not merely as doers of work," Hill wrote.

"These original reactions have been bolstered by everything that has followed in my four full years with the Ottaways — not only in my own personal case, but in my observation of operations at Campbell Hall and all along the line."

"These qualities, I believe, are accepted rather casually by many, but my background also includes 12 years with another, larger group where the strictures imposed from above were numerous and sometimes stifling. I am also aware of the even harsher central control in the days when 'The Boss' sent his messages from San Simeon daily.

"If I had to compress my feeling about Campbell Hall control into one sentence, I would say: The two paramount management requirements are an honest day's work on the part of all employees and the production of good newspapers. These are certainly not hard to live with.

"Their success, I think, has been reflected in the steady growth and product improvement at all locations."

"Until recently, the weakest part of the group operation has been the lack of development of backup people for key positions at virtually all the newspapers. I think the blame falls not only on Campbell Hall, but also on each location."

"There has been, however, a complete turnaround in this area during the last two or three years. At New Bedford, we have an ambitious set of training programs under way. I know that similar programs have started, or are about to start at other locations."

"An important supplement to these on-site programs has been the seminar program at Campbell Hall. Inspired by Lyn Boyd, these sessions have made an invaluable contribution to the group."

"I discovered, during my tenure with the program, that its good went far beyond the cerebral sessions with experts in every field of newspapering. I found that Ottaway people from Plattsburgh to Pocono, from Cape Cod to Middletown, get to know each other and learn that their problems are not peculiar but universal. This one development sent people back to their home publications relaxed and ready to apply the lessons learned at the seminar — with an opposite number's face and name to call for assistance or advice.

"The seminars also give Ottaway people a chance to see Campbell Hall as it really is and to dispel the fiction that it is a 'memo factory.' To say nothing of the valuable contacts with the men who make up the executive team.

"Another plus factor for the group is the exchange of personnel. It gives one the feeling of belonging to something much larger than his own newspaper; to an organization that rewards ability and encourages good performance."

John Ackerman, veteran of both the Brewer-Lewin and Ottaway regimes, acclaimed Jim Jr's "competent and compassionate" leadership in a look-back written 19 years after the acquisition:

"At the *Standard-Times,* we knew the newspaper was for sale. But to whom? What would any new owners do? What would they change? We knew the *Standard-Times* would survive. But in what guise? Would it be the newspaper we knew? Would it be the newspaper where we had enjoyed working for many years?

"We were relieved when we heard the Brewer family had resolved to sell the paper only to some company that would, in effect, keep the *Standard-Times* as it was, a model small city daily where a staff united by respect and camaraderie would continue to put out an exemplary product. We rejoiced that the paper would not be sold to the equivalent of a Rupert Murdoch. And we were elated to hear the Brewers had turned down offers from such sorts.

"When the news came that the Ottaways were buying, I must confess it did not reassure us at first . . . until we were told about the Ottaway family of newspapers, their credo with respect to their newspapers, their belief in local autonomy and their dedication to good newspapering. It rapidly became apparent to us that the Brewers had kept their word; they sold the *Standard-Times* to a company that shared the ideals, the goals, the outlook of the New Bedford daily. Reassuring too, was the announcement that Charles Lewin would continue to manage the newspaper.

"That plan tragically never came to pass; Lewin died in 1965. Jim Jr. became publisher; Dick Early became editor. For those of us on the staff, the transition was unbelievably smooth. Jim, as he quickly became to all of us, proved a competent and compassionate leader, one who went out of his way to familiarize himself with every aspect of life in New Bedford and with every detail of the *Standard-Times*. A man of taste, education and culture, he fitted the Lewin mold and that of Lewin's predecessors. He was, accordingly, welcomed to New Bedford.

"Some things did, of course, change . . . for the better. Staff salaries and benefits began a climb that still continues. Led by Jim, guided by Early, the *Standard-Times* continued to offer superior news coverage, continued to be a respected medium of information.

"The newspaper acquired a new publisher, Gerald Tache, when Jim Ottaway left New Bedford. Jim was missed and still is, by many of us who knew him. Under Tache, the newspaper began to move into the electronic age, a move that began to pick up speed after Dick Early retired in 1975 and James Ragsdale took over the editorial command.

"Linotypes, familiar for more than a century, bowed out before photo-offset

170

cold-type techniques. The old press that had shaken the building since the 1930s fell silent forever when a brand new printing plant offering color capabilities was built and opened in Fairhaven. (One of the first triumphs of color came with the *Standard-Times* Bicentennial issue of July 4, 1976.) The newspaper was altered to take advantage of the new color capabilities and the superior reproduction afforded by offset printing. The newspaper was redesigned and the word 'graphics' was much in evidence as pages began to brighten with the introduction of colorful maps, charts, illustrations and color photos.

"But, in essence, 19 years after the Ottaways took over, the *Standard-Times* remains what it was . . . a first-class small city daily, covering its beats with the same fidelity it has always mustered."

Mass Air, Inc. was a Basil Brewer creation. It was formed to insure same-day delivery of the *Standard-Times* to the islands, Nantucket and Martha's Vineyard. Besides ferrying newspapers it provided charter service and flight instruction.

But Mass Air never flew, profitwise.

During the long merger discussions with Dow Jones the Ottaways discovered that their air force would not be a part of the transaction. Just as Bill Kerby had ruled that Ottaway must sell his radio stations, citing "too much governmental control," so did he insist that the family dispose of Mass Air. The same concept prevailed.

"To clean up the deal," as Jim Jr. put it, "Ruthie, David and I bought it." The Ottaway children ran it for five years, finally selling to Executive Airlines, a northeastern commuter operation.

"We sold the assets and took back a mortgage on the five aircraft. Within a year Executive went bankrupt. The day before, Executive's lawyer called and urged us to 'get those planes out of the hangar before it's padlocked.' We wheeled them across the airport and hid them behind some trees. Finally we sold them for $90,000 to satisfy part of the debt."

Late in the 1970s New Bedford relinquished its island circulation to the *Cape Cod Times*. The papers now were going to the islands aboard a Massachusetts Steamship Authority vessel, which sailed from Woods Hole. Scott Himstead closed both bureaus and eliminated carrier delivery. Circulation on

171

the islands always had been an out-of-pocket luxury item.

One of the most glittering Ottaway dinner parties took place at a perfumed French restaurant during the American Newspaper Publishers Association (ANPA) convention in New York City in 1966, the "New Bedford year."

The affair began in the Ottaway suite in the Waldorf Astoria where his corporate executives and field marshals were liberally sluiced with cheering potions. Jim Ottaway now was the proprietor of eight newspapers and three radio stations, all profitable. He had attained major league status.

The celebrants made their way to Le Voisin in limousines (except for Jim Jr., who insisted the Kings join him on a bus for the ride uptown. "Taxis are too expensive.") The food was Lucullan, covering the alphabet of gastronomy from asparagus to zwieback. The service was impeccable. And the tab reflected the ambience. As some might say, it was out of sight.

Ottaway turned to Boyd. "Got any money?"

"About $30."

Boyd knew what he had to do: open a corporate charge account on the spot. The party thanked the host, unaware that once again the chief had entertained on empty pockets, also in world class style.

Since May 1966, the framed doggerel below has hung in Jim Sr.'s office. It was typed on a *Standard-Times* letterhead.

> Dear Father:
> I want to send you an important statement: To Dad
>   When I was just a little boy,
>   You filled me with ambition —

And then you took me in the firm
and gave me a position;
Secretly, behind your back
Your stock I have acquired;
I now own 51 percent
And guess what Dad?
You're fired!

Sincerely,
Jimmy

P.S.: Perhaps we can work out a deal by which
you could be retained as a New Bedford office boy.

The playful spoof was just that, no more. Jim Jr. did not personally own 51 percent. "I was kidding my father, who had set up our family stock holdings to be sure that one person was in charge if he died. He didn't like an unequal division of his estate among three well-loved children, but he feared dissension over dividends, capital spending and management decisions that we see all the time in family-owned newspapers that are put up for sale as the final solution to family arguments."

The guest list for the 1966 Buck Hill Falls get-together for Ottaway executives predictably included Vivian and John Hannon. After dinner on the opening night of the three-day stand, corporate officers, publishers and general managers discovered that the lanky man of mortgages had a penchant for communal singing. Hannon's boundless repertoire included everything from traditional barber shop ballads to the most recent tunes of Broadway.

Hannon didn't sing alone. His minstrelsy was contagious. Time was on the side of the bourbon old-fashioneds. There was nowhere to go until tomorrow. People forgot he was a banker. They reveled in the sing-alongs that echoed among the Pocono hills.

Hannon performances over the years took on the same urgency as golf, tennis or bridge. Call him the Mitch Miller of the money tree.

14 Boyd becomes president

It was a time to catch a corporate breath.

The years 1967 and 1968, from an acquisition standpoint, were torpid. The next acquisition would not come until April 1970, preceding by two weeks an agreement to merge Ottaway with Dow Jones & Company, Inc.

Ottaway did have an opportunity to buy the *Fall River* (Mass.) *Herald News* but with the Anthony acquisition he had reached the limit of his borrowing power.

But the chief had not run out of surprises.

In 1967 Gene Brown's 1952 prophecy came to pass. Lyndon Boyd was moved up to the presidency. Jim Ottaway became chairman of the board, Brown vice chairman.

Francis Brinkley, who had been a vice president for radio and treasurer, was named financial vice president and treasurer.

"I never, never believed I'd be president," Boyd said.

Boyd's home phone rang one night in mid-spring. It was Ottaway, who said he'd like to stop by for a few minutes. Why at this hour, Boyd wondered.

Ottaway drove up the steep dirt road to the Boyd aerie and broke the news. They toasted the promotion with 25-year old brandy. The chairman always liked to surprise his associates.

"There were no substantial changes during my presidency," Boyd said. "Jim never wanted to return to direct operation after I took over."

Boyd said that from the day he was appointed Ottaway's assistant, back in the 1950s, he "never wanted to intrude." Even as president, he said, he felt "that looming figure of Jim Ottaway in the background."

175

Boyd's term lasted three years. He had planned to retire in 1968 and even had bought a home in Myrtle Beach, South Carolina, that year. But Ottaway prevailed on his president to stay until 1970. "I'll never ask you to postpone retirement again." Then, as part of the arrangement with the chairman, Boyd entered a relaxing routine: work in the morning, golf in the afternoon.

Boyd's deep commitment to his publishers and general managers was underscored not long after he became president. To further reward the field generals he provided each with a company car with all attendant expenses paid.

The cars were not in lieu of periodic salary increases; they enhanced them.

Well before retirement Boyd appeared in the chief's office and announced, "I have chosen my successor."

"I've talked to some of our publishers," he told Ottaway, "and they want Jimmy."

"You're just trying to polish the apple," the chairman retorted.

"You know damn well I've never done that," Boyd shot back.

Boyd thought Ottaway was surprised.

In Boyd's mind Jim Jr. would get the seasoning he needed in New Bedford.

"I was going. It was obvious a change was coming. It would have been pointless to have an interim president. The question was simple: 'Who would be the best?' Jimmy was the logical choice."

What did Jim Jr. think of the lame duck president's proposal?

"I'm hearing about it for the first time," he told the author in late 1984.

Lyn and Eda Boyd went south at the end of August 1970, a few weeks after the merger with Dow Jones.

Publisher Elton Hall had been drafted from Oneonta to fill the corporate vacancy at Campbell Hall caused by Bill Lundquest's move to Cape Cod. Don Clifford succeeded Hall, but as general manager.

In Middletown King was named publisher, the third general manager to receive the title. Van Kleeck moved up to assistant GM. Concurrently, Allan Meath was promoted to general

176

manager in Danbury.

Ed Somers became the fourth and last radio general manager to move into the print medium. Boyd had assigned him to Middletown for a stepped-up training program. Within five months Somers went to Port Jervis as general manager, and in a couple of weeks added the title of editor when he parted company with Dan Dwyer.

"I also swept the floor and helped deliver papers," Somers recalled.

Before Boyd's promotion he had announced a realignment of organizational responsibilities at Campbell Hall.

Lundquest had been named vice president of the New England division of ON-R and Steve Ryder had been given a similar role involving the New York and Pennsylvania properties.

Ottaway and Boyd, the memo said, would be responsible for "overall operations."

The purpose, Boyd said, "was to achieve more active management. Jim was looking for a better program to achieve better newspapers."

The program lasted only six weeks, ending when Lundquest went to the Cape. Even so Ottaway told Boyd he had misgivings about the sort of "competition" that plan might foster.

"In short," Boyd said, "we restored the monarchy."

On January 1, 1968, minutes of the annual meeting of ON-R stockholders report the dissolution of the trusts in behalf of Jim Jr., David and Ruthie. The shares were transferred to the beneficiaries, who now would vote them personally.

Common shares were held as follows:

James H. Ottaway Sr.	168
Ruth B. Ottaway	48
David B. Ottaway	743
James H. Ottaway Jr.	914
Ruth Ottaway Sherer	532
Eugene J. Brown	128
Trust of children of Ottaway Jr.	600

The following June shareholders and directors convened at Campbell Hall, the former representing all first and second preferred and all common stock.

Ottaway reported that under the existing capital structure of the corporation the value of each share of common had become worth approximately $1,650, which he called "unwieldy and difficult to deal with." He recommended a 20-for-1 split, which was approved.

Executive shuffles continued in 1968.

Van Kleeck's stay at the *Times Herald-Record* ended in April. He was transferred to Campbell Hall as an assistant vice president. In turn, Milt McLean came to the *Times Herald-Record* as business manager. Dick Barker moved to the Hall as an administrative assistant and moved out in months to be assistant to Gerry Tache in New Bedford.

In 1968, a presidential election year, Jim Ottaway was drawn into an endorsement he later described as "one of the worst mistakes I ever made."

He had greatly admired the cut of Nelson Rockefeller's jib.

But that was long before the late Republican governor of New York said to a senior aide on the occasion of Democrat Hugh L. Carey's first inauguration: "Poor Hugh. I spent all the money. It's no fun being governor of New York if you haven't got the money."

The total state budget was $1.9 billion in the 1959-60 fiscal year, the first spending plan Rockefeller put together after his election in 1958. By 1972 the budget had soared to $8.7 billion. Even that does not tell the complete fiscal history of the Rockefeller era. The state debt was $1.24 billion when Rockefeller took office, $14.2 billion when he left. There had been eight general tax increases.

As governor of the nation's then most populous and prestigious state, scion of one of the few legitimately imperial families of the nation, he considered it his birthright to be president.

Before the 1960 presidential election he had considered Richard Nixon's lead insurmountable. He fought for the 1964 nomination, but his divorce and remarriage helped lead to a Barry Goldwater victory. At first Rockefeller backed Michigan's George Romney for the 1968 race. But Romney faltered——badly.

Rockefeller's announcement that he would run set the stage for an unprecedented Ottaway personal endorsement.

Before the Miami convention his publishers and editors received an editorial, written and signed by the chief himself, urging Rockefeller's nomination.

Legend has it that the endorsement was to appear on Page 1 at all locations. Not so. But the order was clear: Run it. Which all points did.

Not surprisingly some publishers assumed that the spirit of local autonomy had flown on gossamer wings. Lyn Boyd typically set things straight: "Endorse whomever you wish, but run the Ottaway article. He owns the newspapers."

It would be five years before the extent of Rockefeller's spending would be known. In 1968 he hadn't even begun the South Mall in Albany, which would cost $1.2 billion, enough to build a high school for each of the 700-plus districts in the state.

By that time Ottaway's admiration had turned to a galling distaste for the fiscal policies of the governor.

Ottaway's editorial never was intended to preempt his publishers.

His position on endorsements was clearly stated in October 1960. With Ruth, he was visiting Jim Jr. and Mary in Greece. Their wedding trip was about to end.

Gene Brown cabled the chief from Danbury. He was considering endorsing John F. Kennedy, locked in a close battle with Richard Nixon. "Should I?" he asked, uncharacteristically.

Jim and Jim Jr. left their hotel for the cable office. The chief's reply was right to the point: "Make up your mind."

Ruth nearly wept. Jim Jr. also was upset.

"That," Ottaway counseled, "is what local autonomy is all about."

(Brown's version of the episode appears in Chapter 23 as a part of his 1979 valedictory on the occasion of Jim Ottaway's retirement as chairman of ONI.)

179

Jim Jr.'s reaction to a 1972 endorsement by the Middletown paper proved that the spirit of local autonomy, if anything, was even stronger.

As a simple matter of courtesy King phoned Campbell Hall to advise the president that the *Times Herald-Record* would support George McGovern over Nixon. (It was the only paper in the group that did.)

"I'm glad someone is," he replied.

☆ ☆ ☆ ☆ ☆ ☆

On May 22, 1969, a totally unexpected all-points message from Campbell Hall announced a "new assignment" for Gene Brown. Effective June 1, the notice said, he would "relinquish" his post as publisher in Danbury and "assume the presidency of Ottaway News Service." The message was signed by Ottaway.

The eighth paragraph of the advisory said that Brown "will continue in his overall corporate position as vice chairman of the ON-R board."

In effect, a new title had been created for Brown, now 63. ONS had never had a president. "Basically," Ottaway wrote, "Gene will oversee the activities of this division of ON-R, including our Albany and Washington coverage, but, most important of all, his prime activity will be devoted to his own love, writing."

Bob Van Fleet, for six years ONS chief, presumably had a new layer of authority between himself and President Boyd. Concurrently Allan Meath replaced Brown as publisher. John Van Kleeck, who had moved to Danbury the first of the year, was appointed general manager.

It is clear that the decision to move Brown laterally was a crushing blow to the 25-year veteran of the Ottaway wars.

"It is one subject I will not discuss," he told the author.

Intimates suggest that his silence was a gesture of undiluted loyalty to the Ottaways and Boyd. He accepted his new post with apparent cheer. If there was rancor, it never surfaced.

His associates in Danbury agreed that Brown most wanted to be at the helm during the coming once-in-a-lifetime transition to offset and a move to a new plant.

Nor was Ottaway willing to say much about the shift. "Gene wasn't training people; he wasn't bringing them along," was the chief's only comment.

Boyd, to whose lot it fell to break the news to Brown, said "several" matters led to the change.

Interviews with Meath and Van Kleeck indicated the break came during a circulation strategy meeting with Brown, during which the publisher said he had "little faith" in the new general manager's ability to handle a promotion project.

"Essentially," Meath said, "I felt John had been destroyed."

Brown set up an office at Campbell Hall, adjacent to Van Fleet's, and commuted from Danbury a couple of days a week.

"I never received any direct orders from Gene," Van Fleet recalled. "Whatever he had in mind for stories came in the form of suggestions. Occasionally we traveled together, doing research for several series of articles.

"Although Gene's presence at Campbell Hall didn't last very long, he took to his new assignment with characteristic vigor."

The end of 1969 also saw ON-R exercise its long-standing stock repurchase agreement with Brown, who held 42 shares of first preferred, 256 shares of second preferred and 2,560 shares of common. Brown's holdings, estimated to be worth $350,000, were the last outside the Ottaway family.

Brown did not retire formally until after the merger with Dow Jones, when he became managing director of Seamount Radio.

His dedication to Ottaway is reflected in a letter dated May 3, 1970, just after the merger agreement was signed.

"I am as excited and enthusiastic about the prospective merger as if I were still on the firing line. Certainly I shall always be available for any personal contribution that I can make to you and the family."

Brown also submitted an undated resignation from the Ottaway board.

"Even during the interim period," he wrote, "there may be subjects coming before the board which will be of such nature (to) require discussion among those who will participate in future management."

His resignation letter was sent "with gratitude for the many years of pleasant association.''

Not the words of one harboring resentment.

Meantime on Cape Cod, Bill Lundquest, 57, asked to be relieved, citing poor health. Thirty years had passed since he joined Ottaway in Endicott. He was succeeded by Al DeLuca, who moved to the *Cape Cod Standard-Times* from Plattsburgh as publisher. Ben Turnbull was named publisher of the *Press-Republican.*

And in another display of corporate generosity, the Ottaways sold the WENE building in Endicott to the First Southern Baptist Church for $50,000. The property had a market value in excess of $160,000.

As far back as January 1966 the ON-R board was discussing the inevitable: a new plant, press and related equipment for the *Danbury News-Times*. At the time, the minutes show, Gene Brown said he wasn't prepared to recommend a new letterpress or a shift to offset. But to protect the price, at least until mid-1967, he put down a $10,000 binder with Goss, which froze the price of a six-unit letterpress at $757,000 and a six-unit offset press at $856,000. Back then the anticipated expense for the project was pegged at $1.4 million, which included purchase of the First National Stores (Finast) building on Main Street. The store would become the nucleus of the new plant.

With clearance from Bankers Trust, Ottaway borrowed $1.1 million from the City Trust Company of Danbury, with interest pegged at ½ percent over prime. The financing was to cover the Finast remodeling, five and one half units of Metro offset and related equipment, photo composition in the composing room and the additional construction.

The press cost $773,869, not counting installation. Fourteen years later the *Danbury News-Times* would add two and a half more Goss units at double the price of the first five and one half.

Total expenditures for the massive 1969 project topped $1.8 million.

William Webb Sunderland, son of the architect who designed the old *Danbury News* building in 1893, and grandson of its builder, was chosen architect for the conversion of the market and the spacious additions that would be needed for the circulation and mechanical departments. The new plant would become the largest taxpayer on Main Street.

Richard A. (Dick) Myers, a friend of Meath's from their St. Petersburg, Florida, tours, joined the *News-Times* in 1968 as retail advertising manager. He was ad director of the *Quincy* (Mass.) *Patriot- Ledger*. In mid-1969 he was promoted to ad director. Forrest C. Palmer also came aboard in 1968 from the *Waterbury* (Conn.) *Republican* as executive editor, mainly overseeing the news operation. The veteran Steve Collins was in charge of the editorial page.

Both Myers and Palmer would, in turn, become publishers of the *News-Times*.

As 1969 drew to a close Meath sold the soon-to-be abandoned historic nineteenth century plant for $124,000. It had served nobly for more than seven decades.

On January 19, 1970, the paper made the switch to photo composition, offset printing and a six-column format.

September 1969 also saw the appearance of the *Sunday Record* in Middletown. King had received a green light the preceding May following protracted research, which included interviews with publishers from all areas of the country who recently had launched Sunday papers. Their advice was threefold: "Don't expect an immediate increase in retail display linage. You will get one seventh more classified automatically. And force home delivery to a seven-day set up, i.e., no six-day subscribers."

The advice was prescient. Financially, the *Sunday Record* was not an immediate success. Circulation didn't languish very long, but principal advertisers either spurned the new product or shifted display linage from midweek to Sunday.

It would be months before revenues matched the major additional expense incurred by a seventh work shift, new hires (mostly on the news side) and, of course, newsprint.

Out-of-pocket losses were in the high five figures.

In retrospect King and most others felt that the voluminous Sunday sports report is what finally carried the day. It could not be matched by the New York City dailies, with their early deadlines.

But the stress on sports wasn't King's idea. Flipping through a pre-publication 64-page tab mock-up, Ottaway came upon eight pages relegated to weekly stock tables, mutual funds and related tabular matter.

His reaction can only be described as on the tart side:

"Your readers don't want stocks. They want sports."

Today the *Sunday Record*'s circulation surpasses by far any other wholly-owned Sunday (or daily) in the group. By design, it has never carried the nameplate prefix *Times Herald* as does the daily. The simplified logo reflected what most people called the *Record*.

Even as the *Sunday Record* made its appearance, Boyd warned the ON-R board of a "potential need" for a new press in Middletown. The ever troublesome Hantscho was simply not able to handle ever-mounting circulation. Even fairly stiff newsstand and home-delivery price increases, some deliberately posted to slow growth, did not blunt it for long. The advertising arms of the *Record* were exultant. Display and classified rates could be raised with few advertiser outcries because the cost per thousand net paid remained stable.

Boyd's report confirmed that the price of Goss Metro offset presses indeed were climbing. Five units and related equipment would cost $200,000 more than the units then being installed in Danbury. The board voted to place a contingent order with Goss for five units at a price of $981,405, the price to be protected to July 31, 1971.

General manager in Middletown during the Sunday start-up was Ed Somers, who had been transferred from Port Jervis in April. Milt McLean replaced Somers as GM of the *Union-Gazette* and was promoted to publisher the same year. Another GM to attain publisher rank in 1969 was Don Clifford in

Oneonta.

During the Somers and McLean regimes in Port Jervis, which roughly encompassed five years, the *Gazette* shook off respectable profits.

The Somers-McLean era gave birth to a sense of manifest destiny, which, in effect, dictated first that the time had come to end the *Gazette*'s tenancy in the ancient pile on Pike Street. Somers had even found railroad passes issued well before the turn of the century to Fred R. Salmon "in consideration of advertising in the *Port Jervis Union*." The passes, issued by the New York, Lake Erie and Western (which became the Erie Railroad) turned up behind front office wainscoting. Conductors' punch marks indicated that Salmon often rode the rails.

Somers began the search for a modern plant, but his reassignment to Middletown left the quest to McLean. In 1969 McLean found an adaptable building on Fowler Street, which had been an automotive repair depot and which had been repossessed by a bank. He snapped it up for $27,500. Refurbishing two floors cost another $28,000. McLean didn't stop there. He left the *Gazette*'s primordial office furniture and fixtures at Pike Street and installed new equipment, severing the moldy ties of almost a century.

That wasn't the end of McLean's dream as publisher. Manifest destiny also had dictated a new offset press and a photo composition composing room.

But a printing plant was not in the cards. Money had run out.

It would not be until 1974 that the *Gazette* would have its own press and composing room. Middletown would continue to set the type and print the product.

By then McLean had been named publisher of the *Sunbury (Pa.) Daily Item*. Robert S. (Bob) Widmer took command of Port Jervis operations late in 1972, and would guide its destinies for a decade.

Widmer's career started in Stroudsburg in 1949 as a reporter. He shifted to advertising and then circulation, becoming business manager of the *Pocono Record* in 1970.

185

15 Sunbury

The golden noontide of the Ottaways' destinies as a privately held company came late in 1969 with earnings at an all-time high. At their last meeting of the year directors voted an extra dividend of 15 cents a share on the outstanding common.

There were two other reasons for euphoria in the Campbell Hall boardroom. One was of heroic dimensions, the other of somewhat lesser import.

Discussions had been under way since the spring of 1968 on a merger of Ottaway with Dow Jones. The months of tough bargaining with Bill Kerby seemed to be approaching fruition.

And Ottaway had reason to believe he was about to clear the last barriers that stood between ON-R and acquisition of the 24,000-circulation afternoon *Daily Item* in Sunbury, Pennsylvania, which lies in the Susquehanna Valley, geographic hub of the commonwealth.

For the first time an Ottaway acquisition file contained correspondence to and from non-Ottaway executives. The chief still was calling the shots, so to speak, but understandably was keeping Kerby posted, in addition to Dow Jones Vice President Warren Phillips and DJ counsel.

In effect, Ottaway was wearing interchangeable negotiating hats, one of which had to be worn to meetings with Kerby, the other during negotiations with the Sunbury stockholders. The latter must not know a merger with DJ was shaping up. Patently, the asking price would escalate. Didn't everyone think that DJ had deep pockets?

"I felt uncomfortable with the situtation," Ottaway reflected. "But there was nothing we could do."

Ottaway had been tipped as far back as 1962 that owners of the Daily Item Publishing Company were considering selling. George J. Cooper, a broker-consultant who had become affiliated with the ailing Allen Kander, was the source.

Bill Lundquest had been dispatched to Sunbury in July 1962 for a preliminary market study. He also examined the newspaper plant and equipment and in company with Basse Beck, general manager, repaired to Beck's home for rundowns on key personnel and a glimpse at the shroud of discontent that cloaked the shareholders.

The first daily newspaper in the community was the *Sunbury Daily,* created in 1872 from a weekly. In 1893 another daily was born, the *Sunbury Evening Item.* Harry H. Haddon and Basse A. Beck acquired 48 percent of the *Item* in 1927, the balance in 1933. In 1937, depression economics resulted in a merger of the *Item* with the *Sunbury Daily,* one of whose founders was William L. Dewart.

Thus Haddon, Beck and direct descendants of Dewart held a solid majority of the 3,000 outstanding shares of the *Daily Item,* the surviving property.

Beck was general manager until health forced his retirement in 1966. In 1969 Haddon held three titles: president, treasurer and managing editor. Lewis Dewart IV, a grandson of William L. Dewart, was vice president.

Beck thought little of Haddon. Haddon and Dewart seldom spoke to each other.

Supreme indifference to each other had marked their newspaper comings and goings.

The Lundquest market study was updated in 1969 by Elton Hall, now a Campbell Hall operating vice president from Oneonta; Phil Blake from Pocono; and Ed Hill, an assistant vice president, who had moved to the Hall from New Bedford.

The pursuit by Ottaway began in the winter of 1963, with Haddon as the quarry. Haddon held 30 percent of the 3,000 outstanding shares. Correspondence suggests Ottaway may have been rushing things. He assured Haddon that "we have no interest in pushing you," and apologized for calling Haddon's home from New York three times in 24 hours, blandishments that apparently did not set well with Mrs. Haddon.

Further contacts were sporadic until the spring of 1969. Ottaway now was avidly courting Haddon, the Dewarts and the bedridden Beck (through Mrs. Nita Beck).

Ottaway, having exhausted his borrowing power in the Massachusetts acquisitions, asked Kerby if Dow Jones would consider a role as banker, and if the merger discussions collapsed, accept a role as partner in the Sunbury venture. Kerby flashed a green light.

On June 16 in a letter to Hadden, Ottaway formally offered $3.25 million for the property, which equated to $1,083.33 per share. The price was equal to almost 18 times anticipated 1969 net earnings.

"It would undoubtedly be egotistical and impolite for me to outline our concern for the present employees, our concern for the future of the area that the *Item* serves and our concern for being good citizens of the Sunbury-Northumberland area," the accompanying message read. "In all of our publishing ventures we have done our level best to publish quality newspapers and to allow those in charge of an individual publication to set its editorial policies and to reflect the needs and desires of the local area that it serves."

It was the basic Ottaway set speech but it was the kind of talk the owners wanted to hear. There had been other suitors over the years, but as Mrs. Beck wrote Ottaway, "our confidential negotiations with you are motivated by a repugnance to resort to the open market, and our desire to choose our buyer with assurance that the security we have provided our employees and the service we have rendered the community might be continued."

Mrs. Beck had one other thing to tell Ottaway: She wanted $1,200 per share for the family's holdings.

It became clear in late summer that the Ottaways, senior and junior, and Cooper, would have to negotiate separately with the Becks, Haddon and Dewart IV. The Becks were the least of their worries. They were quite willing to sell. Haddon and Dewart ran hot and cold, but by late August the pieces seemed to be fitting together. Employment contracts for Haddon and Dewart, Ottaway and Cooper reasoned, just might be the keys.

But discussions were to continue another frustrating six

months.

Haddon, picking peaches on August 25, fell off a ladder, breaking a leg. He was 71.

Haddon had been ambivalent about his future. At first he said he wanted to retire quickly. On October 24 he told Cooper he liked the idea of staying on under Ottaway and "tapering off slowly." He said also that a job guarantee for Dewart might swing Dewart around. Three weeks later Haddon, exhausted by continued therapy, told Jim Jr. he was "more anxious than ever" to push stockholders to a conclusion by December 1. He suggested that he use "a soft sell" on Dewart. Haddon had committed himself to sell.

Dewart wrote to Jim Jr. on December 31 that "(I) don't feel I have reached a point where I'm ready to stop trying to make a go of it," alluding to the deep friction within *Item* management.

The elusive break came on January 12, when Dewart decided to sell. His decision, oddly enough, followed a long discussion with Haddon. The broken silence between the two antagonists meant victory for Ottaway (and Dow Jones). Concurrently Mrs. Beck backed off her demand for $1,200 per share.

The sale agreement was announced April 1 and on the 15th the *Daily Item* became the ninth member of the Ottaway group.

In the end Ottaway did not have to call on Dow Jones for financial assistance. By December 31, 1969, the original $12 million Bankers Trust loan of 1966 had been shaved to $8.4 million. Bankers advanced $3 million and ON-R paid the balance, plus a five percent broker's fee to Cooper, $162,500. Dow Jones guaranteed the Ottaway note to Bankers.

There were some glum faces among some former *Item* shareholders when the Dow Jones-Ottaway merger was announced just two weeks later. But the finger-wagging ended in short order.

Phil Blake, publisher of the *Pocono Record,* was chosen to guide the *Item*'s destinies. But there was a brief skirmish over his title. The Ottaways wanted Blake to move in as general manager, leaving Haddon with his old titles as president and managing editor. The GM title had been unused since Beck's retirement.

Blake balked, reasoning that this division of titles would

indicate that Haddon still was boss. On second thought he was named publisher, Haddon managing editor.

"The Ottaways didn't want Haddon and Dewart to be upset," Blake said, years later. Indeed they didn't, the files indicate.

Haddon, whose top salary had been $24,000, was given a three-and-one-half year contract that called for $30,000 a year over the first 30 months, plus $15,000 during the final 12. Dewart, whose salary peak had been $13,000, was given a five-year contract at $20,000 a year. Dewart was to be "operations/personnel manager and coordinate the work of the mechanical departments with the advertising and news departments."

Haddon retired at 74 after two and a half years. Dewart lasted a year and a half and left voluntarily. A private pilot, he had affixed a sign to his office door bearing the prophetic legend "I'd rather be flying." Blake wasn't sorry to see either one take his leave.

When Blake arrived at the 200 Market Street offices, he set up shop in what can only be described as a broom closet and a seedy one at that. Haddon and Dewart had the choice locations. No move was made to place the new chief in executive trappings. Blake stayed put until his lowly diggings were discovered by Lyn Boyd, who didn't share the Ottaways' apparent desire to cosset their nonspeaking holdovers.

Blake also found himself without a working editor. Haddon's only input as ME was the editorials. After hiring and firing two editors, Blake called for help. It arrived in the form of a "loan" from Danbury, Robert E. (Bob) Lauf of the *News-Times* copy desk. The loan became a fixture. Lauf stayed.

Professional life under the old regime left much to be desired, Cyril A. (Mike) Kane, managing editor, recalled.

"In 1970, I thought the *Daily Item* was a better-than-average small hometown newspaper. Just how good or bad we were was difficult to judge as we didn't, except for the few smaller dailies we competed with, really know what was going on outside of our own operation. Generally speaking, most employees were reasonably happy with their jobs.

"Actually, the *Item* was pretty much of a 'one-man-gang' type operation. Harry Haddon was the dominant force.

"Haddon was my idol. However, beginning in April 1970, when the Ottaways acquired the newspaper, I learned that Harry was human and that he had weaknesses.

"It soon became apparent that Harry had not kept abreast of changing methods in producing a newspaper. For example, no one in the editorial department had ever seen a page dummy. No one in the newsroom had ever attended a workshop or seminar. In-house training was nil. Copy editing was almost non-existent.

"Compensation was at the sweatshop level. Until the labor department caught up with the owners a year or so before the paper was sold, some of us were expected to work 45, 50 and 55 hours a week without overtime or time off.

"Editorializing in the news columns and in headlines occurred.

"While there are bittersweet memories about the family-owned operation, the working lives and life styles of most employees began changing for the better with the Ottaway takeover.

"The old management wasn't always in the habit of informing employees of what was going on in-house. In fact, that very situation led to the first and only strike at the paper in 1966.

(The strike involved some members of the production department, which never has been unionized. They were goaded into a walkout by organized printers of the nearby *Shamokin - Mount Carmel News-Item.*)

"Visits by members of the Ottaway family and later by Bill Kerby and Warren Phillips and their assurance of better things to come all helped during the transition. Phil Blake was tough but fair and earned our respect.

"From all of them we learned that the new owners really cared about employees and were sincere about putting out a good newspaper.

"The openness on the part of the new owners with employees was a key to the successful transition and all of the good things that have happened since, in my opinion. Resources and prestige of the Dow Jones connection have helped make our jobs more exciting and have added to our stature in the community.

"It wasn't easy learning all the new methods the Ottaways brought with them. A few people quit rather than learn.

"Gradually we came to appreciate the many changes that took place and took pride in helping to make them work and produce a good newspaper. Among other things, the Ottaways brought organization and professionalism to the operation."

In June 1972 the burghers of Central Pennsylvania discovered that the often stated Ottaway commitment to public service was no facade. When Hurricane Agnes struck in mid-month, Sunbury and neighboring communities along the Susquehanna

191

River suffered what many considered the worst flooding in a century.

On Tuesday the 20th, the *Daily Item* published what would be its last normal edition for a week. On the 21st, police closed all bridges across the river, marooning those staffers who lived on the western side. Phil Blake was one of the last to cross to Sunbury. Bob Lauf was stranded.

Mike Kane, toiling with a skeleton staff, produced bobtailed editions on the 21st and 22nd. The *Item* did not publish on Friday the 23rd because city authorities closed the plant, fearing the Sunbury flood walls might collapse.

Help arrived on Saturday the 24th in the form of a chartered helicopter, which delivered Lauf and other stranded staffers to the newsroom. On that day the *Item* published the first of three successive eight-page editions, which were delivered by the chopper to flood-isolated communities, along with prescription drugs. The paper made up for the lost day by publishing Sunday, the 25th.

The flood editions contained no advertising and were given away.

With the helicopter came reportorial assistance from Ottaway News Service headquarters, then in Campbell Hall. The beleagured *Item* staff could use help. It was virtually exhausted. Chief Robert (Tim) Metz and staffer Edmund Klein responded. They were on the scene until the 28th.

Bill Toland, sports editor, showed up each day to put out his page, even though his home had been wracked by the flood. He was living in an evacuation center. Other staffers, unable to get to the office before the chopper arrived, filed stories by phone — when the phones were working.

Sleeping at the *Item* became a way of life for some. Sunbury accommodations were jammed by stranded travelers.

Legend has it that the *Item* was the only Pennsylvania paper on the Susquehanna to publish six of the seven days that the crisis was at its worst.

Publishing returned to normal on Tuesday the 27th. The helicopter left, bridges reopened and advertising reappeared.

Blake's audacious generalship on the flooded front lines had been inspiring. No less so was the stance taken at corporate headquarters: "To hell with the expense. Cover the story!"

If you ever wondered about the public's concern for their newspaper," Lauf wrote, "you should have seen the stranded people waiting in the streets for the helicopter to drop off the bundles. I will never forget the sight."

The ever increasing demands on Francis Brinkley, financial vice president and treasurer since 1967, dictated a talent search for an executive assistant.

One source tapped by Ottaway and Boyd was Alan Boers, a partner in Ernst & Ernst, the long-time Ottaway accounting firm. Boers was stationed in the Syracuse, New York, office. He placed a help-wanted ad in the *Herald-Journal* there.

The ad led directly to discussions with John S. (Jack) Goodreds, the budget manager of Bristol Laboratories (a division of Bristol Myers Company) in Syracuse. Goodreds, carrying a master's degree in business administration, also had been associated with General Electric. He had no professional newspaper experience.

Goodreds came aboard January 5, 1970, as assistant treasurer.

Days later Brinkley was dead, victim of a heart seizure.

Goodreds was elected treasurer in February, the first step in a series of promotions that would lead him to the No. 2 position in the Ottaway hierarchy by 1980.

Ottaway and Boyd did not tell Goodreds about the merger discussions with Dow Jones until after he was hired.

"They told me only that the company had reached its borrowing capacity and that Ottaway had two choices, to go public or merge with a compatible organization. I was assured that in either case the character of the company would not change."

The start of the 1970s decade saw Ed Hill in yet another shuttle move, this time from Campbell Hall back to New Bedford at Gerry Tache's request. Hill was installed as general manager. Dick Barker was assistant GM.

"I wasn't comfortable with the title," Hill said, "because my real mission was to keep Tache and Editor Dick Early apart. I wasn't even a shadow GM. Barker was doing most of the work."

J. Richard Early had been named *Standard-Times* editor by Jim Jr. in 1966. He had been executive editor under the former ownership. Interviews suggest his relationship with Jim Jr. was cordially productive. But the Tache-Early relationship suffered because of procedural and personality differences. Apparently Early did not relish the idea of reporting to a superior with mostly an advertising background.

At the same time, Allan Meath was brought to Campbell Hall from Danbury as a corporate vice president. John Van Kleeck moved up to the *News-Times*'s publisher's chair.

☆　☆　☆　☆　☆　☆

It is the author's opinion (one that well might raise the hackles of those who presently guide Middletown's destinies) that the apotheosis of *Times Herald-Record* enterprise reporting was achieved in August 1969.

The then editor, Al Romm, agrees.

Here are his recollections of the three-day Woodstock Festival:

"Coverage represented a high point in newsroom preparation and reporting under extreme pressure. The package was of Pulitzer Prize quality — and, we were told later, we missed by a hair.

"Advance sales and other clues told us that Max Yasgur's famous 600-acre site in the Sullivan County Town of Bethel would be hopelessly overcrowded. So we prepared. We rented a trailer, complete with food and grill, a teletype to our Monticello office, a telephone, walky-talkies for each assigned reporter, and a radio link to state and local police networks. We hired an off-duty policeman as a motorcycle courier for film. And we rented a helicopter for photography.

"To his credit, Publisher Charles King approved the hefty expenditures without blinking.

"Although we planned carefully — better than any other news medium or

194

governmental agency, or the festival planners themselves — the crush of 350,000-450,000 rock fans forced us to improvise.

"Like thousands of ticket-holders, some reporters never made it to the site. No matter. We pressed into service every off-duty staffer or friend who had come for the show. I had driven to the scene with my wife, Ethel, Thursday night, just to check arrangements. I stayed on to direct the coverage and Ethel did some fine reporting. We didn't leave until Sunday afternoon, several deaths and thousands of bad drug trips later. A dozen reporters, photographers and volunteers worked alongside us, with almost no sleep.

"We published an 'extra', distributed on Sunday, August 18, and followed through with coverage long after the last person had left the muddy scene.

"Mythology sprang up about Woodstock before our very eyes. Most news media, lacking our resources, concentrated on reporting the unprecedented array of superstar performers in the natural amphitheater. We covered that, too, with our music reviewers and others, but we also covered the drugs of all descriptions, the deaths, the public sex, massive police problems, the inadequency of water, food and sewage services, the instant urbanization of a small tract of rural land, the promoters and the populace who exploited the emergency for personal gain and the many hundreds who donated their skills, their food and their time to cope with an unprecedented demographic and medical emergency.

"The *Times Herald-Record* editorially had been supportive of the festival, standing against those who first had rejected a festival site in Scotchtown, adjacent to Middletown, and who then argued vainly against the next choice, Bethel. We did a forthright about-face in mid-festival. We called it a mixture of Sodom and Disneyland and argued that a multi-day festival of that sort, with all rules and laws unenforceable, simply could not be authorized or condoned.

"And I testified in Albany, effectively, for legislation that would prevent such man-made disasters.

"Others may have fond, possibly drug-softened, memories of those few days in August 1969, as the youth phenomenon of a troubled decade. It was that, of course. But I remember Woodstock for our newspapers' finest and most perceptive performance, achieved under the most trying of circumstances."

16 Merger with Dow Jones

The New Bedford and Cape Cod acquisitions in 1966 and the costly ongoing betterment programs throughout the group had placed the Ottaways in a virtual corporate cul-de-sac in 1969. Further expansion now was impossible. Financing for acquisitions was not their only concern. The industry was about to enter another revolutionary era in newspaper production in which electronics would speed the various processes to achieve immense reductions in costs. The group would have to adapt.

To gain access to financing for acquisitions, the future state-of-the-art equipment and what Jim Jr. called "the new technological know-how that we lacked," two options were open: Merge or go public.

The Ottaways had explored two merger possibilities in the mid-1960s. One was with Whitney Communications, whose president, Walter Thayer, had supported the $12 million New Bedford loan as a Bankers Trust board member. Jim and Jim Jr. lunched with John Hay (Jock) Whitney and Thayer, but came away feeling that they were principally "running a financial empire" in which newspapers were held to be "inanimate." To the Ottaways, newspapers were flesh and blood.

An actual merger offer came from Reno-based Speidel Newspapers, which owned the *Poughkeepsie* (N.Y.) *Journal.* The proposal called for 60 percent ownership by Speidel, 40 by Ottaway. The discussions were dropped.

And there was an out-of-the-blue phone call from Gulf & Western Industries. "Not interested," Ottaway replied.

"The family was in no financial trouble," Ottaway said.

196

"None of us was in need."

The most fortuitous development the Ottaway family could have wished for was about to unfold.

In the late spring of 1968 Ottaway received a letter from William F. Kerby, president of Dow Jones. Kerby told Ottaway that Dow Jones wanted to expand its economic base by diversifying into the area of general newspapers published in small and medium-sized cities. (A few years before a sort of "trial marriage" between Dow Jones and Gannett had been developed for the same reason, but a stock interchange arrangement collapsed.)

Kerby, like the Ottaways, owned a cottage at Buck Hill Falls. Theirs was an intimate relationship covering two decades.

Various departments of Dow Jones — editorial, advertising and circulation — had convened at Buck Hill over the years. Ruth and Jim Ottaway often had been invited to cocktail parties at the Kerby cottage or at the Inn and had gotten to know (and admire) top- and middle-level executives.

Specifically, Kerby wondered, would Ottaway let him know if a potential acquisition turned up that Ottaway couldn't handle?

Kerby's memoirs*, published in 1981, describe his approach to Ottaway as a "spur-of-the-minute phone call," and quote Ottaway as unhesitantly replying: "How about a group? How about the Ottaway papers?"

Two books on the *Wall Street Journal*** published the following year, curiously attribute identical language to Ottaway. It did not happen that way.

It would have been totally out of character for him to have implied instantly and unilaterally that the family business could be purchased.

Kerby's letter did not contain a merger proposal.

That possibility developed in continuing conversations between Ottaway and Kerby as each sought solutions to his own problems.

The Ottaway family sorted through the pros and cons of merger as a corridor to further growth.

"Your newspapers are of medium size, well run, with high

* "A Proud Profession", William F. Kerby, Dow Jones-Irwin, 1981.
** "Inside the Wall Street Journal", Jerry M. Rosenburg, Macmillan, 1982.
** "The Wall Street Journal", Lloyd Wendt, Rand McNally, 1982.

editorial standards," Kerby told his friends. "And they're run by people we know."

Kerby's enthusiasm was matched by the Ottaways' own.

There had been a plenary family session at the Ottaway Campbell Hall home in January 1969. No opposition developed to the principle of merger, nor would any arise later.

But there were nagging questions that had to be answered during the summer of 1969 when discussions became serious.

Jim Jr. felt there were at least 17 possible reasons not to merge. His handwritten list, dated July 8, 1969, includes these questions:

"Would Ottaway lose its independence, its status? Would it lose its separate identity? Would Ottaway become a financial acquisition to be run for profit first instead of second? Would Dow Jones primarily push for profit performance at the expense of editorial freedom and quality?"

Jim Jr. also wondered if DJ executives and its directors would "look down their noses at Ottaway's percent of profit when they are used to 18 percent after taxes." And he was concerned about outside pressure on Ottaway executives.

Finally, he thought, if an understanding could be reached with Kerby, with whom would Ottaway be dealing after Kerby stepped down?

On the positive side Jim Jr. ticked off 11 reasons why he thought merger would be propitious. Implying that agreement had been reached in principle to achieve a tax-free merger through an exchange of stock, he cited the obvious advantage in converting the Ottaway family holdings into "valuable, marketable stock paying substantial dividends."

"Sooner or later," he told the author, "there could be family arguments over the traditional Ottaway philosophy of management, shareholder discontent over plowing profits back into existing properties and acquiring new ones."

(Jim, Jim Jr. and Ruth, of course, had been drawing salaries and dividends, David and Ruthie dividends only.)

Jim Jr. also alluded to ready Dow Jones financing for acquisitions and modern equipment and DJ's world-wide reputation for research and development.

The discussions eventually included Warren Phillips, who

would succeed Kerby as president and then chairman.

Most of the talks were about operational procedures.

"We didn't want Dow Jones calling us up from 30 Broad Street and telling us what to do," Ottaway said.

Kerby also wrote that agreement was reached after "many, many months of hard and at times rather acrimonious bargaining." But the Ottaways had no recollection of any caustic exchanges.

In retrospect the discussions from the start boiled down to a matter of price. "We were sold on the principle and on the people with whom we were dealing," Ottaway said, "it was all done on faith and promises. Both companies had much in common, particularly their emphasis on news quality. We wanted to take the same road to modernization. And we admired Dow Jones's integrity."

Thus the final agreement consisted only of economic language. Mutual trust covered everything else.

Before the agreement-in-principle was announced on May 1, 1970, Ottaway called what he described as a "summit meeting" in New Bedford, where Jim Jr. had been publisher since 1966. "It was designed," he said, "to give Jimmy all the pros and cons of merger and to make sure that he had a complete feel of the situation."

"It was not a whether-we-do-or-whether-we-don't meeting. I simply wanted all the facts laid out. Merger made sense for the family."

Alan Boers, an Ernst & Ernst partner with intimate knowledge of the Ottaway newspapers, and attorney Bill Carey, Ottaway's merger counsel, were present. Boers addressed himself to tax implications, Carey to legal matters.

After the meeting Ottaway turned to his son ("Father looked me squarely in the eye") and said:

"It's your decision. It's your life. I'm nearing the end of my career."

The verbal agreement to merge was reached in March 1970, a few weeks before the announcement of the Sunbury acquisition. The Ottaways shook hands with Bill Kerby and Warren Phillips in a hideaway in the then new west wing of The Inn at Buck Hill Falls.

The salient non-economic points of the compact neatly dissipated any of Jim Jr.'s earlier concerns. He would be president. Ottaway Newspapers would be a separate subsidiary and would retain the name. Headquarters would remain in Campbell Hall. Jim Sr. would remain as chairman until retirement. There would be no major changes in staff or leadership and Ottaway would have full management authority. Perhaps most important was the promise of editorial independence.

Jim Ottaway also would operate Dow Jones's acquisition arm.

"The senior Ottaway," Kerby wrote, "had a wide acquaintance among publishers and was universally liked and respected. Given Dow Jones's financial resources, I visualized him as the man who could round up additional desirable acquisitions."

The agreement also called for DJ to continue the Ottaway retirement plan.

The Ottaways received 914,038 shares of Dow Jones stock for their properties. At the then market price that equated to $36 million, or roughly 24 times Ottaway's projected 1970 earnings of $1.5 million.

"There was nothing between us but a handshake," Kerby wrote.

At one point Kerby had offered to buy 80 percent of the Ottaway stock. "He thought we might like to keep 20," Ottaway said. "But that idea, however thoughtful, didn't appeal to us."

The ties of mutual trust soon were tested by a fickle stock market. Before a written contract could be signed, the market plunged.

In mid-March the stock was 46½ bid, 47¼ asked. By May 1 it had fallen to 40 bid, 43¾ asked. On July 31, the day of the merger closing in New York City, it had dropped to 27¾ bid, 28¼ asked.

"The Ottaways," Kerby wrote, "had every excuse to at least seek a renegotiation, but to their everlasting credit, neither father nor son even mentioned their eroded purchase price."

(At the time Dow Jones was traded over the counter. Soon it would be listed on the New York Stock Exchange, which would
200

provide a better market and add prestige to the listing.)

The family distribution of Dow Jones shares follows:

James H. Ottaway Sr.	51,867
Ruth B. Ottaway	17,475
James H. Ottaway Jr.	4,427
David B. Ottaway	3,992
Ruth Ottaway Sherer revocable trust	3,761
Ottaway family voting trust dated 5/3/68	653,416
Trust for children of James H. Ottaway Jr.	179,100
Total	914,038

As of December 31, 1970, reflecting pre-merger holdings, Jim Jr., his family and family trusts held 49.93 percent of the overall Ottaway family shares. Jim's and Ruth's wills were to give Jim Jr. the added stock needed for clear control.

Jim Jr. was present when his father's employment contract was being discussed. "I guess they had to offer one to me," he recalled, "and when they did, I found myself in quite a dilemma. I felt I'd be better off without a contract and trusting that if I did a good job, Dow Jones would treat me fairly. I never have regretted the decision. Everyone has been treated fairly. They have more than lived up to their promises. In the last 15 years, for example, DJ has not turned down a single capital expense request."

Ottaway senior was given a $95,000-a-year contract for "at least" six years at full time. He would retire in 1976 and act in a consulting capacity for "the rest of his life." And he would have a seat on the Dow Jones board.

Immediately after the May 1 agreement was signed, the Ottaways typically took to the road to explain "the facts behind the merger." They talked frankly and in detail to related groups of employees at each of the nine newspapers. During the summer Bill Kerby joined Ottaway in a second round of meetings, designed to prove, among other things, that the Dow Jones president "didn't have horns."

Right off the bat, they found employees who thought Dow Jones was an investment company.

"Dow Jones is going down each day. Won't this affect our newspaper?"

Patiently, Ottaway explained that the Dow Jones Index was a composite listing of market prices and that Dow Jones was a publishing company.

Ottaway stressed at the May meetings that "there was no compulsion to merge."

"Dow Jones had gotten along without the Ottaways since 1882, and the Ottaways without Dow Jones since 1936," he said. "Ottaway is financially sound. However, the combination (of DJ-Ottaway) gives employees five to six times more security than existed before."

One of the employee questions that arose repeatedly was whether an individual newspaper would be taking orders directly from DJ in New York City.

Ottaway found himself underscoring the vital point that Ottaway Newspapers, Inc., would be the operating company, with Jim Jr. as the new president and with the same operating officers at Campbell Hall.

This salient point — corporate separation of the new subsidiary from the parent — was the core of his message.

Unionized production employees at the *Pocono Record* asked if their contracts now would be negotiated with Dow Jones.

"Negotiations will be completely local," he replied.

In response to questions at other locations, he also laid to rest any ideas that DJ employee benefits would be extended to Ottaway papers, citing the "very liberal" Ottaway pension plan and medical plans geared to each location.

The message was either misunderstood or ignored by one group of employees. In the months ahead, some Middletown editorial employees not only sought union representation, but initially demanded a contract embodying nothing less than Dow Jones wage scales, substantially above Ottaway's highest. Their vehicle was the Independent Association of Publishers Employees, which represented most DJ editorial and technical personnel.

It is clear that the Middletown cadre approached IAPE,

202

which guided a successful organizational effort and at first even supplied a chief negotiator and its own legal counsel. In time Dow Jones IAPE participation dwindled and the *Times Herald-Record* unit continued bargaining on its own.

The two major concerns of the Middletown unit were what it called job security and economic benefits the group thought should spin off promptly as a direct result of the Ottaway-Dow Jones alliance.

Negotiations dragged on for more than a year. The contract that was signed in November 1971 bore little resemblance to the original IAPE proposals.

The Middletown unit decertified IAPE in May 1974 by a 33-1 vote, then cast its fortunes with the International Typographical Union.

The unforeseen alliance between the Middletown and Dow Jones newsrooms was not the sort of interplay the Ottaways had envisioned. It was not only an acute embarrassment to them, but both were irritated, especially Jim Jr. Publisher King and Editor Romm also were embarrassed and annoyed. Hadn't their editorial staffers been the only ones to seek an instant financial Valhalla in the wake of merger?

In 1970 Jim Ottaway was elected to the board of directors of the Associated Press. He was defeated in a re-election bid two years later.

Also in 1970 Bob Van Fleet, chief of Ottaway News Service since its founding in 1963, was appointed an assistant vice president. Van Fleet's promotion and the subsequent vacancy led to the first editorial talent interchange with Dow Jones.

Historically, Ottaway always had sifted its own ranks to fill vacancies, but in this case Jim Jr. and Van Fleet could not find the right individual (who was willing to take the job). So they turned to Dow Jones.

The talent search turned up Robert T. (Tim) Metz, a *Wall Street Journal* reporter, who arrived at Campbell Hall in

December 1970.

Jim Jr. hailed the move as a "fitting symbol of our merger with Dow Jones, where high-quality news and editorial content has always been a first priority, as it is with Ottaway." Jim Jr. and Van Fleet also felt that it was an ideal time to have someone from DJ to help integrate the existing ONS Washington and statehouse reports with the vast amount of new material flowing from the *Wall Street Journal* and *Barron's Business and Financial Weekly*.

"Dow Jones never pushed the Metz choice, nor did it ever ask us to pick anyone," Jim Jr. said. "It definitely was our choice and decision."

Metz reported directly to Van Fleet.

Metz was one of only two Dow Jones staffers to come to work for Ottaway during the first 15 years of merged operations. The other was James D. (Jim) Hitchman, a veteran of seven years in various production management posts, including the *Asian Wall Street Journal* in Hong Kong.

Hitchman arrived early in 1980 as understudy to Tom Purcell, Ottaway vice president for production. Purcell, who retired late in 1981, had come to Campbell Hall from Danbury in 1970, where he was production manager and composing room foreman. For years after his retirement Purcell was retained as a production consultant.

Back in 1970 Jim Jr. had hoped for frequent interchanges, but it was not to be. Only three Ottaway staffers had joined Dow Jones, and one of those returned to his home newspaper in a relatively short time.

When Dow Jones closed its money-losing weekly, the *National Observer,* in June 1977, Jim Jr. tried to hire a few of its editorial personnel, but most were at salary levels substantially above what the smaller Ottaway papers could offer. The salary differential always has been a major block for DJ people who otherwise might join the group.

Homesickness for the *Wall Street Journal* overcame Metz late in 1972. He declined an Ottaway offer to enter a management training program in Danbury and in March 1973 left to become the *WSJ*'s first bureau chief in Toronto, Canada.

Between 1963 and 1966 Ottaway News Service was virtually a

204

one-man operation in the person of Van Fleet, who spent a couple of days a week in Albany while the New York State Legislature was in session. Occasionally he had now-you-see-it, now-you-don't assistance, while writing for the New York papers.

When the legislature wasn't sitting, Van Fleet was filling story requests for all of the six papers then in the group.

He also organized task forces to augment local coverage of major stories around the circuit, drafting reporters from various Ottaway papers.

When New Bedford and Cape Cod entered the fold in 1966, the Ottaways and Van Fleet inherited a Washington news bureau of sorts, which then was shared by about 12 other small and medium-size newspapers, mostly in the northeast. Its proprietor was Donald R. Larrabee. Larrabee's staff consisted of youngsters who aspired to reporting stardom in the Federal City. They were content to work at wage levels far beneath those of their established counterparts in the Senate Press Gallery.

During the decade Larrabee served Ottaway, his staff averaged five reporters. Like David Ottaway, who worked in the bureau in 1968-69, most went on to become recognized and respected bylines.

Larrabee's primary mission was parochial: coverage of personalities, issues and commerce involving each client, stories that would not normally be handled by either of the major wire services.

The Griffin-Larrabee News Bureau, as it was formally known, was promptly engaged by Ottaway to service the other six papers in their group.

The bureau was established by Bulkley Griffin, son of a renowned editor of the *Springfield* (Mass.) *Republican.* Larrabee joined Griffin in 1946 and bought the operation following Griffin's death in 1967.

Larrabee was the featured personality at the 1966 Buck Hill Falls seminar of Ottaway publishers, general managers and editors. The chief was justifiably proud of the fresh dimension of coverage he had conferred upon his field marshals and exhorted them to use it to the full, recapturing the investment in even better local and regional news reports. "Tell us what you want; give us story ideas," Larrabee urged.

The arrangement worked and it didn't. Larrabee's having added six Ottaway papers to his stable of clients patently increased the work load on his small staff, geographically and topically. And Larrabee's financial well-being was proportionally contingent on a lean payroll servicing a fat clientele. Led by New Bedford, some papers used G-L often and well. Others complained of poor service or no service at all. Personality clashes developed between some Ottaway copy desks and the somewhat harried Washington staff. Van Fleet was forever mending fences.

During his brief stay with Ottaway, Metz established an ONS bureau in Harrisburg, Pennsylvania, which beefed up the statehouse reports for Stroudsburg, Sunbury and Sharon. He picked John Moore of the *Daily Item* as the first bureau chief.

Metz was succeeded as ONS chief by Edmund P. (Ed) Klein in February 1973. Klein, who had joined the expanding service in 1970, was legislative correspondent for Ottaway's four New York papers and the *Danbury News-Times,* whose circulation reached into New York's Putnam County. Klein had been regional editor in Middletown. During his regime Klein upgraded Albany to a full-time operation and established a year-round Boston bureau to protect New Bedford and Cape Cod.

Thus the Metz-Klein era began a decade of ONS expansion under Jim Jr. that would see the formation of an Ottaway bureau in Washington and a further heavy investment in a sophisticated communications network linking all properties.

Even during the Stone Age of ONS, presidential nominating conventions were not overlooked. Van Fleet assigned himself to the 1964 conventions in San Francisco and Atlantic City, which produced the Barry Goldwater-Lyndon Johnson non-contest. Van Fleet had an assistant on the West Coast: Ruthie Ottaway Sherer, who commuted from her home in Los Gatos.

In 1968 Van Fleet supervised coverage of the Miami and Chicago conventions, which nominated Richard Nixon and Hubert Humphrey. But this time he had substantial assistance from Don Larrabee's staff. Larrabee sent half his reporters to

Miami, the others to Chicago.

In 1972 the conventions that nominated Nixon and George McGovern were handled by Metz, Klein and the Larrabee staff. If any Campbell Hall supervision was needed, Van Fleet did it from his desk there. His duties were gradually shifting from the daily pursuit of news quality. For one thing, he was writing a training manual for new reporters.

17 Sharon

The 26,000-circulation *Sharon* (Pa.) *Herald,* an afternoon publication, in 1971 became the 10th newspaper to join the Ottaway group.

A tip led to the courtship. Within a few months Ottaway and the Sharon Herald Company were altar-bound. The acquisition had none of the off-again-on-again hang-ups that had dragged out negotiations in Sunbury.

The tip came to Jack Goodreds, then financial vice president of Ottaway. Goodreds, in turn, tipped Jim Ottaway. Ottaway turned to George Cooper, the broker, who had helped in the Sunbury struggle.

Dominant figure on the *Herald* was Gerald A. (Gerry) Harshman, president and editor.

Some of Harshman's contemporaries said Cooper's first approach was by phone. Harshman thought it was by letter, or, possibly a follow-up letter to a phone call. No matter. Legend has it that Cooper got right to the point: Was the *Herald* for sale? Legend has it further that Harshman said it was not. The chances are he did. Harshman said he had been getting about "a letter a week" from brokers on fishing expeditions. All had been consigned to the wastebasket.

But Harshman did accept Cooper's invitation to an exploratory discussion of the ever-rising values of desirable newspaper properties and possible compatible buyers.

That Harshman even agreed to talk with Cooper underscored the validity of the out-of-the-blue tip Goodreds had received. Their first meeting was at the Pittsburgh International Airport, 70 miles southwest of Sharon.

During his high school years Goodreds was a resident of Greenville, Pennsylvania, just north of Sharon. He was on the staff of the school paper, which was printed in the *Herald's* job shop. But Goodreds had no direct ties to Harshman or to any of Harshman's colleagues. (Identity of the tipster remains a Goodreds secret.)

Research on the Sharon (Mercer County) market was handled by Ray Shaw, at the time assistant general manager of Dow Jones, the Ottaways, Steve Ryder and Goodreds. The consensus: the *Herald* was nowhere near its potential either in circulation or advertising sales.

The Harshman-Cooper dialogues bore fruit in rather short order.

Harshman provided Cooper with financial data. Cooper talked about the *Herald's* market value, the soaring prices commanded by desirable newspapers. Eventually Cooper went a step further. "He told me who was interested," Harshman said.

In an interview in December 1984, Harshman said that selling the *Herald* "was sort of in the wind" in the late 1960s. All evidence suggests that when Cooper revealed that the would-be suitor was Dow Jones-Ottaway, the die was cast. (During preliminary negotiations Harshman told Ottaway he had had feelers from Gannett and Thomson Newspapers, but no firm offer.)

Cooper had fulfilled his assigned role. The door was open. He would receive a finder's fee for his efforts. From now on Harshman would deal directly with the Ottaways.

In an over-the-masthead story on April 2, 1971, the Sharon Herald Company board announced an agreement to merge with Ottaway in an exchange of stock that would give Herald shareholders four shares of Dow Jones for each share of Sharon Herald.

At the time 23,510 Herald shares were outstanding, each with a book value of approximately $80. Thus book value of the *Herald* was estimated internally at about $1.88 million.

The Ottaway offer was 94,040 shares of Dow Jones, which, at the the close of the market April 1, equated to $4.5 million. DJ was quoted at 47½ bid, 48 asked.

In mid-May the *Herald* employee shareholders voted overwhelmingly in favor of the tax-free merger. Fifty four of 60 attended the ratification meeting. The vote was 23,460 to 50.

The merger became effective on June 30, 1971.

(As the result of Dow Jones two-for-one stock splits in April 1981 and July 1983 *Herald* employees effectively received 16 DJ shares for each share of Sharon.)

Thus, on the basis of the April 1 DJ market price, Ottaway paid roughly $190 per share, about 17 times the *Herald*'s previous three-year average earnings after taxes.

Also acquired in the transaction was a *Herald* subsidiary, Allied Newspapers, based in Grove City, east of Sharon. The unit consisted of the weekly *News,* with a paid circulation of 3,600. It was published Mondays. A free-distribution *News* was circulated to 12,000 homes on Thursdays.

Ottaway always has looked upon Allied as a training ground. Robert W. (Bob) Parks, former general manager, was promoted to GM in Port Jervis in 1982 and to GM in Ashland in 1985.

James R. (Jim) Lane, who preceded Parks as Allied GM, in 1979 was promoted to assistant general manager and marketing director of the *Pocono Record.* In 1981 he was named retail advertising manager of the *Joplin* (Mo.) *Globe* and was advanced to sales and marketing director in 1983.

Allied was acquired by the *Herald* in 1965.

In 1944, when Jim Ottaway bought his second property, the *Oneonta Star,* there were 76 newspaper groups controlling 368 dailies. At the time of the Sunbury acquisition in 1970, there were 157 groups, controlling 879 dailies.* The advent of the 1970s brought ever-escalating prices. Independent and small chain publishers were being overwhelmed with fat offers. Some publishers cheerfully encourgaged "auctions." They sold to the highest bidder with little or no concern for a purchaser's need to cut costs to increase profits to pay for the investment, usually lowering a newspaper's standards.

The *Herald* began life as a weekly. It became a daily in 1909.

*"The Newspaper Business in the 1980s", Benjamin M. Compaigne, Knowledge Industry Publications, Inc., 1980.

In a mid-depression merger, it absorbed the *Sharon News-Telegraph* in 1935, taking over the *N-T* building on South Dock Street.

A. Walter McDowell, one of four who bought the weekly *Herald* in October 1907, became president of the merged company. Claude B. Lartz, the *Herald*'s first full-time reporter, who became vice president and general manager of the *News-Telegraph* in 1925, became McDowell's business manager.

Credit for the merger, by all accounts, went to McDowell and Lartz. The McDowell career had been on the business side, Lartz's on the editorial. Tom Perjol, a *Herald* reporter now retired, compiled a history of the *Herald* in 1964, its 100th anniversary. He wrote of the two:

"McDowell had been born to 'father' a paper and Lartz to instill it with personality and character."

A few years after Lartz's death in 1956, the *Herald* established the C.B. Lartz Memorial Awards, presented annually to editorial staffers for exceptional editorial achievements.

Harshman advanced to the president's chair in 1957 when McDowell resigned as chief executive officer and became chairman. McDowell died in 1968.

Harshman, like Lartz, was on the staff of the *News-Telegraph* at the time of merger.

Herbert E. Hetu was a vice president and treasurer. Edward M. Hyde was a vice president and advertising director.

Exactly 11 years after the merger, May 13, 1946, Herald management decided to sell stock to the employees. Neither the A.W. McDowell nor the Claude Lartz families had heirs who could take over the property.

The stock distribution, McDowell wrote, "is the first step in a move to guarantee that ownership and control of the *Herald* shall remain in the hands of those who create it."

"Under the program," he added, "the employee as well as the community, will be safeguarded against the danger of outside interests purchasing control and substituting outside management."

The employee ownership plan extended to all departments,

211

all jobs. Employees bought stock by payroll deductions at book value, which was computed annually. Obviously, higher-paid employees were able to accumulate more than others. Seventy eight individuals immediately became stockholders.

Seven in management positions and 44 other active employees held stock at the time of the Ottaway purchase.

The record indicates that as late as February 1971, Ottaway favored a cash transaction. Exactly when the discussions turned to an exchange of stock is not clear.

There were advantages for both sides in a stock exchange. Dow Jones would not have to advance up to $5 million in cash. Sharon shareholders would not have to pay immediate capital gains taxes. Both large and small Sharon shareholders would receive more dividend income from Dow Jones common, assuming the DJ dividend remained at $1 per share, than they were getting at the Herald's dividend rate of $3 per share.

Why did Harshman sell?

"I was concerned with the *Herald*'s long-term future," he said. " I thought we should take advantage of what Ottaway and Dow Jones had to offer. It was the smartest thing we ever did."

Harshman also cited the Ottaway traditions of local independence and editorial autonomy.

A few *Herald* executives said that Harshman's decision must have been linked directly to the escalating market prices of newspapers. "All the stockholders ever had discussed was the book value of the *Herald,*" they recalled. "Attitudes changed when we were exposed to its potential market value." (Book value is the net worth of a business, or the value of its common stock as shown by the excess of assets over liabilities.)

At the time of merger the Herald board consisted of Harshman; James A. (Jim) Dunlap, managing editor; George D. Lanier, controller; Edward M. (Eddie) Hyde, vice president and advertising director; and Dr. Robert E. Lartz, son of co-founder Claude Lartz.

Dr. Lartz was the largest stockholder, with 5,240 shares. The second largest block, 2,880 shares, was held by inactive McDowell interests. Retired employees held 5,785 shares. Thus non-employee holdings controlled 59.1 percent of the outstanding shares.

The seven top operating executives controlled 25.9 percent, the other employees 15, for a total of 40.9 percent.

This apparent imbalance, with control by "outsiders" and retirees, had nothing to do with the sale, Harshman said. "I never analyzed it on that basis."

But it was clear that several major shareholders eventually would incur estate problems. (Sharon by-laws stipulated that upon death stock must be sold back to the company at book value. An estate would realize far less under continued Sharon ownership that it would under the final tax-free Ottaway-Dow Jones purchase formula.)

During 1969 and 1970 the *Herald* spent $1.8 million for a 27,500-square foot addition to its Dock Street building, and, somewhat surprisingly, a second-hand 124-page Scott letterpress.

The *Herald* had been setting display advertising matter via the cold type, or photo composition process since 1959, but news matter was still the traditional hot type operation at the time of merger. The plant addition had ample space for a completely cold type composing room and an expanded engraving department, needed to convert photo compositon paste-up pages to letterpress plates.

With the industry-wide conversion to offset in full flower, why did Harshman elect to buy what staffers called the "blue monster" from the Dayton (Ohio) newspapers? Why not offset, which would be eminently more compatible with the photo comp operation?

"A few Western Pennsylvania papers had gone offset," Harshman recalled, "and they were having a terrible time. And there was the Davenport, Iowa, mess. It scared me off. I felt that we could get offset quality with the wrap-around plastic plates then being developed. It looked like the easiest way to go. I just didn't have the foresight. I would not do it over again."

That portion of the March 1971 market study devoted to *Herald* equipment commented that ". . .we would have to complete the transition (to photo composition) spending $125,000 for new equipment in the composing and engraving areas. Further capital expenditures would be necessary to improve printing quality by changing to direct printing with

213

thin wrap-around plates, a process Dow Jones perfected at its Riverside, California plant before going offset."

The "blue monster" would print the *Herald* for almost a decade after merger and did a creditable job after the bugs were eliminated.

Sharon's switch to offset came about in 1981 in a prime example of what Bill Kerby liked to call "synergistic" action. Hearing that Dow Jones was going to close its Cleveland printing plant, Jim Jr. urged the parent to build a replacement near Sharon, which could handle both the *Wall Street Journal* and *Herald* requirements. Nearby West Middlesex was chosen as the site. Some Cleveland printing went to Bowling Green, Ohio.

Had DJ not agreed to the West Middlesex location, Jim Jr. felt that Sharon still would be using the "blue monster," what with the area's continuing economic recession.

Ottaway and DJ share in the capital cost and depreciation expense of the press, reducing costs for both partners.

Between acquisition and December 31, 1983, capital improvements costing $1,685,000 were lavished on the *Herald*. In 1984 a new business system was installed. The price tag was $100,000.

Another entry in the Ottaway work book sized up top management in Sharon as appearing to be "of higher caliber . . . than you usually find in a paper of this size." The key executives, the book suggested, "are capable of managing the newspaper without immediate need for an Ottaway executive on the spot full time."

Which is exactly what happened.

Harshman was retained as chief executive officer until his retirement at the end of 1973. He was succeeded as publisher-general manager by George Lanier. In early 1985 Lanier was one of only three publishers in the group not an Ottaway import.

Lanier never had aspired to be a publisher. During the war he found himself assigned to an Army overseas replacement depot in the aptly-named hamlet of Transfer, Pennsylvania, a few picas north of Sharon. A church social hall in Sharon frequented by off-duty soldiers turned his life around. There he met Cecilia

214

Dickson, a *Herald* employee. They became engaged before Lanier went overseas.

Marriage and an accountant's job in a Georgia bank followed war's end. But Ceil was homesick for Sharon. Lanier came north for an interview with a Sharon banker, who steered him to Herbert Hetu and the *Herald*. "He's looking for an accountant; it's a better opportunity than you'll have at the McDowell Bank."

During the first year of the Harshman administration Jim Ottaway Jr. was the Sharon liaison with Campbell Hall.

Jack Goodreds then was assigned as headquarters point man, Jim Jr. suggesting it would give him an opportunity "to become more familiar with our operating system."

"I'll never forget the first time we (the Sharon Herald board) met the Ottaways," Lanier said. "We were at the Sharon Country Club. In walked Jim with his scruffy tan briefcase. Jimmy was wearing what looked like a suit from his freshman year at Yale. Both were down-to-earth persons. We liked what we saw."

18 Traverse City

The tide of conquest swept northwestward in 1972.

On August 11 Ottaway Newspapers signed an agreement to buy the Herald and Record Company of Traverse City, Michigan, publishers of the 18,500-circulation *Record-Eagle*. On September 29 the afternoon paper became the 11th member of the group.

Understandably there was jubilation in both the Dow Jones and Ottaway board rooms. Jim and Jim Jr. once again had outmaneuvered a clutch of would-be buyers and the purchase price was well under the agreed-upon ceiling.

Traverse City lies on the lower peninsula of Michigan, known as the Grand Traverse region, and carries the sobriquet "Cherry Capital of the World." Lumbering, which was begun in 1847 by the first white settlers, dried up before the turn of the century. The vast stands of pine were no more. The cherry industry replaced the sawmills and has dominated the area economy since. Tourism is another major dollar catalyst.

The *Record-Eagle,* a 76-year-old daily, was born of a merger on October 31, 1910. The *Daily Eagle,* first daily in the Grand Traverse region, was established in 1893. The *Evening Record,* which began life as a morning paper, was first published in 1897. The Herald and Record Company soon found itself in severe financial trouble. On February 2, 1917, the *R-E* was sold to four men who operated the *Battle Creek* (Mich.) *Moon Journal.* One of them was Austin C. Batdorff.

Batdorff and one Richard T. Allen were dispatched to Traverse City to run the *R-E*. Allen eventually withdrew from active participation in the partnership. Batdorff continued as

216

president and general manager until his death in 1963.

Austin Batdorff was the father of two sons, Robert A. and John H. Upon the father's death Robert became president and publisher. John served as vice president and general manager. John Batdorff died in 1970.

In the early spring of 1972 the *Record-Eagle* ostensibly was not for sale, in the sense that Bob Batdorff wasn't actively seeking a buyer. But, according to Maurice K. Henry, a broker, it was for sale — if.

Henry had become affiliated with Ottaway's old friend, George Cooper, who helped in the Sunbury and Sharon acquisitions.

On May 3 Henry met with Batdorff in Traverse City for the third time. A written advisory to Cooper said, in part, that "...he (Batdorff) would sell if the buyer offered him his price."

Henry, trying to get a handle on Batdorff's thinking, suggested $2.5 million.

"Hell no," he quoted Batdorff.

Then Henry went to $3.5 million. Batdorff, he said, smiled, but did not address himself specifically to that figure.

Henry remembered Batdorff saying, "If we get an offer near my thinking, I will not do the negotiating but send the buyer to see my accountant. He will advise me what to do." (Batdorff's accountant's offices were in Battle Creek, south of Traverse City.)

Henry probed possible methods of payout: Stock, cash or cash in installments.

"I like cash," Batdorff said, "but my accountant will have to advise me what to do."

Toward the end of the conversation, Henry reminded Batdorff that "Jim Ottaway is interested in Traverse City." Batdorff agreed to meet with Ottaway.

"If Ottaway goes to Traverse City based on previous research of the market and newspaper, he will have to be prepared to make an offer," Henry wrote. "If the offer comes within Batdorff's range, he will send Ottaway to the CPA. This is a cat-and-mouse situation, but the only way a meaningful situation can be developed is for the game to be played this way with Batdorff in order to get to the CPA for nuts-and-bolts

217

conversation. Batdorff does not want a lot of prospects run past him. He hopes for only one."

Henry's allusion to "previous research" by Ottaway apparently covered a preliminary and rather sketchy look at the market, because the formal study was not completed until late in June. It was compiled by Jim Jr., Peter E. Hartley, Steve Ryder and Jack Goodreds. (Hartley became administrative assistant to Jim Jr. in January 1972. He had been classified manager of the *Cape Cod Times*. When he returned to the Cape a year later he was posted as a special assignments reporter. Hartley died early in 1982.)

"Evidence of commercial growth is particularly apparent on U.S. 31, south of Traverse City," the report said, "and in the vital downtown commercial district. Residential growth is apparent in the entire area around the city. Real estate is booming."

The study concluded that the *Record-Eagle*'s display advertising rates were unrealistically low as was the home-delivered price of 50 cents a week. Batdorff's classified pages carried no display ads. "With the bullish real estate market, the possibility for classified growth is almost unlimited," the study concluded.

The two principal negative factors were the crowded *R-E* plant and "relatively low" pay scales except in the mechanical departments. The research team alluded to the eventual (and costly) need to correct both deficiencies.

Ottaway, Batdorff and Henry met for the first time on June 14. Steve Ryder accompanied the chief. A typical Ottaway bread-and-butter note followed, assuring his host that "I have a feeling that you and I see eye-to-eye in regard to the philosophy of local newspaper publishing and also in regard to maintaining the 'human touch' in dealing with employees and with the public."

Ottaway also took pains to reassure Batdorff that he would play the game according to Batdorff's rules:

"As promised, our financial vice president and accountant will be glad to go to Battle Creek next week (or whatever time you indicate) and talk with your accountant. And, at the same time, if agreeable with you, Jim Jr. and I would very much like

218

to come to Battle Creek so that he could have the opportunity of meeting you and the three of us could talk together again."

The chief returned to Traverse City on June 23. In his briefcase was the agenda he hoped to cover, which carried the legend "We want to do business." Item No. 1 covered the possibility of a tax-free exchange of stock, a review of Dow Jones earnings and a replay of the 1971 stock swap in Sharon. Ottaway also had eight major questions to ask Batdorff, most of them economic.

Meantime Jack Goodreds met with Batdorff's CPA in Battle Creek.

The Herald and Record Company was capitalized at 1,700 shares of $100 per value, 1,300 of which were outstanding. Robert Batdorff was the largest individual stockholder, controlling approximately 38 percent.

The acquisition file indicates that Batdorff had made up his mind in late June to sell to Ottaway, leaving only price and terms to be decided.

On July 6 Ottaway extended his opening offer: 75,400 shares of Dow Jones stock, which equated to 58 shares for each Herald and Record Company share. He arbitrarily placed a floor of $40 per share and a ceiling of $50 on the DJ stock, which that day closed at 42¾ bid, 43¼ asked on the Over-the-Counter Market. A median $45-per-share offer would have equated to $3,393,000.

Batdorff, reportedly against the advice of his attorney, Harry Calcutt, declined the offer.

Meantime several other valid proposals, some in the $4 million range, had reached Batdorff and Calcutt. Henry's May 8 memo alluded to "three other brokers or prospects, including the Michigan Booth operation" having visited Traverse City.

Other known suitors included Frank A. Daniels Sr., board chairman of the *Raleigh* (N.C.) *News & Observer* and *Times;* Harte-Hanks, Ridder, Thomson, Lindsay-Schaub, the *Detroit News*, Carmage Walls of Montgomery, Alabama, and Newhouse's *Huntsville* (Ala.) *News*.

On one of his visits to Batdorff, Ottaway met Daniels at the Cherry Capital Airport. Daniels understandably wondered aloud why the chief happened to be in the Grand Traverse area. "Oh, I have relatives in the vicinity," Ottaway said, tongue very much in cheek, "I'm a Michigan native. Born in St. Clair."

Ottaway soon would see Daniels again, but under different circumstances. In Raleigh during one of his fund-raising expeditions for the American Press Institute the chief gave Daniels the full pitch, after which Daniels handed him a prepared check for $7,500. Ottaway asked why Daniels listened to the set speech if his mind had been made up. "I just wanted to see if you knew what you were talking about," Daniels retorted.

Next time Ottaway and Daniels met was at an API function. Daniels remarked that he had been happy to give Ottaway the $7,500 but was not at all happy about losing the *Record-Eagle*.

Ottaway and Batdorff shook hands on July 19. They had cut a deal.

Purchase price came to $3.9 million cash, or $3,000 per Herald and Record share. In addition Ottaway gave Batdorff an employment-consulting contract calling for $5,000 a month from October 1 to January 31, 1973, and $22,500 a year for the next decade.

Ottaway Newspapers used $1 million of its own cash and $2.9 million borrowed from Dow Jones, bringing the total owed the parent to $5.94 million.

The brokerage fee to George J. Cooper Associates (including Maurice Henry) came to $125,000. Ottaway also picked up the check for Harry Calcutt's legal fees: $30,000 over three years.

Ottaway Newspapers as a rule borrowed from DJ only for acquisition purposes - and always at the prevailing prime rate. It paid its own way for capital improvements from the start of the merger.

Why did Bob Batdorff sell?

"I was getting tired. I wasn't feeling my best," he said.

Why did he sell to Ottaway?

"I was very impressed with James and James Jr. They seemed sincere in their efforts to accommodate me in my wishes . . . and they didn't come on too strong. Basically I wanted to do business with people I liked and respected. Traverse City is my town. I did get a higher offer, but Ottaway Newspapers seemed best for me and for Traverse City. I have not been disappointed in my choice."

In a separate letter to the author, Batdorff described his dealings with the Ottaways as "memorably pleasant." Since the transaction, he wrote, "they have honored, absolutely and without exception, every pledge and arrangement that they promised. Honorable men, both of whom have earned my absolute respect and admiration.

"I guess that I will always remember several occasions when the lawyers for both sides were battling out details in another office, while Jim Sr. waited with me and seemingly expressed impatience at the amount of time attorneys took with such trivial details. But I felt aware that he was fully cognizant of every little detail that was being thrashed out. He had run the course before, while I hadn't, and I was just hoping that my small-town lawyer could hold his own against such big city legal expertise."

The purchase by Ottaway marked the first time the *R-E* had been owned and operated by anyone other than a Traverse City resident. The fiercely parochial community possibly had looked upon Austin Batdorff as a carpetbagger when he arrived in 1917. But he quickly blended with the Grand Traverse coterie that historically made things happen — or saw to it that they didn't. His sons also mixed well. Robert started his *R-E* career in 1938 as a reporter. John joined the staff in 1955 as business manager.

On the surface, at least, the Ottaway takeover was greeted mostly with tepid approval. But some segments of the community, long accustomed to the Batdorff's benign (some would call it protective) daily news report, stridently criticized what they called the new "absentee ownership" and "revolving-door" management. Pockets of resentment linger to this day.

The *Record-Eagle* of September 1, announcing the agreement of sale, quoted Ottaway: "During our discussions with Bob Batdorff we found that we share many of the same basic newspaper publishing philosophies. . ."

Many. But not all.

Batdorff's was based on a live-and-let-live, don't-rock-the-boat credo. If possible, his *R-E* sidestepped controversy. "The only waves here are out on Lake Michigan," one editor

221

said.

Martin D. Sommerness, a summer reporter intern (1974-77), wrote in a master's thesis* that "If . . . it is the duty of a newspaper 'to print the news and raise hell,' this study shows the *Record-Eagle* under the Batdorff family took care to print little that would raise even a reasonable facsimile of hell."

Sommerness's thesis explored the news, entertainment and opinion content of the *R-E* before and after its purchase by Ottaway.

The period immediately following the sale was passed over by Sommerness "because it was a time of flux for the newspaper in general and its editorial department in particular."

Indeed it was.

When news of the impending acquisition circulated at Campbell Hall headquarters in late August, Elton Hall asked for a meeting with Jim Ottaway, who was relaxing at Buck Hill Falls.

"I know what he wants," Ottaway told his neighbor, Bill Kerby. "He wants to go to Traverse City."

Ottaway was right. Like a few other corporate officers before him, Hall preferred a publisher's chair. He was tired of travel, for one thing. Hall took over from Batdorff on October 1. His tenure lasted two years. He died unexpectedly in his office October 28, 1974. Hall had been the only immediate Ottaway import.

Hall was succeeded by Don Clifford, publisher of the *Oneonta Star*. Clifford, now senior Ottaway publisher, served until 1979, moving to New Bedford to succeed Gerry Tache, who had been named a corporate vice president.

The third Ottaway publisher in seven years was Orren Robbins, who moved up from general manager of the *Cape Cod Times*.

"Some people are still asking 'Who's running the paper?' " Robbins said early in 1985. "They feel as though they've had 10 different publishers. That perception insists on lingering."

Perhaps changes at the general manager level also con-

---

*"*Northern Michigan's Greatest Daily*" accepted by the School of Journalism, Michigan State University in partial fulfillment of requirements for a master of arts degree, 1979.

tributed to the precept.

Gilbert A. (Gil) Bogley was assistant GM and GM under Hall. He was succeeded in 1978 by Francis A. (Frank) Perretta, who, in turn, was replaced in 1981 by Brenda J. Tallman, former classified manager. Ms. Tallman was the first woman to become an Ottaway GM.

Bogley and Perretta moved to other Ottaway properties. Both would become publishers.

A cavalcade of editors also filed through the West Front Street portals between 1972 and 1980. Editor for the Batdorff family since the mid-1930s was William Smith, who resigned in April 1974. After 18 months he decided he could not cope with Ottaway's brand of community journalism.

Lee Lapensohn, editor of the *Plattsburgh Press- Republican,* was tapped to replace Smith. The Fates did not smile on the appointment. Lapensohn underwent heart bypass surgery eight months after reporting.

Then started what some Ottaway watchers call the "editor-of-the-month club." The month of January 1975 was protected by Bob Lauf, on loan from Sunbury. Ed Klein covered during February, temporarily leaving Ottaway News Service without a chief. Frank Perretta arrived from Oneonta to mind the store during March.

Klein finally was selected as Lapensohn's replacement.

A Batdorff holdover, the indefatigable Marge Cotter was managing editor during Elton Hall's regime. She was replaced by John P. Kinney, who arrived from Ottaway News Service in 1976. Kinney became editor when Klein returned to ONS in 1978. Upon Kinney's departure for New Bedford in 1980, James Herman ascended to the editor's post.

"Newswise (under Batdorff) school board meetings were covered by the public relations man for the schools," Ms. Cotter recalled. "And the majority of the other stories seemed to be those that walked into the office. Katy Carroll, society editor, used to peddle the paper in the afternoon on a motor route. Obviously pay has improved since the Ottaways took over."

Ms. Cotter believed that "too many of the chicken dinner items have been removed, with too much space devoted to wire news."

223

Sporadic vocal resentment over "absentee management" by Traverse City's Old Guard was (and remains to a degree) a phenomenon Ottaway executives never had faced. With Smith as his editor for 18 months, Hall had little to worry about. The *R-E* news report ran in pre-acquisition style, which is to say on the flaccid side. There were no axes to be ground by the holdovers.

But with the advent of Lapensohn and his successors, it became clear that the Batdorff way of life was on the way out. Reader perceptions began to change immediately. Hall's death left Publisher Clifford, Gil Bogley and Frank Perretta to take the first major onslaught of criticism.

Batdorff himself echoed some of the community's feeling in a memo prepared for this book. He described his own feelings as "unbiased and otherwise."

"There is no doubt," he wrote, "that the *Record-Eagle* has improved in many ways. I'm not quite sure that it is a better 'small town' newspaper, but it is truly a fine paper, and by all measurable criteria it is better. Perhaps my feelings are tempered somewhat by the fact that I have never fully subscribed to the now-popular theory of 'investigative reporting.'

"I believe that the publishers who have guided the fortunes of the *Record-Eagle* over the past 10 years have been excellent, each one in his own and slightly different way. . .

"My enthusiasm has been slightly less warm regarding some of the editorial staff imports, some of whom have seemingly seen fit to start dissecting Traverse City before they memorized the name of the street on which they lived. I'm a little sad that some residents might conceivably view the paper with a little touch of fear and trepidation rather than affection. But it is very difficult to dispute success, and I feel that the *Record-Eagle* has achieved that."

Martin Sommerness's thesis concluded that "under absentee ownership" the *Record-Eagle* "had become a better newspaper."

It alluded to an increase in total content and local information, a greater variety of opinion and entertainment matter and "much more aggressive editorial stance."

224

The study also proves, Sommerness wrote, that the *R-E* has "a particular orientation to its home community that was lacking in its locally-owned days."

The *R-E*'s own 1977 readership survey indicated readers were "generally satisfied" with the overall newspaper product.

Nevertheless, "product" and "ownership" have never meshed in public opinion.

Sommerness concluded that "as long as the *R-E* continues its aggressive news and editorial policies and as long as an embittered group of merchants and bureaucrats long for what one man called 'the good ol' days,' the ownership will be a bone of contention for many."

Perhaps the outstanding *Record-Eagle* public service story of the 1970s was its investigation of a child pornography operation, reportedly based on an obscure island in Lake Michigan. It not only typified the aggressive newsroom policy under Editor Klein and ME John Kinney, it underscored the Ottaway policy of get-the-story-and-worry-about-the-bills-later.

This is Kinney's recollection of a staff effort that burgeoned into an expose with nationwide implications:

"Sometimes the 'big story' falls into outstretched arms and an eager newsroom has the good sense to run with it. Occasionally, the story lies just outside your reach. You have to scratch for it and rely on that peculiar mix you sometimes find in newsrooms, a strange brew of compulsiveness, tenacity, fair play, balance and dogged determination.

"In 1977, the way the *Record-Eagle* landed its 'big story' — an expose of a nationwide child pornography network — fell into the scratch-and-dig category. And, yes, the strange brew mentioned above was there in sufficient quantity and diversity to land the story. It started with a tip that a boy's camp on an island in Lake Michigan was the setting for a child pornography operation. It was a tip all right, the tip of the iceberg. But we couldn't get below the surface until Marilyn Wright, the *Eagle*'s feisty police reporter, got the name of an inmate in downstate Jackson Prison who was connected to the locale in question, North Fox Island.

"Four or five staffers went to work on other aspects of the story and Wright went to prison — to prison — to interview the inmate. She came back goggle-eyed with a story spilled by an embittered man and a chart of what appeared to be a nationwide "boy love" organization. We got to work attempting to prove or disprove the allegations. We found even more information. Using a religious name as a cover, the supposed boys' camp was, in fact, run by an organization that put male juveniles in sexual situations and filmed them. We found similar camps in Florida and near New Orleans. We uncovered dummy corporations and a trail of aliases that led to the ringleaders, one of whom was the scion of a prominent Detroit area family.

"In a matter of weeks, Wright was trading information with police agencies throughout the country, including the New Jersey Crime Commission. With the help of Ottaway News Service and friends within other news organizations, we'd tracked corporate records in several states and detailed a nationwide web of individuals and organizations that were victimizing young males and distributing films and magazines.

"After several spot news stories, we had enough for a comprehensive series. The series was picked up (and, in some cases, ripped off) by other newspapers and wire services. Some of the main actors in this seamy drama were driven underground, one fled the country. The camps were shut down.

"The capper came when Michigan Gov. William Milliken recognized the *Record-Eagle*'s efforts by taking an unprecedented step — he signed a landmark child pornography bill into law right in the *R-E* newsroom.

"Since the mid 1970s the newspaper's share of state and regional public and community service awards has been significantly larger than its circulation suggests it should be. This is due largely to a commitment to community service. It is a commitment that generally results in local news and feature stories that examine issues, events and personalities on a wide range of local topics.

226

"However, because the paper was willing to follow a 'local' story through its national ramifications, the pornography series carried much more than a local impact. It had an impact on Michigan law, enforcement of pornography laws in many other states and it helped to drive at least a segment of a nationwide child pornography operation underground or out of the country."

During the 1970s the *R-E* underwent a major expansion program, which almost doubled the size of the physical plant, and replaced its 55-year-old Goss letterpress with offset equipment.

Since the acquisition Ottaway Newspapers has lavished $3.4 million on *R-E* capital improvements.

Even so, the specter of what some critics have called the "East Coast liberal establishment" refused to vanish.

As late as September 1984 Jim Jr. was reminded of the lingering community resentment over *R-E* editorial policy — 12 years after the acquisition.

In Traverse City for the company's annual party, he played one of his now infrequent rounds of golf with Robbins, Richard A. (Dick) Myers, corporate liaison with the paper and ex-U.S. Senator Robert J. Griffin, a lawyer.

After the match the quartet repaired to the club house for a drink. Attorney Calcutt joined the gathering.

Gently but firmly Griffin and Calcutt told Jim Jr. they weren't at all happy with the retooled *R-E*. It was 1972 all over again.

There were these other major developments with roots in 1972:

Bill Kerby visited Plattsburgh with Ottaway early in the year. During a ride through the city they passed the downtown Margaret Street properties that Al DeLuca bought in the mid-1960s for $80,000. Before driving to the Clinton County airport Kerby asked if he might have a second look. Publisher Ben Turnbull was more than delighted to comply.

"Things moved fast after that," Turnbull said.

ONI board minutes show that on March 17, $865,000 was authorized for a new plant and $221,000 for a Goss Urbanite press.

The *Press-Republican,* Turnbull was always quick to say, paid out-of-pocket for all construction costs. In exchange, Campbell Hall waived *P-R* service charges until the new plant opened in the spring of 1973. Since 1973 the *P-R* has updated electronic production equipment three times and in 1981 built a $200,000 addition to its plant.

In 1975 an advertising windfall descended on Plattsburgh. The Pyramid Mall increased the *P-R* linage 35-40 percent. The inelegant old rabbit warren on Clinton Street never could have handled the bonanza.

Al DeLuca resigned May 1, 1972, at age 59 as publisher of the *Cape Cod Standard-Times.* A long-overdue physical examination indicated his health was beginning to fail. Scott Himstead moved up.

DeLuca resettled in Florida. Betty DeLuca died of cancer in March 1976. Then, in a move that surprised few who knew him well, the ex-publisher turned to the Roman Catholic priesthood. He was accepted as a candidate by the bishop of Davenport, Iowa. After preparatory studies he was ordained in Sacred Heart Cathedral March 23, 1978. Father Albert was assigned to St. Joseph's Church in What Cheer, Iowa, a mission church of Keswick, Iowa. He died of a heart attack in the rectory May 23, 1982.

Elton Hall's appointment as Traverse City publisher left a corporate vacancy at Campbell Hall. Jim Jr. brought in Phil Blake from Sunbury. (Blake lived across the Susquehanna River in Hummel's Wharf, on whimsically-named Easy Street). Milton McLean moved west from Port Jervis to replace Blake. The Port Jervis slot was filled by Robert S. (Bob)

Widmer, business manager of the *Pocono Record*. Also in 1972 Dick Barker became general manager of the *New Bedford Standard Times*.

There was rejoicing in Middletown, too. Installation of a Goss Metro offset press was near completion. The days of the unpredictable Hantscho were numbered. Before the year ended it was sold to the Inland Newspaper Machinery Company for $80,000. There is no known record of its whereabouts today. There are few, if any, who care.

19 Medford

"My friendly source tells me that Harte-Hanks made a pass at the Medford (Ore.) Mail Tribune but was rebuffed because the little lady who owns it didn't like their style or Harte-Hanks stock. The paper has a circulation of 24,000-25,000. The owner, Mabel W. Ruhl, is a widow in her 70s with no one coming on."

The terse advisory, dated July 18, 1972, was directed to Jim Ottaway at Campbell Hall. It was signed by Ray Shaw, then director of development for Dow Jones. Shaw's "friendly source" was not identified.

Thus began an odyssey that in less than a year would see the Ottaway corporate ensign fluttering for the first time on the West Coast.

Ottaway immediately lateraled Shaw's tip to George Cooper, the broker, who flew west. Cooper discovered that the primary conduit to Mrs. Ruhl was her attorney, Otto J. Frohnmayer, a partner in the redoubtable Medford firm of Frohnmayer & Deatherage.

Would Mrs. Ruhl be willing to meet with Jim Ottaway?

Frohnmayer suggested that first it might be helpful for him to learn more about Jim Ottaway and his newspapers. On August 3 the chief wrote to the attorney, advising him that he and Ruth periodically traveled west to see their daughter, Ruthie, who lived in Los Gatos, California, "and that it would be very simple to come up to Medford if I were welcome."

Ottaway also told Frohnmayer that Jim Jr., president of ONI, and Cleveland (Cleve) Twitchell, news editor of the *Mail*

230

Tribune, were classmates at Phillips Exeter Academy and had worked together on the newspaper there.

Besides the letter Frohnmayer received a package that included an updated corporate informational flyer, "This Is Ottaway Newspapers," and copies of the Cape Cod, New Bedford, Danbury and Pocono papers, which, Ottaway discreetly wrote, "you and Mrs. Ruhl possibly might like to examine."

At the same time Peter Hartley was dispatched to Medford for a preliminary market study. Hartley's research embraced only cold statistics. If he had any reactions, they were not recorded.

Medford, county seat of Jackson County, is the major retail and wholesale trade center for Southern Oregon and Northern California. The southern border of the county forms part of the Oregon-California border.

All evidence indicates that the Ottaway overtures were placed in Frohnmayer's deep freeze during the summer and most of the fall of 1972. Finally, a date was set for a meeting with Mrs. Ruhl: December 7.

But just a few days before Ottaway and Jim Jr. were to fly west on separate aircraft, a telephone call, two visitors and a snowstorm contrived to fashion what would become a warm Medford welcome.

Since Ottaway acquired the *Oneonta Star* in 1944, the paper's annual party has been held on the first Saturday in December. So it was on December 2, 1972. Ruth and Jim were there to help celebrate their 28th year of ownership. Jim Jr., Mary and family were in New Hampshire, on Phillips Exeter business.

The phone rang in the Ottaway's Oneonta motel room on Friday, December 1. The caller was Mrs. Herbert Simmons of Dorset, Vermont. Roxane Ruhl Simmons identified herself as a daughter of Mabel Ruhl and cheerily added that she had been told Jim and Jim Jr. were going to Medford on December 7.

"We'd like to meet you. We'd like to visit you tomorrow."

Jim and Ruth left Oneonta early, arriving at Campbell Hall in what turned out to be a storm verging on blizzard proportions. The Simmonses arrived on schedule.

The storm, in effect, made the Simmonses a sort of captive

231

audience. They stayed the night, and, as Ottaway recalled, "We got to know each other well."

There was more than conversation. Ottaway wheeled out those corporate vice presidents he could round up. One of them, Steve Ryder, didn't know it at the time, but his long-term future was being shaped that day.

Roxane Simmons took to Ruth and Jim Ottaway and their lieutenants. She not only liked what she saw, she liked what she heard about their publishing philosophy. When she returned to Vermont she called her mother in Medford and told her so.

As if the serendipitous snowbound meeting wasn't enough for entree to Mrs. Ruhl's Medford living room, yet another typical Ottaway gesture came from Jim Jr. Before returning home from Phillips Exeter, he drove to the Simmons home in Vermont. The measure of affection with which he was received might be gauged by Roxane Simmons's final word of caution: "Remember when you meet mother that she is deaf in her left ear. Try to talk into the right. She won't admit she's deaf."

Mrs. Simmons had told the Ottaways that she and her sister, Mrs. John R. MacArthur of Medford, were "very anxious" to sell the *Mail Tribune* to a group. "If we sell it to an individual he'll sell it to a group later anyway." Primary reason for sale, she said, was her mother's age, 87. (Shaw's source had misstated Mrs. Ruhl's age.)

Mrs. Ruhl would say 11 years later that she sold because "I had no interested children or grandchildren and I didn't feel I was doing justice to the paper and Medford people to keep it. But I didn't want to sell the paper just to sell it."

Mabel Works Ruhl was the widow of Robert W. Ruhl, publisher of the *Mail Tribune* and president of Medford Printing Company until his death at 87 in August 1967.

Robert Ruhl had been a Medford resident since 1911, when he bought controlling interest in the *MT* and a sister paper, the *Sun*. He consolidated the two immediately, discontinuing the *Sun* in 1919. Ruhl retired from active writing in 1958.

During his stewardship, his obituary said, "the *MT*'s editorial policy was known for its liberal attitude and vigorous expression. He fought the revived Ku Klux Klan in the early 1920s and the so-called 'Good Government Congress' in Jackson

232

County in the early 1930s. It was for his editorials during this period, marked by ballot stealing, violence and other civic disturbances, that the *Mail Tribune* was awarded the Pulitzer Prize in Journalism in 1934 . . . for 'disinterested and meritorious public service'."

His editorials always were signed "R.W.R." The tradition of signed editorials continues.

Otto Frohnmayer met the Ottaways at the Medford airport on the morning of December 7 and drove them to the Ruhl home. With Mrs. Ruhl were Mrs. MacArthur and Herbert G. Grey, retired advertising director. Grey was a minority shareholder, the only one outside the Ruhl family.

Jim Jr. did not get the conversational position that would give him access to Mrs. Ruhl's right ear. To accomplish this, Ottaway asked if he could use the "family facilities," and so maneuvered his son into a more favorable spot. While Jim Jr. and Mrs. Ruhl chatted, Frohnmayer had some questions for Ottaway:

"Why are you interested in Medford? What percent of Ottaway profits go to Dow Jones? Are you interested in a stock exchange? Would the stock be restricted? What is your relationship to Dow Jones? How do you operate at Campbell Hall?"

Then Jim Jr. addressed himself to the current newspaper operations, his relationship to the publishers, Campbell Hall's relationship to the individual newspapers, the Ottaway publishing philosophy and the Ottaway relationship to Dow Jones.

Mabel Ruhl had a sense of humor. One day while driving through Medford she pointed to a tract of parkland she and her husband had given the city. Turning to Ottaway she said "Don't get any idea I'm going to give you the newspaper!"

George Cooper was assigned to follow up with Frohnmayer.

There was no further word from Medford until February 6, 1973, when Mr. and Mrs. Frohnmayer returned from an extended European trip. In a note addressed to "Dear Mr. Ottaway" the attorney said he and the Ruhls "are favorably impressed with the company and its management. We expect to have further discussions in the very near future." It would not be long before Ottaway and Frohnmayer were on a first-name basis.

Memories are blurred on whether Steve Ryder was present at the first meeting with Mrs. Ruhl on December 7. He thought he was. But his name does not appear in Ottaway's detailed recapitulation of who said what to whom. Nonetheless, Ryder was very much in attendance subsequently and was the author of a remarkably detailed market study completed March 15. Sterling (Jim) Soderlind of Dow Jones also researched the market. Both studies came up pro-acquisition.

The same subliminal corporate chemistry that interreacted favorably with Roxane Simmons also attracted Alicia MacArthur and Mrs. Ruhl.

"There's one condition I have to put on the sale," Frohnmayer soon would say, as buyer and seller approached agreement. "Steve has to be publisher."

It was a case of unabashed trust and admiration.

Ryder thus became the second Ottaway acquisition hostage. Jim Jr. had been part of the New Bedford-Cape Cod purchase.

Acquisition correspondence does not refer to Gerald T. (Jerry) Latham, *Mail Tribune* general manager, until mid-April. Apparently Latham, then 60, called Ottaway at Campbell Hall on April 13 and proposed that *MT* management "continue exactly as it is." The chief replied that "we are counting on you to continue as general manager," and assured Latham that "what other changes that might take place we certainly will discuss with you in advance."

A cash offer of $7.5 million for all of the stock of Medford Printing Company, including the newspaper and its marginally profitable radio station KYJC was made shortly after a two-day visit to Medford by the Ottaways and George Cooper on March 30 - April 1.

Frohnmayer called the offer "satisfactory," but on April 3 cautioned that two other possible purchasers would be interviewed and that price alone would not be the determining factor. Frohnmayer said he and his principals were concerned about the "quality of the newspapers, treatment of employees and their own pride in the community where they will continue to live."

234

Frohnmayer did not identify the two remaining suitors, but in all likelihood they were the Lee Newspapers and the Speidel group, which were known to have had an interest.

Medford Printing was capitalized at 600 shares of $100 par value, with 400 shares issued and outstanding. Mrs. Ruhl owned 50½ percent.

On April 4 Frohnmayer asked Ottaway how fast a deal could be made.

"We had discussions about spinning off the radio station," Ottaway wrote to Bill Kerby. "He said there were some local people who were anxious to buy it. I told him that if he accepted our offer of $7.5 million cash (and cash was what they wanted, nothing else) that Frank Parker (a Dow Jones attorney) and I could head for Medford right away and that we ought to be able to sign an agreement within a matter of two weeks."

Station KYJC was eliminated from the package by mid-April for the benefit of both sides. If Ottaway bought Medford Printing and KYJC, months might pass before a buyer could be found for the station and transfer of license. This would delay an Ottaway takeover of the *Mail Tribune* indefinitely, which neither buyer nor seller wished. In effect, a portion of the proceeds from the eventual sale of KYJC would be applied to the $7.5-million original offer.

On April 27 the *Mail Tribune* became the 12th member of the group. The purchase price shook down to $7.35 million less proceeds from a forthcoming sale of KYJC. As foreordained, Ryder was named publisher.

(KYJC was not sold until April 30, 1974. It brought $325,000. Frohnmayer and George Cooper handled the transaction.)

The entire staff of the *MT* was retained. Jerry Latham, as promised, stayed as general manager with the additional title of executive vice president. Eric W. Allen Jr. remained as editor, a post he had held since 1958.

Allen, then 52, is a son of the late Eric Allen, long-time dean of the School of Journalism at the University of Oregon. Allen joined the *MT* as city editor in 1948 and became managing editor in 1956. He had worked for newspapers in California and Oregon and in two West Coast bureaus of the then United Press.

Allen and his wife, Betty, were vacationing in Italy at the

235

time of the sale. Here are his recollections of receiving news of the acquisition by Ottaway Newspaper via overseas telephone:

"It was at about 9 p.m. Rome (Italy) time, as my wife and I were getting ready for bed in our hotel, that I received a call from the overseas operator announcing a call from Medford, Oregon, U.S.A.

"It was Otto Frohnmayer and Mrs. Ruhl, calling to advise me of the sale of the *Mail Tribune* to Ottaway Newspapers, of which I had never heard. They reassured me about my job and future. Nonetheless, sleep was scarce that night.

"En route home I had scheduled a stop in Washington, D.C., to attend the annual meeting of the American Society of Newspaper Editors. Our flight, due to mechanical difficulties, was some 10 to 12 hours late, and we arrived at the hotel at about 4 a.m., exhausted.

"Later in the morning I found a note in my box asking me to call one Steve Ryder in Medford, of whom I had never heard. I called, and was welcomed back to the states, to the Ottaway organization and to the *Mail Tribune*.

"Soon thereafter I began meeting Ottaway editors, the first being Bob Lauf from Sunbury, whose wife took my wife under her wing. We were reassured by the Laufs and others that, after the initial shock of the acquisition, being in the Ottaway group wasn't bad at all.

"It was at the same meeting that I first met Jim and Jimmy Ottaway, and Warren Phillips and Ed Cony, and other Ottaway and Wall Street Journal types, all of whom were friendly and welcoming.

"Upon our return to Medford, Steve reaffirmed his welcome, and we began feeling each other out. This was a process that continued for some months, with gradually increasing mutual respect and friendship, which continues to this day.

"Under Steve, and later under Gil Bogley, the *Mail Tribune* has received strong leadership, and excellent representation in the Ottaway organization. Changes have been many, and most of them for the good.

"The tradition of editorial autonomy had been preserved, and only in the business office, and in procedures such as budget preparation and action plans, has ONI made its presence known operationally.

"The substantial investments made by ONI in the *Mail Tribune*, for remodeling, new equipment and additional staff have made possible the progress of the *Mail Tribune* - progress which I view with applause and some pride, even as I have withdrawn into a rather more circumscribed role than in earlier years.

"Today we have a strong staff, sensitive leadership, good morale, hard workers — the net result of which is a strong paper of increasing excellence.

"I have been proud to have had a part in the growth and development of the *Mail Tribune* over the past 35 years, and particularly during the past 10 under Ottaway auspices."

In October 1983 Mabel Ruhl, now in her 90s, reminisced over

tea with Steve Ryder. At the author's request Ryder asked how she felt about Ottaway stewardship since 1973.

"Why Steve, you know I've never been sorry. Ottaway has shown as deep a commitment to the public as we did. Bob (Ruhl) always played it straight with everybody and I think you have. Jim Ottaway and Jimmy, too, inspire respect. I've always felt they would carry on in the right way."

While seeking an acceptable buyer, she said, she had subscribed to many newspapers owned by groups, but in the name of Alicia MacArthur, so no one would realize what was going on. "I read all the editorials in all the papers to see what they stood for. Then I finally shook it down to four or five, but was drawn to the Ottaways all the time because I felt they would carry on the way they should."

Mrs. Ruhl carried the title of publisher for about five years after her husband's death, but was relatively inactive at the paper, kept no office there and visited it infrequently.

She said she felt increasingly inadequate in responding to decisions she was being asked to make by Latham, de facto operating head of the *MT*.

Ottaway wasted no time going offset. ONI board minutes show that in September 1973, $1,377,000 was authorized for a Goss Cosmopolitan press. In 1980 almost $1 million more was allocated for advanced production equipment. Meantime the *MT* itself was undergoing change: elimination of column rules, down-style headlines and reduction of page width.

Mrs. Ruhl, Ryder recalled, was totally supportive. "She was quick to tell her establishment friends that the paper never looked better. I recall one day she said 'Steve, you and I are the only publishers in town. We have to stick together.' That kind of support was hard to beat."

Perhaps the high point of Ryder's stewardship came in 1976 with the totally out-of-the-blue First Amendment Award of the Society of Professional Journalists, Sigma Delta Chi. The *MT* was the first newspaper to be so honored. The *MT* was cited for obtaining an injunction barring the sequestering of criminal records in Jackson County.

In 1975 the Oregon legislature had enacted a law limiting unwarranted access to criminal records. Some exceptions inadvertently were omitted from the bill. As passed, the law barred release of any information about arrests, trials, detentions, previous records, releases and paroles.

Hours before the new law went into effect, the *MT* obtained a temporary injunction against enforcement in Jackson County. The law was repealed four days after it became effective, but Jackson County was the only area in Oregon where criminal information was available for those four days.

☆ ☆ ☆ ☆ ☆ ☆

Ever since his elevation to the presidency in 1970 Jim Jr. had been concerned with the ever-diminishing ability of corporate headquarters to provide Ottaway publishers and editors with quality in-depth critiques and consistent helpful tearsheet comments on news content.

In December 1972, in an all-points message, he wrote, "I don't want us to become, as we grow larger, like some other newspaper groups which devote all their managing attention to revenues, profits and production problems and forget their people, editorial quality and community service."

By the end of 1972, the group included 11 daily and four Sunday publications. One man — Bob Van Fleet — was responsible for helping the operational vice presidents, publishers and editors in their quest for quality in news, editorial, photography and typography. Van Fleet was swamped.

Jim Jr.'s message was a background explanation of his December 12 announcement that Charles King would relinquish the publisher's chair in Middletown to become a corporate vice president in 1973, reporting to the president. King was to take over most of the projects on which Van Fleet had worked since 1970. These included daily reading of all Ottaway papers, tearsheet comments of praise, criticism and suggestions for improvements, special studies of the editorial quality of one paper over a period of time and reports on how all papers handled major news stories. King also would produce *Ottaway*

238

News Extra, the bi-monthly house organ, and would oversee the news service.

Hopefully, Jim Jr.'s memo said, "this will free Bob Van Fleet as an assistant vice president, to travel to our newspapers where he will be a consultant upon request helping to implement the new reporter training program, editorial department policy manuals and doing special projects which may be requested."

Lest the order be construed as a departure from the basic Ottaway philosophy of local autonomy and editorial independence, Jim Jr. bluntly told his field marshals that "neither King nor Van Fleet will become editorial directors or chief editors. They are as anxious as I am to avoid that conflict with our basic philosophy. But we must not be so afraid of that ghost that we fail to invest time, talent and treasure to help our newspapers that need to ask for help on news problems."

John Van Kleeck succeeded King as publisher in Middletown. Ed Somers remained as general manager. Van Kleeck was fresh from a triumphal Sunday *News-Times* start-up in Danbury the previous September. Unlike the Middletown Sunday launching in 1969, the Danbury product paid its way from the beginning. Dick Myers was promoted to publisher and general manager. Forrest C. Palmer, *N-T* editor, also was named assistant general manager.

Just weeks after the Medford signing, Jim Jr. enunciated publicly for the first time his basic philosophy of mechanical modernization and automation as it related to "publishing high-quality newspapers more efficiently." His approach would affect the disbursement of millions of dollars over the next decade and beyond. His views were presented to a group of securities analysts:

"Conversion to photo-composition in composing rooms for from $50,000 to $200,000 per newspaper, depending upon its size and the sophistication of computerized type-setting equipment, produces the most dramatic savings in people and payroll.

"We purchase new offset presses when old letterpresses wear out and have been depreciated over a period of years, so that we don't have to take large book value losses when we write them off. This can cost from $300,000 for a 40-page Goss Urbanite to $2 million for an 80-page Goss Metro and does not produce dramatic savings by itself.

"We will convert to direct printing from plastic plates on younger letterpresses still in good condition and still on our books at relatively high dollar amounts. Plastic plate costs and printing quality have improved greatly in recent years and produce newspapers of almost offset printing quality. Plastic plates allow us to convert composing rooms to photo-composition, and get big savings there without the major capital investment needed for offset presses and new plants.

"We research and purchase similar photo-composition, platemaking and press equipment in all of our newspapers. Common production systems give us group discounts, more pressure on suppliers for better service, more in-house experts able to fix our own machines with common spare parts, emergency back-up units and the future potential of shared central computer systems when they become economical for our newspapers.

"We constantly work to improve the management and productivity of existing old hot type and new photo-composition mechanical departments. We have substantially improved productivity in newly-acquired and existing composing rooms — hot and cold type — by better training of foremen and supervisors and closer management control of worked hours and overtime.

"We measure productivity by reductions in the number of worked hours required to set one full page in a composing room. Ten years ago our average hot type composing room took about eight hours to set one page. Today our five photo-composition shops have cut this in half to a four-hour average, while our six hot type shops now average about six worked hours per page.

"We maintain good relations with the 19 unions with which we have contracts. Ottaway Newspapers has had only one strike in 35 years. We treat our unions fairly but firmly and have generally received the same respect in return.

"We provide production, plant construction and new process conversion expertise from our central headquarters production director, Tom Purcell, and experienced ex-publishers working as operating vice presidents with local publishers. They coordinate group research, purchasing of major new production systems and mechanical trouble-shooting for all papers.

"We invested in so many new pieces of photo-composition and offset equipment during the 1960s that we are very cautious about plunging into the very latest new technology. Our problem is to be certain that new equipment will do what it is supposed to do every day; that it will actually save money; that it won't sell for half as much three months from now; that convincing salesmen are backed up by trained servicemen available when you need them (which many suppliers can't provide today); that the company you buy from will actually be in business a year from now.

"This is an exciting time in the newspaper business with production technology changing so rapidly. It is also an easy time to lose your head, and make very expensive mistakes when selecting new equipment. With the help of our association with Dow Jones and their technological experts, we think we are steering a sensible course through uncertain waters."

240

In April 1973, the new plant of the Plattsburgh *Press-Republican* was unveiled. The minute book set the final price tag at $1,459,000 for building, press, furniture and fixures.

Concurrently the ONI board was discussing a $700,000 capital investment in Oneonta, which would bring the *Star* into the age of offset.

The idea of a printing plant in Wareham to serve both New Bedford and Cape Cod surfaced in 1973, but was dropped. So was a plan to buy 9.69 acres from the New Bedford Redevelopment Authority for a New Bedford printing center. Before the end of the year, directors had more or less decided to build in an industrial park in Fairhaven, just across the Acushnet River from New Bedford.

Ottaway's smallest paper, the Port Jervis *Union-Gazette*, was thinking big, too. Middletown still was printing the *U-G*, but at an annual estimated out-of-pocket loss of more than $80,000. As 1973 drew to a close, the board agreed to equip the *U-G* with a new Goss Community offset press and some hand-me-down typesetting and camera equipment. Milt McLean had provided the building. Now Bob Widmer would complete the homecoming.

Late in King's stewardship of the *Times Herald-Record,* he became impressed with the management potential of a young dayside pressroom foreman who had joined the paper as an apprentice after military service. John Del Santo had simply been looking for a job. That it was on a newspaper happened to be coincidental.

King moved Del Santo into the composing room as a general trainee. Del Santo's next stop was classified sales, then to accounting and finally to circulation. When Van Kleeck replaced King, Del Santo advanced to assistant to the publisher. In 1975 he was named assistant general manager of the *Pocono Record* under Publisher Alan Gould Jr. The man of reels, tensions and pasters had come a long way in a very short time. He was destined to go much further.

241

Sunbury's Richard J. (Dick) Anthony was named general manager in Middletown late in 1974, succeeding Ed Somers. Somers was promoted to publisher in Oneonta, filling the vacancy caused by Don Clifford's reassignment to Traverse City.

In May 1974 the *Oneonta Star* changed its nameplate to the *Daily Star* underscoring its emergence as a regional newspaper covering most of four counties. The typographical format was changed to six columns from eight with the arrival of photo-composition equipment. A five-unit Goss Urbanite also was installed. Planning for the changeover had begun two years before in the Clifford regime. Total outlays came to $737,000.

November 1974 was a particulary sad month for the Lundquest and Ottaway families. Bill Lundquest, a company servant in a myriad of high-level assignments, died at 62 of a heart attack. He had been with the organization since 1939 and had seen it grow from the once anemic *Endicott Daily Bulletin* into a radiant showcase of 12 dailies.

"To know Bill Lundquest was to know one of God's great human beings," Ottaway wrote. "Dedicated to his family, to his friends and to his newspaper, he pursued his publishing duties with rare dedication toward creating the best possible daily newspaper.

"He never knew the clock. He always had time to help out his associates and friends. He was possessed of a delightful sense of humor and an unusual warmth. Those who knew him will never forget him."

Also in 1974, Orren Robbins, general manager at Plattsburgh, was reassigned to the Cape in a similar capacity. Robbins had been a central figure in the *Press Republican* building program and conversion to cold type and offset. He would perform similar duties under Publisher Scott Himstead. There was board room talk of the *Cape Cod Times* going offset. In 1976 ONI would authorize a $1.4 million outlay for four secondhand Goss Metro press units that were for sale in Sacramento, California.

With the Traverse City conversion to photo-composition in 1974, only Sunbury remained a hot-type operation. Preliminary board discussions heralded an early changeover.

242

Late 1974 board minutes indicated negotiations had begun for properties in Mankato and Owatonna, Minnesota. But the *Free Press* and *People's Press* would not become members of the group for another five years. And minutes also alluded to the *Santa Cruz* (Calif.) *Sentinel*, which Ottaway had been courting for years. Acquisition of the *Sentinel* was eight years distant.

Forty two months would pass between the Medford acquisition and the triumphal Ottaway entry into Joplin, Missouri, in late 1976. But even as Jim Ottaway, George Cooper and Maurice Henry relentlessly pursued leads seeking a geographical diversity for the group things were humming at Campbell Hall and around the circuit.

☆ ☆ ☆ ☆ ☆ ☆

As ONI expanded, so did the need for swifter executive transportation. In May 1975 the company retired its first off-the-shelf aircraft, a Piper Navajo. It was replaced by a twin-engine Cessna. The $317,000 outlay (including trade-in) was a pittance in the overall capital expenditure of $4.24 million that year.

The Navajo, with Ed daSilva and Rich Messina at the controls, did a lot more than ferry corporate and line officers on their occasions of business around the circuit. During the original American Press Institute building fund drive in 1973-74, it first carried Jim Ottaway across New England in the company of Mal Mallette. Later, with Turner Catledge aboard, the aircraft called at points between West Virginia and Eastern Alabama. Catledge at the time was the retired executive editor of the *New York Times*. and chairman of the API Building Committee. He died in April 1982.

Ottaway and Catledge brought home a substantial number of equally substantive pledges. They claimed, elfishly, to have had an unbeatable routine: One would jangle a tambourine, the other would extend a collection basket.

"Jim Ottaway," Mallette said, "was exceptionally successful as an API fund raiser for at least two reasons. He was widely known, respected and liked. And prospects knew that his own newspapers were exceptionally generous toward API."

Mallette had other points to remember:

"One of my most vivid personal recollections is that of a fast-paced flying trip through New England. This was the first time either of us had sallied forth in search of contributions. The future of API hinged on the fund campaign, and we were uneasy, not knowing how publishers would respond to our blandishments. The first stop was Pittsfield, Massachusetts, and the *Berkshire Eagle,* where we were greeted warmly and pretty much assured of a contribution. We left Pittsfield feeling a bit more confident.

"Then we flew to Worcester, there to meet Richard (Dick) Steele, publisher of the *Evening Gazette & Telegram.* The Worcester newspapers had always been generous in supporting API, and Jim and I viewed this as a key visit. It was one matter for newspapers to contribute annually to the sponsorship fund that subsidizes the operating budget. It was quite another to ask for big dollars for a building. Dick Steele welcomed us with approximately these words: 'I know what you fellows are. You're pickpockets. But I've dealt with pickpockets before. Please sit down.' All this with a big smile. Within moments we had assurances of a major contribution. And we had even more than that: We had confidence that publishers in general would respond to API's needs."

In the post-merger years through 1976, total Ottaway capital outlays came to a whopping $18.3 million, not counting acquisitions. The betterment programs all were financed internally. In 1975 the directors agreed it would be prudent to reduce, at least temporarily, betterment outlays in order to build up reserves for acquisitions and acquisition debt repayment. However the pace slackened but little.

When Ed Klein was appointed editor in Traverse City in April 1975, King reached out to Sharon for replacement to run

Ottaway News Service. The new chief was Cornelius P. (Doc) Adams who had been news editor of the *Herald*. The primary challenge facing Adams and King was the development of a more efficient news transmission system, linking Campbell Hall to its Washington, Albany, Harrisburg and Boston bureaus and 12 group locations.

20 Joplin

Jim Ottaway always held that a convenient swimming pool was one of the greatest of the amenities, ranking in social importance with suites at the Waldorf-Astoria, Jack Daniels bourbon, Dunhill felt-tip pens and winters in the Caribbean.

Pools were not merely for exercise or relaxation. Pools were a perfectly acceptable environment for business discussions. This became clear to two generations of Ottaway associates and some overnight guests at Campbell Hall. No one ever had to decline an invitation to swim because he lacked trunks. Jim Ottaway had spares in all sizes.

"Jim's idea of the best time to do business was at 7 in the morning," Gene Brown recalled, "or at just about any other time if it was done at poolside. When I was swimming, he'd follow me back, forth and around the pool. He didn't have to chase Lyn Boyd. Boyd never swam."

There were house rules for in-pool conduct. No splashing, for one. One entered the pool via steps at the shallow end. One ill-advised and rather portly publisher, the author recalls, chose to dive into the deep end, sending sheets of water onto the deck. Ottaway spent the next 20 minutes grimly blotting up the outfall with beach towels. One was supposed to g-l-i-d-e through the water.

Ottaway also was enamored of swimming while away from home. The acquisition trail found the chairman in many a lodging place with an attractive pool. Thus swimming trunks were as much a standard part of his traveling wardrobe as shaving equipment. It would have been unthinkable for him to have checked into the Marriott Inn at St. Louis's Lambert

Field, for example, and have to buy a one-shot set of paper trunks at a drugstore.

The date was September 4, 1975. Ottaway and Maurice Henry, the broker, had arrived in St. Louis the night before. Henry had arranged for what he thought would be no more than a routine get-acquainted meeting between Ottaway and Fred Hughes, president and general manager of the *Joplin* (Mo.) *Globe*. Henry had been trying for more than a year to arrange the introduction. Up to now Hughes had declined.

Ottaway and Henry spent the morning of the 4th going over other acquisition prospects in the care of Henry and his colleague, George Cooper. In the mid-1970s the portfolio of possibilities was formidable.

Hughes arrived at noon. The trio lunched in his suite that just happened to overlook the Marriott pool. Possibly Henry was thinking of a letter he had received from Hughes the previous July in which Hughes had written, "I would be pleased to talk with Jim Ottaway with the understanding that I would be seeking information only for possible use at some undetermined date in the future."

Hughes was an admirer of Dow Jones. He had studied the Ottaway group. He liked what he had learned and said as much. It was clear that now he wanted to get to know Jim Ottaway.

As far back as October 1974, Hughes wrote to Henry, "I recognize that he (Ottaway) represents one of the outstanding publishing organizations in the country and . . . I appreciate his interest."

The Marriott pool, Hughes recalled, was the milieu in which they "became acquainted." Ottaway had suggested a swim before serious conversation. He, of course, was prepared. Hughes bought a set of paper trunks.

No thawing out was necessary. An immediate kinship developed when each discovered the other was a Michigan native. Hughes grew up in Grand Rapids. We have seen how Ottaway's geographic background helped set the tone of the Traverse City acquisition effort.

Hughes talked about the recent history of the *Globe*, its organizational setup, building, press and photo-composition equipment and said he was seriously considering installing

247

VDTs and computers. In turn Ottaway described the group's relationship with Dow Jones and answered a host of questions about Campbell Hall's relationship to its individual newspapers.

Informational discussions continued back in Hughes's suite. At about 3:30 he invited Ottaway to tango: "Jim, we've come a long way. If everything is going to be confidential we ought to get everything out on the table." Out came the *Globe* financial statements.

"As far as I'm concerned," Hughes told the author, "the sale of the *Globe* was consummated in the swimming pool. Jim and I never had any arm's-length negotiations. When all the facts were in, we came to an agreement in 15 minutes. It was a natural."

Hughes, then 60, was concerned about the *Globe*'s future. His principal associate was Harrison Lang Rogers, 56, who carried the titles of publisher and editor.

Both Hughes and Rogers had sons-in-law on the payroll. Gregory Taylor, who married a Hughes daughter, had the title of assistant to the general manager and was primarily involved in mechanical operations. Robert Haugen, Rogers's protege, an Arizonan whose business background was in banking, was assigned to the promotion office.

Hughes's chief concern was what the future held for *Globe* stockholders. Who would run the *Globe* if anything happened to him and Lang Rogers? Diversified and absentee shareholder interests could create what Hughes called a "chaotic" situtation over who would manage the property.

Hughes had been romanced by acquisition suitors for several years. One had offered $2 million above the final Ottaway price without even examining the *Globe*'s books.

"It wasn't the type of ownership we wanted," he said.

The *Globe* family tree goes back to 1872, at the height of the Joplin area lead and zinc mining boom. The first daily, the *Mining News*, shortly became the *Joplin News*. Then came the *Joplin Herald*. The *News* and *Herald* merged in 1901. The *Globe* was founded in 1896 and was incorporated as a stock company in 1899.

Shortly after, Gilbert Barbee, a mining operator, builder and a colorful Democratic politician gained controlling interest in the *Globe*.

Heated rivalry marked the operations of the *News Herald* and *Globe* in wide open Joplin. With saloons, love stores, gambling and horse racing, it became an oasis for alcoholically dry Kansas, Oklahoma and Arkansas, attracting, as one history said, "its full share of outlaws."

A third newspaper, the *Joplin American,* made a brief appearance in 1905. It was financed principally by Alfred Harrison Rogers, grandfather of H. Lang Rogers. A.H. Rogers built and was president of the Southwest Missouri Railway, an interurban streetcar system linking Joplin with district mining towns. The *American* lasted nine months in Joplin, then moved its operation to Fort Smith, Arkansas.

A centennial history of Joplin as recorded over the years in its various newspapers, was published by the *Globe* in March 1973. In a masterpiece of understatement it said only that "in 1910 Mr. Rogers purchased controlling interest in the *Globe* and became president." What it didn't say was how A.H. Rogers wrested control from Gilbert Barbee, his arch-foe in Joplin.

On one melancholy occasion, when a girl was struck and killed by one of Rogers's streetcars, Barbee's *Globe* led Page 1 with the screaming headline 'A.H. ROGERS A MURDERER.'

A libel action wasn't the way they avenged slurs in Southwest Missouri in 1910.

Rogers and several of his closest friends in the mining industry quietly started to buy up *Globe* stock. (Barbee held roughly 45 percent.)

Soon the cabal had somewhat more than 50 percent. At that point Rogers, accompanied by Harrison and Robert, his sons, both wearing six-shooters, strode into Barbee's office. Rogers slapped the stock on Barbee's desk and told the publisher he had 24 hours to leave the building. He did.

The story was told to the author by Lang Rogers.

Barbee retired temporarily from publishing but returned to start the *Joplin Tribune*. It closed after 18 months.

A.H. Rogers died in 1920. He was succeeded as president of the *Globe* by Harrison C., who served until his death in 1946. Robert had died at 18, the victim of a heart attack.

249

Harrison Rogers, in turn, was succeeded by Clay Cowgill Blair, who had become general manager in the early 1920s. Blair, as farm editor under A.H. Rogers, made newspaper history by founding the first full-scale farm department of any daily in the country. During the heyday of lead and zinc mining, the *Globe* operated a newsroom mining department.

After a protracted printer strike in 1922, the *Globe* acquired the financially ailing afternoon *News Herald* and moved its operation into the *Globe* plant. The *News Herald* was discontinued in August 1970.

Fred Hughes became affiliated with the *Globe* just after World War II. He had married Rebecca (Becky) Blair, C.C.'s daughter, in the early 1940s. They met while they were students at the University of Missouri. Hughes practiced law, then served with the Federal Bureau of Investigation during the war. He joined the *Globe* as assistant to the general manager, the latter one of Blair's titles. His first assignment was to seek new sources of newsprint, which at the time was in short supply.

Hughes became president and business manager at the time of Blair's death in 1966. *Globe* bylaws stipulated that the president be the chief executive of the company.

Lang Rogers was the son of Harrison C. He started as a cub reporter in 1936, working summers while in high school. At the outbreak of war he enlisted as a private first class, entered a Marine Corps officer training school, served with distinction in several Pacific area campaigns and was mustered out a major. He then entered the active reserve.

During the Blair regime, Rogers occupied all the traditional newsroom chairs on his way to the top.

The initiative to sell the Globe Publishing Company came from Hughes.

Lang Rogers, virtually to the end, opposed the move. History must record that Rogers was emotional about his journalistic lineage, which went back to 1910 and old A.H. Rogers. He thought of Hughes, if you will, as a sort of latecomer.

The tenuous relationship between the two was simply a well-understood fact of life at the *Globe*.

Lang Rogers's own family held 25 percent of almost 39,000

outstanding shares. A cousin, Mrs. Katherine Rogers, who lived in Los Angeles, held 31 percent. She never visited Joplin. Fred Hughes's family and Hughes relatives had 27 percent. The remaining 17 percent was minority spread.

(Katherine Rogers's last name was coincidental. Divorced twice, she married a Rogers with no ties to the newspaper family.)

Katherine Rogers and the minority shareholders were perfectly content with Hughes's administration and generally went along with his policies and programs. In effect, Hughes controlled the votes. Rogers had little choice but to swim with the tide, strong links to the past notwithstanding.

Maurice Henry wrote to Ottaway immediately after the Marriott meeting, assuring the chief that Hughes "prefers being associated with Dow Jones and Ottaway if they make a sale." He cited Hughes's concern over what future roles Hughes, Rogers and their sons-in-law would have in the event of a sale. Hughes also told Henry that he and Rogers would want to end up with the *Globe*'s one-third interest in television station KOAM-TV in Joplin. Midcontinent Telecasting, Inc. was founded in 1953.

The correspondence, dated September 6, indicates that Rogers was not yet aware of the Marriott discussions.

"We have to dress our proposal out basically to his satisfaction because he then, in turn, could recommend it to his associate, Rogers, and the other stockholders. Hughes has told me several times that 'other stockholders are always in agreement with me when I make a recommendation to them.' "

During a second head-to-head meeting between Ottaway and Hughes December 1-2 — this time in Joplin — the ties grew stronger. Ottaway was an overnight guest in the Hughes home. Again Hughes pressed for details on how Ottaway would operate the *Globe* "if we made a deal." Becky Hughes told Ottaway that there was an obvious emotional issue involved, citing her father's long presidency and her husband's close ties to the community.

Lang Rogers wasn't in Joplin at the time. He was attending an American Press Institute seminar in Reston, Virginia. Coincidentally, two of his fellow participants were Jim Ottaway

251

Jr. and Steve Ryder. Hughes urged Ottaway to meet Rogers in Reston, which he did on December 3 after the API evening session had ended. Hughes warned Ottaway that he didn't know how Rogers would react to the possibility of a sale, but added "that with the fragmentation of the various families, stock ownership was being divided more and more and (I) feel that the time has come to do something if the price is right and we can feel comfortable with the new ownership."

Rogers's reaction was predictable. After the API session he wrote to Ottaway, "I really do not have any current aspirations directed toward the sale of our family s interest in the *Globe*." And as late as June 1976, as negotiations were jelling, Rogers told the Ottaways he had "a kind of pain in the stomach when it came to selling because of my family's long association with the newspaper."

Meanwhile on June 20, 1976, Jim Ottaway stepped down as chief executive officer of ONI. He was about to reach age 65. Jim Jr. succeeded his father.

Ottaway received another honor that year. He and Paul Miller, chairman of the Gannett Company, were the first named as members of the New York State Publishers Association Hall of Fame.

"They are unusual and rare men, devoted to the profession of journalism and its highest ideals, men who cast large and inspirational shadows," the citation read.

The acquisition came in two steps. In August 1976 Hughes, Rogers and Ottaway announced an agreement in principle for ONI to purchase an 83 percent interest. On November 1 Jim Jr. announced from Kansas City that ONI had acquired 100 percent of the *Globe* stock, making it the 13th member of the group.

At the time the *Globe* had a daily circulation of 40,000 and just under 42,000 on Sunday Hughes and Rogers, each with an eight-year contract, remained at their desks. So did their sons-in-law, Greg Taylor and Bob Haugen.

The purchase price came to $12,028,000, with $3.1 million down and the balance over 10 years at seven percent. George Cooper's finder's fee was $69,000. For his work Maurice Henry was paid $24,000. The sale did not include KOAM-TV. Hughes and Rogers took over the *Globe*'s one-third interest in the station.

☆ ☆ ☆ ☆ ☆ ☆

The *Globe* was not an attractive editorial product, at least by Ottaway standards. Ottaway had commissioned three market studies in the fall of 1975, one a quickie by Bob Van Fleet. The others were done by ONI's Ed Hill and William (Bill) Clabby, then managing editor of AP-Dow Jones and in 1985 vice president of DJ's Information Services group.

Hill alluded to the paucity of regional news, what with the *Globe*'s normal area of circulation responsibility into parts of Kansas, Oklahoma and Arkansas — not to mention Missouri. He also panned the press work, "caused, perhaps, by the absence of quality control." Hill found "dirty" pages, poor photo reproduction and blurred type to be the rule rather than the exception.

Clabby concluded that from a "quality of product" standpoint, the "Joplin paper seems to be years behind the times." "To put it bluntly," he wrote, "The paper is hard to read and is stiff and unattractive. There's nothing to convey a feeling of breeziness or modernity about it. Worse yet, the content is woefully lacking. The paper depends heavily on press association copy to fill its pages, while good local copy is at a premium. I looked at a week's papers and can say there wasn't anything imaginative in the way of features to be found."

Globe executives agreed that the printing was not uniformly acceptable. The letterpress was a 96-page, six-unit Hoe Colormatic, which began life on Long Island in the 1950s with the ill-fated *Suffolk County Sun.* The press was the keystone of a $1 million, 24,000 square foot expansion program started in 1972.

Why not an offset press? Cost considerations precluded such an investment with the building program in progress. The new pressroom was equipped with knockout panels against the time offset would become financially prudent. The *Globe* Colormatic never ran with hot metal printing plates. Plastic plates were the norm.

Nowhere in the transcripts of discussions with Hughes or Rogers did the Ottaways allude to the *Globe*'s editorial product, responsibility for which was divided. Rogers oversaw the news report, but the editor of the editorial page reported directly to Hughes.

Middle-level newsroom staffers conceded that all was not well during the four years preceding the acquisition.

"We were undergoing a organizational effort by the International Typographical Union, firing line leadership was weak and the pay was low," was the consensus.

The staff understandably was apprehensive about Ottaway ownership at first.

"But after we got to know Jim Jr. and his colleagues, the tension eased," said James (Jim) Ellis, the recently-named managing editor. "We had opportunities for training, we found out that Ottaway editorial independence meant just that and almost immediately our wages and benefits increased.

"Just as important was the resurgence of strong newsroom leadership, additions to staff and knowing exactly what we were trying to do."

Ottaway seminars at Campbell Hall, American Press Institute seminars and regional and national meetings of journalism societies exposed *Globe* editors to a world they'd hardly known. They also relished tearsheet critiques from headquarters and welcomed the periodic Van Fleet-King newsroom workshops.

The $400,000 newsroom budget of 1976 exceeded $1.12 million in 1984.

Almost $5.5 million in capital improvements have been made at the *Globe* in the past decade, including a new five-unit Goss Headliner offset press.

The press conversion cost a bit more than $3 million, well under budget. In another example of Dow Jones-Ottaway synergism, DJ released excess press equipment and a

254

second-hand folder, which Goss mated with new custom-built offset units. In effect the *Globe* saved approximately $2 million.

The Ottaways moved swiftly to dispel any apprehension over their new ownership. Right after the Kansas City closing, they toured the plant with Hughes and were introduced individually to every employee. Then came a typical Ottaway gesture. He invited all the department heads to dinner at the Rafters, one of Joplin's best restaurants. Out came his reassuring set speech on local control and other philosophical basics. The group of 20 was charmed.

The Ottaway personality was a constant. Only minute details were variables.

Weeks later there was a follow-up dinner at Twin Hills Country Club for community leaders, department heads and wives. By now Ottaway was a *Globe* household word. But on this occasion there was an impressive new ingredient: the top brass from Dow Jones. In attendance were Bill Kerby, Warren Phillips and Ray Shaw.

Not surprisingly some *Globe* people still talk of Phillips's need to leave the party early and the fact that the DJ jet would have him in New York before they finished dessert. It was an unobtrusive example of the economic truism that time is synonymous with money. Hurry was not a way of life in Joplin's corner of Missouri.

Dick Barker, general manager of the *New Bedford Standard-Times* was appointed GM of the *Globe* in June 1977 and reported the following September.

Technically, Fred Hughes still was chief executive officer, retaining the title of president but yielding the GM role. Rogers's duties did not change. He reported to Barker.

In June 1979 Barker was named publisher and Hughes received the title of chairman of the board. Full command had passed to an Ottaway-trained executive.

Greg Taylor was assigned to the *Danbury News-Times* in 1977 for further management training. At the same time Bob Haugen moved to Cape Cod for training at the *Times*. After a year Taylor returned to Joplin as general manager. Haugen elected not to continue in newspapering. His marriage having failed, he returned to Arizona.

Hughes and Rogers stepped down in the fall of 1984, their employment contracts having expired.

"Let me tell you about two of Jim Ottaway's peccadilloes," Hughes said to the author in 1984. "For one thing I couldn't read his handwriting. I had to phone him to find out what he was saying. One day he told me his father had placed him before a typewriter at about age five, so he'd never learned penmanship.

"And on one visit to Joplin he took Becky and me out to dinner, but when the check came he had no money. I picked up the tab. Several weeks passed and no reimbursement from Jim. So I sent him a bill. Then a second bill. Finally I received a check, which I held — also for weeks, waiting for him to react.

"Selling the newspaper to the Ottaway group was great. But just as great was the friendship with Jim that resulted."

21 Essex County Newspapers

"You're right. The time has come to have some fun!"

Philip Saltonstall Weld had, in effect, chosen to continue his love affair with transatlantic sailboat racing. The time had come, he concluded, to chart the orderly transition of his Essex County (Mass.) Newspapers (ECN) group to a compatible publisher.

Weld's decision was reached in mid-spring of 1976. In April he had been rescued from his 60-foot trimaran Gulf Streamer, which had capsized in the Atlantic Ocean off Cape Sable, Nova Scotia, in the crush of a 40-foot rogue wave. He was 61.

Weld's closest associate and minority owner of ECN was Alexander N. Stoddart. Instinctively, Stoddart knew what the first order of business had to be as soon as Weld returned from his ill-fated voyage. Was the principal proprietor going to continue his avocation of blue water sailing, with its obvious attendant perils? If so, the future of the newspaper properties and their employees well might be headed for heavy seas.

Weld and Stoddart took a long drive along the Massachusetts coast, threaded their way into New Hampshire and visited their weekly operation in Hampton. They talked about Weld's fortuitous rescue by a British container ship, and more to the point what could have happened had Weld not survived.

Phil Weld had had plenty of time to reflect on the melancholy possibility of death at sea. He (Weld) was not surprised, Stoddart discovered, when the inevitable question was posed: Publishing or sailing?

Stoddart was not surprised at Weld's reply: Sailing.

He knew his colleague reveled in challenges. Phil Weld was

257

an adventurer, whose greatest sea-going triumph would make headlines around the world.

Both knew that the Commonwealth of Massachusetts had one of the toughest trust laws in the country. Had Weld been lost, his widow would have had to sell to the highest bidder. There would have been no opportunity to choose an appropriate buyer. A loyal staff well might face a disagreeable future. Chaos might result.

"You don't build for 27 years and then dump everything," Weld remarked. The course had been set: "Let's find the right buyer."

On May 25, 1977, Jim Ottaway took an out-of-the-blue call from Stoddart, who said that he and Mrs. Stoddart were going to be in Vermont over the Memorial Day weekend and that he would like to come to Campbell Hall on the 31st "to get some advice."

Stoddart knew both Jim and Jim Jr. Their paths had crossed at the American Press Institute. He also had talked with Jim at publisher meetings. "Jim Ottaway," Stoddart said, "preached our philosophy."

Weld was enthusiastic when Stoddart suggested an approach to Ottaway. He, too, knew Jim Sr.

"A publisher," Weld said often, "must have the highest sense of purpose."

Stoddart and Ottaway got right down to business. His visitor assured the chief that he and Weld had not talked to any other prospective buyer.

The Essex County properties at the time consisted of the *Gloucester Daily Times*, the *Newburyport Daily News*, the *Beverly Times* and the *Peabody Times*. All were printed in the modern Beverly plant, which contained eight units of Goss Urbanite offset press and two folders. And there was the *Hampton* (N.H.) *Union*, a weekly, two year-round free shoppers and a free summer tabloid. ECN also printed the New England edition of the *Christian Science Monitor* under contract.

Hampton is located in Rockingham County, just across the Massachusetts border. Stoddart pointed out that it was one of the fastest-growing areas in the U.S. and in the not too-distant future well might be able to support a daily newspaper. Five

258

years later Ottaway would acquire the *Exeter* (N.H.) *News-Letter,* then in direct competition with the *Hampton Union,* setting the stage for just that sort of eventuality.

Stoddart, then 50, also made it clear that he wanted to stay with the business if it was sold. Weld owned 90 percent of ECN, Stoddart 10.

The conversation went further after a luncheon, which Jim Jr. attended. Stoddart said he envisioned a 9-11 percent after-tax profit for the current year on a gross of approximately $6 million. He also said that Weld was interested in a stock exchange to avoid capital gains taxes, but that he might want some cash.

As for timing on a sale, Stoddart said there was no particular hurry, but he "suspected Weld would like to complete a deal by fall."

He said that an appraisal of the ECN properties was about to begin and that he and Weld would like to have it in hand before proceeding further.

At the end of his first communique to Bill Kerby and Warren Phillips, Ottaway wrote "Stoddart impresses Jimmy and me very much . . . We think he is the kind of person who would not only be excellent in running ECN, but would be a fine addition to our organization."

Ottaway promptly commissioned three market studies, one in great depth by Ed Hill, the others, comparatively brief, by Allan Meath and Bob Van Fleet.

None of the researchers liked everything they saw. But there were no suggestions that the project be dropped.

The main concern was the proximity of Beverly and Peabody to the then 31,000-circulation *Salem Evening News,* which outsold ECN on some of ECN's own turf. Salem, the Ottaways learned from Weld and Stoddart, was a mismanaged property, wracked by incredibly lavish and stifling union contracts of Boston dimensions.

From the start, however, Ottaway showed an interest in adding Salem to the ECN properties, built-in labor problems notwithstanding.

A consultant letter from Weld to Jim Jr. in August 1979 suggested "it would be much more fun for your group to be

259

expanding what you've got as opposed to making further acquisitions of established properties."

Weld favored establishing a daily in Southern New Hampshire rather than going after Salem.

But pressed on the Salem question by Gerry Tache, Campbell Hall liaison with ECN, Weld early in 1980 said Salem "is a prize worth working for." Tache's notes quote Weld as saying that by combining Salem with ECN, Ottaway would have the potential of becoming the fourth largest newspaper market in Massachusetts."

Weld, Tache wrote, felt strongly that if Salem did come into the Ottaway group the ECN should continue to publish five separate newspapers, but that "eventually" Salem-Peabody-Beverly could be melded into a single market.

Would it be possible to acquire Salem, just a river's width from Beverly? Not now, Stoddart advised Jim Jr. Stoddart was fairly close to C.J. (Cy) Newbegin and Damon Lyons, president and vice president, respectively, of the *Evening News*. Stoddart would put Ottaway in touch with them. He did. Jim Jr. and Newbegin golfed in September 1982 at the venerable Myopia Hunt Club. The only tangible result was the outcome of the match. Newbegin won.

Phil Weld took over negotiations once Stoddart had arranged the meeting between seller and prospective buyer. Some sessions were held on the veranda of Weld's gracious home on Dolliver's Neck, overlooking Gloucester harbor. On a clear day the negotiators could see the Boston skyline.

Weld, graduate of Milton Academy and Harvard College, was a Brahmin who took the best of everything for granted.

"No," Stoddart told the author, "make that a maverick Brahmin. Phil didn't follow the code 100 percent."

Weld issued two caveats at the outset: the price had to be fair and Ottaway had to agree not to reduce the editorial departments, which were purposely overstaffed to protect Weld's penchant for special assignments.

In mid-July Allan Meath spent a day with Stoddart in the latter's office at the *Beverly Times,* and submitted a detailed report to Campbell Hall on the deployment of personnel in all ECN departments.

"A quick analysis," Meath wrote, "would indicate that there certainly is some overstaffing."

Ottaway researchers apparently were surprised to discover that each of the ECN papers had its own editorial staff. Meath suggested also that "a revamping of the news operation be of primary concern."

What no one in Ottaway seems to have recognized immediately is that the architects of ECN over the years obviously knew what they wanted the end result to be: a group that could withstand metro challenges and prosper. To do this ECN units had to be different. They had to have their own personalities. It was the Weld-Stoddart way of saying, "We know who it's for and what it's for."

Phil Weld's first newspaper job after graduation from Harvard was on the *Chicago Daily News* as a general assignment reporter. During World War II he served brilliantly with Merrill's Marauders in Burma.

Upon his discharge in 1945, Weld knew he wanted to return to newspapering — but in New England. He entered the old *Boston Herald's* promotion department. Then came an opportunity to join a group interested in starting a new daily in Manchester, New Hampshire, home of the late William Loeb's *Union Leader*. A pro forma budget indicated the group would need at least $300,000 for the first 18 months of operation. But wartime price controls ended, the price of newsprint soared and Weld backed off. The start-up estimate was no longer valid.

Then, Weld said, "I talked my way into a job as executive assistant to the lawyer managing the affairs of the failing *Boston Post,*" and had a "wonderful education in how not to run a newspaper."

During hostilities, Weld had written to his wife, the former Anne Warren, that his principal ambition was to become his own proprietor. In the late 1940s he discovered that a 35 percent interest could be bought in the *Gloucester Daily Times* and *Newburyport Daily News* for $114,000. Weld borrowed from his mother and wife, added his own resources and took the plunge.

Weld's and Stoddart's stars came into conjunction in 1950.

For three summers, 1949-51, Weld published the *Cape Ann Summer Sun,* a free distribution weekly designed to serve the resort business. At the time Stoddart was attending Johns Hopkins University in Baltimore and working nights on the *Baltimore Sun*. The Stoddarts summered in Gloucester.

"I wrote to Phil on a *Sun* letterhead," Stoddart recalled, "asking him for a job." Weld's reply was succinct: "You're the editor." But Stoddart soon discovered he had other duties. "I was just about everything," he said.

The *Summer Sun* according to Weld, never did more than break even, "but it introduced me to Roger W. Babson, Gloucester's wealthiest and most celebrated native son and the most important man in my business career."

Roger Ward Babson, statistician and economist, perhaps is remembered most for the Babson Institute, near Boston, a two-year school devoted to business training. His own theory of business cycles, based on the Newtonian law of action and reaction, reached its apogee of credibility in 1929, when he forecast an imminent drop in stock prices. Within two months the market collapsed, touching off the Great Depression.

Babson also was a vehement dry and ran for president on the Prohibition Party ticket in 1940.

Weld's introduction to the goateed man of graphs and charts came by way of a phone call. Somehow Weld's distribution system had contrived to leave a bundle of 50 *Summer Suns* on his kitchen steps.

"I enjoy your paper, but one copy is enough," he told Weld.

Weld drove the company jeep (bearing the legend, "Make hay while the *SUN* shines") to the Babson residence to retrieve the unwanted 49 copies and somewhat surprisingly, found himself in the kitchen discussing Weld's dreams of the future.

"There began a friendship that gave me a business education as well as access to the $300,000 I needed to complete the purchase of the Gloucester and Newburyport properties," Weld wrote in 1981.

The interest on the 1952 loan was pegged directly to the newstand price of the papers. Three cents a copy equated to three percent interest. But Weld's father convinced the new publisher to set a cap of 10 percent on what Babson could charge. Twelve years later single copies sold for 10 cents, but by then the debt had been retired.

Stoddart was named advertising manager of the Gloucester and Newburyport papers when Weld completed the acquisition. In 1960, when Weld embarked on a 18-month sabbatical as publisher of the European edition of the *New York Herald-Tribune,* he named Stoddart publisher of his papers. On Weld's return from Paris, Stoddart began to acquire shares in ECN.

On January 2, 1964, Weld and Stoddart acquired the *Beverly Times,* and two years later bought the weekly *Peabody Times,* converting it to a twice-a-week paper, then to daily status in 1976. The *Hampton Union* came into the fold in 1975.

A purchase and sale agreement between Ottaway and the ECN partners was signed February 22, 1978, in Boston.The price: $10 million. There had been a handshake agreement the previous December 18.

"The price is a fair one," Weld told his staffs. "We'll never know if it was the most we could have gotten because we didn't try to find out. Out aim was to choose the most appropriate new owners. We decided on the Ottaways because of their demonstrated devotion to newspaper excellence in communities of the same size and character as ours. We liked their belief in leaving authority in the hands of the local publisher."

The sale was completed May 30 for cash and promissory notes. Weld stepped down as president but agreed to remain in a consulting capacity. Stoddart was named president and publisher.

At one point in the negotiations Ottaway and Weld discussed a possible exchange of stock, but that foundered because Ottaway's offer was based on a per-share price below the current market. "Phil was upset," Stoddart recalled, "but considering the Dow Jones two-for-one splits in 1981 and 1983 he would have been well ahead." Ottaway's reasoning was that the DJ shares surely would increase in value.

Ottaway and Stoddart never discussed a stock swap. The new president was paid in cash.

Weld and Stoddart were among the very few sellers who published the sale price.

"It's a lousy publisher who doesn't run the price," Stoddart said tartly. "It's part of the news."

Alex Stoddart's 30-year business relationship with Phil Weld was a way of life that now was to vanish. Their executive duties were clearly defined. Each did his job. Neither interfered with the other. If Weld wanted to race sailing craft and not appear in the office for five or six weeks, so be it. Stoddart managed nicely, thank you, with a system of his own devisings.

With the advent of Ottaway control, there arrived from Campbell Hall operational vice presidents, a strange new chart of accounts, detailed budget preparation, monthly profit-and-loss analyses and a haystack of other paperwork. The former "one-man band," as Stoddard called himself, began to feel as though he was between the jaws of a corporate vise.

Stoddart's relationship with The System began to erode 18 months after the signing. An individual of patrician bearing, he was a willing acquisition hostage but a not-so-willing conformist. He had turned down an extended employment contract, settling with a handshake for three years. "If I go I want to go as a friend," he told the Ottaways.

In June 1980 he wrote to Jim Jr., "I confess to fighting the system to a degree, sometimes consciously, sometimes not. There is a basic philosophic difference in our modes of management." Stoddart pledged "every effort to conform to policy" and suggested he and Jim Jr. take another look a year hence. "If it's not working, we should admit it."

On February 13, 1981, Stoddart and Ottaway met at the Hyatt Regency in Cambridge and decided to terminate the relationship. "I fear our modus operandi was fated never to be compatible," Stoddart wrote afterward. "You gave me a fair shake all the way."

In a somewhat whimsical coda, Stoddart alluded to what Jim Jr. called a "lack of communication" by ECN: "There were 446 written messages in 30 months. That's one every 1.7 working days, not counting telephone calls!"

Stoddart's resignation was announced February 19. He stepped down at 54 on March 1 with a consulting agreement that would run for 10 years.

"I would still choose Ottaway," he said.

Stoddart wasn't the only acquired CEO to wag an imperious finger at The System. But he was the only one who openly viewed it somewhere on the spectrum between awe and disdain. A few others simply floated off silently on the tide of cash or stock paid for their properties.

Since 1961 an outrageous exhortative metaphor had guided Ottaway's field generals: "Put it on the Erie-Lackawanna* and see if it gets off at Campbell Hall!" It wasn't always easy for the newcomers. Yesterday's hometown bravura was subject to the checks and balances inherent in any publicly-owned corporation.

Under an agreement reached at the very first Ottaway Newspapers board meeting, for example, ONI vice presidents, publishers or general managers theoretically had authority to spend up to $10,000 without asking questions. Approval of the chairman or president of ONI was required for an outlay between $10,000-$50,000. The ONI board itself could authorize up to $100,000, but anything above that had to go before DJ directors. By 1985 the limits had been increased substantially.

Frank O. King succeeded Stoddart as president and publisher of ECN. King came to the group in 1964 as an advertising salesman, moving up the ladder to assistant publisher in 1979.

King made but one change in the executive line-up, bringing in James A. (Jim) Wells from Cape Cod as general manager of ECN. Wells subsequently defected to Gannett's *USA Today*. Wells eventually was succeeded as GM by Peter Watson, ex-editor of the *Gloucester Daily Times* and later the *Beverly-Peabody Times*. Ralph W. Gibbs continued as group comptroller, retaining his title of GM in Gloucester. William L. (Bill) Plante Jr. remained group executive editor and GM in Newburyport. The overlapping GM titles preceded the acquisition and would be eliminated by attrition.

*Now, of course, Conrail

In March 1981 Stoddart — now a consultant — received a call from Charles Thayer, 42, editor, co-publisher and vice president of the Exeter (N.H.) News-Letter Company, publisher of the *News-Letter,* a paid 8,000-circulation weekly; 10 free weekly shoppers; and a flourishing commercial printing shop.

Thayer told Stoddart that he and his brother Harry, 45, had "probably" decided to sell, because they were too undercapitalized to take advantage of their potential market. Stoddart had maintained sporadic contact with the Thayers well before the advent of Ottaway.

"It is my feeling," Stoddart wrote to Jim Jr., "that the *News-Letter* is worth quite a bit to Ottaway, as with Hampton's 6,000 circulation right next door it would certainly have daily potential for the area."

Jim Jr. hurried to Exeter, home of Phillips Exeter Academy, where he had prepared for Yale in the 1950s. He paled at the Thayers's asking price of $2.6 million but found plenty of reasons to try to negotiate a "reasonable" deal.

"The geographical fact," he wrote, "is that the Exeter weeklies and our Hampton weekly and the *Newburyport Daily News* fit together quite neatly. It should be a natural merger, creating a strong base for two or one weekly newspaper which could be expanded to two times or three times a week quickly, with the strong possibility of starting a morning daily. . .

"The *News-Letter* printing plant is publishing 400 tabloid pages a week now, so it could print 200 standard pages a week without any strain or new equipment. This would allow start-up of a daily newspaper averaging 40 pages five days a week. It would probably allow printing of the *Newburyport Daily News* in Exeter to take pressure off the Beverly plant. It would allow going morning . . . in Newburyport . . . without disturbing the other Essex County newspapers' afternoon publication."

Another statistic that intrigued Jim Jr. was Rockingham County's population growth. From 1970 to 1980 it shot up 37 percent, compared to 24.8 percent for the state of New Hampshire and 11 percent nationwide.

By October 1981 serious negotiations were under way. At that point Jim Jr. wrote to Ray Shaw, now president of Dow Jones, "We estimate we could start a daily two years after purchase of the *News-Letter* and build it to 10,000 circulation within two

266

years, with a potential 20,000 circulation by 1990."

In May 1982 Jim Jr. requested board approval of an agreement to buy the News-Letter Company for $1.5 million cash and notes, with $500,000 down at closing and the balance over five years at 10 percent. ONI also would assume $250,000 of the company's long-tem debt.

The closing took place on July 30.

John P. Kinney, assistant to the publisher in New Bedford, was tapped as general manager of Rockingham County Newspapers (RCN), which included the three paid and the 10 unpaid weeklies. Kinney had been editor of the *Port Jervis Union-Gazette*, Ottaway News Service bureau chief in Albany and editor of the *Traverse City Record-Eagle*.

Harry Thayer was appointed business manager and Robert M. (Buzz) Herbert, fomerly business manager and editor in Hampton, was named editor of all RCN weeklies. Charles Thayer found employment outside the publishing field.

By 1985 the number of RCN free weeklies had been reduced to three.

☆ ☆ ☆ ☆ ☆ ☆

In late 1981 Ottaway commissioned a survey of Beverly and Peabody readers in an effort to determine if they were unhappy with the products and if so, why. Campbell Hall and ECN management were, in effect, shooting for better penetration at the southern end of the ECN crescent.

The survey turned up what readers described as an appetite for more regional news. Accordingly, in mid-June 1982 the strategies consolidated Beverly and Peabody into one regional edition.

The idea wasn't new. Just before the combination appeared, Stoddart wrote to Jim Jr., agreeing that "overall, it makes sense." He recalled that he and Weld had considered a somewhat similar move, but had abandoned the idea as too expensive.

The Weld-Stoddart plan would not have actually combined

267

the papers because, as Weld wrote, "the cities are not compatible nor contiguous and we did not want to lose what identity we had in both areas."

Their solution would have been a North Shore Times containing a third section with "many common pages and some replates for the four communities of Beverly, Peabody, Salem and Danvers. The front page of the third section would be the *Beverly Times* in Beverly, *Peabody Times* in Peabody and so on."

Stoddart described the 1982 venture as a "calculated risk but one worth taking if the penetration problem is to be solved." To which Jim Jr. added a marginal note: "Amen."

Just before Christmas Jim Jr. wrote to Weld that the "combo is gaining steadily." But his cheery report belied what lay ahead.

Instead of penetration gains, the combination product suffered a severe circulation setback, especially in the Peabody area.

The very subscribers who called for more regional news now complained that the ECN brass had taken away their hometown papers or "the area identity" that had so worried Weld and Stoddart.

"There simply wasn't enough punch in the product," one ECN executive would say. We should have driven Salem back into Salem. If we had been able to get 1,000 new starts, Salem would have panicked."

The combo package lasted until October 1983.

Beverly regained most of its lost circulation. Peabody did not.

In the frenetic, hurrying world of Ottaway, if only one hand was busy, there always was something for the other to do. So it was during the 24 months preceding acquisition of the Essex County group.

As far back as 1974 Jim Ottaway had been courting Jared

268

How, owner of the Free Press Company with papers in Mankato and Owatonna in southern Minnesota. Ottaway and How signed an agreement of sale in August 1978. The closing took place early in January 1979.

At the same time the Ottaways were zeroing in on the *Ashland* (Ky.) *Daily Independent,* which would become the 20th member of the ONI group on April 30, 1979.

The Minnesota and Kentucky stories will be told in succeeding chapters.

The mid-seventies found ONI a radiant showcase of vastly-improved news quality and presentation, especially among the johnny-come-latelys. Board minutes of late 1976 recorded a statistic that warmed the hearts of the accountants at Campbell Hall: Seven of the then 13 papers achieved an operating profit of $1 million before taxes. Middletown and New Bedford each came near the $2.5-million mark.

And there was talk about a new Goss Urbanite offset press and related equipment for Traverse City. Estimated cost: $1.117 million.

During 1977 capital investments totaling $3,589,000 were authorized. Prime beneficiaries were Cape Cod, for pressroom, mailroom and circulation office construction; Traverse City, for ad composition equipment; Sunbury for land acquisition for a press building; and Danbury, for newsprint warehouse expansion, a mailroom and loading dock.

A new executive slot was added to the corporate framework at Campbell Hall early in 1978, directly related to ONI's growth and the virtually limitless permutations of legal, semilegal and money management affairs.

"Although we have received top-notch legal advice from Bill Carey, Bruce Becker and Frank Parker," Jack Goodreds wrote to the headquarters staff, "we need someone with legal and business background and training available for advice and counsel without the need of telephone calls, memos and mail delays to our outside experts."

Goodred's message was by way of announcing the imminent arrival of Peter G. Stone as in-house counsel, who would carry the titles of assistant secretary and assistant treasurer. Stone was a graduate of Columbia Law School and the Wharton

School of Finance in Philadelphia.

The need (for Stone)," Goodreds added, "has become even more apparent . . . with an acceleration of acquisition work, more union contracts to review . . . and a number of other matters . . . which should receive expert legal attention at Campbell Hall."

Stone, in private practice, had answered a want ad placed by Dow Jones and soon found himself in an interview with W. Gilbert (Gil) Faulk, a DJ vice president for legal matters.

"Dow Jones wasn't for me," Stone said. "But evidently Faulk thought well enough of me to keep my name on file. Eight months later I received a call from Jack Goodreds. He and Jim Jr. came to my law office to look me over."

In November 1979 Stone was elected treasurer of ONI, replacing Goodreds. He continued as assistant secretary and as a member of the Management Committee.

Just three months after Stone's arrival, the number of daily papers in the group had jumped to 17 with the ECN acquisition. One of his first moves was to set up a centralized zero-balance checking account and an electronic fund transfer system.

There was idle money in a score or more of checking accounts around the circuit, on any one day amounting to as much as $2 million. Stone put it to work and in 1985 was earning in excess of $100,000 a year.

Jim Jr. acclaimed Stone's promotion as "particularly timely" in the light of the need for more attention to cash management and forecasting and banking relations with "today's extremely high interest rates."

Board minutes of 1978 show that the Ottaway acquisiton arm had much more than the Essex County Newspapers in its hope chest. A laconic entry noted that the Dow Jones board had authorized investment of a cool $38,250,000, which, the board hoped, also would bring the *Everett* (Wash.) *Herald* and the *Coffeyville* (Kan.) *Journal* into the fold. But the wishing well turned up dry. And there was talk of a blind date with the *Morgantown* (N.C.) *News-Herald*.

And of the $3,583,000 earmarked for betterments in 1978, Sunbury began to take the lion's share, $3.3 million for a new offset press and a structure to house it.

☆ ☆ ☆ ☆ ☆ ☆

The news service was undergoing top personnel and transmission changes in the late 1970s. ONS Chief Doc Adams left Campbell Hall in September 1977 for an executive position with Kaepa, his brother's shoe manufacturing firm based in Texas. Ed Klein returned from Traverse City to take charge of ONS for the second time. During his 11 months at the ONS tiller Klein designed, equipped and supervised installation of computerized telecommunications system that supplanted the primordial teletype units.

Quite aware of the problems inherent in the shared Griffin-Larrabee Washington operations, Jim Jr. had as early as 1974 turned his thoughts to a pure Ottaway bureau, run by an Ottaway staff to serve Ottaway papers. In 1975 he dispatched Charles King to Washington to work up a cost estimate. King's report concluded that a major six-figure financial commitment would be necessary to cover payroll, rent, communications and related start-up expenses.

"Don't try to operate a Washington office with a stranger to the city," King was warned. "Hire someone who knows his way around. And you're going to have to pay to get a competent bureau chief."

With the cost estimate in hand, Jim Jr. decided not to act immediately. But he never scratched the basic idea.

The break came in 1977. The governor of the State of Maine wanted to open a Washington office and asked Don Larrabee, an old friend, if Larrabee would be interested in running it. Larrabee accepted on a trial basis and turned over the operation of his bureau to one of his veteran reporters, Knight A. Kiplinger. Kiplinger was a son of Austin H. Kiplinger, proprietor of Washington Editors Inc., publisher of six newsletters and the magazine *Changing Times.* The Kiplingers, father and son, were co-authors of *Washington Now,* a profile of the capitol, published in 1975.

In March 1978 Larrabee's job extolling the virtues of the Pine Tree State became permanent and he placed his news bureau on the market. For a time Kiplinger considered buying it.

Meantime Ed Klein had received an irresistible offer from Middletown to become managing editor of the flagship *Times Herald-Record*.

Now Jim Jr. and King had no alternatives. They needed a replacement for Klein. Kiplinger was the obvious choice. But with his encyclopedic knowledge of Washington, why bring him to Campbell Hall? Hadn't the time come for an Ottaway bureau in the capital? Wouldn't it make sense to run the entire news service from Washington? Would Kiplinger take the post?

Yes he would, if Jim Jr. was willing to pay a salary reasonably commensurate with Washingon standards for a news service chief responsible for 17 papers in seven states. Kiplinger's asking price was well in excess of budget, but Jim Jr. went along. The news service had come of age.

In 1974, the earliest year for which ONS records still exist, the news service budget was $80,874. Eleven years later it had soared to $650,000.

Kiplinger's staff during his first full year as chief consisted of three reporters. As the Ottaway group expanded, so did the Washington staff. Most of the bureau people were transfers from group papers.

During the years framing the Joplin and Essex County acquisitions, executive personnel shifts continued apace.

Donald R. (Don) Micozzi, circulation manager in Sunbury, in May 1976 was promoted to assistant to the the general manager in New Bedford. He was named GM in mid-1978. Two assistant GMs were named early in 1977: Saturno L. (Sam) Marocco at Plattsburgh and John M. Szefc in Middletown. Marocco would advance to GM in Oneonta and would attain publisher status first in Owatonna and then in Mankato, Minnesota. Szefc was named Middletown GM in November 1978. For several years Szefc also carried the title of editor, having stepped in after the separation of two top newsroom executives. Szefc succeeded Richard J. (Dick) Anthony, who moved to Plattsburgh as GM under Ben Turnbull.

In 1977 Gilbert A. (Gil) Bogley was named GM in Medford, succeeding retiring Gerry Latham. Frank Perretta succeeded Bogley in Traverse City.

Some intra-company transfers wound up duds. So it was in Port Jervis in 1974. An import from New England was badly miscast as editor of the *Union-Gazette*, creating staff and community unhappiness — and a vacancy. Joseph Richter, of the Danbury copy desk, was asked to take over and repair the damage. Richter came to the rescue in 1975 and after 18 months of rebuilding the U-G, he was promoted to assistant to Ed Somers, publisher in Oneonta. A. Timothy (Tim) Dodson replaced Richter.

In late 1978 Richter was named director-editor of a joint Dow Jones-Ottaway cable television experiment, which operated from an office in the *Danbury News-Times*. The purpose was to determine if viewers would be interested in local news and advertising originated by *News-Times* reporters and sales personnel. The experiment, one of the first of its kind in the United States, drew publishers from coast to coast. Approximately $80,000 was invested in equipment, Richter recalled.

After five-year leases on two Danbury area channels expired, the project was dropped. Viewership surveys were all negative.

And at the end of 1978 two more retirements took place. Ed Hill stepped down as assistant to Jim Ottaway Jr. and Homer Somers left as director of Ottaway Advertising Sales.

Responsibilty for Ottaway national linage fell to Branham Advertising Sales in mid-1976. Concurrently, Somers was told that OAS would be dissolved. Somers took on a new role, as he put it, "keeping Branham honest, checking on sales calls and suggesting primary account possibilities in areas covered by Ottaway papers. I also made calls on Branham's behalf when the agency needed help."

Somers clearly recognized that the vast geographical diversification of Ottaway locations at the time precluded survival of OAS.

A new two-state approach to regional linage at the distributor level came into being, sponsored by Middletown and Danbury.

Somers said he was offered the job, but decided to retire. The assignment went to William A. (Bill) Cangi, Middletown advertising director, who had come to the *Times Herald-Record* from Plattsburgh in 1970.

Things were humming in Stroudsburg. Publisher Alan Gould and staff were putting the finishing touches on the Sunday paper, which made its debut in January 1979 just as the Minnesota acquisitions were completed. The *Pocono Record* was the eighth Ottaway Sunday product.

22 Mankato/Owatonna

The Ottaway corporate flag was planted beneath the Big Sky of Minnesota on January 2, 1979, when the Mankato Free Press and the Owatonna People's Press became the 18th and 19th dailies to join the group.

George Cooper, the indefatigable broker, for years had been calling on Publisher Jared How. On November 5, 1974, How called Cooper. He was ready, he said, to discuss a possible marriage of The Free Press Company with Dow Jones-Ottaway, an arrangement Cooper had championed from the start.

Less than two weeks later How flew east from Minneapolis for a rendezvous with Ottaway at LaGuardia Airport. It turned out to be more than a typical Ottaway welcome. Driver Charlie Glynn pointed the Cadillac south along the East River Drive to a prearranged luncheon at 22 Cortlandt Street in Manhattan, then the Dow Jones headquarters.

Awaiting How and Ottaway were Bill Kerby, chairman; Warren Phillips, president; and Ray Shaw, vice president. How, Ottaway recalled, said little during the meeting despite an effervescent welcome.

"I think the reason he was reticent is because he was shy," the chief wrote to Kerby. "But he certainly loosened up later. He has great warmth."

Indeed How did thaw, far more quickly than Ottaway might have imagined.

After the collation the chief ferried his guest to Campbell Hall headquarters, where they were joined by Jim Jr. Those corporate officers on premises were introduced. Dinner was served in the Ottaway home.

"After dinner," Ottaway said, "I gave Jared two choices: Have a highball, talk a little and go to bed, or, visit the *Times Herald-Record* in Middletown." How chose the latter.

The second floor of the Ottaway home contains a guest bedroom and bath at one end and a snuggery at the other. Perhaps the most salutary social appurtenance in the latter is a well-ordered bar. Seating is conducive to productive conversation. There's television for one not about to talk acquisition.

When Ottaway and How returned from Middletown, they retired to the den for a nightcap. Gone was How's earlier restraint. He talked about newspapers in general and Minnesota in particular and asked questions about Ottaway's publishing philosophy. At one o'clock in the morning How excused himself, went to his bedroom and reappeared with his October balance sheet and a year-to-date financial statement. Patently, he liked what he had seen and heard.

In 24 hours Ottaway and How had developed a friendship based on trust and mutually compatible goals. The eventual corporate marriage was a perfect expression of the time and the spirit that gave rise to its emergence.

The Free Press acquisition file correspondence alludes but briefly to How's decision to sell. He was quoted by Cooper in a letter to Ottaway only as saying "his banker and accountants have told him that he ought to get his affairs in order." That was in 1974.

How's testimony before the Minnesota Senate Committee on Small Business in August 1975 indicates clearly something of what was on his mind. He said, in part:

"When I inherited the majority interest in the company about 19 years ago, the value of the company was modest. The estate taxes payable were tolerable. Today, partly as a result of inflation and partly as a result of the great group newspaper operations and very impressive advances in technology, the market value of our company . . . has increased tremendously.

"The trouble is, my business . . . involves a very valuable asset, does not throw off enough income to pay estate taxes on top of the cost of operating and modernizing the business. The

276

value in the marketplace is far greater than the value to my heirs.

"If I can't lay up enough cash during my lifetime to pay my estate taxes, what should I do? I am better off to sell out to a large publicly-owned company in a tax-free reorganization. This will give me marketable stock that can be sold to pay my estate taxes. However, this means that there is no guarantee of family continuance in the operation of the company.

"My responsibility, as publisher of a privately-held newspaper, is to myself . . . "

Scores of other independent publishers shared How's views and sold. Theirs was a no-win situation.

Ottaway and Cooper paid the first of many visits to Minnesota in January 1975. They had three possible purchase plans to discuss with How: cash, an exchange of stock or a term payment arrangement. It would take a few years for How, his lawyer and accountants to sift the options. But first How would have to come to grips with nine minority shareholders. Of the 944.5 shares outstanding, How owned 655. Ottaway, of course, needed at least 80 percent of the stock if a deal was to be cut.

Meantime two market studies were commissioned. Bob Van Fleet for Ottaway and Jim Soderlind for Dow Jones drew the assignments. Both were moderately enthusiastic.

Before its emergence as a daily, the *Mankato Free Press* had a weekly history that reached back to the 1850s. It first was issued under its present name in 1880, the product of a merger of two weeklies, the *Mankato Union* and *Mankato Record*. The *Free Press* became a daily in April 1887. In 1919 it bought out the *Daily Review,* a long-time Democratic rival, and plunged into an internal expansion program that saw the advent of full leased-wire Associated Press service and the establishment of a sports section, market reports and comic strips.

James A. Callahan, a native Mankatoan who had achieved journalistic prominence on the West Coast with the Hearst organization, returned home in 1933 and bought a controlling interest in the *Free Press.* His doctors had advised him to slow down. The little hometown paper, he decided, would be just the vehicle for a more relaxed business routine. Callahan became publisher. President was M.D. Fritz, who had joined the

277

company in 1901. Fritz stepped down to the vice presidency in 1934 and Callahan added the title of president. Fritz died in 1940.

James Callahan was a brother-in-law of How's mother. He died unexpectedly of a heart attack aboard a train in December 1943. Clifford H. Russell, editor since 1927, who had succeeded Fritz as vice president, was elected publisher. At the time Mrs. Callahan was named president. After Russell's death in August 1956, How became publisher and vice president.

Mrs. Callahan died in January 1962, at which time How became president and publisher, inheriting her stock.

Jared How, according to contemporaries, "saw the world" before World War II, among other things hiring on as a cargo hand on an ocean-going freighter. He was given an early wartime discharge from service because of poor eyesight and cast his lot with his uncle's *Free Press*.

Kenneth E. (Ken) Berg, who started his *Free Press* career as sports editor in 1943, and at this writing was opinion page editor, remembered How as an excellent reporter, covering city hall and the courts for the most part.

"His first love was the courts, but his experience was varied," Berg said. "Back in those days everybody did everything."

Circulation of the *Free Press* stood at 22,000 in 1962. How's first year as publisher. By 1970 it had passed 24,000 and at the time of its acquisition by Ottaway stood at 28,000.

How's regime was marked by several acquisitions of his own. In 1961 the Free Press Company bought the *Twin Falls* (Ida.) *News-Times* and in 1968 acquired the *Owatonna People's Press*. How sold the Twin Falls property later that year.

In 1976 the Free Press Company moved into the Minnesota weekly field, buying the Hallock, Red Lake Falls and Middle River properties. The weeklies were operated by the Record Printing Company division of the Free Press.

In 1970 How completed a $1.2-million modernization program in Mankato as the *Free Press* entered the world of offset. Building expansion costing $400,000 was for a six-unit Goss Urbanite press costing $515,000 and $290,000 worth of related photo-composition equipment. The paper went on line with offset in July.

How's prescience and investment in the area of advanced technology was one factor that would make the *Free Press* a compellingly attractive acquisition. Necessary capital improvements would be minimal.

The *Owatonna People's Press* began as a weekly in September 1874. Its proprietor, Benjamin E. Darby, loftily proclaimed that "we intend to build up a paper of an immense circulation and one of which every subscriber may be proud. No slang or immorality will enter either our reading or advertising columns and the paper will be one all can properly take into the family circle."

A durable institution, the *People's Press* survived the challenges of 27 other publications that started and folded since the community was settled.

Darby was joined by his three sons in the 1890s. The weekly thrived, expanding to daily morning publication in March 1916. It was the only morning paper in Minnesota outside the Twin Cities of Minneapolis and St. Paul. But Darby coppered his bet. He continued the weekly until December 1917 when it was absorbed by the daily without public announcement.

The *People's Press* was a rarity in that it was published Tuesday through Sunday. The shift to Sunday publication instead of Monday came in December 1916. Darby's reasoning was that employees should rest on the sabbath, and besides, he thought the news potential on any given Sunday (for a Monday morning newspaper) was not worth the candle. There is no record of reader reaction. Letters to the editor were not part of the paper's content at the time.

After 93 years in the Darby family the *People's Press* was acquired by How, who converted it to offset in 1971. There were other dramatic changes, including, incredibly, establishment of an eight-hour day. In pre-How days, when employees asked for a raise, they were simply told to put in more hours. How also instituted a vacation plan and health insurance. During the later Darby days, no one was entitled to more than a week's rest.

Harlo A. (Tommy) Thompson was named business manager of the *People's Press* at the time of the How acquisition and the following year was made publisher and general manager.

Thompson, a native of Minneapolis, was no stranger to southern Minnesota, having attended Mankato State College. He was an advertising salesman for the *Bemidji* (Minn.) *Pioneer* and served two tours in the ad department of the *Free Press*, having left at one point to sell drapery.

At the time of his assignment to Owatonna, Thompson was retail advertising manager.

Ottaway's first proposal to How early in 1975 involved a stock exchange combined with a pooling arrangement. Nothing materialized.

In March Ottaway fired off a letter to Jim Jr. from his vacation base in Barbados, asking for a copy of the Soderlind market study and suggesting that the Inland Daily Press Association (based in Chicago) linage reports "might give some idea of where Mankato-Owatonna stands compared to other midwest and Minnesota cities."

Something else was on his mind.

Evidently the chief had just received the Dow Jones annual report. Even though it carried tidings of joy for shareholders, he told Jim Jr. he felt that publicity-wise it had "short changed Ottaway Newspapers."

"It ought to give our total circulation daily and Sunday, similar to the *Wall Street Journal, Barron's* and the *National Observer*. It also ought to list our newspapers and locations. If you knew nothing about Ottaway, you would never find out reading this report," he observed somewhat testily.

"Perhaps you ought to talk to Warren (Phillips) about this so that it is better in 1976. It also ought to give some idea of where we are going."

Whether Jim Jr. filed a complaint is lost to memory.

On November 5 Ottaway made another offer: 130,000 shares of DJ for the 655 Free Press shares owned by How. The offer was contingent upon How's acquiring the 289.5 shares owned by nine minority stockholders at a cost to the Free Press not to exceed $700,000.

The offer carried a deadline: How would have to accept by December 19.

In a cover letter Ottaway restated his offer of an employment contract and pension plan, adding, "I am sure if you accept our
280

offer that we can have a delightful and productive publishing life together. Jim Jr. and I respect you not only as a man of great integrity but as one who is really dedicated to publishing top quality newspapers."

Ottaway then alluded to How's son, James: "We will be delighted to have Jim continue with the *Free Press* under your direction or give him additional training at other Ottaway newspapers."

In an intra-office memo that fall, Jim Jr. felt a need to remind his father and Jack Goodreds that the Dow Jones acquisition arm had all it could handle — and more.

"We have four live prospects," he wrote in October, "possibly five if the Jacksonville, North Carolina, visit produces results.

(The others were Mankato-Owatonna, Escondido, California; Joplin and Grand Junction, Colorado.)

"Warren Phillips has suggested and I think we must concentrate our limited acquisition energies on two, at the most, of the most attractive markets and newspapers we have a good chance of making a deal with in late 1975 or early 1976. Otherwise we are wasting a lot of our time chasing flies we can never catch. Dow Jones will not agree to buy four papers at once and we sure can't handle more than two in the next year. Even that will be a tough assignment."

In mid-December How called Cooper and declined the November 5 offer. Cooper relayed the message to Ottaway, saying, "How thinks the Free Press Company is worth more than we have offered." Cooper also reported that How would start to buy out his minority stockholders. How said he felt he could do this within two years.

Negotiations were sporadic for most of 1976. In January Ottaway tendered a "first refusal" offer for How's stock and at the same time advised the publisher that an authorized issue of Dow Jones preferred would be approved at the annual meeting in March.

"This stock," Ottaway wrote, "could be convertible to common . . . and might easily resolve the differences that we have had in regard to the number of common shares that we could issue for your stock due to the dilution factor." And it would be a tax-free deal.

On November 11 Ottaway formally proposed a stock exchange based on DJ preferred. He met with How that day in Minneapolis. On the 12th they drove to Mankato.

At luncheon the chief was introduced to Robert (Bob) Girouard, How's son-in-law, and chief editorial writer for the Mankato paper. Jimmy How was in Iowa, selling advertising for the company's new farm paper, the *Land*.

Ottaway's follow-up letter suggested that he sensed a breakthrough on the horizon:

"First and foremost, Jared, if you decide to accept our offer and become a part of the Dow Jones-Ottaway family, it seems to me it is extremely important that we make sure this is going to be a happy situation for you, Kat (Mrs. How), Jimmy, Tommy Thompson at Owatonna and all your employees at both locations.

"The Free Press has become part and parcel of you, Kat, Jimmy and all the members of your family, the same as we feel in regard to our newspapers. We all like to make a good profit . . . but we are mutually committed to publishing top-quality newspapers with the idea of having a fair return on our investment, but not such a high return that newspaper quality is sacrificed."

The letter suggested that How and Ottaway families meet at Campbell Hall for another "heart-to-heart" talk before How decided to accept or reject the latest offer.

The November 11 discussions at the Sofitel Hotel at Minneapolis Airport led to a tentative solution. How and Ottaway signed a memorandum of agreement in January 1977. It provided for an exchange of 60,000 shares of DJ preferred for 100 percent of the Free Press stock. The consideration also included a $250,000 cash payment at closing and an improved employment-pension agreement.

The agreement stipulated that all conditions be carried out by April 30 and that it was subject to a purchase agreement.

One of the last Free Press minority stockholders to sell back to How was John (Jack) Mullowney of Twin Falls, Idaho, who had been a director and shareholder since 1965. Mullowney held 80 shares.

In September 1977 How received a letter from Mullowney advising that he was going to sell his stock for $400,000, equating to $5,000 per share. How had been buying up other minority holdings for $2,000 a share.

Mullowney told How's lawyer he couldn't reveal the name of the buyer. Was it a bluff? A way to force How to buy back the stock at Mullowney's price? How guessed it was even odds that Mullowney was bluffing.

Ottaway told How that if he had to buy the 80 shares, ONI would step in and "work something out" in regard to the difference in price, $219,000 over the $181,000 that How had offered.

On September 29 Ottaway and How came to agreement: ONI would pay $400,000 for the Mullowney shares over four years and How would give ONI "first call" on his 655 shares. Thus Ottaway became a 10.9 percent owner of the Free Press Company.

How volunteered he would like an Ottaway to sit on his board of directors, replacing Mullowney. First he suggested Jim Sr.

"After a few drinks in the evening," Ottaway said, "the more he thought about it, the more he thought he would like Ruth better than he liked me. That's not difficult to understand."

The January 1977 stock exchange proposal came to naught. The April deadline came and went. It was not until April 20, 1978, that How was able to sit down with Ottaway to tell him that a stock exchange would be a "great disadvantage." Ottaway had been scheduled to meet with How right after the first of the year, but Katherine How had been seriously ill.

How's accountants told him that under the new estate tax law, which went into effect December 31, 1976, (and which wasn't explained fully until well into 1977) the Dow Jones stock he received for Free Press shares would take the value of the Free Press Company stock at the time How acquired it. Should How die, his heirs would be faced with a capital gains tax on the difference between the original value of the company and the value of Dow Jones stock at the time of death, plus estate taxes.

"This," he told Ottaway, "puts an entirely new light on a stock exchange."

At this point, Ottaway's summary of the April 20 conversation alluded to earlier offers by Hoile Newspapers and Park Communications, Inc. Hoile reportedly had offered $15 million without even looking at How's books. Park had offered $12 million.

How told Ottaway he now was interested only in a cash transaction. He dropped a figure, $10.7 million, and said he was willing to consider a term agreement. He also would sign a letter of intent.

Jack Goodred's pro forma to the DJ board on May 5 was modestly upbeat.

On May 10 Jim Jr. formally offered $10.7 million for the Free Press Company. ONI would pay $3.2 million at closing with the balance in four equal annual payments at seven percent. ONI further agreed to employ How as president of the Free Press Company from the date of closing through December 31, 1981, and thereafter provide a life pension.

The arrangement also called for an annual stipend for five years after How stepped down as publisher December 31, 1982. He would serve as chairman, consultant and acquisition advisor.

How signed the agreement June 15, right on deadline.

"I assume," he wrote Ottaway, "that the lawyers can now go to work and get to the point where it 'is' rather than 'ain't.' "

In mid-July How transferred a total of 60 shares to his four children, who, in turn, sold the stock to Ottaway at the same price called for in the original agreement.

Thus cash and notes to How totalled $9.7 million. The Laurie How Krosney Trust, the Jared How Jr. Trust, James J. How and Nancy How Girouard would divide the balance over the four-year payout.

On July 18, 1978, the acquisition agreement was signed in Minneapolis.

Besides the Mankato and Owatonna properties, the purchase included the weekly papers in Hallock, Red Lake Falls, and Middle River, all in northwest Minnesota and the bi-monthly tabloid farm magazine the *Land*.

Completion of the transaction came on January 2, 1979.

The bound acquisition record contained two other agreements. The first involved Jim How and Bob Girouard.

284

Each was given an employment contract for 10 years. The second granted Jared How the right to buy back the weekly newspapers. He did, in 1980.

Jim How entered management training at the *Cape Cod Times* with the title of marketing coordinator. But Girouard left the *Free Press* in 1979 to become editor of the opinion pages of the *Minneapolis Star*. When the *Star* merged with the *Minneapolis Tribune,* Girouard resigned and joined the *Cleveland Plain Dealer* as chief editorial writer. He died March 17, 1983, of a heart attack.

☆ ☆ ☆ ☆ ☆ ☆

Jared How, by any measurement, was an individual of upper case gentility. But there were times when his bonhomie turned sour.

Those on the *Free Press* closest to the publisher were all too well aware of his affinity for cigarettes and his sporadic efforts to stop smoking. Over several years How and one of his friends outside the newspaper were riding occasional $500 bets on which could stay off cigarettes the longest.

Employees came to dread the wagers because, as one department head put it, "Jared would become sullen, even surly." His friend was not above entering the *Free Press* unannounced at odd hours, so Jared couldn't carry cigarettes, and at times wore the furtive look of a felon. How often was observed palming a butt from a newsroom ashtray and sneaking a few puffs. A little-used lavatory in a rear storage room was his smoking asylum several times a day.

"There was always something incongruous about a distinguished publisher in an expensive sport coat recycling butts," another executive recalled.

How was very strict when it came to customer delivery service. At times carriers slipped a cog or two. More than a few subscribers were reassured of the paper's high-level benevolence when How dropped off the *Free Press* from a Cadillac or a Mercedes. But not in springtime.

Springtime in Minnesota often brings nearly impassable roads. Motor route drivers sometimes miss deliveries. And farmers, with little to do before planting, occasionally marched into the *Free Press* to complain.

As a result, an unwritten office rule was in effect between March 1 and April 30: "If someone comes in the door wearing a seed corn cap, keep him away from Jared."

The staffs both at Mankato and Owatonna received the news of the sale in good spirit. The Ottaway background, the Dow Jones connection and their shared publishing philosophy based on local control overcame any doubts.

But there was lingering speculation about the easterners from Campbell Hall. What were they like?

First envoy through the door happened to be Phil Blake, who would be Minnesota liaison with ONI. Blake happened to be wearing a black pinstripe suit. He carried a briefcase in one hand, a cigarette in the other.

As one department head remembered it, a barely audible voice said, "My gosh, he looks like a Mafia hit man!" It was unlikely that anyone at the *Free Press* ever had seen a Mafia hit man, but for a brief moment Blake was perceived as one.

Heir apparent to How's office was Harlo Thompson. In December 1980, Thompson was named assistant publisher and general manager of the *Free Press*. John N. Wilcox, *Free Press* marketing and circulation director, replaced Thompson in Owatonna with the title of general manager.

On January 1, 1982, Thompson was named publisher and chief executive officer in Mankato. How remained as president.

A year later Wilcox was promoted to general manager of the *Danbury News-Times* and Saturno L. (Sam) Marocco moved in from Oneonta as publisher-GM in Owatonna. At the same time Joe Richter was appointed GM in Mankato. Richter had been serving as director of seminars and research at Campbell Hall.

The *Owatonna People's Press* was printed on a News-King

press, one of the very few ever manufactured. There were so few News-Kings that they didn't carry serial numbers. They were given names. Owatonna's was christened George.

Wilcox said he used to dread the ringing telephone in the early morning hours.

"It usually meant that Old Unreliable had broken down again. The pressroom foreman called one bleak winter morning to say that the main 880-volt relay had popped out and wouldn't make contact to start the press.

"The relay was an imposing thing and everyone gave it plenty of room as it sat there humming and spewing off ozone. An electrician was called, but he couldn't do anything without special parts.

"There has always been a lot of pride at the *People's Press,* especially in the pressroom, and no one relished calling on a neighboring paper to pull our fat out of the fire. So I had a brainstorm. I suggested that if someone would just push in the relay with a well-insulated object, like a handy two-by-four, we could hold it secure through the 45-minute press run.

"Everyone said that I was the perfect candidate for two reasons: I had thought of the harebrained scheme and I was only the publisher and therefore most expendable.

"So I grabbed the four-foot two-by-four, put it to the humming relay, gulped and pushed. Lo and behold the press started, and we finished the run. It was truly the most electrifying experience of my tenure at Owatonna."

23 Ashland

Jim Ottaway learned way, way back that acquisition tips were not to be brushed off, whatever the origin. At the very least one stroked a rabbit's foot and hoped. Just as Jack Goodreds's tipster had pointed Ottaway toward the *Sharon* (Pa.) *Herald,* so did an out-of-the-blue tip touch off the quest for the *Ashland* (Ky.) *Daily Independent.*

It came in mid-July 1972 to Phil Blake, publisher of the *Sunbury Daily Item,* a member of the group since 1970. The Ashland file shows that Blake relayed the message to Jim Jr. In his memo Blake identified the tipster only as a "Kentucky friend."

Broker Maurice Henry, who helped in the Traverse City and Joplin acquisitions, was assigned to check out the report. Before retiring and selling his own newspaper in Middleboro, Kentucky, Henry had become fast friends with the Norris and McCullough families, majority owners of the *Independent.* Blake's tipster was on the money. Henry reported back to Jim Jr. early in August that the owners "had not come to a final decision on whether or not they wished to sell the newspaper." He said also that there was "considerable uncertainty among the owners of the course they should take," and suggested that Ottaway "keep in touch, but not press the issue at this time."

There was other evidence that the owners were thinking of selling, but more to the point, selling to Dow Jones-Ottaway. Three documents, dated August 3, 4 and 10, show that an Ashland bank executive had been assigned to ask lots of questions about the DJ and Ottaway financial structures, the type of relationship between DJ and Ottaway and what it was like for a community newspaper to become a member of the Ottaway group.

The reports that came back to Kentucky must have fluttered the pulses of the prospective sellers. Typical was the banker's recap of a conversation with the late George S. Warren Jr., then chairman of the board of the McDowell National Bank in Sharon, Pennsylvania. Sharon had joined the group in 1971.

"Talked with Mr. Warren concerning the Ottaway group and its effects on management and the operation of the *Sharon Herald* after the purchase by Ottaway. Warren described the Ottaway group as 'good people — very capable newspaper people.' Warren very impressed by all people associated with Ottaway.

"They made no local management changes. Ottaway had made some operational recommendations which local management has followed. Local management appears quite satisfied with their association with Ottaway. Ottaway has furnished temporary top-flight operation people to work out operational problems.

"Warren was familiar with other Ottaway purchases since their bank did a similar check on Dow Jones — their trust department apparently owned local stock. Reason for selling was that majority stockholders not involved in operation of the paper. They wanted out. Paper at that time was doing fine — new plant, equipment.

"Warren could not have been more complimentary about Ottaway group. They invited Ottaway Jr. on their board after Harshman retired."

(Gerald Harshman stepped down as *Herald* president at the end of 1973.)

It would be more than five years before Ottaway had his first face-to-face meeting with the Kentuckians.

Ashland is located in the northeastern corner of Kentucky, five miles from the West Virginia border and separated from Ohio by the half-mile wide Ohio River.

Henry was at Campbell Hall in mid-March 1975 for a periodic conference on acquisition possibilities. His recapitulation of the properties discussed shows that he believed Ashland was "at least five years away."

289

Other possibilities on Henry's list were Chico, California; Brunswick, Georgia; Anderson and Terre Haute, Indiana; Paducah and Bowling Green, Kentucky; Petoskey, Michigan; Willmar, Minnesota; Joplin, Missouri (acquired in 1976); Chapel Hill, North Carolina; Muskogee, Oklahoma; Danville, Kentucky; and the Seaton group of newspapers, with headquarters in Coffeyville, Kansas.

Henry was prophetic. It was not until June 23, 1977, that James T. Norris Jr., president of the *Independent*, called Henry to say that the Norrises and McCulloughs were in agreement on a sale "provided certain things can be worked out, including employment for Robert A. Jr. and Ben F. McCullough." Norris Jr. told Henry he was not sure if he wanted to continue to work.

Henry also discovered that James T. Norris, Sr. in 1975 had given his son and a daughter stock in the *Independent*. Norris Jr. wondered if it was best to wait out a three-year deadline for an Internal Revenue Service review of the gifts.

Bob and Ben McCullough represented the third generation of their family to help guide the destinies of the *Independent*, then with an evening circulation of 26,000 and 27,000 Sunday. Their father, Robert A. McCullough Sr. was president of the company from 1964 until his unexpected death Sept. 2, 1972, just a month after Blake's tipster called. Their mother, the late Julia Edna Forgey McCullough, was the daughter of the late Colonel B.F. Forgey, a co-founder of Ashland Publishing Company, who remained at the helm until his death in 1960.

Jim Norris Jr. was a second-generation executive. He succeeded Robert McCullough Sr. as president in 1972 and also carried the title of editor. James Norris Sr. began his career with the *Independent* in 1921, as one of the incorporators of Ashland Publishing. He recalled that "we bought the paper from the old Ashland Independent Publishing Company for $60,000." In his 90s in 1985, he was the only living incorporator.

In 1924 Colonel Forgey became president and editor and Norris Sr. vice president and associate editor. Norris Sr. was elected president and editor in 1952 when Forgey became board chairman. C.E. Forgey, a son of the colonel, was named vice president and managing editor, and Robert McCullough Sr. became associate editor. Norris became chairman of the board

290

in 1964 and was succeeded as president by McCullough Sr.

Norris, a widower, in 1972 married Georgia Blazer, widow of Paul Blazer, founder of Ashland Oil, Inc.

The executive lineup in the fall of 1977 consisted of Norris Jr., 47, president and editor; Bob McCullough Jr., 41, director of advertising and circulation sales; and Ben McCullough, 45, production manager. Bob McCullough, Henry told Ottaway, was a "good candidate for future general manager or publisher."

Nowhere in the encyclopedic acquisition file is there a clue as to why three majority shareholders, all in their 40s, were seeking a compatible buyer for a healthy property.

The McCullough brothers, in fact, were not eager to sell.

Norris Jr. was the moving force. He was tired of the pressures inherent in newspaper publishing. And he was the only one in the Norris family with working ties to the *Independent*.

As late as April 11, 1978, Maurice Henry wrote Ottaway, "In my last two conversations with Bob McCullough, he said 'If I had my druthers, Ben and I would not sell, but since Jim Norris Jr. wants to sell we will go along with him and his family.'"

The McCulloughs at one point decided to try to buy out Norris, but they couldn't raise the money.

In September Bob Van Fleet compiled an in-office market report showing basic circulation, population, housing units and retail sales growth, based on census reports and other printed material. In October, John Szefc, then editor and assistant general manager in Middletown, visited Ashland for three days, talking incognito to the chamber of commerce, utility, retail, school, industry and labor sources to learn all he could about the community, the economy and the newspaper itself.

Still another market study was made in November, this time by Ruth Jarmul of Dow Jones. Her findings underscored Szefc's: It was basically a smokestack economy in reasonably good health.

Barney Calame, *Wall Street Journal* chief of bureau in Pittsburgh, reported that the Armco steel mill at Ashland was one of Armco's most modern and pollution-free installations.

Van Fleet went to Ashland in 1978 to update the Szefc and

Jarmul reports and found the economy "looking even better."

What exactly does the ONI acquisition process embrace? Market studies come first. Does it look healthy, growing? Does the newspaper control its market? Is it reasonably isolated? Is there a growth trend in population, housing and jobs?

Assuming positive answers, does the price range needed to buy the property make economic sense? Can the paper move into the black in three years? Does it have a chance to return 20 percent on invested capital before taxes, such as Ottaway has done for Dow Jones, or at least 14 percent minimum? Some guesswork and risk are inherent.

ONI also looks at possible cost savings, price increases, better management to increase advertising and circulation sales and improved quality of news content.

"We take the gradual approach," Jim Jr. said. "No changes overnight!"

"After all the market and financial data is digested," he added, "you come down to good newspaper business instincts, hunches and best judgments."

On September 1, 1977, Henry met with the *Independent* principals in Ashland and convinced them to talk only with Dow Jones-Ottaway. At this point Ottaway learned that the Knight-Ridder organization, based in Miami, had approached the owners. The Knight-Ridder bid died, possibly because no top executives appeared. The Norrises and McCulloughs were insulted.

"It is axiomatic that potential sellers want to talk with chief executives of the purchasing company, who will make the important negotiating and later management decisions," Jim Jr. wrote later.

On October 10 Ottaway and Jack Goodreds, accompanied by Henry, met with the Norrises and McCulloughs for the first time. "I think we hit it off quite well," Goodreds wrote in his summary of the day-long session.

Norris Jr. led the morning discussion, which centered on the industrial complexes of Armco, Ashland Oil, Allied Chemical, National Mine Service and the Chesapeake & Ohio Railway, which just west of the city, operated the largest marshaling yards in the U.S. in addition to a large car repair installation.

292

"Downtown seems to be a viable business area," Goodreds wrote, "and there doesn't appear to be any vacant stores or empty offices. In fact Ashland Oil grabbed whatever empty office space became available for their needs. A year or two ago a high-rise condominium office building was put up and purchased by Ashland Oil before it was completed."

Each market study also sang the praises of Ashland Oil, which took its name from the city and became its biggest employer, with 4,500 on the payroll. Without AOI, one city activist said in 1979, the area "would be a dry hole."

The metaphor applied in another way. In all of Eastern Kentucky, prohibition was then the law. If Ottaway and Goodreds wanted a restorative or two at the end of the day, they had to drive across the Ohio River into the state of that name. It was precisely the reason the only acceptable motel lodging lay on the side of the Buckeyes.

Ottaway and Goodreds found that like Jared How at Mankato-Owatonna, the Ashland owners had switched to offset in 1970-71 and had installed a front-end system with 10 news and two classified terminals.

Norris made it clear that any deal with Ottaway would have to honor the *Independent*'s commitment to its mechanical employees, which guaranteed no layoffs because of new equipment. Norris's strategy was to offer early retirement bonuses to hasten attrition.

After lunch Ottaway settled back and, according to Goodreds, "gave the litany of ONI." As usual, the chief stressed autonomy, services available from Campbell Hall and ONI's unique relationship to Dow Jones.

The sellers had another major concern: Could the McCulloughs stay on in key management roles? Bob aspired to a publisher's or general manager's chair. Ben wanted to continue as production director. Jim Norris Jr. agreed to stay for a brief transition period. Ottaway suggested that the McCulloughs have a face-to-face discussion with Jim Jr. and assured them that Campbell Hall didn't have a long list of personnel ready to send in to a newspaper it had just acquired.

The Norrises and McCulloughs "who we liked and trusted immediately and who seemed to return the feeling," said they would decide by early 1978 on a sale price and terms and make a verbal agreement they would pledge to honor until everything could be committed to a written agreement and signed sometime after February 15, 1979. The date would mark the end of the deadline for IRS review of the Norris Sr. stock gifts to his children.

"This was an unusual and risky way for us to do business," Jim Jr. said. "We feared that other purchasers would make higher bids, which could upset verbal agreements made with the best intentions."

Still stroking the metaphorical rabbit's foot, the Ottaways launched their now-familiar soft sell, stressing the virtues of the smaller ONI group with its reputation for publishing good newspapers, treating employees well and being a good corporate citizen, all backed up by the good name, editorial quality and financial strength of Dow Jones.

Norris Jr. and his wife visited Campbell Hall, met the headquarters staff and spent the night with Ruth and Jim Ottaway. Then they met Mary and Jim Jr. during Parents Weekend at Rosemary Hall-Choate School in Wallingford, Connecticut. Jim's oldest son, Chris, was a sophmore at Choate. The Norrises had two daughters at Rosemary Hall.

"We watched his sophomore daughter play soccer," Jim Jr. recalled. "Newspaper acquisition work has many interesting side benefits."

Bob and Sue Carol McCullough soon followed the Norrises to Campbell Hall, met the staff and were overnight guests of Ruth and Jim. Ben McCullough never made it to Ottaway headquarters. He didn't believe men were meant to fly.

Jim Jr. visited Ashland for the first time March 8 and 9, 1978, and concluded that "while it is not a boom town, it seems to be fundamentally healthy and growing steadily."

One exhibit he brought back was the Ashland Publishing Company's stockholder list. It showed that of the 600 shares outstanding, the Norris family held 260½; the McCullough family, 287½; and the Mulligan family, 52.

The Mulligan stock stemmed from a 1921 investment by Ralph Mulligan Sr. of the firm of Mulligan & MacDonald, national advertising representatives. When Ashland Publishing

Company was formed that year its founders came up short of cash and invited Mulligan to participate.

Jim Jr. also picked up much more detailed information about the newspaper, salary levels, union contracts, editorial content and personnel.

"This," he said, "helped to solidify the relationship with the younger generation of Ottaway after JHO Sr. had softened the beachhead. The sellers were convinced that we would treat their employees well, that we would not have layoffs as Gannett had in nearby Huntington, West Virginia, and that we would be good citizens so they could live in Ashland after the sale and hold their heads high."

The sellers kept their word. They resisted efforts by other newspaper groups to make higher bids and held to their verbal agreement for almost a year with no written commitment from Dow Jones or Ottaway that ONI indeed would buy the *Independent* at an agreed price. Early in 1978 Scripps-Howard also had sought to interest the sellers.

In late March, following a strategy meeting at Campbell Hall, Maurice Henry met with Norris Jr. and the McCulloughs and offered $9.2 million for the property. Norris suggested that the offer should be "about 10 percent more."

"If another firm somehow gets into the Ashland picture," Henry counseled Ottaway, "you will have to make the decision to equal its bid."

Norris wrote to Henry on April 8, "I feel that a price of $11.8 million is a reasonable expectation." He said the Ottaways "are our first choice to be owners of the *Independent*. However, because there are many other stockholders involved, we must take a long, hard look at the money offered and satisfy ourselves beyond reasonable doubt that it represents a going market price."

On April 11 Henry wrote to Ottaway, "If you really want Ashland, I feel you are going to have to go basically with what Jim Norris has put forth. . . if Gannett or Harte-Hanks get their foot in the door the situation becomes very hairy. What shall we do?"

Henry was familiar with basic Ottaway acquisition philosophy, which in effect held that ONI would probably not pay the highest possible price because Ottaway didn't want to tear a paper and employees apart to get an unjustified investment back in a reasonable time.

In late April ONI made a firm offer through Henry: $11.2 million, with 29 percent cash down at the closing and notes from five to ten years at seven percent.

A two-day negotiation session followed on June 28-29 at Greenbo State Park Lodge, 20 miles from Ashland. "It was," Jim Jr. said, "the largest negotiating group we had ever encountered . . . 11 people around one large table. Not ideal conditions for delicate negotiations."

ONI opened with a new offer of $11,450,000 and raised the interest rate to eight percent. After a post-dinner caucus, the ONI team raised the offer by $100,000 to $11,550,000 payable over five years.

The morning after the negotiations, Jim Jr. and Jack Goodreds met with the McCulloughs and hammered out employment arrangements, assuming that the purchase would be completed by April 1979. Bob would become president and publisher; Ben production director and vice president of the company. Norris Jr. would continue for a year as consultant to ONI and Bob McCullough.

During the summer of 1978 one minority shareholder announced that the price and interest rate offers were too low. She held 10 shares in a trust and 10 on her own. She had been told by John Park, a newspaper broker who lived three doors away in Raleigh, North Carolina, that he could easily sell the *Independent* for $15 million.

"He probably could in today's market," Jim Jr. observed.

Norris Jr. began to worry about not getting the highest possible price. He also fretted about minority shareholder suits and whether he was doing the right thing for the children beneficiaries. They wouldn't care who bought the *Independent*. He also began to worry whether he could deliver 80 percent of the stock, which Ottaway wanted to be certain of at that point. Norris even considered letting a local bank sell the newspaper to the highest bidder.

On December 11 Franklin (Frank) Parker, a Dow Jones-Ottaway lawyer, saved the day. He produced a convincing opinion that a minority shareholder could not challenge the sale sucessfully as long as each shareholder got the same price. No law requires selling to the highest bidder.

Meanwhile Norris Jr. took a decisive step. He met with John Park during the Southern Newspaper Publishers Association in Boca Raton, Florida, and told him he did not want to sell the *Independent* through him "at any price."

Norris Jr.'s indecision stretched into 1979 — briefly.

He told Maurice Henry on January 4 that "he had not come to a decision" on the $11,550,000 offer. Henry told Ottaway that he couldn't find out exactly what was bothering Norris.

Ottaway called the next day and among other things offered to raise the interest rate from eight to nine percent.

"Very generous," Norris said, "but I can't say that it will have any bearing on my decision."

Three days later the die was cast. On January 8 Norris called Ottaway and said he had decided to accept. At the same time he declined an offer of a $35,000 consulting fee for the first year after the sale. He said he wanted only $1,000 and would step down December 31, 1979.

"A clear sign of his integrity," Jim Jr. observed.

On January 15, Ottaway Sr. met in Ashland with the principals, their attorneys and bankers to work out the details of the agreement. (Jim Jr. observed that nine percent interest would cost ONI $443,000 more over five years than the original seven percent offer.)

The ONI board approved the purchase price January 23. The Dow Jones board approved it February 21.

Jim Jr. signed the agreement with the majority shareholders, representing 63½ percent of the stock. It was the first time ONI had a signed agreement. Next day ONI letters went out to minority shareholders, offering to buy their stock at the same price, $19,250 per share. ONI now had 20 newspapers on its roster.

On February 22 Jim Jr. and Phil Blake, senior vice president, toured the plant with Norris and Bob McCullough to announce the sale, and as Ottaway put it, "explain ourselves to the employees."

Closing took place in Ashland April 30. By that time all

minority shares were in the Ottaway fold.

Bob McCullough was named president and publisher, reporting to Campbell Hall through Blake. Although he didn't carry the title, McCullough in fact had been general manager under Norris. Ben McCullough became vice president and production manager. As he indicated he would all along, Norris soon departed.

It would not be until October that the *ADI* management team was complete. John Del Santo, who had been promoted to general manager of the *Pocono Record* the previous March, was assigned to Ashland, also as GM.

By then McCullough needed help in the worst way. As a fledgling publisher he faced a period of civic turmoil, perhaps unparalleled at any other Ottaway location.

Community shock and dismay followed disclosure August 23 by Ashland's Oil's senior management that there were "serious questions" as to whether AOI should "continue to grow" in the Ashland area. Orin E. Atkins, chairman and chief executive officer, told the *ADI* that "over the last several years the perception of Ashland as a community in which to live has gone steadily downhill." Specifically, Atkins cited the financial difficulties of the Ashland Public Library, the city school system, lack of transportation and the lack of adequate hotel and restaurant facilities." The last reference may be translated as AOI's annoyance over the liquor statutes, which inhibited its ability to do business the way business is done nearly everywhere else.

Siding with Atkins the next day, and *ADI* editorial admitted that "perhaps we are too late . . . if this happens we have only ourselves to blame."

On May 27, 1980, AOI announced plans to move an oil division, a computer sciences and services division and several adminstrative groups to Lexington. The lost payroll would top $10 million annually.

The bombshell proved, if nothing else, Jim Jr.'s 1978 observation: "Some guesswork and risk are inherent" in an acquisition.

The *ADI* fought back on several fronts. A utilities tax for educational purposes was defeated in 1979, but passed the

298

following year. The Ashland Public Library became the Boyd County Library and remodeling and expansion funds voted. And in 1981 four Ashland precincts voted wet.

Six weeks after the closing, the time came for an ONI executive breather in the form of a three-day get-together at Shangri-La, a resort of Lucullan dimensions on the man-made Lake of the Cherokees in eastern Oklahoma, 60 miles from Joplin. Never had so many traveled so far for fun and frolic. Those who arrived aboard Ottaway and Dow Jones aircraft landed on the resort's own airstrip. Those on commercial flights rented cars at Joplin's airport.

The ponderous logistical problems fell to the lot of Emmanuel (Manny) Fuchs, who recently had replaced Ed Hill as assistant to Jim Jr. Fuchs for 18 years had been chief photographer for the *Middletown Times Herald-Record,* then had engaged in film-making with his brother in Paris. Fuchs was admirably fitted for the sensitive headquarters post. His urbanity and innate tact stood the Oklahoma test, even surviving an encounter with a group of beer-sodden yahoos, whose unscheduled presence dampened the final night's activites.

The Ashland and Owatonna publishers thus were introduced to the annual rite of Ottaway appreciation for executive jobs done well. Mankato wasn't represented. Jared How's wife's illness prevented them from attending.

An added attraction was the reappearance of Gene Brown, Jim Ottaway's quarter-century associate of pre-merger days, known to many at the get-together only as a shadowy but towering figure in company lore. Brown sported a snowy tuft of beard under the chin.

On Friday evening, June 15, cocktails were served alfresco in a sort of amphitheater patio. Accompanying a prophetic Sooner sunset came the announcement that Jim Ottaway, now 67, on July 31 would retire as chairman of the board of ONI, but would continue as director on both the Ottaway and Dow Jones boards. Jim Jr., 41, would succeed his father and continue as president and chief executive officer. Jim Ottaway had led the way for 43 years.

Warren Phillips said it well:

"Jim's contributions to building Dow Jones as well as Ottaway Newspapers, have been immeasurable. But he also has done much, as past chairman of the American Press Institute, an Associated Press board member and an active participant in other newspaper organizations, to advance the profession as a whole. We don't look upon Jim's retirement as a parting in any sense, for as a Dow Jones director he will continue to be active in our corporate affairs, in our acquisition exploration and as a close collaborator in other ways."

Gene Brown said it better.

Taking center stage and flourishing a scrolled manuscript, Brown delivered a eulogy marked at once by deep personal affection but laced with elfin trivia. Longtime Ottaway watchers knew Brown had captured the full spirit of the transfer of authority. Newcomers to ONI now understood how much the past had played in developing a new generation of leadership.

Brown's tribute, in a sense, was distillation of Ottaway history:

"This evening is dedicated to you, Jim, and as your first honor we welcome you to membership in the Shangri-La Branch Institute of the American Senile Seniors which is also my alma mater. At this very moment, however, we regret to advise, while you are so signally honored, you are also being firmly nudged out of your position of chairman of the board as your successor, James H. Ottaway Jr. (a close relative) waits impatiently in the wings and plots corporate change from a a benevolent democracy to a ruthless dictatorship. But let us ignore conspiracy.

"We are here tonight, Jim, in this lush land, to present you with a symbolic bouquet of nostalgia which may look suspiciously like 'forget-me-nots.' We now recall, briefly, those wonderful days when you were laying the foundation stones for this amazing group of newspapers. (The more our memories fail, Jim, the better were those good old days.) In more lucid flashes we remember those good old days of our early operations as hovering between catastrophe and cataclysm (including domestic strife) all of which were only saved by the grace and goodness of the Ottaways. I am not sure that I am correct in adding the phrase 'domestic strife,' but it does give nostalgia a nice family touch.

"Though the growth of Ottaway newspapers represents in the main, the personality and drive of one man, your success was buttressed by the support of such stalwarts as Ruth, your wife, your children, Jimmy, Ruthie and David plus their families, plus the efforts of several universities and your own loving

300

father and mother who bequeathed to you the genes and qualities of their own lives.

"In Ruth and the kids you have a family who truly believe that if there were a great stone to block you, Jim, from emerging from a cave representing possible failure, you would have moved that stone in one day instead of the biblical three.

"And you and Ruth, in turn, with understanding and discreet discipline guided your kids into the real world of hard work and corporate P&Ls. Way back in Endicott, New York, when the children had paper routes, there were days of inclement weather or childish apathy when you and Ruth gallantly peddled those routes yourselves in your Lincoln Continental as an example of parenthood and good journalism . . . even if such elegant delivery was an economic disaster.

"It is only right and just to reveal that most of both new and old people here are successful because of Jim's uncanny faculty of selecting good people to help these papers grow. There were times when Lyn Boyd, his right hand, and I, the rear spear carrier from Caesar's Legions, would sit around Jim's swimming pool and talk about each of your future careers with Ottaway. Frankly, I wouldn't have given a plugged nickel for most of you, but Jim visualized your hidden potentialities and started you on the upward ladder. At the end he also asked for my plugged nickel.

"We moved into the big time when John Hannon, here today, came to our rescue. That was before he became president of Banker's Trust. He placed his reputation on the line by spearheading approval of a vast loan to Jim. He put his reputation on the line at a time when he was addicted to rendering in public, a litany of ribald songs which made his reputation somewhat moot . . . in banking as well as musical circles.

"Johnny did help him get the money and Jim went on persuading good people to work for him 'for honor and pittance.' Many an evening, Margo and I would sit down at the table and I would ask 'What's for dinner tonight?' And she would reply: 'For an entree we have Ottaway honor, dear, for dessert we have Ottaway pittance.' She always said, dear.

"In Charlie King's last astute and perceptive bi-monthly bulletin to the news departments of the group, he reprinted the answer of an Ottaway editor to a reader questioning our editorial independence.

"This leads me to an incident concerning individual paper independence, a creed of our papers.

"When I was running Danbury, as a Democrat I came out with an editorial supporting John Kennedy for president and then cabled my decision to Jim, Ruth and Jimmy who were in Greece at the time.

"When they read the cable announcing my support and decision, Ruth wept in Republican frustration, Jimmy winced at this end of this world but Jim said as he always has to me and others: 'Gene is running the show; it's his decision.' (I might add a bystander later wrote me that he also heard Jim mutter to himself as he reread the cable) 'What do you expect from a Democrat ?'

If one were to select one of the outstanding qualities about the Ottaways, it would be their sincere and personal interest in the lives of the rank and file who worked on the papers. Jim and Ruth remembered names. They remembered upcoming babies and incidents about the lives of their employees with uncanny accuracy.

"I have been on parties with both of them when they personally spoke to, chatted with, danced around and drank with two hundred employees and families. All this was done because they liked the people and the people liked them. Even today wherever I go (and don't overly show my disdain for the lower classes) people recall with me how much it meant to them to feel that the Ottaways treated them as members of the family. What an amazing characteristic this is . . . this ability to make people belong to one another . . . and Jimmy is of the same hue.

"Now before Captain Hook and all the assembled vice presidents reach out to haul me away from this podium, I have another honor, not mine to bestow but one which represents the combined admiration of your friends, associates, publishers, general managers, wives, special guests and anyone on a remittance status. We are assembled here to express in a more tangible fashion, our admiration for you, Jim.

"How can we express admiration and afffection for a man who has nothing except 10,000 friends? But the inspired people here did come up with a delightful idea. It is to participate in a fund which will be donated in your honor to the American Press Institute building fund.

"You have been acclaimed numerous times for your outstanding contribution to the finances and growth of API but our special fund represents the admiration of the people who have deemed it a great privelege to be a part of your life, then and now!

"This is indeed an outpouring of deep respect and love for what you have done for journalism and its people.

"The sum to be raised for API by the group is subject to further speculation. Allan Meath phoned me one morning about this great event and I asked in my pragmatic fashion (taught to me by one JHO) what sum we were talking about. He replied: 'Well if you have six children in college and a mistress who is pregnant, you undoubtedly will have other uses for your contribution.'

"There was a long pause on both ends of the wire (a somewhat pregnant pause.) Finally I breathed a sigh of relief and said to Allan: 'Well, that lets me out.'

"Permit me to finish with this last memory: Nostalgic it is, but typical of your early years of when you bought your second paper in Oneonta, New York. It was over 35 years ago and your mother was helping you financially to such an extent that she remarked that you were so deeply in debt she wondered if you would ever be a success, but never deterred, she kept on helping.

"Now here you are, Jim, the recipient of heartfelt honor, retiring soon as the head of a burgeoning newspaper group, basking in the plaudits for your contributions to the API . . . and I believe you are now very much out of debt. All these events occurred and yet you and your family remain the same fine people you were when you started borrowing from your mother in 1936.

"I wish she were here to see this ceremony, for with her delicious sense of humor she would have listened to the presentation of this gift being given in your name to API and she well might have whispered to Ruth: 'Well if they are going to give this money to API for James, could they at least name the gentlemen's lounge in his honor?'

"And Jim, you are just modest enough and self deprecating enough to echo your mother's remark . . . quote 'just inscribe JHO on the gentlemen's lounge.'

"Since there are no further questions, Jim and Ruth, we thank you for now, the past and the future."

302

Now the Ozark gloaming had set in. But there was one more ceremony before dinner. Gerry Tache, New Bedford publisher, presented Ottaway with an oil painting of the chief by Jack Lanigan, a *Standard-Times* staff artist. It hangs in the Campbell Hall guest reception area.

(The API fund to which Gene Brown alluded provides tuition, room, board and travel for a college-level educator to attend a seminar each year. Typically, the Ottaway family later added to the fund.)

☆ ☆ ☆ ☆ ☆ ☆

Promotions and new assignments for a host of executives were announced during 1979.

Phil Blake and Allan Meath were named senior vice presidents for newspaper operations. Jack Goodreds became a senior VP for finance and development. Tommy Purcell and Bob Van Fleet VPs for production and research and training, respectively. They had been assistant VPs.

Dick Barker became president and publisher in Joplin, effective June 4. On August 1 Greg Taylor was named general manager of the *Globe*. He had been assistant to the publisher in Danbury. At the same time Frank King advanced to assistant publisher/vice president of Essex County Newspapers.

In September Gerry Tache moved from New Bedford to a Campbell Hall vice presidency. The transfer touched off two other major appointments. Don Clifford came east from Michigan to be publisher of the *Standard Times* and Orren Robbins moved into the Traverse City vacancy. Robbins had been general manager at Cape Cod.

Jim Lane was promoted from GM of the weekly *Allied News* in Grove City, Pennsylvania, to assistant GM/marketing director in Stroudsburg and Robert (Bob) Parks succeeded Lane. Parks had been assistant classified manager in Sharon.

On October 8 came another end-of-an-era resignation. After serving 43 years as an Ottaway director, Ruth B. Ottaway stepped down. She was succeeded on the ONI board by Phil

303

Blake.

Other second-generation executive promotions were Keith Edinger to GM in Sunbury and Sam Marocco to GM in Oneonta. David B. (Dave) Regan, production director in Middletown, was named assistant to the publisher.

Meantime, Peter Stone advanced to treasurer of ONI, retaining the title of assistant secretary.

In between the workhorse Navajo and Ottaway Newspapers' entry into the corporate jet age was a sleek Cessna 402, which was phased out in mid-1979 as a trade-in on a Cessna Citation II, which cost a cool $1,568,000.

With the arrival of the Citation came a realignment of the ONI Aviation Division, under the corporate guidance of Allan Meath. Daniel (Dan) Carroll, with more than 7,000 pilot hours to his credit, was named chief pilot and director of the division. Of his total flight hours, Carroll had flown 1,500 in a Citation.

Ed daSilva remained a captain until late 1982. He had come to Ottaway January 1, 1972, from service with Massachusetts Air Industries.

24 Santa Cruz/Riverside

During the great acquisition decade of the 1970s, 14 newspapers were added to the Ottaway muster roll, four with Sunday editions. Negotiations often overlapped. At times Jim, Jim Jr. and Jack Goodreds were dealing simultaneously with as many as four potential sellers.

Directing the symphony of expansion was supremely delicate. The French horns of Oregon must not intrude on the oboes of Minnesota. The percussion instruments of Essex County Newspapers and the violins of Kentucky had to blend into the composition. The maestri wielded their batons superbly.

A muted trumpet joined the ensemble in 1971. The sound wafted eastward from Santa Cruz, California, on fabled Monterey Bay. It seemed to suggest that the 19,000 circulation *Sentinel,* daily and Sunday, sooner or later might come on the market.

Warren Phillips, in 1969 executive editor of the *Wall Street Journal,* that year asked Managing Editor Edward R. (Ed) Cony "to see if anything was loose on the West Coast." Dow Jones President Bill Kerby was pushing diversification. Cony held a master's degree in journalism from Stanford University in Palo Alto and in 1961 was a Pulitzer Prize winner for national affairs reporting.

The silver-thatched Cony turned to an old friend, Chilton R. (Chic) Bush, former dean of Stanford's Graduate School of Journalism. Did Chic Bush have any leads? Bush, retired, had been very active in the California Newspaper Publishers Associations (CNPA). He still was knowledgeable about

305

acquisition possibilities.

The trail in the spring of 1969 led to Santa Cruz and Frederick Duncan McPherson Jr., president and publisher of the *Sentinel,* who represented the third generation of the family in top management. Cony had relatives in Aptos, a community 10 miles south of Santa Cruz.

A two-page, double-spaced memo indicates that Cony first visited McPherson on May 21. Presumably his report went directly to Kerby and Phillips. It would be another year before the Dow Jones-Ottaway merger and Jim Ottaway's commission as the acquisition chief for DJ and Ottaway Newspapers.

"Ed said he just wanted to get to know us," McPherson recalled. "Somewhere along the line he suggested that if we were ever interested in selling the paper, Dow Jones might be interested."

Evidently Cony at least inferred on May 21 there was, indeed, some interest.

"McPherson doesn't want to sell right now," Cony reported. "One, he wants to keep on working and two — most important — he'd like to pass the paper on to his two sons, age 26 and 28. Both are working on the paper now. One is Fred D. III. But, as we know, he considered selling the paper a couple of years ago, and I got the definite impression he's not above changing his mind. In fact he said that in a year or two he might change his mind. He suggested that he wasn't yet sure his sons were committed to careers at the paper, and I thought I detected some doubts also as to their ability to run it. But he won't sell — in any case — to just anyone. He indicated a great distaste for 'ruthless chains' that buy up papers just to make money."

Patently, McPherson had enjoyed Cony's visit. He invited his Dow Jones caller to return next time Cony was in California.

The Cony visit might have accomplished more than he imagined.

The second memo in the Santa Cruz folder is dated January 14, 1970. It was from Chic Bush, who reported to Cony that he had been reading California Newspaper Publishers Association bulletins, one of which reported in October 1969 that Howard Publications, based in Oceanside, California, had sued

306

McPherson on September 25.

The complaint said that on May 11 (just 10 days before Cony's first visit) McPherson had agreed to sell the *Sentinel* to Robert S. (Bob) Howard for $3.5 million but had "reneged" on June 20. McPherson, the CNPA bulletin said, had issued a public statement on September 27: "Negotiations between the owners of the *Sentinel*, a newspaper broker, and the proposed buyer were never completed." A *Sentinel* news story said that "the owners indicated that proposals were not made in the best interest of the people of Santa Cruz or the employees of the *Sentinel*; thus the sale offer was rejected."

(Howard Publications had 20 properties on its roster in 1985).

"I suspect," Bush wrote to Cony, "that Fred (McPherson) is prepared to believe that ownership by Dow Jones would be much better for the people of Santa Cruz than Howard. And probably for the employees."

Thoughts of selling in the 1960s followed a severe downturn in business, a changing community and "more and more" operating (labor) problems, according to McPherson. Generally a buoyant, optimistic individual, he said he became dismayed, even somewhat discouraged, at times.

On July 18, 1970, McPherson stepped down as publisher after a 44-year career. His successor was Jack M. Banks, former business manager of *Watsonville* (Calif.) *Register-Pajaronian and Sun*. McPherson remained as president. Banks held a five-year contract. McPherson didn't think his sons were "ready."

The Cony and Bush documents reached Jim Ottaway's desk in mid-January 1971, six months after the merger. He now headed the DJ-ONI acquisition arm.

"I will be delighted to go out there with you to see what we can do if you can get an appointment," he wrote to Cony, who in 1970 had been promoted to executive editor of Dow Jones publications and news services.

Then Ottaway homed in on the Howard suit against McPherson.

He chose as factfinder George Cooper, the broker. Cooper went directly to Howard, also one of his clients, and told him about the DJ-ONI interest in Santa Cruz. Howard was

307

forthright. He said a California broker told him Santa Cruz was for sale and that he (Howard) had sent the owners a letter of intent offering $2.5 million for the paper, plus a $200,000 agreement for McPherson not to compete and $750,000 for the new *Sentinel* building, including assumption of a $500,000 mortgage.

Cooper said he suspected that the coast broker also offered the property to at least two other newspaper groups, suggesting he was an "auctioneer." (Some brokers do not represent individual buyers. If they find a paper is for sale, often it is sold to the highest bidder.)

Howard told Cooper that all three of the McPherson family owners signed the letter of intent, "apparently agreeing to sell."

Howard also said he had more or less lost interest in the *Sentinel,* but that he had offered to settle on the basis that if McPherson ever did wish to sell, Howard would have first option. Ottaway then asked Cooper if he thought Howard would bow out if DJ-ONI decided it could do business with McPherson. Cooper said he probably could arrange such a move.

Roots of the *Sentinel* go back to June 2, 1855, when John McElroy started a weekly in Monterey called the *Monterey Sentinel.* Just over a year later McElroy decided that the thriving Santa Cruz area had superior possibilities. He moved his equipment across Monterey Bay aboard a schooner and on June 14, 1856, published the first issue of the renamed *Pacific Sentinel.* To the McPhersons, that is Volume 1, Number 1.

Over the next eight years there were several changes of ownership. In 1864, Duncan McPherson, great-grandfather of the present publisher, acquired the weekly and renamed it the *Santa Cruz Sentinel.*

Duncan McPherson came to Santa Cruz in 1856 from a hamlet near Rochester, New York. He was a logger, hauling lumber from the Santa Cruz mountains by ox team.

The *Sentinel* became a morning daily in 1884. A competing daily, the *Santa Cruz Evening News,* began publication in 1907. On July 1, 1941, the *Sentinel* bought the *News* and operated both papers individually. The *News* was published Monday through Saturday evenings, the *Sentinel* on Tuesday through Sunday

308

mornings. Shortly after World War II, the papers were merged into the *Sentinel-News,* with publication Monday through Friday afternoons and Sunday morning. In 1956, its centennial year, the paper again became the *Santa Cruz Sentinel.*

Duncan McPherson was publisher from 1864 until his death in 1921. He was succeeded by his son, Fred Duncan McPherson, who died unexpectedly in 1940.

Fred McPherson Jr. that year was a $40-a-week beat reporter. He literally was thrown into the publisher's office. A fourth generation of McPhersons was in the wings, so to speak, when Cony made his first approach in 1969.

Fred Jr. was a Republican conservative, who, his sons recalled, "grew more conservative by the year."

(All the Frederick McPhersons preferred the abbreviation "Fred.")

There is abundant evidence in the acquisition file that McPherson Jr. not only was an innately affable individual, but also was one who graciously made himself available to acquisition suitors even though he knew he would be giving carbon copy replies to carbon copy questions.

Jim Ottaway, who would be probing discreetly (but without letup) over the next decade, had his first meeting with McPherson February 8 and 9, 1971, at the *Sentinel* offices and over lunch. Cony, who had arranged the get-together, was with Ottaway. In 1971 McPherson was 70.

McPherson and Ottaway trusted each other from the start. "Jim Ottaway's reputation preceded him," McPherson said. They were much alike outside the realm of business. Both liked to contemplate the cheering restoratives that would cap a day and give and take.

"I liked Jim," McPherson said. "He maintained regular inquiries, friendly relationships, yet never pushed. I developed a great personal leaning toward Jim and Ruth, and later, Jimmy."

Right off the bat McPherson turned aside any notion that he would discusss a possible sale. He said "there really wasn't much he could do" because of the Bob Howard lawsuit. His lawyers, he said, felt he had a good case. But Ottaway and Cony pushed on. Would McPherson sell after the suit was settled?

McPherson was noncommittal.

Neither Ottaway nor Cony was favorably impressed with the news content of the 1971 *Sentinel*. "Pretty bad on local news," Cony wrote. "Very heavy on wire service material."

A typical Ottaway thank you letter to McPherson was lyrical in its praise of the *Sentinel* plant and predictably ended with the assurance that "I am most anxious to see you again."

Two matters intrigued the chief. Why was a publisher (Banks) imported with two McPherson sons coming along? And could George Cooper help untangle the McPherson-Howard snarl without branding Ottaway and Cony as meddlers?

McPherson said years later that he wanted to be sure his sons would have an opportunity "to grow in the newspaper if they deserved it." He meant that they had to show interest themselves and demonstrate skills, "not just be given positions because they happened to be McPhersons."

At Cony's suggestion, Chic Bush called McPherson as a sort of amicus curiae follow-up to the February meeting. McPherson told Bush he wasn't ready to sell until he could find out "what the future holds." Besides the Howard suit, he told Bush, he had to settle his wife's estate. Mrs. McPherson died in November 1970.

Ottaway and Cony returned to Santa Cruz early in May to find that McPherson thought there was a possibility the Howard suit might be settled out of court. Ottaway tactfully suggested that since George Cooper had handled transactions both for ONI and Howard, it was conceivable that Cooper could talk to Howard to convince him to "drop out of the picture" if McPherson wanted him to. Cony suggested, and McPherson agreed, that his visitors talk to McPherson's lawyers in San Francisco.

Next day Ottaway and Cony called on J. Hart Clinton, a partner in the firm of Morrison, Foerster, Hollaway, Clinton & Clark. Clinton also had an interest in the *San Mateo* (Calif.) *Times and News Leader*. (Cony, not known to miss a bet, talked to Clinton in 1969 about a possible sale. Clinton said he was not interested.) Clinton, of course, was handling the Howard suit.

Ottaway told Clinton he was ready to approach Cooper if Clinton wished, stressing that ONI didn't want to become involved. The chief also said that he hadn't seen any *Sentinel* financial statements "and had no idea, except for a general interest, of whether we would be in a position to pay the price Howard had offered."

Ottaway wrote to Kerby that he felt "we have done everything we can," adding that Santa Cruz "looks like a second Cape Cod."

Jim and Ruth Ottaway spent Thanksgiving 1971 with the Dunham Sherers (daughter Ruthie) in Los Gatos. Next day the chief lunched with McPherson and learned that Howard had offered to settle the suit if he received a first call purchase option.

Meantime, Jim Soderlind's "long-range" analysis of the market concluded that there were no "strong pluses or minuses."

Ottaway and Howard met in April 1972 during the American Newspaper Publishers Association convention in New York. Ottaway's report indicated that their conversation was cordial. Howard said he expected to settle with McPherson within a month and told Ottaway that once an agreement was reached, ONI would be free to talk to McPherson. However, Howard said, he was interested in recapturing his legal fees, which he estimated at $30,000.

Apparently Cony alone maintained contact with McPherson during 1972, who said during a late August meeting that he had "all but reached agreement" with Howard. The arrangement, Cony reported, was that if McPherson decided to sell any time in the next six years, he must start by naming his price to Howard. Howard then could make a counter offer. McPherson would not have to accept that, but he could accept an offer from anyone else, provided the offer was more than 50 percent of the gap between the McPherson price and the Howard bid.

McPherson said the family was not keen to sell, but that the death of any of the three principals "could change matters." Besides Fred, there was a brother, Dr. Mahlon McPherson, and a sister, Mrs. Lillian Rouse, widow of Robert P. Rouse.

Might Cony report back to Dow Jones-Ottaway that if the *Sentinel* did come on the market, McPherson would let him know? "Absolutely," McPherson replied. He told Cony that

311

"only last week" Paul Miller, chairman of Gannett, had dropped in.

Cony returned to Santa Cruz late in October. The Howard suit had been settled on the terms Cony described. Cony reported McPherson had "no thought of selling right now." (But he did urge Cony to vote the straight Republican ticket.)

Elsewhere in this narrative are references to Jim Ottaway's baffling longhand. If further documentation of its mysteries is needed, Cony provided it. In a letter to Ottaway dated October 30 he wrote:

"I think you should know that someone is writing letters on the letterhead of Brown's Hotel and signing your name to them. Fortunately they are completely illegible so it doesn't matter whatever outrageous statements they contain."

(Jim and Ruth Ottaway had been to England and had stayed at Brown's Hotel in London.)

Ottaway and Cony made no progress during 1973. In February McPherson said again he didn't want to sell until his late wife's estate was settled. He had remarried in 1972.

Ottaway returned to Santa Cruz alone in December. In his pocket was an offer of $4.5 million for the *Sentinel*, its plant and equipment. It topped the early Howard offer by approximately $1 million. But before the chief could lay it on the table, McPherson said he didn't want to talk business because there had been no decision on the first Mrs. McPherson's estate. He then told Ottaway that he owned 54 percent of the company; Dr. McPherson and Mrs. Rouse 23 percent each.

Ottaway did not make the offer. He felt that under circumstances involving the estate, he might "antagonize" McPherson.

But he did meet Mrs. Rouse for the first time. Discovering that she was a world traveler, they chatted about Greece and the Caribbean. He also met Bruce McPherson, then city editor. Fred III, classified manager, was not present.

Apparently Bruce was turning in a superior job. Three years after Cony's dour appraisal, Soderlind wrote, "The *Sentinel* has made a marked improvement in local coverage. But it needs a lot of push for more quality." Soderlind was studying the market for Dow Jones. Steve Ryder and Bob Van Fleet were

312

engaged in a companion study for ONI. The studies were an offshoot of a suggestion by Cony: "If we are to get this property, we have to be more aggressive."

Lurking on the fringes and anxious to pounce should McPherson waver were emissaries of the Donrey, Scripps and *New York Times* interests. That Ottaway was McPherson's stated choice didn't ease the tension.

On September 23, 1974, the chief, accompanied by Cony, formally unveiled the $4.5 million offer he had earlier taken to Santa Cruz, but had not presented. McPherson read the proposal aloud in their presence. He remained noncommittal.

On September 30 Jim Jr. came center stage for the first time. He was in San Francisco at a United Press International editors meeting (Edicon) and drove south for an introductory chat with McPherson and his sons. Jim Ottaway thought a meeting or two between the younger generation principals perhaps would hasten a deal. Jim Jr. answered salvo after salvo of questions about Dow Jones and ONI. Fred III and Bruce made it quite clear that they were concerned about their future with the *Sentinel*.

If Jim Jr.'s visit suggested that aureate destinies might lie around the corner, the vision was dashed on October 24. That day McPherson wrote to Ottaway "that the paper is not for sale." As if that wasn't enough, the Jack Banks contract expired in January 1975. McPherson reclaimed his publishers's chair and promoted Fred III to business manager.

"Where does that leave us?" Cony asked, rhetorically.

Letters from Jim and Jim Jr. flowed to the West Coast during the next two years with the regularity of lunar tides. In June 1976 Fred and Pearl McPherson visited Campbell Hall, something of an Ottaway coup in itself. The McPherson-Howard agreement expired April 1, 1977, giving McPherson a clear shot at selling on his terms.

Also in 1977 Cony became vice president/news of Dow Jones.

But the owner held fast throughout 1977 and 1978, volunteering only that three other newspaper groups were seeking the *Sentinel*: the *Washington Post*, and the McClatchy and Block organizations.

Cony returned to the quest in late May 1979. McPherson

313

volunteered that he had not forgotten his promise to Ottaway and Cony to let them know when he was ready to sell. "Is that day upon us?" Cony asked. "Not right now, but things could change," McPherson countered.

Ottaway followed up on June 2 and discovered that *Sentinel* stock ownership had changed. McPherson's sons each now owned 13½ shares, but their father retained voting rights during his lifetime. The chief also found that the profit picture had changed dramatically. The *Sentinel*'s fiscal year would end June 30. McPherson said he expected to make $1 million before taxes. In 1974, when ONI offered $4.5 million for the property, the figure was $162,000!

"Why don't we see if we can come to an agreement in principle?" Ottaway asked McPherson. "Why don't we make a deal to buy out your 27 percent and the 23 percent each owned by your brother and sister, for a total of 73 percent? Let the boys keep their 13½ each. Or, let us buy 3½ percent each from Bruce and Fred so that we would have 80 percent. Then we would give them an agreement for X period of time, guaranteeing them the same price in case they decided to sell."

McPherson said he and his sons had talked at length about what they should do and for the first time volunteered that they knew that eventually they would have to buy an offset press to compete effectively with the Watsonville paper.

"We began a serious exploration of offset in the late 1970s," he recalled. "The weeklies and other neighboring papers were printed attractively and we felt we must make the move. But interest rates were soaring." McPherson said he estimated up to $7 million would be needed and "that was just too much for us to handle."

"Yes, we probably could have arranged a loan, but it would have been too big a debt to saddle on the family and the *Sentinel*."

At this point Ottaway said he felt that McPherson was beginning to waver. He invited McPherson and his sons to fly east on the Dow Jones aircraft, to discuss a possible agreement consisting of these planks:

ONI was the organization with whom they wished to do business.

314

The type of deal tax-wise that would be best for them.

The amount of stock the sons might want.

A mutually agreeable sale price.

If McPherson indeed was wavering, he kept it to himself. There would be no further definitive action in 1979.

Now the Ottaways felt they had to make an offer. They chose the 1980 ANPA meeting in Hawaii. Their substantially-improved proposal to the McPhersons included employment contracts for Fred Jr., Fred III and Bruce.

It was in 1980, the sons recalled in a 1985 interview, that the McPhersons decided to sell. The decisive family discussions were initiated by Fred III and Bruce, they said, and lasted about a year. They were concerned about Fred Jr.'s age, 79. Their aunt and uncle also were nearing 80. One or more deaths would create sticky tax problems.

There were other considerations: Fred Jr., his sons said, knew they were committed to remaining with the *Sentinel*. They wanted assurance of their future. And the nagging need for an offset press. Where would the money come from?

"We never argued," Bruce said. "Once we made up our minds we never gave it a second thought."

On June 12, 1981, Fred Jr. called Jim Ottaway with the magic message: "We are ready to talk."

Jim and Jim Jr. met with the five McPherson shareholders in Fred Jr.'s Santa Cruz home July 1. Fred Jr. described it as a "meeting of two families." He said he liked the father-son relationship on both sides. Jim Jr.'s presence, as it had many times before, explicitly suggested continuity of the qualities the McPhersons admired in Jim Sr.

The Ottaways again recited what Jack Goodreds liked to call the "litany of Dow Jones-Ottaway" and Jim Jr. described how ONI would work with the *Sentinel* through Steve Ryder, who was to become its West Coast vice president.

Dr. Mahlon McPherson then alluded to the advancing age of the three major stockholders. Three sets of estate taxes would overwhelm the heirs. He said the stockholders wanted Dow Jones stock in a tax-free merger.

At this point in the long-running quest, Jim Jr. emerged as the chief negotiator. His father and Fred Jr. had established the

315

base of mutual trust. Now those of the generation that would continue the alliance would fashion the deal.

There were two purchases to be considered by Ottaway. One was the *Sentinel* itself. The other was the McPherson Land Company, a partnership, which owned most of the city block of land and buildings occupied by the newspaper. The partners, each holding 33⅓ percent, were Fred Jr., Dr. McPherson and Mrs. Rouse. Thus the partners in the partnership and shareholders of the *Sentinel* were substantially the same.

The would-be sellers asked for an offer "as soon as possible," reminding the Ottaways that they were talking to no one else, but that they knew a persistent Gannett would pay them "almost anything."

They promised the required financial information without waiting for the final June 30 fiscal year-end figures.

Concurrently, Bob Van Fleet was assigned to update his 1978 market study. He found it was "growing and vibrant." He also underscored competitive factors in the form of dailies and a host of weeklies and shoppers. But Campbell Hall felt a more aggressive marketing strategy could overcome that threat.

On September 17 the Dow Jones board authorized ONI to negotiate. A week later Ottaway and the McPhersons arrived at a basic merger agreement.

Early in December Jim Jr. proposed that Fred Jr. become board chairman "for as long as he wishes," that Fred III be president and publisher and Bruce editor and vice president. There had been a suggestion that the sons be co-publishers, but Jim Jr. vetoed the plan as unworkable.

ONI in February 1982 launched what it called a "final push" to get a signed agreement, reminding the McPhersons that they would lose the June 1 Dow Jones dividend if there was any significant delay in tying up loose ends.

An agreement of merger was signed April 12.

The announcement was made to department heads at a dinner in Fred Jr.'s home that evening.

The purchase price equated to 355,000 shares of Dow Jones.

The closing took place in San Francisco April 30.

Fred Jr. was given a liberal lifetime pension. His sons each received identical three-year employment contracts.

How does Fred Jr. feel about ONI now?

"I am very happy, without exception," he told Steve Ryder late in 1983. "We're family. We'll continue to live in Santa Cruz and have no interest in leaving."

So, he explained, it was important the newspaper continue and improve in a way of which he would be proud. He said he felt that Fred III and Bruce were doing a good job, that they "sharpened up some of the people who needed a chance," and that they were making the right changes.

In 1985 the "chairman emeritus" still maintained an office at the *Sentinel*, used it a few hours each morning and was quite alert to much that was happening at the paper. But he carefully isolated himself from operations.

The new leadership didn't have to wait very long for an offset press. A benevolent ONI approved a $5 million investment in late 1983 for six units of Goss Headliner and betterments in the circulation and distribution areas. Installation of the press began in early 1985. It replaced a six-unit Goss letterpress, manufactured in 1937 for a Canadian publisher, and purchased by Fred Jr. in 1963 for $300,000.

The *Sentinel*'s present plant was built in 1966 at a cost of $800,000 and occupied early the following year. All its old typesetting equipment was moved into the new plant. Some cold type operations began in 1970; and March 1976 saw the arrival of the first computers.

The Santa Cruz acquisition was not ONI's first successful venture in California.

In 1981 it acquired 20.1 percent of the Riverside Press-Enterprise, Inc., comprising of the morning *Enterprise,* the evening *Press* and the Saturday-Sunday *Press Enterprise*. Morning circulation was 72,000; evening 33,000; and Sunday 105,000.

Riverside is located 53 miles east of Los Angeles. The county of the same name — almost as large as the state of New Jersey — boasted the fastest growth rate of any in Southern California.

The *Press* and *Enterprise* were founded in the late 1800s. In 1981 Arthur A. Culver was president, co-publisher and general manager. Howard H. (Tim) Hays was co-publisher, editor and vice president. In 1968 the *P-E* won a Pulitzer Prize for meritorious public service for an expose of corruption in connection with the handling of property and estates of an Indian tribe in California.

Ties of the Culver and Hays families to the Riverside newspapers reach back into the 1920s. The Press-Enterprise Company was formed through a merger in 1932. Hays took over the editorship on joining the then 18,000-circulation papers after World War II.

Hays, his two brothers and their children held the majority interest, 57½ percent. The Culver family holdings were substantially less.

In retrospect, it could be deemed inevitable that word would first reach Jim Ottaway that a minority shareholder was anxious to sell. Interwoven professional and personal friendships and reputations clearly cast the die.

Warren Phillips had succeeded Tim Hays as president of the prestigious American Society of Newspaper Editors in 1975. Dow Jones has a printing plant in Riverside. And Hays had succeeded Ottaway as chairman of the board of the American Press Institute in 1978.

Jim Ottaway always had considered "using" API friendships for acquisition purposes a breach of trust.

Late in May 1981, Tim Hays and his wife, Helen, had attended an API board meeting in Boston. They accepted an invitation from Ruth and Jim Ottaway to spend the night of the 27th at Campbell Hall en route home.

Next morning Hays confided to Ottaway that Arthur Culver had advised him that his daughter, Deborah Culver Lawlor, wanted to sell her stock, and that he had been talking to Bankers Trust Company. Deborah Lawlor lived in Australia. Her holdings were 13.1 percent of the outstanding shares.

Meantime, the Bankers Trust brokerage arm approached

318

Jack Goodreds separately, reporting that in 1979 the Culver family had indeed discussed the possibility of selling. Culver told BT that Dow Jones-Ottaway was the type of company to which he would sell — if there was to be a sale.

A. Anthony (Tony) Culver, Arthur's son, in a new development, indicated that he would grant Ottaway an option to buy seven percent of his holdings, also 13.1 percent. Tony Culver was administrative assistant and corporate secretary of the P-E Company.

On August 13 Dow Jones and the *Press-Enterprise* jointly announced the DJ purchase of the Lawlor 13.1 minority interest, adding that ONI negotiated an option to buy an additional seven percent of the common stock from Tony Culver by October 30.

Ottaway Newspapers exercised the option in mid-September, becoming the largest minority shareholder with 20.1 percent. The Culver family holdings thus were reduced to approximately 12 percent.

Price tag for the two transactions was in excess of $8.4 million. DJ-ONI subsequently acquired another small block from a minority shareholder. In mid-1985 it held 21.5 percent.

The Culver and Hays families once held an equal number of shares, amounting to about 90 percent of the stock. In 1974, Hays recalled, the Culvers sold a similar block of its holdings, which was bought up by the *Press-Enterprise*, leaving the Hays family with the dominant interest.

Why didn't the company snap up the Lawlor and Culver stock now owned by Dow Jones-Ottaway? The *Press-Enterprise* was in the midst of a $7 million expansion program — building, press and related equipment. It simply didn't have the cash.

Ottaway recalled that Tim Hays was present but stayed out of the direct negotiations with the Culvers and stressed that ONI "is not involved in management of the *P-E* in any way. It is a very friendly arrangement." Jim Jr. was named to the *P-E* board, representing DJ-ONI.

Not unexpectedly some newspaper analysts suggested the investment was but the forerunner of further buy-ins. "It doesn't make a lot of sense as an investment unless there is hope later of a controlling interest," one told the *Los Angeles*

319

Times. "I doubt that Dow Jones would be interested unless somewhere down the road they could pick it up."

"It was an excellent investment," Ottaway Sr. insisted. "Some day we might be able to acquire other holdings."

Hays told one interviewer that he regretted seeing "the historic pattern of family ownership disturbed" by the buy-in, but he stressed that the change would not affect the papers' management.

Jim Jr. underscored Hays's view:

"Our goal is to be helpful minority partners in one of the best newspapers in the country. This was by no means an unfriendly takeover bid."

One of his first moves was to hook Riverside into the Ottaway News Service network.

Hays, then 64, said publicly that he did not intend to sell any of his stock and "hoped that the papers would remain independently owned and managed. I'm sure that no Hays shareholders have any intention of selling."

"My family," he said, "is quite determined to hang on to its interest — and the Dow Jones people know that."

Hays also applauded his link to Dow Jones as a productive way to keep up with the technology innovations sweeping the publishing field. "The affiliation would ease any transition for the company," he said. "We wouldn't be among the papers caught napping."

Early in September 1981 the *Press* and *Enterprise* dropped their separate names after a half century as the hyphenated *Press-Enterprise*.

The change in ownership had no bearing on the move, Hays said, adding that it was done principally for promotional and marketing reasons. He did acknowledge that the consolidation identity would make it easier to fold the smaller aftenoon edition eventually, but insisted that was not the company's intention.

However, on October 1, 1983, the *P-E* converted from its morning-evening-Sunday format to morning and Sunday.

☆ ☆ ☆ ☆ ☆ ☆

Ottaway Newspapers capital expenditures in 1979 totalled $5.75 million, the highest yearly outlay since the 1970 merger. More than $1.55 million was allocated to Sunbury, where an offset press installation in a new press-newsprint building was under way. Sunbury had received $1.48 million the previous year.

Starting in 1980, Middletown was the recipient of more than $10.5 million over five years, covering a front-end system, five offset press units, a newsprint warehouse and office expansion, by far the highest outlay lavished on a single operation. In the first 15 years of alliance with Dow Jones, capital outlays totaled $77.5 million. Of that sum the *Times Herald-Record* drew down almost 20 percent. "The investment," Jim Jr. told the ONI board, "would see our fastest-growing and most profitable paper into the next century."

The Sunbury and Middletown press installations each involved five units manufactured by Tokyo Kikai Seisakusho, Ltd. The Japanese firm was "discovered" by Dow Jones, which also purchased TKS equipment. Two major reasons dictated the foreign investment. The first was cost. TKS at the time was pricing its products substantially under those of the leading U.S. supplier, the Goss Company. The second reason was a sharp reduction in installation time, often by months. Unlike Goss, TKS assembled its presses, tested them and shipped the completed units to the U.S. in crates.

Engineering considerations precluded the purchase of TKS units for some Ottaway locations.

Other major investments during 1980-84 were additional Goss Metro press units and front end systems for Danbury and Cape Cod, and Joplin's authorization to spend $3.5 million for five Goss Headliner units.

Capital outlays topped $10 million in 1982 and reached a 15-year peak of $12.6 million the following year.

Barely discernible in the staggering tally was Campbell Hall's sorely-needed new conference center built in 1980, which came in at $280,000. Not surprisingly, it was named after Jim Ottaway Sr.

ONI board minutes alluded to three acquisition possibilities in the early 1980s. The sterile prose said only that the

Gainesville (Ga.) *Times* was "being considered." The next year ONI "was willing" to bid a substantial sum for the *Sarasota* (Fla.) *Herald-Tribune*. And there was fleeting reference to the *Dickinson* (N.D.) *Press*.

Retirements and appointments at the executive level continued to make Dow Jones and Ottaway corporate news between the Ashland and Santa Cruz acquisitions.

In 1980 Bill Kerby resigned after 10 years on the board of ONI. He was replaced by Cony.

Jim Hitchman came to Campbell Hall as assistant to Tommy Purcell, vice president for production, and John Kinney moved from Traverse City to New Bedford as assistant to the publisher.

Jack Goodreds rose to the No. 2 position in ONI in October, becoming executive vice president in addition to his roles as chief financial officer, coordinator of acquisitions and a corporate director. Allan Meath's resignation as a senior vice president followed. Meath went to Park Communications, based in Ithaca, New York, as executive VP.

Meath was replaced by Dick Myers, publisher in Danbury. Forrest Palmer became publisher of the *News-Times*.

In December King stepped down as news quality VP but remained on a part-time schedule as editor of *Ottaway News Extra*.

ONE is an in-house publication that chronicles what its subtitle describes as "hits and misses" by Ottaway editorial personnel. It started in 1967 as the result of an informal staff session at Campbell Hall. The idea was Jim Ottaway Sr.'s. Early issues were on four pages of 8½ x 11-inch stock. As the group expanded, so did *ONE*, presently requiring 24 tabloid pages to fulfull its mission. It is used as a teaching tool in most major schools of journalism.

Staffers with hits to their credit are identified, along with their newspapers. Those who commit errors are mercifully unnamed.

Bob Van Fleet was appointed VP for news and research and training; Al Romm moved to Campbell Hall from Middletown as director of news quality and training and Joe Richter became director of seminars and research. Richter had been assistant to the publisher and director of the CATV project in Danbury.

Frank Perretta, GM in Traverse City, was appointed GM in Danbury under Palmer.

Phil Weld, who with Alex Stoddart sold the Essex County Newspapers to Ottaway in 1978 because he preferred the challenge of transatlantic sailboat racing, achieved his greatest victory in 1980. In June Weld sheared two days and 14 hours off the record for the 3,000-mile Plymouth, England, to Newport, Rhode Island, solo race, the Observer Singlehanded Transatlantic Race (OSTAR). His vessel was the 51-foot trimaran Moxie, which was disdained by the traditional monohull sailors of New England's yacht clubs.

Four years later Weld would die at 69 of a heart attack in Harvard Square in Boston.

In January 1981, ONI sold its East Stroudsburg, Pennsylvania, Sun Litho-Print operation to Richard (Pepper) Lyons, a commercial printer based in Middletown. James A. (Big Jim) Somers, general manager of Sun for 21 years and before that manager of the old Commercial Printing Department of the *Pocono Record,* helped in the transition of new ownership, then took early retirement.

The sale of Sun Litho-Print was prompted by Ottaway's announced unwillingness to make major new capital investments in larger and faster presses and "because ONI's major company purpose is to publish newspapers."

Also in 1981 Brenda J. Tallman was named general manager in Traverse City, succeeding Perretta. The first woman in the Ottaway group to become a GM, Ms. Tallman was ad director and assistant to the publisher of the *Record-Eagle.*

At the same time Jim Lane moved from Pocono to Joplin as retail ad manager.

Tommy Purcell retired in November and was succeeded by Hitchman, with the title of national production director.

David (Dave) Regan advanced to assistant GM in Middletown.

And Jim Jr. made an unsuccessful run for a seat on the board of the Associated Press.

The following year he was successful, also winning a second

term in 1985. He was named second vice chairman and a member of the Finance Committee in 1984, becoming chairman of the Finance Committee in 1985.

Jim Jr. also served on the United Press International Advisory Board 1974-1978 and was vice president 1977-1978.

More executive shifts, promotions and a retirement took place in 1982.

Bob Parks was named general manager of the *Port Jervis Union-Gazette,* replacing Bob Widmer, who became general manager of the *Pocono Record.* Parks had been GM of *Allied News,* the Grove City, Pennsylvania, weekly.

One of Park's achievements was a complete restyling of the *Gazette,* including a name change. In September it became the *Tri-State Gazette,* with a high-priority commitment to detailed local/area coverage of its traditional circulation area, encompassing small parts of three adjoining states; New York, Pennsylvania and New Jersey. To open the newshole to expanded local reportage, the *Gazette* dropped its United Press International pony wire, using a portion of the *Wall Street Journal's* national/international roundup, "What's News," and the Ottaway News Service regional file from Albany, Harrisburg and Washington.

In May, Steve Ryder was appointed vice president of the *Medford* (Ore.) *Mail Tribune* and Ottaway's western operations, working as liaison with the *Santa Cruz Sentinel.* Ryder relinquished his responsibilities as *Mail Tribune* publisher, but remained a director of ONI. Gil Bogley was promoted to publisher and GM.

In September, John Kinney became general manager of the Rockingham County, New Hampshire, weeklies.

On December 1 Alan Gould stepped down as publisher of the *Pocono Record.* He was succeeded by Frank Perretta.

The winds of corporate personnel change did not abate in 1983.

Beverly Jackson became general manager of the *Cape Cod Times* in January, the second woman to achieve that rating. Ms. Jackson joined the *Times* two years earlier. Her career in publishing began in 1973 as a book publishing house acquisitions editor. She later served on weeklies and dailies in New

324

Hampshire and Massachusetts.

John Wilcox left Owatonna to become GM of the *Danbury News-Times*. He was replaced by Sam Marocco, who became publisher and GM from GM in Oneonta. At the same time Joe Richter was reassigned from Campbell Hall to Mankato, also as a GM.

Less than three months after Wilcox's arrival in Danbury, the *News Times* switched from afternoon to morning publication. In April 1984 the *Cape Cod Times* followed suit.

Jim Jr. acquired a new assistant in 1983, who replaced Manny Fuchs, appointed promotion director in Middletown. He was John J. (Jack) McMahon, who was executive director of public affairs at Orange County Community College, based in Middletown.

Out in Joplin Jim Lane was advanced to sales and marketing director from retail ad manager.

Dave Regan went west to Santa Cruz as GM and another *TH-R* comer, James L. (Jim) Fournier was chosen business systems manager of ONI. Fournier was a son of retired John Fournier, who joined the group in 1952 in Plattsburgh and who came to Middletown in the early 1960s.

At Essex County Newspapers, Publisher Frank King appointed Peter Watson as his assistant. Watson had been editor of the *Beverly/Peabody Times* after a tour as editor of the *Daily Times* in Gloucester.

When Knight Kiplinger took over as chief of Ottaway News Service in 1978, he did so with the explicit caveat that within five or six years he would leave to join his family's business, Kiplinger Washington Editors.

The call came in late summer of 1983.

It fell to Bob Van Fleet to find a replacement for the versatile Kiplinger, who, with unrelenting persistence, had brought ONS a sophistication in Washington coverage it never had known. Kiplinger also teamed with Tommy Purcell and Associated Press technicians to upgrade the ONS transmission system.

Van Fleet's selection was William F. (Bill) Schmick III, who had joined Gannett's Washington operation as special projects director after six years as city editor of the *Baltimore Sun*. Schmick's father had been publisher of the *Sun*. Schmick took over the news service in September, as it expanded to cover the regional requirements of the then 21 community newspapers in 10 states.

Capital spending in 1983 set a record of $12.6 million.

The Ottaway Citation II jet was replaced by a used nine-passenger Hawker Siddeley that carried a price tag of $3.6 million, not including the trade-in. The jet's superior speed was further proof that to the Ottaways time equated to money. Besides, it had a completely enclosed lavatory, the comforts of which were not lost on the officers.

The same year saw Gerry Tache become a member of the board of ONI.

Also in 1983 DJ-ONI submitted a stock offer for the *Chico* (Calif.) *Enterprise Record*. Nothing materialized.

25 Sun City

"The old order changeth, yielding place to new . . ."
—*Alfred, Lord Tennyson*

On April 18, 1984, a laureate Jim Ottaway stepped down from the Dow Jones board. Technically he was to have retired the previous December 31, the year he became 72. But DJ tradition holds that directors serve until the annual meeting the following spring.

His departure was marked by a directors' dinner at the 21 Club in New York City, also attended by Gene Brown and Lyn and Eda Boyd. The Boyds flew north in the Ottaway jet from their retirement home in Camden, South Carolina. Next day the Boyds came to Campbell Hall for visits and a dinner with many of his old comrades of the 1950s and 1960s.

On May 2 Jim Jr. announced his father's retirement from the Ottaway board. The announcement was made at an ONI board meeting in the Ritz Carlton Hotel in Montreal during the American Newspaper Publishers Association convention. Ottaway, the minutes reveal, was invited to stay on. He declined, agreeing to continue to serve the company as founding director, but without a vote.

The board thanked Ottaway for 48 years of service to the company and 14 years as an ONI director, acclaiming the "extraordinary grace and skill with which he arranged and executed the transition from his leadership to that of the younger generation."

Exactly 29 days later some Dow Jones-Ottaway watchers thought they had reason to perceive a dramatic departure from

327

one of the cardinal acquisition precepts laid down by the founder in 1936. Ottaway always had preached a gospel of reasonable market isolation.

On May 31 came an announcement that Ottaway Newspapers had acquired the *Sun City* (Ariz.) *News-Sun*, a six-day afternoon paper, serving what Sun City's developers describe as the "world's premier adult resort community." Sun City lies in the northwest quadrant of the greater Phoenix metropolitan market, less than 15 miles from Eugene S. Pulliam's power base from which flow the redoubtable *Arizona Republic*, daily and Sunday, and the evening *Gazette*.

The Pulliam papers actually match *News-Sun* circulation in the latter's retirement enclave. But *News-Sun* philosophy has always been "not to worry" about the metro presence. Its owners over the years fashioned an "aggressively provincial" publication, carefully tailored to the interests of the well-to-do retirees. As a result the *News-Sun* carved out its own submarket and has shown spectacular growth since it became a daily in 1977.

News-Sun circulation historically peaks in the winter, nudging 19,000, but falls off to about 12,000 in the summer, averaging more than 15,500. Total revenues increased 20 percent in 1982 and again in 1983.

Within 15 miles of the *News-Sun* are at least a dozen shopping centers, 10 of them in Sun City and Sun City West. Two new centers were under construction in Sun City West in 1984. Sun City residents traditionally stay close to home to shop because they dislike traffic congestion in downtown Phoenix.

"If we are to seriously consider this opportunity," Jack Goodreds told the Ottaway board, "we must be willing to take a larger than normal risk, accept a longer than normal payback and pay a high price. Obviously offsetting these risks and drawbacks is the opportunity to buy a paper in a premier area of the country with great long-range potential."

Coincidentally, Ottaway corporate officers, publishers and general managers were playing war games at Campbell Hall at the time Sun City became an acquisition possibility. The seminar on long-range and strategic planning was divided into groups to study theoretical problems. But one group had what

328

Goodreds called "a real live one." It was the *News-Sun*.

Steve Ryder and Bob Van Fleet did the market research. Goodreds and Roy Meyer, Ottaway controller, covered the financial aspects.

The *News-Sun* came into existence in 1957 as the monthly *Youngtown News,* a mimeographed chronicle dedicated to covering Youngtown, Arizona, which some consider the first U.S. retirement community. Youngtown was founded in 1954. The little paper gradually developed into a semi-monthly tabloid. When Sun City opened in 1960, its publisher, Syd Lambert, changed its name to the *Youngtown News and Sun City Sun.*

In July 1960 the property passed to two visionaries who had virtually no tangible assets, but who were rich in talent and faith in the future of Sun City. They were Burton and Ursula Freireich.

The Freireichs met while journalism students at the University of Illinois. He was graduated in 1948 after distinguished military service. Freireich's first job was with the *Springfield* (Ill.) *State Journal.* After a two-year hitch there, he joined the *Phoenix Gazette* as a copy reader, and after 30 months entered the sports department.

Why Arizona?

"I was stationed near Phoenix while in service," Freireich recalled, "and I liked the climate."

Freireich paid $7,500 for the property, putting $1,500 down and signing notes for the balance. His apparently tenuous cash position at the time was underscored by a need to borrow $1,000 on a G.I. life insurance policy to help cover the down payment.

At the time of purchase Sun City had but 300 residents. Today it has 50,000. A second development, Sun City West, was founded in 1978. It is more than a third occupied. It, too, is expected to become a city of about 50,000.

Freireich had entered right on cue. He was in the right place at the right time.

The first issue of the *News-Sun* (Freireich had shortened the name upon taking ownership) was published July 22, 1960. The Freireichs operated out of their home. Not until April 1961 would they acquire an office in a just-completed Sun City shopping center.

A brochure published in 1985, commemorating the 25th anniversary of the founding of Sun City, told of Freireich's postgraduate problems in journalism. "He was secure in his writing and reportorial abilities," it said, "but when it came to photography he admits he didn't know one end of the camera from the other, nor did he know anything about display advertising, but now he was doing both."

Evelyn Barber, editorial page editor, said that "photography never quite got to be Freireich's thing." In the early days, she recalled, he acquired the epithet "fanny photographer," always managing to capture a rear view of a player in action.

Ms. Barber had another memory of the publisher. "I was fired periodically, only to be told to come back after lunch."

The author's reference to "Ms. Barber" wouldn't have passed muster with Freireich. He insisted on "Miss" or "Mrs." on second reference.

Freireich, she said, was a sought-after speaker, with a reputation for a deep sense of humor. But he was serious when he repeated one of his favorite dicta: "The publisher of any newspaper is a dictator. You'd better hope that he's a benevolent dictator."

Ursula Freireich took over bookkeeping, classified advertising and circulation.

"Ursula," Mrs. Barber recalled, "was always known as a stickler for details. After years of working side by side with Burt, writing and supervising ad-taking, she finally was able to confine herself to being office manager and writing a column, which became popular. Once, when she overheard a clerk exaggerate the *News-Sun*'s circulation, she reacted with a stern reprimand. Circulation was quoted each week at its exact figure.

"As the publisher's wife she often was the last resort for people who expected special treatment. They'd call her at home, expecting favored treatment. What they received was a polite hearing and a referral to the proper individual at the office. I'm sure she still receives calls from oldtimers who want her to put in a good word."

The *News-Sun* became a weekly in 1962. No one, Freireich

recalled, told him it couldn't be done.

Until the shopping center location became available, all office work was handled by the family. The Freireich children, Elliott and Debra, helped mail out-of-town papers. The only machinery at the start were typewriters and a hand-cranked Addressograph.

The Freireichs live in Litchfield Park, a little south of Sun City. Their dwelling is on the 14th fairway of a golf course. When they bought the newspaper, neither had reached 50 and so were barred from settling in the retirement community.

Until 1969 all composition and printing were done under contract. The *News-Sun* first was printed in Peoria, then in Glendale, next in Mesa and finally in Scottsdale. All are suburbs of Phoenix.

About 1967 the newspaper operation moved into its own building, at the same time renting space to an attorney and a real estate firm. It soon needed all three rooms.

DEVCO, a subsidiary of the Del E. Webb Corporation, which developed Sun City, offered to sell land to the Freireichs a couple of years later as business continued to expand. When their office opened in 1969, the *News-Sun* began to do some of its own composition, the Freireichs having bought some basic electronic typesetting equipment and a vertical camera.

The astonishing growth continued.

In 1970 it became clear that larger quarters would be needed. The Freireichs soon traded their property for a larger DEVCO lot in Sun City's lone industrial zone. A complete printing plant, in effect, went on the drawing board. None too quickly. In October 1971 the *News-Sun* became a twice-a-week publication.

An 8,300-square-foot cinder block and stucco building arose, housing the Freireichs' first press, a six-unit Goss Community offset. The first issue came off that press in August 1972.

The *News-Sun* became a daily in October 1977, reflecting the continually burgeoning population of the retirement communities.

That year a second floor was added to the front portion of the building for offices. The payroll was growing, too. In 1969 DEVCO sold a second building to the Freireichs, located about 200 yards from the main structure. More than $900,000 was invested in building, furniture and fixtures in 1969. A thumbnail history of the *News-Sun* recalled that the owners incurred "only $200,000 of debt" in the process.

Burt Freireich was 58 at the time of the sale to Ottaway.

Why did he sell?

"I was tired of working," he said. "Each of us has a perception of himself. I felt I was no longer a newspaperman. I felt like a manufacturer and I didn't relish it. A basic point was that I worked very hard, and I was the only millionaire I know who didn't have any money. Now I can do anything I want."

Ursula Freireich was happy, too.

"No more telephone complaints," she said. "What a relief to get only personal calls!"

Freireich said he was not averse to discussing the price and terms hammered out in negotiations, but declined "because my wife would balk. Let's just say it was well in excess of the $7,500 I paid for the original property."

Indeed it was.

Almost a year had passed since the Santa Cruz acquisition. In February 1984 Steve Ryder, ONI vice president of western operations, received a call from one of the many western publishing executives he had met and cultivated since his arrival in Medford in 1973.

Ryder's contact said that the Freireichs were discussing divestiture and suggested he call Sun City to express Ottaway's possible interest in the property. The identity of the tipster must remain a vault secret. The Borgias of medieval Italy would have applauded the behind-the-scenes action.

Freireich said that a newsprint salesman — a "very close family friend" — knew of the decision to sell and was the original source of the information that began to circulate in the Southwest, then in the Midwest.

"When I was contacted by Ottaway," Freireich said, "some prospective buyers had dropped out. There was one other party in the running."

Ryder made contact with Freireich immediately and spent almost three days with the publisher late in February. The first evening Freireich arranged a family dinner so that Ryder could meet Mrs. Freireich, their son, Elliott, and his wife, Marquita.

Ryder discovered that the Freireichs owned 85 percent of the 10,000 shares of the *News-Sun* corporation. Elliott and his sister, Debra, owned the balance. Ryder also found that Elliott was not altogether pleased with his father's decision to sell, and that he aspired to stay on as general manager under any new ownership.

Ryder correctly sensed that Freireich was in a hurry.

"Why should I wait if I have a good offer?" he replied.

On February 25 Ryder's thank-you letter assured Freireich that "we definitely are impressed and interested." Ryder promised to call within a week "to give you the status of what I believe will be an attractive offer."

A year after the *News-Sun* acquisition Ryder recalled that the first Dow Jones-Ottaway reaction to the prospective purchase was less than enthusiastic. "It took some persuasion," he said, "because Sun City was a totally different market."

One of Jim Jr's concerns was the two separated buildings constituting the *News-Sun* plant. Newsprint storage was in one, the press room in the other. He felt pressures would build to consolidate "sooner than we would like to believe," which could represent more than a $2 million investment in new offset press units and building addition. Jim Jr. even probed Dow Jones's long-range plans for a printing plant in the Phoenix area as a possible solution. Perhaps in the early 1990s, he was advised.

The first cash offer to Freireich was dated March 9 and included assurance that Elliott would continue as general manager. It was delivered by Jim Jr., who arrived at Phoenix International Aiport the next day. He was en route to Nepal in the Himalayas for a few weeks of mountain climbing. Nothing less would account for the haystack of baggage he brought along.

Jim Jr. and Ryder dined and chatted with the Freireichs Saturday and toured the area and continued negotiations on Sunday. Jim Jr. departed the United States the next day. Jack Goodreds then joined Ryder in the quest.

It was the first time negotiations had taken place without Jim Ottaway Sr. More than a year later the Freireichs had not even met the founder.

In less than two weeks Ryder and Goodreds, at a breakfast

333

meeting in Sun City, presented a revised offer, which addressed itself to questions Freireich had posed, including his son's future. Patently, Freireich liked what he heard. He signed the letter of intent Goodreds brought along.

Goodreds's summary of the meeting quoted Freireich as believing that in three or four years the *News-Sun* would be worth "at least $1 million more."

"Ottaway will double its money by the year 2,000," he predicted a year later.

Signing of the purchase and sale agreement took place May 30. The *News-Sun* became the twenty-second daily in the group.

Tapped as publisher was Ed Somers, since 1974 chief executive of the *Oneonta Daily Star*. He had joined Ottaway in 1951 as a radio time salesman.

With the Freireichs, Jim Jr., Ryder and Somers made the announcement to department heads at dinner in a semi-public restaurant stall, where Jim Jr. said, "I had to whisper loudly the story of Ottaway and Dow Jones without being overheard. A terrible way to break the news, but it came off reasonably well and we had a very friendly dinner, with Steve, Ed and me answering questions and explaining ourselves and the transaction in more detail.

Somers, who was to go to Sun City after the closing in June, was well received that evening and again next day, when the old and new owners toured the plant to meet employees.

In 1984 the annual Ottaway executives' get-together was held in mid-June at the renowned Chatham Bars Inn on Cape Cod. After the wind-up clambake, the solicitious farewells to Ed and Lucie Somers suggested they might never be seen again. "Remember," several Ottaway wives cautioned Lucie, "not to put anything in the moving van that will melt. It is h-o-t in Arizona!"

Was there any reason other than price that Burt Freireich sold to Dow Jones-Ottaway?

"Dow Jones had nothing to do with my decision," he said, "but it didn't hurt any. I was impressed with Steve Ryder, Jim Ottaway and Jack Goodreds. They are good hands. But the other people who sought to buy the *News-Sun* were not undesirable."

334

Freireich thought the Ottaway lawyers were, if anything, overmeticulous. "They make you prove you're alive," he volunteered. "I would have done the whole thing on a handshake."

Retirement age readers acclaim the gerontological typography of the *News-Sun*. Younger readers, examining the paper for the first time, might be excused for assuming the staff included a geriatrist, or at the very least an ophthalmologist.

Body type is 10½. Headlines are in type sizes normally inconsistent with the relative importance of a given story. The crossword puzzle is three columns wide. Classified line ads are set in oversized measure.

New York Stock Exchange listings also appear in larger-than-usual type. The *News-Sun* promotes itself as "delivering what the *Wall Street Journal* promises," by printing the four o'clock closing prices during the months most of the country is on daylight saving time. Arizona never strays from standard time. As a result the three-hour time difference enables the *News-Sun* to run closing prices and still get a 1:30 press start. When New York returns to standard time, the *News-Sun* must be content with three o'clock listings.

The promotional puff invoking the *Wall Street Journal*, Somers was quick to say, was a Freireich creation.

Somers discovered early in his stewardship that *News-Sun* classified pages are hot items in more ways than one. There's a daily lineup at the door at press time, mostly used furniture and antiques dealers, panting to get to yard, garage and private sales. Sun City used merchandise, he said, is noted for its quality and reasonable pricing. The same holds true for used cars.

And there have been cases of other less patient traders showing up at the pressroom door, offering as much as $10 for a hot preview copy.

A retirement community, Somers also discovered early in the game, has its own way of life, hewing close to a portion of Benjamin Franklin's proverb from *Poor Richard's Almanac*: "Early to bed and early to rise. . ."

The folks are breakfasting at King's Inn as early as 5:30. But

335

the conversation doesn't tend to center on the latest in the morning *Arizona Republic*. Rather the seniors are preoccupied with colostomies, arthritis, incontinence and pacemaker implants. Oatmeal, bran flakes and prune juice top the food sales charts. Conversely Sun City pulls in its sidewalks early. By 9 p.m. its bars are empty. That is not to say consumption of spirits is low. The cocktail hour begins in early afternoon. It is pleasant to contemplate the quantities of bourbon that may have crossed the service bars.

And Sun City may have the only Diabetes Lions Club in the U.S. One must be a diabetic to join.

Anyone who achieves a hole-in-one on any of the 20 golf courses in the area automatically rates a picture in the *News-Sun*. At the height of the season aces run from three to 10 each week. In another departure from the norm, the *News-Sun* occasionally will run a page of poetry.

"We could be accused of being a bulletin board paper," Somers said, "with all of the notices, meetings, golf starting times, bridge tournaments and the like. No question we're guilty. We're trying to find ways to make it more palatable."

Burt Freireich's eclectic approach to local news lives on.

"I never thought I'd want to hug my P & L and budget," Somers said. "But if you come to a place where they haven't existed, you'll know what I mean. Accounting was done partially in the office and partially by an outside firm. This arrangement meant that basic figures often did not appear until the 20th of the following month. Record keeping for linage and accounts was virtually nonexistent."

Dick Anthony was tapped to replace Somers as publisher in Oneonta. He had been general manager under Ben Turnbull in Plattsburgh.

January 1984 saw five promotions at Campbell Hall.

Peter Stone was named vice president/finance and law with responsibilities as chief financial officer, in addition to his

336

duties as treasurer and legal counsel of ONI.

Jim Hitchman became assistant vice president/production. Al Romm was appointed assistant vice president/news and David P. Stewart became assistant treasurer in addition to his duties as insurance manager. Catherine D. Paffenroth was appointed benefits manager.

In July Ruth and Jim Ottaway celebrated their 50th anniversary with a family gathering at Brown's Hotel in London, England. Logistically speaking, it was a jet-assisted triumph for the far-flung clan.

David and Marina Ottaway flew in from Cairo, eight hours distant. The *Washington Post* bureau chief didn't want to be any farther from his base. The Dunham Sherers (Ruthie) flew from California via a stopover in Spain. Jim Jr. arrived from New York. Mary Ottaway couldn't make the party. With some of the grandchildren, there were 12 at the get- together.

The annual party in Oneonta on December 1, 1984, marked the 40th anniversary of the purchase of Jim Ottaway's second newspaper.

Jim Jr. saluted what he dubbed "the *Daily Star* School of Journalism," which had incubated an Ottaway president (Lyn Boyd); 10 publishers (Gene Brown, Ed Somers, Milt McLean, Alan Gould Jr., Ben Turnbull, Steve Ryder, Don Clifford, Sam Marocco, John Van Kleeck and Frank Perretta); and two general managers (Joe Richter and Brenda Tallman.)

That same month the Dow Jones board authorized Ottaway to enter a bid for the Herald Publishing Company of Rock Hill, South Carolina, publishers of the *Evening Herald*. But the News and Observer Publishing Company of Raleigh, North Carolina, took the prize. Presumably its pockets had been deeper.

Publishing great newspapers was not the only criterion by
which the Ottaways judged their executives. Right behind the
two top priorities — editorial excellence and profitability — in
that order — came community involvement of the sort that
reflected a comfortable mix of moral principle and
pragmatism.

The Ottaway family set the tone and the pace. Its noblest
contribution was the establishment of the Nicholas B. Ottaway
Foundation, described earlier.

Their tradition of community service started in Endicott, the
first power base. After the move to Campbell Hall the family's
generous investment of time in civic affairs continued.

In a 1985 interview with the *Middletown Times
Herald-Record* Ottaway said he "took a dim view of some . . .
editors and publishers who feel they should sit on a pedestal and
not become involved in community affairs because they would
have some sort of conflict of interest."

"When I was president of the Chamber of Commerce in
Endicott and Ruth was active in Girl Scouting and the
Community Chest, if we got into some position where there was
a conflict, well, we just bowed out."

Apparently few, if any, conflicts did arise. Ruth even saw her
way clear to work on the 1940 Willkie-for-President campaign.

The community service Ottaway regarded with the most
satisfaction was his affiliation with the Orange County Citizens
Foundation, which is dedicated to orderly growth, or, as he put
it, "to keep the county from becoming a field of asphalt," as in
neighboring Rockland County.

Ottaway also helped Orange County establish a system of parks. He was a charter member of the Parks Commission, serving as vice chairman from 1963-1970.

Jim Jr.'s involvement in community affairs started during his tenure as publisher in New Bedford and included service as a trustee of St. Luke's Hospital; secretary of the Urban Coalition, a group dedicated to indentifying and solving problems of minorities; and a member of the Governor's Committee on Law Enforcement and Administration of Justice. He moved to Goshen, on becoming president of Ottaway Newspapers in 1970 and for several years served as president of the Arden Hill Hospital Foundation there.

In June 1985 Jim Ottaway Sr. received the prestigious First Amendment Freedoms Award of the Anti-Defamation League of B'nai B'rith. The award recognized Ottaway for "a career that combined journalistic achievement with civic responsibility."

In a brief but moving acceptance speech at a dinner at the Hotel Thayer at West Point Ottaway said, "It is my hope that in each of the 22 communities in which we publish daily newspapers, we have contributed to making these cities better communities in which to live."

Typically, Ottaway suggested that the award "rightfully belongs to the 2,500 men and women who publish our newspapers."

"They are the ones who make sure that our reporting is unbiased as humanly possible; that we speak out editorially on subjects of current interest and guarantee that those who disagree with us have a right to be heard in our news columns.

"We have always strongly believed that freedom of the press is not a privilege belonging only to newspaper men and women, but to everyone in this free country. We believe a newspaper is, in a sense, a sacred trust and that freedom of speech and of the press is vital to democracy. It is particularly important to minority groups whom you work so hard to defend.

"As in all professions the newspaper business has its heartaches and its successes. But there is nothing nearer and dearer to my heart than having our newspapers publish the news of the day as objectively as possible as our contribution to

339

making democracy succeed."

The B'nai B'rith dinner committee thoughtfully invited an old Ottaway family friend to give the invocation, the Reverend Sam Little of the now-steepled Endwell Methodist Church.

Perhaps the most famous corporate maxim of present leadership was set forth by Jim Jr. shortly after he became president:

"Local autonomy isn't a license to publish a bad newspaper, but the freedom and responsibility to publish a great one."

His credo appealed to publishers and editors and more because of another homey saying he used frequently:

"We put our money where our mouth is."

Through 1985, during the first 15 years of its alliance with Dow Jones, Ottaway Newspapers invested more than $88 million on betterments at the group's 22 newspapers and at Campbell Hall. Not a single project was turned down by the parent company.

It was a benevolent way of underscoring the Ottaway philosophy that publishers didn't exist to serve Campbell Hall. Campbell Hall existed to serve them. Ever since the former Ottaway Newspapers-Radio, Inc., was established, Jim Ottaway had tried to develop the attitude that "we are working for our local publishers, not the other way around."

Besides offering a hand in whatever areas help might be needed, headquarters, through the ongoing betterment outlays, predictably has created an atmosphere in which pursuit of excellence thrives. It expects no compromise with mediocrity.

But there is a price tag. Campbell Hall generates no income except earned interest.

With the formation of ON-R a system of business service charges was set up to defray the parent company's operational costs. The original format was devised by Alan Boers of Ernst & Ernst. It has changed little over the years.

Charges to each paper cover administrative and secretarial

340

salaries, the Aviation Department, maintenance of buildings and grounds and 50 percent of the cost of operating Ottaway News Service. Years ago all properties shared the cost of corporate debt. Today only those actually incurring corporate debt are affected.

Charges are computed by averaging three factors: each paper's percent of total ONI revenue, daily circulation and number of full-time employees. There are additional charges for specific services, such as group seminars.

Total full-time Campbell Hall work force in April 1970 was 26, protecting eight newspapers and three soon-to-be-sold radio stations. By 1985 the roster had doubled.

In an era of demonstrably high turnover of support personnel the service record of five of six secretarial staffers in 1985 averaged a remarkable 17-plus years. The sixth, hired in 1961 by Bill Lundquest, left in 1966 but returned 10 years later.

Ms. Bonnie Schoonmaker, now with 18 years of service, made history of a sort in late 1968 when she declined an offer to become Jim Ottaway Sr.'s secretary. Naturally he wondered why. Next day he invited the youngster in for a chat. She explained she felt she was too inexperienced to accept the responsibilites implicit in the job. Ms. Schoonmaker did become secretary to President Boyd and today is secretary to Jim Jr.

The longest service record belongs to G. Beverly Pengel, 21 years.

Between 1936 and merger, Ottaway minute books bristled with details of corporate hopes and fears, achievement and failure, all chronicled in homespun fashion. No longer.

Today the contents are on the sterile side, virtually barren of human interest. They contain not the slightest clue as to individual or collective thinking. For example, only formal offers for newspaper properties are recorded. There are no

341

references to the frustrations encountered in the acquisition arena, where elements of gamesmanship have emerged along with new tax laws and marketing strategy.

It is a matter of record that Jim Jr., Jack Goodreds and corporate staff went into seclusion in 1983 to reexamine their acquisition tactics. During the retreat they wondered if Ottaway had been aggressive enough, enjoying as it was, unqualified support from Dow Jones.

Goodreds, who succeeded Jim Ottaway as chief of the acquisition arm, clings to the philosophy that "buy, buy, buy doesn't always mean good." Goodreds also has found that the day of one-on-one potential buyers and sellers is fast disappearing. "Fewer and fewer owners are asking, 'Would you like to buy this newspaper?' "

One Goodreds yardstick is, "Is this the best situation we're going to see in the next couple of years? Is it the best property we have a chance of buying?"

The *Santa Barbara* (Calif.) *News-Press* came on the market in the spring of 1985. Several major newspaper groups were invited to bid on the evening and Sunday property.

The Dow Jones board authorized ONI to enter a strong bid for the *News-Press*. But the prize went to the *New York Times*. Its bid was not disclosed.

"It's like a high-stakes poker game," Goodreds said. "Occasionally we have to play. We have been perceived as being too conservative. Sometimes the facts of the marketplace don't support conservatism.

"And, for the record, let it be said that we have been outsmarted on occasion."

One tactic used by Goodreds — although not entirely new — is to give a prospective seller a list of former owners who have sold to Ottaway.

"Check with any of them," Goodreds likes to say.

He has found that several had done just that, not waiting for a list. ONI'S reputation for keeping its word has been an ace in the hole.

Many of the properties sought but not acquired have been tallied in this history. Others include Wichita Falls and Midland, Texas; Allentown and Greenville, Pennsylvania; and

342

Santa Rosa, California.

☆ ☆ ☆ ☆ ☆ ☆

Another acquisition publisher — still in his 40s — stepped down in February 1985. Bob McCullough had guided the destinies of the *Ashland* (Ky.) *Daily Independent* since it joined the group in April 1979.

John Del Santo, general manager, succeeded to the publisher's chair less than two decades after hiring on in Middletown as an apprentice pressman. McCullough was named chairman of the board and received a five-year consulting contract.

The decision to part with Ottaway was McCullough's.

"Jim Jr. treated me more than fairly," he said. "The 'System,' so-called, taught me a lot. But newspaper life used to be a lot simpler. Before Ottaway I never had seen a detailed P&L.

"The daily stress of being a publisher got to me. I remember my father saying 'The public will only tell you when you are wrong.'

"I don't like to wear hats or ties. And I wanted to spend much more time in our Florida condominium."

McCullough also volunteered that the severe economic downturn in the Ashland area was a factor in his decision.

McCullough's retirement followed his brother's by eight months. Ben McCullough also owned a Florida condominium. Both were purchased just after the sale of the *Independent*.

In late May Bob Parks, general manager of the *Tri-State Gazette* in Port Jervis, was promoted to GM in Ashland.

Concurrently P. Lea Campbell, assistant GM of Oneonta's *Daily Star,* replaced Parks in Port Jervis. Campbell had been editor of the *Daily Star* before becoming assistant GM. He had been associated with the *Charlottesville* (Va.) *Daily Progress* and *New River Newspapers,* a group of Virginia weeklies, the *Fredericksburg* (Va.) *Free Lance-Star* and the *Bangor* (Me.) *Daily News,* before joining the Ottaway group as city editor of

343

the *Middletown Times Herald-Record.*

There were these other appointments during 1985:

Harlo (Tommy) Thompson returned to Owatonna as chairman of the Free Press Company and as publisher of the *People's Press.* Sam Marocco moved from Owatonna to Mankato as publisher of the *Free Press.*

At Essex County Newspapers Peter Watson was named general manager. He had been assistant to Publisher Frank King.

A retirement also was announced before mid-year. Editor Eric W. Allen Jr., stepped down in March after 37 years with the *Medford Mail Tribune.* In June the Oregon Newspaper Publishers Association twice honored Allen. With three others he was inducted into ONPA Hall of Fame. He also was given the Amos E. Voorhies Award for public service. The Voorhies Award is made only in years when ONPA finds a qualified recipient. First recipient was Allen's father, Eric W. Allen Sr., a former dean of the University of Oregon's journalism school.

There is a third-generation Ottaway coming along, Christopher W., 22, who graduated in June 1985 from Lewis and Clark College, Portland, Oregon. Christopher entered a display advertising training program at the *Riverside Press Enterprise* in October. He is a son of Jim Jr. and Mary Ottaway.

Previously he worked summers for *The Newspaper* in Chapel Hill, North Carolina and for the *Hampton Union* weekly.

Does Christopher aspire to a publisher's chair?

"I would not say he wants to be a publisher yet," Jim Jr. said. "But he sure is learning different parts of the newspaper business."

If there is to be a third-generation Ottaway publisher, it might be conjectured whether he will be presiding over one of the kind of newspapers that brought acclaim to his grandfather and father. Or will we be pushing buttons in our homes to find out what's going on in the world?

Jim Ottaway Sr.'s answer was published in 1983 in *The Bulletin,* a magazine published by the American Society of Newspaper Editors:

"My sense is that those newspapers operated by executives who are publishing live, sparkling and interesting newspapers will be around a long time.

"Still, the newspaper business today is no longer an amateur's profession. Even publishers must be trained!

"All of us must be more creative. We can use beautiful typefaces, horizontal makeup and pretty pictures. But unless we back that up by top reporting and writing, we will fail.

"We need creative editors and reporters, not just those who cover the regular news beats (this is vitally important), but those who have the sense to smell a good news story and dig it out.

"We need to relate to our readers personally as well as professionally. While the 'meat and potatoes' of a newspaper may be covering school boards, city councils and related civic meetings, news stories about human beings — feature stories that tell how our readers live, what they do and how they do it — are what readers love.

"Best of all, they're exclusive."

The winds of corporate change swirled again in October 1985.

Jim Jr. was elected a senior vice president of Dow Jones and on January 1, 1986 became president of its affiliated companies group. He remained chairman and chief executive officer of Ottaway Newspapers.

Concurrently Jack Goodreds moved up to president and chief operating officer of ONI, the fourth to hold the title.

Few were surprised at the changes, at least those close to corporate headquarters.

The Ottaway appointment filled the post held by George W. Flynn, who died in July. Flynn had been ONI's Dow Jones

345

representative and had served 10 years as an ONI director.

"I accepted this new challenge," Jim Jr. wrote in an all-points memo, "because I think I can bring Ottaway even closer to Dow Jones, give Ottaway problems and questions an even more knowledgable ear at Dow Jones, and make a contribution to Dow Jones decision-making from a new perspective."

Predictably Jim Jr. assured his field marshals that there would be no shift in half-century old corporate priorities.

"Jack Goodreds," he wrote, "knows our business and key people well, and is completely committed to our high standard of editorial quality, community service and integrity in everything we do."

Besides ONI, the DJ affiliated companies group includes the Richard D. Irwin book publishing company and newsprint partnerships.

Just days before the Ottaway-Goodreds appointments were announced, Jim Jr. named Al Romm chief of the editorial services department of ONI. Concurrently, he announced the retirement of Bob Van Fleet from full-time duty. Van Fleet was named a consultant on newspaper acquisition and writing/ editing workshops for newspaper personnel.

David E. (Dave) Brace, managing editor of the *Middletown Times Herald-Record,* was appointed director of newsroom training, reporting to Romm.

Brace became ME of the *TH-R* in 1979. Earlier he was Sunday editor and news editor. Before coming to Ottaway Newspapers, Brace was managing editor of three weeklies in New Jersey.

Several weeks after the Ottaway-Goodreds promotions Jim Jr. received a typical Gene Brown congratulatory note:

"Dear Jimmy:
"This is what you call milking an incident to the last pasteurized drop.

"A very fine letter you sent out announcing the Goodreds elevation and your mammoth jump.

"Nepal is nothing compared to the new elevation.

"Love to the family. Gene."

Brown's note contained an excerpt from his column:

"I must have related this item in the past but there has been a development which makes it bearable again.

"When Jimmy Ottaway Jr. . . . was around six years old, some 40 years ago, I taught him how to play gin rummy. On the second round he ginned me. At that point I said to all in my hearing, 'This kid will be president some day.'

"The other day Jimmy Ottaway Jr. was elected a senior vice president of Dow Jones. Obviously this promotion was made to justify my 40-year-old prediction."

Acknowledgements

In July 1980 Stephen W. Ryder, then publisher of the *Medford* (Ore.) *Mail Tribune,* proposed informally that Ottaway Newspapers commission a corporate history. "Just an idea while many sources still are available," he wrote to Jim Ottaway Jr., then in his 11th year as president.

A year later an article in the *Harvard Business Review,* titled "The Value of Corporate History," spurred Ryder to ask again for consideration of his proposal. He and others were thinking of November 16, 1986, a day that would mark the 50th anniversary of the purchase of the semi-weekly *Endicott* (N.Y.) *Bulletin* by James H. Ottaway Sr.

In September 1982 Jim Jr. approved the project.

In the fall of 1985 only Ruth and Jim Ottaway remained of the cadre that brought the *Endicott Daily Bulletin* into being in the 1930s. And a mere handful of others who served the expanding group in the 1940s still were alive.

Despite some blurred memories and differences over details these veterans reminisced vigorously and vagariously, lacing the thematic content with human interest material no corporate secretary would think of recording.

In fashioning a corporate history that offers significance for th present and the future, the author, clearly, must concentrate on those events and decisions that form its essence. A history also should be a way to understand why the present is as it is and what the future might hold.

And such a history should be fun to read.

If I have met the criteria, credit must go to those who providently set a policy of preserving all corporate records from Day One. Legend, folklore and reminiscing merely flesh out the information in the hundreds of minute books and bulging correspondence files, all of which were made available. Even the Endicott file is complete. The *Daily Bulletin* was sold in 1960.

The Campbell Hall headquarters staff responded cheerfully to a host of requests for information. So did publishers, especially those at the oldest newspapers in the group. Their vaults still hold yellowing records from the first day of Ottaway ownership.

I was fortunate to have had three tough editors: Bob Van Fleet, Al Romm and Jack McMahon, all veterans of Middletown newspapering, now in key posts at Campbell Hall. Ruth and Jim Ottaway read the next-to-last draft for factual accuracy.

Jim Hitchman, assistant vice president/production, contributed his knowledge of book publishing. Romm and McMahon coordinated the work with the publishing house.

I am grateful to Barbara R. Wolgamuth, coordinator of corporate research and seminars, for acting as liaison with the *Oneonta Daily Star*, where the history was set in type.

Thanks also to Loretta M. Dombroski, who typed the original draft, and Julia A. Sullivan, for her seemingly countless visits to the vault in search of information.

C.A.K.
October 1985

Here is the decoded letter from Jim Ottaway to the author, which appears among the illustrations in the center of the book:

Water Isle
March 5, 1966

Dear Charlie:

Thank you for your very thoughtful March 1 letter marking your 7th anniversary of our association together.

How the years pass by!!! And what a wonderful 7 years it has been for us and we are glad for you, too.

Much has happened in these 7 years and much has been accomplished, thanks to your ability and drive. For all you have done, we are deeply appreciative.

Ruth (sitting here in bathing suit) sends her very best to Lois and you and joins me in hoping our association will last many, many times 7 years more!!!

We are on our porch off our room. 'tis 8 am and we are having a cup of coffee. I'm not even dressed.

Beautiful morning. So delighted February turned out so well. Congratulations!!!

Cheerio and don't forget to give Lois a Honda for her birthday!!!

Jim O.

Best of all to the TH-R

Index

Newspaper	Circulation*	
	Daily	Sunday
Daily Star, Oneonta, N.Y.	18,815 (AM)	—
Pocono Record, Stroudsburg, Pa.	18,920 (AM)	20,034
Press-Republican, Plattsburgh, N.Y.	22,610 (AM)	—
News-Times, Danbury, Conn.	40,483 (AM)	45,355
Times Herald-Record, Middletown, N.Y.	75,118 (AM)	85,754
Tri-State Gazette, Port Jervis, N.Y.	4,648 (PM)	—
Standard-Times, New Bedford, Mass.	**48,338 (PM)	52,154
Cape Cod Times, Hyannis, Mass.	39,569 (AM)	45,694
Daily Item, Sunbury, Pa.	26,945 (PM)	—
Herald, Sharon, Pa.	27,036 (PM)	—
Record-Eagle, Traverse City, Mich.	24,536 (PM)	—
Mail Tribune, Medford, Ore.	***29,832 (PM)	31,296
Globe, Joplin, Mo.	38,503 (AM)	43,423
Essex County Newspapers:	36,631 (PM)	—
Daily Times, Gloucester, Mass.		
Times, Beverly, Mass.		
Times, Peabody, Mass.		
Daily News, Newburyport, Mass.		
Free Press, Mankato, Minn.	26,976 (PM)	—
People's Press, Owatonna, Minn.	7,474 (AM)	7,637
Daily Independent, Ashland, Ky.	24,806 (PM)	27,137
Santa Cruz Sentinel, Santa Cruz, Cal.	27,735 (PM)	30,686
News-Sun, Sun City, Ariz.	15,846 (PM)	—
TOTAL	**554,821**	**389,170**

*ABC as of 12/31/84
**PM Monday-Friday; AM Saturday
***Does not publish Saturday

Medford •

Santa Cruz •

• Sun City

OTTAWAY NEWSPAPERS, INC.

Plattsburgh

Newburyport
Peabody
Beverly
Gloucester
Hyannis
New Bedford

Oneonta

Mankato

Traverse
City

Owatonna

Stroudsburg
Sharon Sunbury

Danbury
Middletown
Port Jervis

Ashland

Joplin